"With his trademark care and judiciousness, Weima offers a particularly useful interpretive guide to the seven sermons of Revelation 2–3. He asks what Christ's message was to the original churches and what it is to the contemporary worldwide church. Weima provides engaging historical detail but also presents inviting contemporary sermon models based on the sermons of Revelation. Weima's evident faith and compassion make this book a great companion for teachers and pastors."

—**L. Ann Jervis**, Wycliffe College, University of Toronto

"Weima has provided an excellently detailed analysis of the seven sermons in Revelation 2–3, which he clearly demonstrates are not letters. He is fully conversant with the historical context of these sermons and shows both how a judicious analysis of that context illumines our understanding of the text in its original setting and how these homilies can be preached today. Further, he is right on target in saying that these sermons are exercises in truth-telling not in foretelling. Highly recommended."

—**Ben Witherington III**, Asbury Theological Seminary

"With precision and potency, Weima provides an insightful corrective for some misunderstandings of Jesus's sermons to the seven churches in Asia Minor. This is one of the most comprehensive and helpful resources on Revelation 2 and 3, equipping preachers to interpret, communicate, and apply Jesus's timeless instructions for modern listeners. You will want to get your hands on this significant book."

—**Matthew D. Kim**, Gordon-Conwell Theological Seminary; author of *Preaching with Cultural Intelligence* and *Preaching to People in Pain*

"Weima has again written a detailed study of a New Testament text that is both comprehensive and a pleasure to read, both historically informed and theologically focused. He explains the truth of the gospel and assists pastors in their task of preaching the word of God. This is the best commentary on the messages to the seven churches in Revelation 2–3 written in a long time."

—**Eckhard J. Schnabel**, Gordon-Conwell Theological Seminary

T0339326

The Sermons
to the
Seven Churches
of Revelation

A COMMENTARY AND GUIDE

JEFFREY A. D. WEIMA

Baker Academic
a division of Baker Publishing Group
Grand Rapids, Michigan

© 2021 by Jeffrey A. D. Weima

Published by Baker Academic
a division of Baker Publishing Group
PO Box 6287, Grand Rapids, MI 49516-6287
www.bakeracademic.com

Printed in the United States of America

Library of Congress Cataloging-in-Publication Data
Names: Weima, Jeffrey A. D., author.
Title: The sermons to the seven churches of Revelation : a commentary and guide / Jeffrey A.D. Weima.
Description: Grand Rapids, Michigan : Baker Academic, a division of Baker Publishing Group, [2021] | Includes bibliographical references and index.
Identifiers: LCCN 2020049527 | ISBN 9781540960139 (paperback) | ISBN 9781540964359 (casebound)
Subjects: LCSH: Bible. Revelation, II–III—Commentaries. | Seven churches—Sermons—History and criticism.
Classification: LCC BS2825.53 .W45 2021 | DDC 228/.07—dc23
LC record available at https://lccn.loc.gov/2020049527

Unless otherwise indicated, all Scripture quotations are the author's translation.

Baker Publishing Group publications use paper produced from sustainable forestry practices and post-consumer waste whenever possible.

To my grandchildren:
Leo, Graham, Reeva, Elliott, Hendrix, Denver, Clara, and Archer

May you have ears to hear what the Spirit is saying
so that each of you will grow up to be a "Nike" Christian

Contents

Illustrations

Preface

The origin of this book began fourteen years ago. A group of seven pastors from northwest Iowa invited me to join them for the first weekend of May 2007 and proposed the following plan. First, I would share with them as much information as I could within the allotted time about the seven letters of Revelation 2–3. Second, they would divide up the seven letters among the members of the group, and each pastor would write a sermon on their assigned letter. Finally, they would preach their sermon to all seven congregations as each pastor rotated to the different churches represented by the group. By drafting only one sermon in the series, not only did each pastor save a lot of time in sermon preparation, but each congregation got an opportunity to enjoy variety from listening to the insights of six other pastors. A clever and efficient plan indeed!

I was initially reluctant to accept their invitation since until then I had focused my research and writing exclusively on the Pauline Letters and had done no scholarly work on the book of Revelation. However, at that same time I was planning to expand the variety of biblical tours I offered by including a trip to Turkey, which would afford me an opportunity to teach about the seven letters of Revelation while visiting the ancient sites of the churches that received these messages. So I accepted the invitation from the seven pastors, spent much time and effort researching the seven letters of Revelation 2–3, and then shared with them the exegetical and homiletical results of my studies.

After this initial intensive teaching seminar on Revelation 2–3, I traveled frequently to the ancient sites of western Turkey, and this furthered my interest in the seven letters (or, more accurately, *sermons*). Not only did I lead additional preaching seminars on the seven sermons of Revelation 2–3 for pastors all over the United States and Canada, but after recognizing how relevant these seven messages are for the contemporary church, I also began preaching on these texts to churches I visited. Having spent almost fifteen years (1) helping pastors create sermons and teaching series on this material, (2) preaching on these seven sermons to various congregations in North America and abroad, and (3) leading dozens of biblical tours to the ancient sites of the seven churches in western Turkey, I believe that I have developed a unique understanding of this small but special section of Scripture and want to make my insights available to a broader audience.

I gratefully acknowledge the help of others in the long process that led up to the publication of this book. Three people in Turkey deserve special mention. Levent Oral, owner and president of Tutku Tours in Izmir, has played an indispensable role in ensuring the success of the many biblical tours that I have led not only to Turkey but to other biblical and ancient sites around the Mediterranean. Levent is an amazing business partner, whose hard work and attention to detail distinguishes him from others in the religious travel industry. More importantly, he has repeatedly extended a level of hospitality and generosity to my wife and me that has resulted in his becoming a valued friend. Cenk Eronat, vice-president of Tutku Tours, has served often and well over the years as my local guide. He too has become a dear friend whose infectious laughter, compassionate spirit, and inquisitive mind make every trip he guides a joyful experience, regardless of the challenges we may encounter during the tour. Mark Wilson, founder and director of the Asia Minor Research Center in Antalya, is an American biblical scholar who has lived in Turkey for almost two decades. I have appreciated his friendship over the years as well as his ability to use insights from the geography and history of ancient Anatolia to shed light on various aspects of the biblical text, especially on the sermons to the seven churches of Revelation.

Closer to home here in North America, I want to mention Wells Turner at Baker, who again has done a wonderful job editing one of my books, saving me from embarrassing errors, and enhancing the volume's overall quality. Brittain Brewer, my teaching assistant and budding New Testament scholar, compiled the subject index. I am especially thankful to my wife, Bernice, for her constant support of me and my various ministries outside the classroom; she continues to be my best friend and partner in ministry. Finally, I am grateful for my eight grandchildren and for the love, joy, and laughter they bring into my life, and so it is to them that this book is prayerfully dedicated.

Abbreviations

General and Bibliographic

AD	*anno Domini*, in the year of our Lord
ASV	American Standard Version
BC	before Christ
BDAG	W. Bauer, F. W. Danker, W. F. Arndt, and F. W. Gingrich, *A Greek-English Lexicon of the New Testament and Other Early Christian Literature*, 3rd ed. (Chicago: University of Chicago Press, 2000)
BDF	F. Blass, A. Debrunner, and R. W. Funk, *A Greek Grammar of the New Testament and Other Early Christian Literature* (Chicago: University of Chicago Press, 1961)
ca.	*circa*, about
CEB	Common English Bible
cent.	century
cf.	*confer*, compare
chap.	chapter
CIG	*Corpus Inscriptionum Graecarum*, ed. A. Boeckh, 4 vols. (Berlin: Reimer, 1828–77)
CIL	*Corpus Inscriptionum Latinarum*, ed. Deutsche Akademie der Wissenschaften zu Berlin (Berlin: Reimer, 1862–)
ed(s).	editor(s), edited by, edition
e.g.	*exempli gratia*, for example
esp.	especially
ESV	English Standard Version
fig(s).	figure(s)
GNT	Good News Translation
i.e.	*id est*, that is
IGRR	*Inscriptiones graecae ad res romanas pertinentes auctoritate et impensis Academiae inscriptionum et litterarum humaniorum collectae et editae*, ed. R. Cagnat, J. Toutain, G. Lafaye, and V. Henry, Académie des inscriptions & belles-lettres, 4 vols. (Paris: E. Leroux, 1901)
inf.	infinitive

KJV	King James Version
LEB	Lexham English Bible
lit.	literally
LXX	Septuagint (Greek Old Testament)
MOP	Master of the Palace
MT	Masoretic Text of the Hebrew Bible
NASB	New American Standard Bible
NCV	New Century Version
NEB	New English Bible
NET	New English Translation
NIV	New International Version
NKJV	New King James Version
NLT	New Living Translation
no(s).	number(s)
NRSV	New Revised Standard Version
NT	New Testament
OT	Old Testament
par.	parallel
P.Colon.	Cologne Papyrus
P.Oxy.	Oxyrhynchus Papyrus
pres.	present
rev.	revised
RIC	*The Roman Imperial Coinage*, ed. H. Mattingly, 10 vols. (London: Spink, 1923–94)
Sm.	Smyrna
TDNT	*Theological Dictionary of the New Testament*, ed. G. Kittel and G. Friedrich; trans. and ed. G. W. Bromiley, 10 vols. (Grand Rapids: Eerdmans, 1964–76)
Tg.	Targum
TLB	The Living Bible
trans.	translator, translated by
var.	variant reading
vol(s).	volume(s)
v(v).	verse(s)
w.	with

Old Testament

Gen.	Genesis	2 Sam.	2 Samuel
Exod.	Exodus	1 Kings	1 Kings
Lev.	Leviticus	2 Kings	2 Kings
Num.	Numbers	1 Chron.	1 Chronicles
Deut.	Deuteronomy	2 Chron.	2 Chronicles
Josh.	Joshua	Ezra	Ezra
Judg.	Judges	Neh.	Nehemiah
Ruth	Ruth	Esther	Esther
1 Sam.	1 Samuel	Job	Job

Ps(s).	Psalm(s)	Joel	Joel
Prov.	Proverbs	Amos	Amos
Eccles.	Ecclesiastes	Obad.	Obadiah
Song	Song of Songs	Jon.	Jonah
Isa.	Isaiah	Mic.	Micah
Jer.	Jeremiah	Nah.	Nahum
Lam.	Lamentations	Hab.	Habakkuk
Ezek.	Ezekiel	Zeph.	Zephaniah
Dan.	Daniel	Hag.	Haggai
Hosea	Hosea	Zech.	Zechariah
		Mal.	Malachi

New Testament

Matt.	Matthew	1 Tim.	1 Timothy
Mark	Mark	2 Tim.	2 Timothy
Luke	Luke	Titus	Titus
John	John	Philem.	Philemon
Acts	Acts	Heb.	Hebrews
Rom.	Romans	James	James
1 Cor.	1 Corinthians	1 Pet.	1 Peter
2 Cor.	2 Corinthians	2 Pet.	2 Peter
Gal.	Galatians	1 John	1 John
Eph.	Ephesians	2 John	2 John
Phil.	Philippians	3 John	3 John
Col.	Colossians	Jude	Jude
1 Thess.	1 Thessalonians	Rev.	Revelation
2 Thess.	2 Thessalonians		

Old Testament Apocrypha

Bar.	Baruch	Sir.	Sirach
1–2 Esd.	1–2 Esdras	Tob.	Tobit
Jdt.	Judith	Wis.	Wisdom (of Solomon)
1–4 Macc.	1–4 Maccabees		

Old Testament Pseudepigrapha

Apoc. Elijah	Apocalypse of Elijah	Sib. Or.	Sibylline Oracles
2–4 Bar.	2–4 Baruch	T. Dan	Testament of Dan
1–3 En.	1–3 Enoch	T. Jud.	Testament of Judah
Jub.	Jubilees	T. Levi	Testament of Levi
Pss. Sol.	Psalms of Solomon	T. Mos.	Testament of Moses

Other Ancient Sources

Ant.	Josephus, *Jewish Antiquities*	Did.	Didache
b.	Babylonian Talmud	Ign. *Eph.*	Ignatius, *To the Ephesians*
CD	Damascus Document	1QM	War Scroll

Introduction

I regularly give my seminary students—future preachers and Bible teachers—the following advice: "You can't take everything from the study to the pulpit or the classroom." It is easy to agree with such advice in theory; it is much harder to put it into practice. We often get so excited about our exegetical discoveries or insights into a particular biblical text that it can be quite difficult to suppress the natural desire to share all of them with our parishioners and students. Yet the constraints of time and the danger of overloading our audience with details or technical points often make it wiser to leave certain things in the study.

By taking a close look at the seven letters (actually sermons; see "The Genre of the Seven Sermons" below) in Rev. 2–3, this book models the important move from the study to the pulpit or classroom. Each chapter begins with a close examination of one of the seven letters/sermons in order to discover the then-and-there of the text, what Christ was saying through John to the original readers in Asia Minor near the end of the first century AD. The second and shorter portion of each chapter (labeled "The Contemporary Significance") illustrates how the text might be presented in the pulpit or classroom. This second portion is a sermon that emphasizes the here-and-now of the text, what Christ is saying through John to twenty-first-century readers in the worldwide church. This concluding sermon not only summarizes the most important points of the preceding detailed exegetical analysis but also serves as a model of how the pastor or Bible teacher might preach or teach this ancient text to a modern Christian audience.

The advice of not taking everything from the study to the pulpit or classroom is also relevant for the matters taken up in this introductory chapter. On the one hand, several issues preliminary to studying the seven sermons of Rev. 2–3 are important enough to warrant our attention before concentrating on the meaning of these texts. The first issue concerns the *genre* of the seven sermons: despite their almost universal identification as the seven "letters," these seven passages do not exhibit even a single formal feature typically found in either NT letters or secular letters of that day. The second issue deals with the *structure* of the seven sermons: each of these seven messages follows a fixed pattern—so fixed that occasional deviations from this pattern are not accidental but deliberate and thus exegetically significant. The third issue involves the *historical context* of the seven sermons: What is the situation not only of the author, John, on the island of Patmos, but also of the readers located in the seven cities of Asia Minor? The fourth and final issue deals with the *interpretation* of the seven sermons: Do these seven messages foretell seven future church periods, or do they forthtell God's will to seven churches of the past? Do these seven messages involve only common metaphors, which would be readily understood by any community in the ancient world, or do they also contain allusions to local historical, cultural, and geographic features that would be especially meaningful for the specific churches to which they were addressed?

On the other hand, it may be that the preacher who is preparing a seven-week sermon series on these texts simply does not have the time to include these issues in either the first or subsequent homilies. But regardless of whether these preliminary matters are left in the study or included in a sermon or teaching lesson, such issues are important for a proper exegetical analysis of these seven passages from Rev. 2–3.

The Genre of the Seven Sermons

The messages to the seven churches found in Rev. 2–3 are commonly called "letters." This is the designation typically used in commentaries on the book of Revelation. Sermon series on these passages are likewise usually titled something like "Christ's Letters to the Churches" or even "Letters from Jesus." The almost universal identification of Rev. 2–3 as "letters," however, is severely undermined by the fact that this material contains not even one formal feature typically found in letters of that day.

All letters of the ancient world consisted of at least three major sections: the opening, the body, and the closing. Paul's letters have an additional section located between the opening and body: a thanksgiving section, named after its opening words "I/we give thanks . . ." (for a detailed formal analysis of the four major sections of Paul's letters, see Weima 2016). The so-called letters of Rev. 2–3 do exhibit a clear internal structure (see below "The Structure of the Seven Sermons"), but this structure does not in any way follow the typical three- or four-part structure of an ancient letter.

The opening section of every NT letter contains three epistolary conventions that are consistently given in the following sequence: the sender formula (e.g., "Paul, an apostle of Christ Jesus by the will of God," 2 Cor. 1:1 NRSV; "James, a servant of God and of the Lord Jesus Christ," James 1:1 NRSV), the recipient formula (e.g., "To the church of the Thessalonians in God the Father and the Lord Jesus Christ," 1 Thess. 1:1b NRSV), and opening greetings (e.g., "Grace to you and peace from God our Father and the Lord Jesus Christ," 1 Cor. 1:3 NRSV). The so-called letters of Rev. 2–3 not only contain sender and recipient formulas (i.e., "The one who . . . says these things"; "To the angel of the church in . . . , write") that are quite different from other NT letters, but they also give these unique formulas in the reverse order and omit any opening greeting. The reversed order of the sender and recipient formulas happens only occasionally in letters of petition, in which a person of lower status addresses someone of higher rank (Exler 1923: 65–67; Weima 2016: 12). Since Christ is clearly not writing to the seven churches from a position of inferiority, the reversed order of the sender and recipient formulas is yet another nonepistolary feature of the seven so-called letters.

Various epistolary conventions occur in the NT letters and especially in those from Paul, who wrote the most NT letters (for more information about epistolary conventions, see Weima 2016):

> *Appeal formula.* "I/We appeal to you, brothers and sisters, that . . ." (e.g., Rom. 12:1; 15:30; 16:17; 1 Cor. 1:10; 4:16; 16:15–16; 2 Cor. 10:1; Phil. 4:2 [2×]; 1 Thess. 4:1, 10b).
>
> *Disclosure formula.* Two of the six distinct forms of this formula employing the key verb "to know" signal the important transition from the thanksgiving to the letter body, either the negative "I/We do not want you not to know that . . ." or the positive "I/We want you to know that . . ." (e.g., Rom. 1:13; 2 Cor. 1:8; Gal. 1:11; Phil. 1:12; 1 Thess. 2:1).
>
> *"Now about" formula.* There are seven occurrences in 1 Corinthians (7:1, 25; 8:1, 4, 12:1; 16:1, 12) and three in 1 Thessalonians (4:9, 13; 5:1).
>
> *Confidence formula.* There are five examples of Paul expressing confidence in his readers (Rom. 15:14; 2 Cor. 2:3; Gal. 5:10; 2 Thess. 3:4; Philem. 21).
>
> *Vocative as a transitional marker.* Examples include "brothers and sisters" (e.g., 1 Cor. 1:10, 26; 2:1; 3:1) and "dear friends" (e.g., Rom. 12:19; 1 Cor. 10:14; 2 Cor. 7:1).

It is telling that not one of these epistolary conventions occurs in the so-called letters of Rev. 2–3.

A few commentators rightly recognize that the seven sections of Rev. 2–3 do not belong to the genre of a letter. Ramsey Michaels (1997: 64) observes: "The seven communications to the angels (2:1–3:22) are commonly known as the seven letters of Revelation, or the letters to the seven churches. They are not letters, however, in any sense of the word. . . . The communications in chapters 2–3 have none of the formal characteristics of early Christian letters." David Aune (1997: 125) likewise asserts: "Unlike the Pauline-like epistolary framework of Revelation (1:4–5; 22:21), the seven proclamations exhibit not a single characteristic feature of the early Christian epistolary tradition, a fact that must have been the result of a deliberate choice." G. K. Beale (1999: 224) similarly states: "The seven letters do not technically correspond to the typical epistolary form."

But although it is certain that the seven messages of Rev. 2–3 do not belong to the genre of a letter, it is less clear how they ought instead to be classified. Several alternatives have been proposed, including the genre of the "heavenly letter," the "prophetic letter," the "imperial edict," or a type of Greco-Roman rhetoric (for an explanation and evaluation of each of these proposed classifications, see the survey in Aune 1997: 119, 124–29). The best option, however, is to identify the seven messages as "prophetic oracles"—messages delivered by an inspired prophet dealing with a specific situation that currently confronts the people of God (so Hahn 1971: 372–94; Müller 1975: 47–100; Aune 1997: 126; Beale 1999: 225; Keener 2000: 105; Wilson 2002: 258). This classification is supported by the *tade legei* (he says these things) formula that opens each of the seven messages. Though an obsolete form in Hellenistic Greek and thus unexpected in a document dating to the first century AD, this expression appears over 250 times in the Septuagint to introduce messages of OT prophets. The classification of the seven messages of Rev. 2–3 as prophetic oracles gains further strength from a number of important OT parallels: Balaam utters seven oracles of blessing on the nation of Israel (Num. 22–24); the prophet Amos announces seven oracles of judgment against the Northern Kingdom of Israel and its neighboring nations (Amos 1–2); and the prophet Ezekiel proclaims seven oracles of judgment against the enemy nations of the remnant of Israel (Ezek. 25–32). Additional OT parallels are found in Isaiah and Jeremiah, both of which contain a series of prophetic oracles (numbering more than seven; see Isa. 13–23; Jer. 46–51) against various nations and people groups surrounding Israel. (The Septuagint text of Jeremiah, which differs significantly from the Masoretic Text, makes frequent use of the *tade legei* formula.) That the book of Revelation is saturated with OT allusions makes it even more plausible that the seven messages of chapters 2–3 are modeled after OT prophetic oracles.

A modern and more user-friendly designation for a prophetic oracle is "sermon." In keeping with the definition of a prophetic oracle given above, the word "sermon" helps the contemporary audience to think of the seven messages as seven sermons given by the inspired prophet John, which deal with specific situations confronting the people of God in Asia Minor at that time. Consequently, throughout this book we will refer to the seven prophetic oracles of Rev. 2–3 as the seven "sermons."

The Structure of the Seven Sermons

Their Internal Structure

Even a cursory reading of the seven sermons of Rev. 2–3 reveals that they contain a consistent internal structure. A more detailed formal analysis confirms this initial assessment: there are no less than eight distinguishable parts typically found in each sermon.

1. *The commission.* Each sermon opens with the author John being commissioned by Christ to write to a specific church in Asia Minor: "And to the angel of the church of . . . , write." This first element is among the most fixed of the eight identifiable parts within each sermon. Aside from the expected variation in the name of the city location of each church, the only difference in the wording of the commission formula occurs in the first sermon, to Ephesus, which lacks the introductory conjunction "and." In a style more typical of Hebrew than of Greek grammar, the initial "and" joins the six sermons that follow with the first sermon as a literary unit.

2. *The Christ title.* Immediately after the commission, the second item consistently found in each sermon is a descriptive title for Christ, who is about to speak. This Christ title is always introduced by the *tade legei* (he says these things) formula. As noted above, this fixed expression occurs over 250 times in the Septuagint, where it begins the fuller Hebrew phrase "thus says the LORD (Almighty)" and commonly introduces a prophetic utterance. By the end of the first century AD, however, this expression had become an obsolete formula that would have sounded old-fashioned to first-century ears, similar to the old English expression "thus saith" (Aune 1997:141).

Following the *tade legei* formula is a description of Christ. This description typically consists of more than one title (the only exception is Pergamum) taken from the impressive vision of Christ in 1:9–20. These Christ titles anticipate or are linked to later references in the sermon, thereby indicating that John has made his selections from the preceding vision not haphazardly but intentionally so that they better relate to the specific setting and message of each church. For example, the Christ title "he who died and came to life again" (2:8) in the sermon to Smyrna clearly looks ahead to both the challenge of 2:10b ("Be faithful to the point of death, and I will give you the crown of life") and the positive consequence of 2:11b ("The one who conquers will certainly not be harmed by the second death"). As Harrington (1993: 56) observes: "The speaker is Christ, whose titles, mostly from the preceding vision, are relevant to the local situation in each case" (contra Michaels 1997:66, who asserts that "any of the seven self-designations of Jesus could have been used to introduce any of the seven messages. They are not based primarily on the message that each introduces").

3. *The commendation.* The beginning of Christ's words to each of the seven churches is clearly signaled by the verb "I know" (*oida*), which occurs in all seven sermons. This opening "I know" formula is followed five times by the direct object "your works" (2:2, 19; 3:1, 8, 15), whose precise meaning is spelled out in later explanatory clauses. This section of the sermon can be justly labeled the "commendation": here Christ typically acknowledges the positive features of the church being addressed. Even for those churches to which Christ gives a pointed and strong complaint, he first commends those congregations for what they are doing right.

4. *The complaint.* After commending a church for what it is doing right, Christ typically follows with a complaint that highlights what it is doing wrong. This shift from commendation to complaint is marked by the stereotyped phrase "But I have [this] against you" (*alla echō kata sou*). The complaint formula occurs in the first (Ephesus), third (Pergamum), and fourth (Thyatira) sermons (2:4, 14, 20) but is missing from the fifth (Sardis) and seventh (Laodicea) sermons because these latter two messages have no commendation with which the complaint contrasts; instead, Christ proceeds directly to spelling out the grievances he has against these two churches. The complaint formula is also missing in the second (Smyrna) and sixth (Philadelphia) sermons because Christ has found nothing about which to criticize these two churches.

5. *The correction.* The complaint is logically followed by the correction. Christ does not merely rebuke a church and then abandon the believers in a state of condemnation but instead graciously provides a solution to their fundamental problem. Although there is no stereotypical clause that consistently introduces this section, it does contain some common features. One of these is the use of the imperative as Christ commands a corrective course of action

(Ephesus: 2:5 [3×]; Smyrna: 2:10a; Pergamum: 2:16a; Thyatira: 2:25; Sardis: 3:3 [3×]; Philadelphia: 3:11b; Laodicea: 3:19b). The imperative commonly used is "repent," which occurs in every sermon addressed to problematic or unhealthy churches (Ephesus: 2:5a; Pergamum: 2:16a; Thyatira: 2:21 [2×], 22; Sardis: 3:3; Laodicea: 3:19b). The sermons to the two healthy churches, Smyrna and Philadelphia, lack this verb since these congregations are not doing anything for which they need to repent. Another frequent marker of this unit is the inferential particle "therefore" (*oun*). Though common throughout the NT (501 occurrences), *oun* is not found anywhere in the seven sermons except in the correction unit (2:5, 16; 3:3 [2×], 19). This particle highlights the close connection between the correction and the immediately preceding complaint.

6. *The coming of Christ*. After the correction, Christ typically refers to his coming to the church (2:5b, 16b, 25; 3:3b, 11a, 20; lacking only in the sermon to Smyrna). The close link between this unit and the preceding correction is often made explicit by prefacing the reference to Christ's coming with a conditional ("if") clause. Examples include "But if not [i.e., if you do not follow through on the correction], I am coming to you" (2:5b); "But if not, I am coming to you soon" (2:16b); "Therefore, if you do not wake up, I will come like a thief" (3:3b). With one notable exception (3:20), the purpose of Christ's coming is to exact punishment, and thus the statement functions as a warning to the church to correct its sinful conduct.

7. *The conquering formula*. All seven sermons contain the "conquering formula," so named because it involves the key verb "to conquer" (*nikaō*): for example, "To the one who conquers, I will give to that person the right to eat from the tree of life, which is in the paradise of God" (2:7b; see also 2:11b, 17b, 26–28; 3:5, 12, 21). Each conquering formula involves an eschatological promise—the reward given in the end time to those who overcome the spiritual challenges that they are facing in the present time. Thus a contrast is established between the preceding reference to Christ's coming and the conquering formula: the former conveys a negative tone of judgment, but the latter expresses a positive note of victory. The specific reward described in the conquering formula is often closely related to the specific problem the church is facing. For example, believers in the healthy church of Smyrna, who were facing the possibility of death for their faith, are appropriately comforted with the following conquering formula: "The one who conquers will not be hurt at all by the second death" (2:11b). Believers in the unhealthy church of Pergamum, who were rebuked for eating meat sacrificed to idols, are fittingly rewarded with the promise of being given something to eat: "To the one who conquers I will give hidden manna" (2:17b). The location of the conquering

formula varies slightly in tandem with the "call to hear" formula (see below), occurring *after* the "call to hear" formula in the first three sermons (Ephesus, Smyrna, Pergamum) but *before* the "call to hear" formula in the final four sermons (Thyatira, Sardis, Philadelphia, Laodicea).

8. *The "call to hear" formula.* The expression that is most fixed in the seven sermons, occurring word-for-word the same in each message, is the "call to hear" formula: "Whoever has ears, let them hear what the Spirit says to the churches" (2:7a; 2:11a; 2:17a; 2:29; 3:6; 3:13; 3:22). This formula echoes the words of Jesus in the Synoptic Gospels (Matt. 11:15; Mark 4:9, 23; Luke 8:8; 14:35) where, as in the seven sermons, it formally concludes a saying or parable of Jesus (contra Rev. 13:9, where it introduces an oracle). Jesus's use of this "call to hear" formula does not appear to originate with him but in turn echoes the OT prophetic tradition (Ezek. 3:27; 12:2; Jer. 5:21; on the likely influence of Isa. 6:9–10, see Beale 1999: 234, 236–39). The formula, both in Jesus's use of it in the Gospels and here in the seven sermons, is a strong exhortation to the audience to pay close attention to the message that they have just heard. It may also include the additional idea that "Christ's message will enlighten some but blind others" (Beale 1999: 238). The version of the "call to hear" formula in the seven sermons uniquely includes a reference to the Spirit, thereby recalling John's assertion at the opening of the vision of Christ in 1:9–20 that he "was in the Spirit" (1:10) and that each of the seven sermons from Christ has been revealed to him through the mediating work of the Spirit.

The preceding formal analysis reveals that the seven sermons typically contain the following internal structure:

The commission
The Christ title
The commendation
The complaint
The correction
The coming of Christ
The conquering formula
The "call to hear" formula

The strength of this proposed eight-part structure is that it is not artificially imposed on the text but instead emerges from a careful, formal analysis of it. This structure helpfully guides any detailed analysis of the content of the seven sermons.

Although this eight-part structure works well in the study, it is a bit long and cumbersome to work well in the pulpit or most church classrooms. A simplified internal structure consisting of five parts can be used without compromising either the formal analysis done above or the content of the text. The opening and closing elements—the commission and the "call to hear" formula—are by far the two most firmly fixed expressions in each sermon, repeated virtually word for word. The omission of these two formal elements does not negatively impact Christ's *specific* message to each church in any substantive way. The unique features of each message—the description of Christ, who is about to speak; what each church is doing both right and wrong; how they can correct their sinful conduct; and what punishment or reward awaits them—all this is expressed in the remaining formal elements of the sermon. The two other formal elements located at the end of each sermon—the coming of Christ and the conquering formula—form a natural contrast, so these two elements can justly and conveniently be combined under the common heading "Consequence." This overarching heading can then be subdivided into the categories "negative consequence" (since Christ is typically coming to exact judgment) and "positive consequence" (since Christians who conquer their sin are given a reward). The resulting simplified internal structure of the seven sermons is as follows:

The Christ title
The commendation
The complaint
The correction
The consequence
   Negative
   Positive

Some preachers and teachers may wish to preface their sermon or lesson with an overview of the particular city being addressed in the text. The ultimate goal should be to present details pertaining to the history and geographical setting of the city that are relevant for understanding certain local allusions taken up later in the exposition. In this approach, it might be best to refer to the opening "commission," since this unit includes a reference to the specific city and thereby provides a natural occasion to discuss relevant historical and geographical details. An alternative approach is followed in this book: historical details and geographical considerations are presented in the exegesis where they are most relevant for understanding a local allusion, a metaphor, or some other reference to the ancient world.

Their External Structure

The order in which the seven sermons are presented forms a "chiasm." This is a literary device where the various elements of a text are arranged in a balanced order: the elements are first listed in a series (*abc . . .*), and then the same elements are repeated in reverse order (*. . . c'b'a'*). The term "chiasm" originates from the Greek letter *chi*, which looks like an English X and mirrors the pattern of narrowing and expanding that is characteristic of this structure. Any number of elements may compose a chiasm, forming either a balanced scheme (*abcc'b'a'*) or, as is the case with the seven sermons, an uneven-numbered scheme with an isolated center:

A   Ephesus: unhealthy church
  B   Smyrna: *healthy* church
    C   Pergamum: unhealthy church
      D   Thyatira: unhealthy church
    C' Sardis: unhealthy church
  B' Philadelphia: *healthy* church
A' Laodicea: unhealthy church

It is true that many claims about chiastic structures in the biblical text reveal more about the cleverness and ingenuity of the modern commentator than about the actual intention of the biblical author. Nevertheless, a chiasm is a relatively common literary device, especially in the OT, a source from which John frequently draws in the book of Revelation. Support for seeing a chiastic arrangement to the seven sermons lies in the strong parallels that exist between the second sermon (B: Smyrna) and the corresponding sixth sermon (B': Philadelphia). These are the only two sermons that omit the complaint unit, and both churches face attacks from "those who call themselves Jews and are not but are (of) the synagogue of Satan," a striking expression found nowhere else in the Bible. Additional support for the chiastic arrangement is found in the fact that the fourth sermon (D: Thyatira), located in the key center position of this structure, is by far the longest of the sermons.

Two important conclusions can be drawn from the chiastic arrangement of the seven sermons. First and foremost, this structure emphasizes the overall poor spiritual condition of the churches. The five unhealthy churches are located in key positions (beginning, center, and end), and the two remaining healthy churches are not only in the minority but are hidden among the majority of unhealthy churches. As Beale (1999: 226–27) perceptively observes:

"The condition of the churches is presented in the literary form of a chiasm: abccc'b'a'. The significance of this is that the Christian church *as a whole* is perceived as being in poor condition, since not only are the healthy churches in a minority but the literary pattern points to this emphasis because the churches in the worst condition form the literary boundaries of the letters and the churches with serious problems form the very core of the presentation" (emphasis original).

The second important thing to be derived from the chiastic arrangement is how this literary device emphasizes the universality of each church's sermon. This structure places emphasis on the central Thyatira sermon, and at the center of this central sermon is a plural reference to "church*es*": "And all the churches will know . . ." (2:23b). That this is the only use of the plural "churches" in all seven sermons, with the exception of the closing "call to hear" formula ("Whoever has ears, let them hear what the Spirit says to the churches," 3:22), is not likely to be accidental or insignificant. Rather, this plural reference to the "churches," strategically located in the exact center of the central sermon, highlights the expectation that each church hear and heed the sermons addressed to the other churches (note also the presence of the adjective "all" with the plural "churches"). This expectation is confirmed by the "call to hear" formula, which even more clearly shows that each sermon is intended for a wider audience than just the local church that is named.

The number seven further demonstrates the universality of the message given to each church. The number could have been higher; there were many other important churches in Asia Minor at that time, including Troas (Acts 20:5–12; 2 Cor. 2:12), Colossae (Col. 1:2; Philemon), Hierapolis (Col. 4:13), and likely Magnesia and Tralles (churches to which Ignatius writes only 10–15 years later). The choice of seven almost certainly reflects the idea of completeness typically associated with this number, here representing the universality of the churches presented. Elsewhere in the book of Revelation, the number seven is used to indicate the completeness of the things described. This is how the early church understood the significance of there being seven churches addressed (see Aune 1997: 130–31). For example, the Muratorian Canon, dated to the late second century AD, states, "John also, though he wrote in the Apocalypse to seven churches, nevertheless speaks to them all." In his commentary on the book of Revelation written around AD 260, the church father Victorinus wrote, "What he [John] says to one, he says to all" (*Commentary on Revelation* 1.7). So the symbolic meaning of the seven churches as encompassing the church in its universality was recognized early on.

The Historical Context of the Seven Sermons

The Author's Situation

The key details concerning the author's situation are succinctly summarized at the beginning of the book of Revelation: "I, John, your brother, who shares with you in Jesus the tribulation and the kingdom and the patient endurance, was on the island called Patmos on account of the word of God and the testimony of Jesus" (1:9).

"I, JOHN"

Although the author explicitly identifies himself four times as "John" (1:1, 4, 9; 22:8), the question arises: "John who?" The traditional answer is that he is the Galilean fisherman John, who became the beloved disciple of Jesus and a key apostle in the early church. The external evidence in support of this view is early and strong (Justin Martyr, *Dialogue with Trypho* 81.4; Irenaeus, *Against Heresies* 3.12; 4.20.11; 5.30.3; Tertullian, *Against Marcion* 3.14.3; Clement of Alexandria, *Christ the Educator* 2.108; Origen, *First Principles* 1.2.10; Hippolytus, *On Antichrist* 25–26). Nevertheless, some differences in grammar and theology between the Gospel of John and the book of Revelation have caused many to doubt that the apostle John is the author of the book of Revelation. Instead they argue that this final document in the canon was penned by someone identified simply as "John the Elder," an important church leader in Asia Minor about whom virtually nothing is known.

The debate over the authorship of the book of Revelation is complex and involves a wide number of considerations. For our purposes, however, there is no need to review them at great length, since the interpretation of the sermons to the seven churches is not significantly affected by this debate. What Beale (1999: 35) says about the book of Revelation as a whole is perhaps even more true for the study of just chapters 2–3: "The issue [of authorship] is not important to settle since it does not affect the message of the book." We end this brief discussion, then, by noting two salient points. First, the Fourth Gospel shares a number of important similarities with the book of Revelation (see, e.g., Mounce 1977: 29–31; Osborne 2002: 4–6; Tonstad 2019: 32–33), and the differences can be readily accounted for. Second, it seems highly implausible that there were two "Johns" in Asia Minor—one a well-known disciple of Christ, whose presence in that region is widely attested, and the other an unknown person who, despite never being mentioned in these abundant sources, nevertheless had enough stature to write the canonical book of Revelation under his own name and without needing to clarify for readers that he should not be confused with his much more famous namesake (Guthrie 1990: 946; Carson and Moo 2005: 706–7).

The island of Patmos is one of many small islands located close to the coast of Asia Minor. It belonged to the group of islands in the Aegean Sea that were referred to in the ancient world as the Sporades, or "scattered" islands (in distinction from the Cyclades, or "circle" islands located in the middle of the Aegean). The closest major harbor on the mainland was not Ephesus, located about sixty miles to the northeast, but Miletus, situated thirty-seven miles due east. Patmos is seven miles long and three miles across at its widest point, but the total land area (about 14 square miles) is much less than these dimensions suggest. The terrain is rocky and arid, with few natural resources. Some of the lower slopes are flat enough to create small fields for growing crops, and there are a few bays along its rugged coastline where ships can find anchorage and protection from the wind and rough waters of the Aegean Sea.

Many Christians today mistakenly think of Patmos as a kind of modern-day Alcatraz (so Swindoll 1986: 3), as an unhabitable island where John was banished to live either in virtual isolation or in a penal colony where he was forced into harsh labor, perhaps in the quarries (so, e.g., Moffatt 1910: 341; Charles 1920: 22; Lenski 1935: 56; Beasley-Murray 1978: 64; Witherington 2003: 9; D. Johnson 2004: 39). This false scenario of John's situation may have arisen from the over-active imaginations of those reading the comments of nineteenth-century pilgrims who described Patmos as "a barren, rocky, desolate-looking place" (Newton 1865: 223) or as "a wild and barren island" (Geil 1896: 70). This faulty understanding of John's situation was popularized by Ramsay (1904: 83), who conjectured that Patmos was a

Figure I.1. Patmos and the seven churches of Revelation.

penal settlement and that John had been sentenced to hard labor in the mines—a conjecture that many subsequent commentators took as fact.

Archaeological and inscriptional evidence, however, paints a decidedly different picture: when John arrived on the island of Patmos, he came not to a desolate locale but to a populated place that supported significant religious, military, and social institutions (see Saffrey 1975; Aune 1997: 76–77; Boxall 2006: 24–27; Boxall 2013: 232–34). Religiously, the island was closely connected with the worship of Artemis. One local inscription (see figure I.2) refers to a priestess of Artemis and a temple to the goddess. Although this inscription dates to the second century AD, its description of Patmos as "the most esteemed island of the daughter of Leto" (who bore the divine twins Apollo

J. A. D. Weima

Figure I.2. Marble inscription (2nd cent. AD; 100 × 79 × 6 cm) from Patmos claiming that Artemis chose "Vera of Patmos" as her priestess. She was born on "the most esteemed island of the daughter of Leto." Museum in the Monastery of St. John the Theologian, Patmos, Greece.

and Artemis) points to the fact that for some time it had been recognized as a place sacred to Artemis. Another brief inscription, unfortunately impossible to date, was found on a marble altar dedicated to Artemis under her local name "Artemis Patmia." These two inscriptions support a much later local tradition asserting that in the eleventh century, the cleric Christodoulos Latrinos destroyed the great cult statue of Artemis originally housed in the temple and that he built on top of that pagan site a monastery, which still stands on the highest point of the island.

Militarily, Patmos, along with the neighboring small islands of Leros and Lipsos, served as a "fortress island" (Greek *phrourion*) and protected the important nearby harbor city of Miletus on the mainland from naval attack. Patmos was especially well suited to play this military role since it had sheltered harbors on both its east and west coasts. Already in the second century BC, Patmos housed a military garrison and a commandant who functioned as a resident governor under the authority of leaders in Miletus. Ruins of military fortifications built in the Hellenistic period can still be seen on the acropolis of Patmos—not the highest point where the Artemis temple originally stood but an elevated hill (the so-called Mountain of Kastelli) strategically located near the main harbor in the center of the island.

In terms of the social setting on Patmos, a local inscription dating to the second century BC honors a certain Hegemandros, who had served seven times as head of the gymnasium, for his donation of a stone statue of the god Hermes. The inscription also refers to two associations or groups of athletes, one identified as "torch-runners" and the other as "oil users."

In light of the preceding evidence, clearly it is wrong to depict John as writing the seven sermons on the island of Patmos while living either all alone or in a small community of prisoners. As Aune (1997: 77) asserts: "Patmos was certainly not a deserted island." Boxall (2013: 234) similarly concludes: "This inscriptional evidence strongly suggests that accounts of John's Patmos as an isolated penal colony or cultural backwater are historically implausible." A more accurate description of John's situation is that he lived on the island of Patmos among a "decent sized" (Osborne 2002: 81) or even perhaps "thriving" (Boxall 2006: 25) population.

"On Account of the Word of God and the Testimony of Jesus"

The reason John was on the island of Patmos has been the occasion of some debate. The key phrase in 1:9 is that he was there "on account of the word of God and the testimony of Jesus," which has been interpreted in at least three different ways. Some have argued that John traveled to Patmos either (1) to engage in missionary activity (so, e.g., Corsini 1983: 83–84; Harrington 1993: 50; Farmer 2005: 38; see also Tonstad 2019: 51) or (2) to receive a revelation (so, e.g., Schüssler Fiorenza 1991: 50; Knight 1999: 20–21, 38). Both of these interpretations assume that John went to Patmos voluntarily. The traditional view, however, is that (3) John was exiled to the island as a form of punishment.

Compelling evidence supports the almost unanimous reconstruction of John's situation as being exiled to Patmos. Grammatical evidence against the two alternative views is that elsewhere in the book of Revelation (and seemingly also everywhere else in Scripture: see BDAG 225–26) the Greek preposition *dia* with the accusative case ("on account of") never conveys the purpose of an action but always its cause (Rev. 2:3; 4:11; 6:9 [2×]; 7:15; 12:11 [2×], 12; 13:14; 17:7; 18:8, 10, 15; 20:4 [2×]). Furthermore, although the small island of Patmos was not, as demonstrated above, an isolated penal community, its small number of inhabitants would not have drawn someone to go there to do missions, especially with so many other more populated and readily accessible locations on the mainland.

Internal evidence within the text in support of the traditional view is John's identification of himself as one who "shares with you in the tribulation" (1:9), strongly implying a close connection between the affliction or persecution that he and his readers are experiencing and his being on the island of Patmos. Additional evidence from within the book of Revelation is found in 6:9 and 20:4, where the phrase "on account of the word of God and the testimony of Jesus" here in 1:9 is given as the reason why believers were martyred, suggesting that this is also why John received a similar negative fate—not death, but exile on Patmos.

External evidence also strongly supports the view that John was banished to Patmos. Ancient secular sources state that many small islands in the Aegean Sea were used as places of exile (Plutarch, *Moralia* 603b; Tacitus, *Annals* 3.68; 4.30; 15.71; Juvenal, *Satire* 1.73; 10.170). These ancient writings identify some thirteen Aegean islands—including a few close to Patmos—that were either used or considered potential places of banishment (Boxall 2006: 24n8). In fact, these islands were so commonly used as a place of exile that the ancient satirist Juvenal referred to them as "rocks crowded with our noble exiles" (*Satire* 13.246). A later Roman writer asserted that during the reign of Domitian the islands—not just those in the Aegean but also elsewhere—were full of exiles (Philostratus, *Life of Apollonius of Tyana* 8.5). Although these secular sources do not specifically mention Patmos as a place of exile, such silence is hardly surprising since this tiny island is rarely mentioned at all by ancient writers on any subject (only three brief references appear in classical literature: Thucydides, *History of the Peloponnesian War* 3.33.3; Strabo, *Geography* 10.5.13; Pliny the Elder, *Natural History* 4.12.69).

Early Christian sources universally support the view that John was banished to Patmos, though the details connected to that banishment sometimes differ. The earliest witness comes from Clement of Alexandria (ca. AD 150–211), who states that John was released from his banishment to Patmos after the death of "the tyrant" (*Salvation of the Rich* 42). As part of his commentary on Matt. 20:22–23, Origen (ca. AD 185–254) states that "the emperor of the Romans—so tradition teaches—sentenced John, who testified on account of the word of truth, to the island of Patmos" (*Commentary on Matthew* 16.6). In commenting on OT prophecies relating to the antichrist and Babylon, Hippolytus of Rome (ca. AD 170–235) identifies Rome as Babylon, which "sent you [John] into banishment" (*Treatise on Christ and Antichrist* 36). Although these three church fathers confirm that John was exiled to Patmos by Roman authority, they do not reveal which "tyrant" (Clement) or "emperor of Rome" (Origin) or representative of "Babylon" (Hippolytus) was responsible for this action. Eusebius (ca. AD 263–338), by contrast, supplies this detail and more:

> But after Domitian had reigned fifteen years and Nerva had succeeded to the empire, the Roman Senate, according to the writers that record the history of

those days, voted that Domitian's honors should be cancelled, and that those who had been unjustly banished should return to their homes and have their property restored to them. It was at this time that the apostle John returned from his banishment in the island and took up his abode at Ephesus, according to an ancient Christian tradition. (*Church History* 3.20.10–11; see also 3.18.1; 3.23.1–4)

The Roman historian Pliny the Younger confirms that Nerva, who began ruling Rome in AD 96 after Domitian's death, immediately pardoned all of his predecessor's exiles and allowed them to return home (*Epistles* 1.5.10; 9.13.5). Writing in his commentary on the book of Revelation, Victorinus (ca. AD 250–303) supplements the details provided by Eusebius: "He [John] was on the island of Patmos, condemned to the mines by Caesar Domitian, where he saw the apocalypse, which he published after being released on the death of the emperor" (*Commentary on the Apocalypse* 10.3). These statements from the church fathers reflect universal agreement about why John was on the island of Patmos. He did not go voluntarily in order to evangelize or to receive a revelation; rather, he went involuntarily as a form of punishment and exile at the hands of a Roman emperor. There is less clarity about the identity of the emperor, though the only one mentioned by name is Domitian.

The circumstances of a person's exile could vary greatly, and so further clarification is needed about the type of banishment John endured in order to gain an accurate picture of his situation when writing the sermons to the seven churches. Although numerous types of exile are discussed in classical Roman law (see Aune 1997: 79–80), they fall into two main categories. The first, harsher type involved "deportation" (*deportatio*); it was permanent, was issued only by the Roman emperor, and included the stripping of citizenship and property. The second, less severe type involved "relegation" (*relegatio*); this removal could be either permanent or temporary, was issued by the provincial governor (proconsul), and did not normally include the loss of citizenship or property.

The testimony of church fathers who claim that John was exiled by Domitian suggests that the apostle's situation reflected the first, harsher type of exile. Against this view, however, is the fact that, in contrast to Paul, John was not a Roman citizen and so was not entitled to have his case tried by the emperor. The testimony of the church father Tertullian (AD 155–220) suggests that John may have experienced the second, less severe type of exile. Tertullian was a lawyer and thus more likely to have understood the relevant laws. He specifically says that John was "relegated to an island" (*Prescription against Heretics* 36.3). It is therefore more likely that the kind of formal accusation that was brought against Christians in Smyrna and Philadelphia (see the commentary on Rev. 2:9 and 3:8) had also been brought against John. This in turn led the governor of the province to issue a judgment against John of *relegatio ad insulam*—that is, "relegation to an island" within his jurisdiction—in agreement with a ruling recorded in Roman law (see *Digest* 48.22.6–7).

How then should we envision John's situation? On the one hand, John's exile was not the most extreme form of banishment, the apostle was not alone on the island of Patmos, and he was not part of a penal community forced to work as a member of a "chain gang" in a prison quarry. On the other hand, John's exile involved real personal suffering. He suffered physically due to his old age, he suffered socially due to the loss of honor in an honor-shame culture, and he suffered emotionally due to his being separated from fellow believers whom he viewed as his spiritual children. As Ramsay (1904: 85–86; 1994: 62) observed over a century ago: "We might wish to think that in his exile St. John had a mild type of punishment to undergo which permitted more leisure and more ease; but would any milder penalty be suitable to the language of 1:9, 'your brother and companion in the suffering'? . . . The interpretation which gives most power and meaning is the right one. St. John wrote to the churches in those words of 1:9 because he was suffering in the same degree as themselves."

The Recipients' Situation

A proper interpretation of the sermons to the seven churches requires not only an awareness of the author's situation but even more importantly an accurate understanding of the recipients' situation. These recipients are identified by name not only at the beginning of each sermon but also twice earlier in the book of Revelation: there is a general reference in the epistolary-like opening of 1:4 ("John, to the seven churches that are in Asia") and a specific reference in the important vision of 1:9–20 ("I was in the Spirit on the Lord's day, and I heard behind me a loud voice like a trumpet saying, 'Write what you see in a book and send it to the seven churches, to Ephesus and to Smyrna and to Pergamum and to Thyatira and to Sardis and to Philadelphia and to Laodicea,'" 1:10–11). The sermons, therefore, are addressed to seven specific churches, each with its own unique historical context and social setting.

The specific local situation of each church will be examined in later chapters as part of the detailed exegesis of the seven sermons. Here in the introduction I wish to highlight one aspect of the readers' situation that is commonly misunderstood and often undermines our ability to see the relevance of these seven sermons for Christians today. A common reading of the book of Revelation sees these seven churches as healthy communities of Christ followers who are suffering much for their faith at the hands of oppressive Roman authorities, and the book of Revelation is assumed to have been written to encourage these persecuted believers with the good news that Christ will ultimately be victorious and that their faith in him will be vindicated. This widespread but mistaken view of the readers' situation makes it too easy for contemporary Christians to ignore the book of Revelation because our current situation does not similarly involve this kind of persecution, and consequently Christ's message to the seven churches does not seem relevant to our day and situation.

The chiastic arrangement of the sermons noted earlier helps to counter this view that focuses on the positive spiritual condition of the original recipients of John's revelation. As observed above, the external structure of the seven sermons emphasizes the overall poor state of the churches: the five unhealthy churches are located in key positions (beginning, center, and end), and the two healthy churches are not only in the minority but are hidden among the unhealthy churches. The largely unhealthy spiritual condition of the churches is confirmed by a careful analysis of the seven sermons, especially of the "complaint" section, which lays bare the significant problems occurring in five of these congregations. These problems include a failure to love fellow believers and the embracing of idolatry, sexual immorality, false teaching, and complacency—all problems with which the affluent Western church struggles today. Although the central problem for the two healthy churches is persecution, which is not a primary concern for the Western church, opposition to the Christian faith is increasingly an issue for many contemporary churches around the globe. All of this makes the sermons to the seven churches extremely relevant to our times and important texts on which to preach and teach. As Keener (2000: 39) observes:

> Traditionally scholars have viewed Revelation as addressing oppressed Christians facing persecution from the mighty Roman state. Today many emphasize instead that the book addressed "complacent, spiritually anemic Christians." . . . Revelation speaks to churches both alive and dead, but more of the churches are in danger of compromising with the world than of dying from it. This makes the book relevant to North American Christianity today.

The Interpretation of the Seven Sermons

Forthtelling versus Foretelling

As a basic interpretative principle, these sermons should be viewed as *forthtelling* God's word to seven ancient churches. In other words, they are divine

messages addressing first and foremost seven specific churches located in Asia
Minor at the end of the first century AD. However, like all Scripture, these
texts are also relevant to the twenty-first-century church. This interpretative
principle differs from an older, once popular approach that saw the sermons
as *foretelling* seven future church periods. That approach arose primarily
within classic dispensationalism and asserted that the seven sermons were not
so much letters to historical churches as they were predictions of seven future
periods of church history covering the time between Christ's first coming and
his second coming. The churches were typically correlated with key periods
in church history in the following manner:

Ephesus	Early church period
Smyrna	Persecution during the patristic period
Pergamum	Time of Constantine
Thyatira	Middle Ages
Sardis	Protestant Reformation
Philadelphia	Missionary outreach during the eighteenth and nineteenth centuries
Laodicea	Modern period of growing apostasy, leading up to Christ's return

This foretelling approach to the seven sermons was made popular through
the influential study Bible of C. I. Scofield (2003: 1657) in a comment on Rev.
1:20, though he differed on which historical period each church represented:

> These messages by their very terms go beyond the local assemblies mentioned.
> It can be seen that Ephesus (2:1–7), though a local church in the apostle's
> day, is typical of the first century as a whole; Smyrna (2:8–11) characterizes
> the church under persecution, e.g. from A.D. c. 100–316; Pergamos (2:12–17),
> "where Satan dwells," . . . is suggestive of the church mixing with the world,
> e.g. in the Middle Ages; Thyatira (2:18–29) reveals how evil progresses in the
> church and idolatry is practiced; Sardis (3:1–6) is representative of the church
> as dead, yet still having a minority of godly men and women, as during the Ref-
> ormation; Philadelphia (3:7–13) shows revival and a state of spiritual advance;
> and Laodicea (3:14–19) is illustrative of the final state of apostasy which the
> visible church will experience.

John Walvoord (1966: 52), a leading dispensational theologian, describes the
approach this way: "Many expositors believe that in addition to the obvious
implication of these messages the seven churches represent the chronologi-
cal development of church history viewed spiritually. . . . What is claimed
is that there does seem to be a remarkable progression in the messages. It
would seem almost incredible that such a progression should be a pure

accident, and the order of the messages to the churches seems to be divinely selected to give prophetically the main movement of church history" (see also Boyer 1985).

The vast majority of commentators, however, have rightly rejected this predictive approach to the interpretation of the seven sermons. It has been widely criticized for its arbitrary and subjective character, evidenced by the fact that even the proponents themselves disagree about which seven historical periods the churches supposedly represent. As R. C. Trench (1867: 240) noted long ago: "There is no agreement among themselves. . . . Each one has his own solution of the enigma, his own distribution of the several epochs; or, if this is too much to affirm, there is at any rate nothing approaching to a general consensus among them." Hendriksen (1940: 60) makes the same criticism but much more bluntly:

> The notion that these seven churches describe seven successive periods of Church history hardly needs refutation. To say nothing about the almost humorous—if it were not so deplorable—exegesis which, for example, makes the church at Sardis, which was dead, refer to the glorious age of the Reformation; it should be clear to every student of the Bible that there is not one atom of evidence in all the sacred writings which in any way corroborates this thoroughly arbitrary method of cutting up the history of the church and assigning the resulting pieces to the respective epistles of Revelation 2 and 3.

In addition to the arbitrary character of the foretelling approach, this way of interpreting the seven sermons faces other serious problems. There is no statement in the opening chapter of the book of Revelation or within the seven sermons themselves suggesting that they are to be understood as predicting later periods of history. This interpretative approach reflects a Western bias that ignores the significant phases of Christianity's growth and spread in other parts of the world. It also devalues these messages as sources of challenge and encouragement to first-century readers by viewing them instead as coded messages addressed to contemporary believers living in the seventh, climatic Laodicean church age and paving the way for Christ's imminent return. The chiastic structure of this sermon collection provides a different and more compelling explanation for its order and arrangement. It is hardly surprising, then, that even a widely respected dispensational scholar like Robert Thomas (1992: 505–15), after carefully reviewing the arguments in support of the foretelling approach, concludes that it "is beset with difficulties and unsupported by any conclusive evidence" (511).

Local Allusions

I have asserted above that the seven sermons ought to be interpreted as *forthtelling* God's word, that is, as divine messages addressed first and foremost to seven specific churches located in Asia Minor at the end of the first century AD. This assertion in turn raises another debated issue: Do the seven sermons contain local allusions, suggesting geographical, historical, or cultural features that are either unique to or have special significance for the specific church community being addressed? Two scholars have been especially influential in popularizing the use of local allusions in explaining certain features of the text in the seven sermons. William Ramsay in his 1904 monograph *The Letters to the Seven Churches of Asia and Their Place in the Plan of the Apocalypse*, argues: "The letters were written by one who was familiar with the situation, the character, the past history, the possibilities of future development, of those Seven Cities" (1904: 40). Ramsay proposed many local references within the seven sermons; these were reexamined and developed further by Colin Hemer in his 1986 work *The Letters to the Seven Churches of Asia in Their Local Setting*. Hemer strongly affirms the presence and importance of local allusions in the seven sermons, stating about these messages: "Doubtless their general sense and many of their allusions were readily understood by all Asia readers, but each is directed with peculiar force to strictly local circumstances" (1986: 14). Most commentators on the book of Revelation have followed the lead of Ramsay and Hemer, though not always agreeing on each one of their many proposed local allusions.

There have been and continue to be, however, a few dissenting voices. Only a few years after Ramsay published his influential 1904 monograph, Moffatt (1910: 285–86) questioned the legitimacy of local references in the sermons to the seven churches: "We have no reason to assume that the local Christians, who were ardently awaiting a citizenship from heaven, had any vivid civic consciousness, or were keenly sensitive to the historical and geographical features of their cities. The analogies sometimes drawn from the latter are interesting but for the most part specious and irrelevant coincidences. It is modern fancy which discovers in such directions any vital element present to the mind of the prophet or his readers." More recently, Thompson (1990: 203) has offered this assessment of Hemer's analysis of the seven sermons: "As with Ramsay's work, connections between the language of the book of Revelation and the situation of the seven churches are often tenuous and of little individual significance." Koester (2003: 408) agrees with this assessment and summarizes the points of those who have raised doubts about local allusions:

Connections between the imagery in Revelation 2–3 and the characteristics of the Asian cities remain problematic. Critics have pointed out that quests for local allusions often allow the expressions in Revelation to exert too much control over the selection and interpretation of material from other sources. They observe that archaeological and other ancient materials appear as isolated pieces of evidence that are used without adequate consideration of the broader context from which these materials were taken. Appeals to conjecture are common, and some key points rely on circumstantial evidence.

See also the concerns raised by others (Friesen 1995; Prigent 2001: 164–65, 192, 209–11; and Tonstad 2019: 70).

It can be readily conceded that some and perhaps even many of the local allusions proposed by Ramsay and Hemer are indeed questionable and that modern exegetes and preachers should be cautioned against too quickly accepting certain claimed connections to the local setting or overstating their supposed significance for interpreting aspects of the text. Yet this danger is not so great that it requires a rejection of all potential local allusions. The basic approach of recognizing local allusions remains legitimate if done judiciously.

One commonly asserted local allusion may provide a test case for assessing the legitimacy of this interpretative approach. In the sermon to Sardis (3:1–6), the emphatic double reference to being "watchful" (3:2, 3a) and the reference to Christ's unexpected coming "like a thief" (3:3b) are regarded by many commentators as an allusion to the "Croesus tradition" relating to the capture of the acropolis at Sardis. The details of the life of Croesus, the ancient king of Sardis, are presented in chapter 5 below and need not be duplicated here. For now it is sufficient to highlight one aspect of Croesus's life that was universally known and repeatedly retold in the ancient world. His arrogance and complacency led to the capture of his supposedly impregnable acropolis at Sardis. This story was so well known that what can justly be called a "Croesus tradition" developed as the story was repeatedly retold not merely for entertainment purposes but also for education by teachers instructing their students on the dangers of pride and complacency. Aune (1997: 220) observes: "The moral lessons derived from this series of events [in the Croesus tradition] (one must avoid pride, arrogance and over-confidence and be prepared for unexpected reversals of fortune) became a *topos* for later historians and moralists." What made the capture of the Sardis acropolis even more famous was the fact that history repeated itself: the fortress fell a second time, due once again to Sardis's overconfidence and complacency (again see chap. 5 for details).

Because the double capture of the Sardis acropolis was so well known in the ancient world, many commentators attach significance to the doubling of Christ's command "Be watchful!" (3:2, 3a). Mounce (1977: 110–11), for example, asserts, "The exhortations to watchfulness would carry special weight in Sardis because twice in its history the acropolis had fallen to the enemy due to a lack of vigilance on the part of the defenders. . . . As in history, so in life, to consider oneself secure and fail to remain alert is to court disaster." Osborne (2002: 174) similarly claims, "The church is like the city. Twice before, the city had fallen because the watchmen were not on the walls and assailants had climbed the cliffs to let in invaders. The church is being rebuked for the same lack of vigilance." Commenting on the threat that Christ will come to Sardis "like a thief" (3:3b), Keener (2000: 144) notes that "this warning would also prove especially alarming to proud Sardians schooled from youth in the history of their city. Conquerors had never overtaken Sardis by conventional war, but had twice conquered it unexpectedly because Sardians had failed to watch adequately."

A few have questioned the legitimacy of this claimed local allusion. Wood (1961–62: 264) wonders, "Perhaps the Christians in Sardis would have found the words under consideration a less obvious reference to historical disasters, from three to five hundred years previous, than we now suppose." Ramsey Michaels (1997:82) argues that this local allusion is "unlikely" and that "the warning could as easily have been directed to Ephesus and Laodicea, or to the unfaithful in any congregation." To counter such skepticism, Hemer (1972–73) cataloged the abundant references to the Croesus tradition in ancient sources, including texts that mention various aspects of this king's life and the fall of his supposedly unconquerable acropolis at Sardis. These numerous references date to the first and second century AD (and thus overlap with the date of the book of Revelation) and are found not just in pagan sources but also in Christian and Jewish writings. Indeed, the references are so numerous that one can justly label the Croesus tradition as "proverbial" in character. In his later monograph, Hemer (1986: 133) declares that "the case for seeing historical allusion in the letter to Sardis is related to an appreciation of the formative and proverbial character of the [Croesus] event. It is impracticable to reproduce the literary evidence in the present study: there is far too much of it."

The existence of local allusions in the seven sermons in no way restricts either the understanding or applicability of these messages for other believers in Asia Minor whom John expects to be listening in (note the plural "churches" in the "call to hear" formula repeated in each sermon: "Whoever has ears, let them hear what the Spirit says to the churches," 2:7a, 11a, 17a, 29;

3:6, 13, 22). The local allusions would obviously be especially powerful and relevant to the local church being addressed, but they would also be readily understood by any of the Christian communities in Asia Minor. As Scobie (1993: 614–15) has rightly argued:

> We have no good reasons for doubting that the members of the different com-munities would be familiar with well-known characteristics of the other com-munities. The seven cities were situated in relatively close proximity, and travel and communication among them were easy. The fierce civic pride and long-existing rivalry among the cities is well attested, and this is surely something which Christians would not immediately and totally shed with their conversion to the new faith.

Our interpretation of the seven sermons, therefore, will recognize the pres-ence of local allusions. Given John's clear knowledge of the situation of each church, such allusions are to be expected. As Ladd (1972: 36) points out, "The many allusions to local history, topography, and conditions in these churches leads to the inescapable conclusion that John was personally and intimately acquainted with them." Trebilco (2004: 295) similarly concludes, "Given the differences between the proclamations, and their details about people and the circumstances of each community, there seems little doubt that John knew the situation of each of the communities he addresses well." Nevertheless, we must guard against the danger of too quickly accepting every claimed connection to the local setting or of overstating the importance of these local connections for interpreting certain aspects of the text. Many exegetes of Rev. 2–3 have succumbed to this danger out of an honest desire to capture the full and complete meaning of a text with its images and references, which are often not easy to understand. We will therefore carefully examine each claimed local illusion and judiciously weigh the evidence to determine whether it is actually relevant for interpreting the text.

1

Ephesus

The Church of Loveless Orthodoxy

The Christ Title (2:1b)

In each of the seven sermons, the message opens not with the words of Christ through John to the particular congregation but with a title that Christ gives himself. More than one title is typically given, and virtually all of them are taken from the impressive vision of Christ that opens the book of Revelation (1:9–20).

In the sermon to Ephesus, the first of the two Christ titles identifies the one who is about to speak as "the one who holds the seven stars in his right hand." This title conveys Christ's *power* and emphasizes that power in two ways. First, whereas the opening vision portrays Christ in 1:16 as merely "having" (*echōn*) the seven stars, here Christ is "holding" (*kratōn*) the seven stars. This verbal change is significant because the latter term conveys greater power and has a variety of meanings, including "to take control of someone or something" (BDAG 564.3). Jesus not only "has" the seven stars, in the sense of possessing them; he "holds" the seven stars, in the sense of exercising sovereign control over them, which graphically reveals his power.

Second, Christ's power is further stressed by holding the seven stars "in his right hand." Since most people are right-handed, using this hand more than the left, their right hand naturally becomes stronger. This common cross-cultural phenomenon explains why the right hand appears repeatedly in Scripture as a metaphor for power and authority. Both the OT and the NT frequently allude to God's sovereign control and power by referring to his "right hand" (Exod. 15:6; Pss. 16:11; 17:7; 18:35; 44:3; 45:4; 63:8; 98:1; 118:15; 139:10; Isa. 41:10; 48:13; Matt. 22:44; Acts 2:34; 7:55; Rom. 8:34; Heb. 1:3).

The power of Christ conveyed in the first title is stressed even further by the opening main clause, "he says these things" (*tade legei*). As noted in the introduction, this fixed expression occurs over 250 times in the LXX, where it appears as part of the fuller Hebrew phrase "thus says the LORD (Almighty)." By John's day, however, this construction sounded old-fashioned, like the English expression "thus saith" would today (Aune 1997: 141). It would catch the attention of John's audience, however, not just because of its old-fashioned sound but, more important, because it evokes divine power: like the One who spoke this formula in the OT, Christ is the divine and powerful God. Although "he says these things" introduces all seven of the sermons, its presence here supplements the notion of power conveyed by the first Christ title.

It is difficult to determine with certainty the meaning of the seven stars that Christ holds in his powerful right hand. Although the preceding chapter tells us that "the seven stars are the angels of the seven churches" (1:20), this answer simply raises another highly disputed question about what the word "angel" means here. This Greek word for "messenger" (*angelos*) is often used in the NT for God's special envoys, angels. Proposals for what the word means here in Rev. 1:20 fall into two broad categories: *angelos* refers to (1) human beings, either messengers to or leaders of each church, or to (2) supernatural beings, either guardian angels who lead and protect each church or personified heavenly counterparts of the prevailing spirit of each church. Key considerations in this debate include the fact that elsewhere in the book of Revelation *angelos* always (69×) refers to a supernatural being, early Christian texts rarely use *angelos* to refer to a human being, and Jewish writings from this time period frequently depict heavenly angels as guiding and safeguarding the actions of earthly kings and nations (e.g., Dan. 10:13, 20–21). Therefore, the "seven stars," which are the seven "angels," most likely symbolize the guardian angels of each congregation (for a fuller discussion of the options and their relative strengths and weaknesses, see Aune 1997: 108–12; Osborne 2002: 98–99). Happily, our understanding of the first Christ title does not depend on resolving this disputed question. Regardless of what the seven stars refer to, the Christ title in the Ephesian sermon is intended to highlight Christ's sovereign power. The one who is about to speak does not merely possess but firmly grasps the seven stars in his all-powerful right hand.

The power of Christ spotlighted in the first Christ title likely involves a polemic against Rome. Its emperors liked to present themselves on coins as demigods whose power extended beyond earth to control the planets and the stars. After the death of his ten-year-old son in AD 83, Domitian declared that the boy had become a god and that his wife, Domitia, became the mother of a god. He issued a coin to honor his deceased son (*RIC* 2:213) that portrays him sitting on a globe in a position of power over the world. Depicting his heavenly dominion over the whole universe, he holds seven stars, representing the seven planets, in his outstretched arms.

Figure 1.1. *Left*: Domitia, wife of Domitian. *Right*: Deceased son of Domitian seated on a globe and surrounded by seven stars.

Figure 1.2. *Left*: Wreathed head of Hadrian. *Right*: Crescent moon with seven stars.

The later emperor Hadrian (AD 117–138) issued a coin (*RIC* 2:202) with his image on one side and with a crescent moon and seven stars on the other. The not so subtle message is that Hadrian is powerful enough to control not only earthly events but also what happens in the heavens among the moon and seven stars.

Christ's depiction in the first title as "the one who holds the seven stars in his right hand" should therefore be seen as a challenge to Roman power. The Jesus who has already been identified earlier in the book of Revelation as "the ruler of the kings of the earth" (1:5) is once again portrayed as the one whose cosmic power exceeds the claims of Rome. As Beasley-Murray (1978: 70) notes, "When John declares that the seven stars are in Christ's right hand, he is claiming that the sovereignty over this world resides not in the Caesars of Rome but in the Lord of the Church" (for more on the polemic here against Rome, see also Krodel 1989: 95; Beale 1999: 108).

The second of the two Christ titles identifies the speaker as "the one who walks in the middle of the seven golden lampstands." While the first title conveys Christ's *power*, this second title conveys Christ's *presence*. This presence is emphasized by another subtle change from the opening vision of 1:9–20. In

1:13 Christ is seen simply as being in the midst of the seven golden lampstands (the Greek text has no verb); here Christ "walks" (*peripatōn*) among them. The opening vision identifies the seven lampstands with the seven churches (1:20); the second Christ title therefore portrays Jesus as intimately present with the congregations of Asia Minor and walking among them. He has power over life both on earth and in the heavens, and his sovereign control exceeds that of any Roman emperor; yet he is not a ruler who is distant and removed but is present and near his churches, including the Ephesian congregation.

Christ's presence contains a dual aspect of both comfort and challenge. On the one hand, the believers in Ephesus are comforted by the knowledge that they are not alone: the all-powerful Christ is present and "watches over" them as they face false apostles, unorthodox teachings, and other threats to their spiritual well-being. On the other hand, they are challenged by the knowledge that the all-powerful Christ is present and "watches" them, which gives him an intimate knowledge of their spiritual condition (2:2, "I know . . .") and reinforces his warning about the potential need for him to come and remove their lampstand (2:5).

The Commendation (2:2–3, 6)

Christ typically begins his address to each particular church by commending its members for what they are doing well, a pattern that begins here. Yet his praise of the Ephesian congregation is hardly a perfunctory act or token note of politeness before he turns to what he really wants to say in the complaint. Instead, the commendation in the Ephesian sermon is fulsome and strong, and this fact ought not to be downplayed (as, e.g., Wall 1991: 69, who claims that Ephesus, perhaps along with Laodicea, is the most severely condemned of the seven churches). Although Christ commends the church for a number of things, the ultimate characteristic that connects these items of praise together concerns the Ephesian believers' *orthodoxy*—their passion for the truth and aggressive effort not to be misled by the wicked, whether they be false apostles or the Nicolaitans.

The Main Commendation (2:2–3)

The commendation begins with what will become a standard opening formula for all seven sermons: "I know." The choice of the word for "know" is regarded as significant by some. They claim that the verb used here (*oida*) refers to "full or complete knowledge" in contrast to another Greek verb

(*ginōskō*) that "speaks of progress of knowledge" (Thomas 1992: 133). However, this distinction in meaning is not supported by the use of these two
verbs in the rest of the book of Revelation (*oida*: 2:2, 9, 13, 17, 19; 3:1, 8,
15, 17; 7:14; 12:12; 19:12; *ginōskō*: 2:23, 24; 3:3, 9). Nor must we rely on the
verb to convey the idea of Jesus's "full or complete knowledge." The second
Christ title has already introduced Jesus as the one who is walking among
the seven lampstands, that is, the seven churches, and this means that he is
fully aware of the situation of each church and thereby wholly justified in his
commendation and his complaint. The object of this complete knowledge of
Christ is "your works." This same object is used with this opening formula
in all seven sermons except two (2:9, Smyrna; 2:13, Pergamum). To Protes-
tant ears, the word "works" may be associated with "deeds" as opposed to
"faith," to what people do in contrast to what people believe. Yet it is clear
from the seven sermons as a whole that the word "works" refers to both. This
is understandable when we remember that actions are intimately connected
to beliefs. Therefore, all seven sermons deal not only with right and wrong
conduct but with the right and wrong thinking that lies behind such conduct.

The works of the Ephesians that Christ fully knows are clarified as "your
labor and perseverance." The Greek text lists all three nouns in a simple se-
quential manner that literally reads, "I know your works *and* labor *and* your
perseverance." Based on its similarity to 1 Thess. 1:3, where these three nouns
are listed in the same order, some see here not just a triad but "a traditional
Christian triad" (Beasley-Murray 1978: 74; see also Aune 1997: 142; Michaels
1997: 70). However, there are compelling reasons not to view the three terms
equally as objects of what Christ knows but instead to see the second and
third terms as specific explanations of the first generic term: (1) "works"
occurs in the plural, in contrast to "labor" and "perseverance," which are in
the singular; (2) none of the four subsequent sermons that have "works" as
the object of what Christ knows include both "labor" and "perseverance"
(see 2:19; 3:1, 8, 15); (3) the personal pronoun "your" is included with the
first and third terms but not with the second, suggesting that it applies to
the last two terms and that the terms belong together ("your labor and perseverance"); and (4) the second and third terms are picked up and repeated
in the immediately following clauses, but the first term is not. Therefore, the
conjunction (*kai*) that appears before the second term almost certainly has
an explanatory function (BDAG 495.1.c) so that the commendation should
read: "I know your works, *namely*, your labor and perseverance" (as many
commentators agree).

This conclusion is not merely a technical grammatical point but an important clue for understanding the structure of the rest of Christ's commendation

of the Ephesians, as the two explanatory terms are further explicated. The word "labor" is explained in the rest of 2:2, which deals with the church's *active* response to those challenging orthodoxy, and the word "perseverance" is elucidated in 2:3, which describes the church's *passive* response to the situation they face (so Charles 1920: 49; Thomas 1992: 133; Osborne 2002: 112). Forms of these two terms appear in subsequent verses (the noun "labor" in v. 2 has the same root as the verb "to grow weary" in v. 3; "perseverance" in v. 2 is repeated in v. 3). Likewise, the double use of a third term ("to endure" in v. 2 also appears in v. 3) lends lexical coherence to this subunit (i.e., the commendation of 2:2–3) within the sermon. All of these observations strengthen the case that the structure proposed above is not merely imagined by modern exegetes but was intended by the ancient author. This two-part structure of the commendation can be seen more easily when the text is presented as follows:

> "Labor" refers to the Ephesian church's *active* response to those challenging orthodoxy, which is explained in the rest of verse 2: "and you are not able to endure wicked people, and you tested those who call themselves apostles—and they are not—and you have found them false."
>
> "Perseverance" refers to the Ephesian church's *passive* response to those challenging orthodoxy, which is explained in verse 3: "and you have perseverance and you have endured [wicked people] on account of my name and have not grown weary."

The labor of the Ephesian church is first explained as "You are not able to endure wicked people." This church's concern for orthodoxy is revealed in their refusal to tolerate anyone who can be called "wicked." The congregation in Ephesus does not succumb to the temptation to avoid conflict by simply putting up with those in their midst whose character and conduct are evil; instead, the church's passion for the truth makes them unable to endure such folks.

The depth of the Ephesian congregation's defense of orthodoxy becomes even clearer in the second way that their labor is explained: "You tested those who call themselves apostles." The word "apostle" has three different meanings in the NT and early Christian literature. (1) It sometimes refers narrowly to the twelve disciples of Jesus (see Rev. 21:14)—a meaning that is impossible here in 2:2, since it is far-fetched to believe that anyone at this late date would try to pass themselves off as one of the original disciples or that Christ would commend the Ephesian church for discerning such an obvious falsehood. (2) On a few occasions, the word "apostle" refers to those who are simply messengers without any extraordinary status other than the authority of the person or church sending them on a mission (John 13:16; Phil. 2:25; 2 Cor. 8:23). (3) The term "apostle" most often, however, refers to "highly honored believers with a special function as God's envoys" (BDAG 122.2.c). Such apostles include not only well-known leaders such as Paul, James (Gal. 1:19), and Barnabas (Acts 14:14) but also more obscure figures such as Andronicus and Junia (Rom. 16:7) as well as unnamed individuals who claimed divine commissioning and authority (see 2 Cor. 11:5; 12:11). Those whom the Ephesians tested claimed to belong to this third category. They were not merely messengers but missionaries who called themselves "apostles," thereby invoking divine authority for their teachings.

The danger faced by the Ephesian congregation was common in the early church. The Letter of 2 John exhorts its readers not to welcome into their house-church gatherings itinerant preachers "who do not acknowledge Jesus Christ as coming in the flesh" (2 John 7; see also 1 John 4:1–3a). The Letter of Jude addresses the problem of "shepherds" (i.e., leaders, Jude 12) from outside the local church who "have secretly slipped in among you" and "who pervert the grace of our God into a license for immorality" (Jude 4). The Letter of 2 Peter warns its readers that, just as "there were false prophets" among the people of God in OT times, so also "there will be false teachers among you" (2 Pet. 2:1). The Didache, an anonymous Christian treatise dating to the late first century or early second century, provides instructions on how the church should welcome visiting apostles and how to distinguish the false prophet from the true by their behavior (Did. 11.3–11). False prophets in the early church were not only a common danger but also a predicted problem. Some forty or so years earlier, Paul warned the Ephesian elders in his farewell address that "after I leave, savage wolves will come in among you and will not spare the flock" (Acts 20:29). Paul's prophetic warning of heretical outsiders came true, and so the Ephesian church is commended by Christ for not naively accepting the apostolic claims of all itinerant missionaries but instead putting them to the test and finding some to be false—a finding with which the author of the sermon agrees in a parenthetical comment ("and they are not").

Who were these false apostles? Answers to this question vary widely. Some claim that they were legalists like the opponents whom Paul faced in Corinth, whom he similarly describes as "false apostles" (2 Cor. 11:13; see Spitta 1889: 251; Hort 1908: 21). Others reach the completely opposite conclusion, arguing that "the context suggests that self-appointed apostles were antinomians rather than legalists" (Mounce 1977: 87; Hemer 1986: 40). Still other interpreters have viewed these false apostles as Gnostics who appealed to the heavenly Christ over against the earthly Jesus and whose negative view of the flesh led to an anything-goes ethic, thus justifying the earlier description of them as

"wicked people" (Beasley-Murray 1978: 74). These three proposed identifica-
tions all suffer from a lack of compelling evidence.

Many instead connect the false apostles with the Nicolaitans mentioned
later in the sermon, viewing the two groups as identical (so, e.g., Charles
1920: 50; Thomas 1992: 136–38; Kistemaker 2001: 113). There are several
reasons, however, why this proposal is also unconvincing. First, each group
seems to have threatened the Ephesian church at different time periods: the
congregation in Ephesus "tested" and "found" (past tense) these apostles to
be false, whereas they "hate" (present tense) the works of the Nicolaitans.
Second, the strong adversative "but" (*alla*) that introduces the Nicolaitans
in 2:6 more likely marks the beginning of a new reason for commendation
rather than a restatement about the false apostles mentioned in 2:3 (Aune 1997:
147). Third, if the Nicolaitans were in fact the same as the false apostles, this
would render 2:6 redundant: there would be no need for Christ to commend
the Ephesians for hating the practices of the Nicolaitans if he had already
praised them a few verses earlier for testing this group and finding them to
be false. Fourth, those claiming to be apostles have come from outside the
Ephesian church, whereas the Nicolaitans appear to be heretical insiders.
It is most probable, therefore, that the "false apostles" and Nicolaitans are
two separate subgroups of the larger category of "wicked people" whom the
Ephesian church is not able to tolerate.

Identifying the false apostles is less important to the commendation than
highlighting the Ephesians' demonstrated track record of defending orthodoxy. This concern for truth was not a fleeting interest but a long-standing
passion of the Ephesian church: they demonstrated it in the *past* by testing
false apostles (note the past tense of "tested" and "found"), in the *present* by
not tolerating wicked people in general and the practices of the Nicolaitans
in particular (note the present tense of "not able to endure" and "hate"), and
even into the *future*. A short time later (perhaps only a decade), the church
father Ignatius of Syrian Antioch cites the bishop of Ephesus, Onesimus,
who praised the Ephesian church because "all of you live according to the
truth and no heresy resides among you. On the contrary, you no longer listen
to anyone, except one who speaks truthfully about Jesus Christ" (Ign. *Eph.*
6.2; Ehrman 2003). In the same letter, Ignatius further writes, "I have learned
that some people have passed through on their way from there with an evil
teaching. But you did not permit them to sow any seeds among you, plugging
your ears so as not to receive anything sown by them" (Ign. *Eph.* 9.1; Ehrman
2003). The "labor" of the Ephesian church for which Christ commends them,
therefore, concerns their orthodoxy—their passionate and persistent defense
of the truth.

After fleshing out the first key term, "labor," Christ's commendation goes on to explain the second key term, "perseverance": "And you have perseverance, and you have endured on account of my name, and you have not grown weary" (2:3). The word "perseverance" (*hypomonē*), which occurs six other times in the book of Revelation (1:9; 2:2, 19; 3:10; 13:10; 14:12; the verbal form does not appear), refers to "the capacity to hold out or bear up in the face of difficulty" and can be variously translated as "patience, endurance, fortitude, steadfastness, perseverance" (BDAG 1039). Just as the general term "labor" in 2:2 is clarified by the clause that immediately follows, so also here the general term "perseverance" is made clearer by the next statement: "and you endured on account of my name." The verb "endure" is repeated from the preceding verse, where its object was "wicked people." Even though no object is explicitly stated here in 2:3, the same object can be assumed: "and you have endured *wicked people* on account of my name." The perseverance for which the Ephesians are being commended, therefore, does not refer broadly to any and all types of hardships (so the NIV) but instead specifies the danger of visiting missionaries and itinerant preachers who claim to be authoritative apostles. The final clause "and you have not grown weary," expressed in the emphatic perfect tense, suggests that "the problem of false teachers faced by the Ephesian Christians was no temporary crisis but one that exerted a severe test of their steadfast adherence to the gospel. Here was a church outstanding for her doctrinal purity" (Ladd 1972: 39).

The Additional Commendation (2:6)

Literary, grammatical, and contextual considerations all show that the commendation comes to a close in 2:3. Literary evidence for this is found in the *inclusio*—the framing device—formed by cognates of the key term "labor." The noun form (*kopos*) opens this section (2:2), and the verb of the same root (*kekopiakes*, you have not grown weary) closes this section (2:3). Yet as noted above, this unit also repeats a second key word (the noun "endurance" and the verb "to endure"), thereby giving this commendation lexical coherence. A new unit in the sermon starts in 2:4, as signaled grammatically by the strong adversative "but" (*alla*) and contextually by the shift from commendation to complaint ("I have this against you . . ."). With these boundaries of the commendation so clearly marked, it is surprising to find a resumption of Christ's praise for the Ephesian church later in 2:6: "But you have this, namely, you hate the works of the Nicolaitans, which I also hate." This resumption of the commendation is signaled not only by Christ's words of praise but also by the linking key word "works": the "works" that Jesus knows and for which he commends the Ephesians in 2:2–3 ("I know your works . . .") include the fact that they hate the "works" of the Nicolaitans.

The additional commendation of 2:6 reveals even further the depth of the Ephesian church's preoccupation with orthodoxy. Compared to the earlier descriptions of their response to those advocating falsehoods, their passion for the truth comes out in the more intense language of the verbs used here. Not only were the believers in Ephesus "not able to endure" wicked people and actively putting "to the test" those claiming to be apostles, but they were also aggressively hating the works of the Nicolaitans. As Osborne (2002: 119) notes, the language here "is much stronger than 2:2–3. There they found the false teachers to be 'false,' but here they 'hate' their 'works.'"

In our contemporary pluralistic and relativistic society, such a response may seem intolerant. Christ's commendation of the Ephesian church's hatred may also appear to contradict Christ's complaint in the preceding verse that they have "abandoned the love [they] had at first" (2:4). But Christ is praising the believers in Ephesus for their hatred, not of the Nicolaitans themselves, but of their "works." The common distinction between "hating the sin" and "loving the sinner"—though criticized as illegitimate by some and not always practiced by those who too glibly cite it—nevertheless appears to be supported by this sermon. After all, Jesus not only praises the Ephesians for hating the works of the Nicolaitans, but he himself hates what they hate. There is no justification from any NT text for pitting Christ's emphasis on love for others against his hatred of the sinful acts that people do. God said of his Son: "You have loved righteousness and hated wickedness" (Heb. 1:9). The same Jesus who commanded his followers not to hate but to "love your enemies" (Matt. 5:43–44) is also described as an "avenger" who will one day return to punish people for their sin (1 Thess. 4:6). Similarly, there is an appropriate way for followers of Jesus to demonstrate love for others while at the same time hating the sinful actions of others. Christ thus further commends the Ephesian church for demonstrating their orthodoxy by their hatred of the works of the Nicolaitans.

Who were the Nicolaitans, and what was the nature of their hate-inducing works? They are mentioned only twice in the Bible, both instances occurring here in Rev. 2. The present reference in v. 6 to "the works of the Nicolaitans" is cryptic, and the mention in 2:15 of "the teaching of the Nicolaitans" in the sermon to Pergamum is similarly obscure. Although Rev 2:6 offers no clues about the identity of this group, 2:14–15 connects the Nicolaitans with the behavior of Balaam, who caused Israel to eat food sacrificed to idols (the sin of idolatry) and to commit sexual immorality. The immediately follow- ing sermon to Thyatira refers to Jezebel, another infamous OT villain, who likewise caused Israel to commit these same two sins (2:20–23; the order of these closely linked sins is reversed), so this text is also potentially relevant for understanding the identity of the Nicolaitans.

After the two references in the book of Revelation, Irenaeus contains the earliest mention of the Nicolaitans. He claims that they were followers of Nicolaus, one of the seven "deacons" of Acts 6:5, and that they led lives of "unrestrained indulgence" (*Against Heresies* 1.26.3). But Irenaeus describes their libertine lifestyle by citing the two sins mentioned in Rev. 2:14, which suggests that he did not have any additional information about the Nicolaitans beyond what is given in the Pergamum sermon. Other church fathers also make comments about the Nicolaitans (see Hilgenfeld 1963: 408–11), but their claims involve "a heavy mixture of legend and imagination" (Aune 1997: 149) and so are not much help in determining the identity of this heretical group that existed within the churches of Asia Minor.

Irenaeus elsewhere asserts that the Gospel of John was written to repudiate the error of Cerinthus and his Gnostic cosmology, adding that this error was held "a long time previously by those termed Nicolaitans, who are an offset of that 'knowledge' falsely so called" (*Against Heresies* 3.11.1, *ANF* 1:426). The "knowledge falsely so called" is an allusion to 1 Tim. 6:20 and refers originally to erroneous teachings in Ephesus, about which Paul was warning Timothy; yet Irenaeus attributes the same *gnōsis* or false knowledge to the Nicolaitans. The reference in the Thyatira sermon to "the so-called 'deep secrets of Satan'" (2:24) may indicate a Gnostic background for the teaching of Jezebel and thus also of the Nicolaitans. These are some of the reasons why many modern scholars have concluded that the Nicolaitans were Gnostics (so, e.g., Harnack 1923; Schüssler Fiorenza 1973; Prigent 1977; Beasley-Murray 1978: 74).

But though Gnostic—or more precisely, proto-Gnostic thinking like that opposed in 1 and 2 John and the Pastoral Letters—is a possible characterization of the Nicolaitans, there is too little reliable information available to be certain about the teachings of this group (see the concerns raised by Hemer 1986: 93–94; Aune 1997: 148–49). Furthermore, a Gnostic theology is not necessary to explain what we can be certain about, which is their practices. The Pergamum sermon makes clear (2:14–15), as does the Thyatira sermon (2:20), that the Nicolaitans encouraged others to join them in two activities explicitly forbidden at the Jerusalem Council: eating food sacrificed to idols (the sin of idolatry) and committing sexual immorality (see Acts 15:20, 29). Their justification for doing such things likely involved reasoning similar to that of the Corinthians who engaged in the same two forbidden activities. They claimed that because there is only one true God and that all other so-called gods do not really exist, all who possess knowledge of these truths have a right to participate in cultic meals with impunity (1 Cor. 8:1–11:1, esp. 8:4–6). About the Nicolaitans, Mounce (1977: 89) states, "Broadly speaking, they had worked out a compromise with the pagan society in which they lived."

What must not be lost sight of in the debate over the precise identity of the Nicolaitans is that their actions were hated by the Ephesian church, and Jesus commends them for this hatred. In sharp contrast to some in the Pergamum church "who hold to the teaching of the Nicolaitans" (2:15) and others in the Thyatiran church "who tolerate that woman Jezebel" (2:20) and her Nicolaitan-like practices, the Ephesian church aggressively rejected the works of this heretical group, thereby providing further evidence of their passionate pursuit of orthodoxy.

The Complaint (2:4)

After commending a church for what it is doing right, Christ typically follows with a complaint that highlights what it is doing wrong. This shift from commendation to complaint is marked by the stereotyped phrase "But I have [this] against you" (*alla echō kata sou*). The complaint formula occurs in the first (Ephesus), third (Pergamum), and fourth (Thyatira) sermons (2:4, 14, 20) but is missing from the fifth (Sardis) and seventh (Laodicea) sermons because these latter two messages have no commendation with which the complaint contrasts; Christ simply proceeds directly to spelling out what grievances he has against these two churches. Similarly, the complaint formula is missing in the second (Smyrna) and sixth (Philadelphia) sermons, but in those cases it is because Christ has nothing to criticize about these two churches.

Christ's lengthy commendation of the Ephesian church is followed by his brief but pointed complaint: "But I have this against you: you have abandoned the love you had at first" (2:4). The key exegetical issue concerns the object of this abandoned love: Has the Ephesian church abandoned its love for God and/or Christ or its love for fellow believers?

Several, mostly older commentators, choose the first of these two options. Tait (1884: 147), for example, asserts: "Now the Angel, as the representative of the Church at Ephesus, is reminded of the early devotion of that Church to God." Walvoord (1966: 55) similarly concludes about the Ephesian congregation that "though they had not departed completely from the love for God, their love no longer had the fervency, depth, or meaning it once had had in the church." Proponents of this view frequently appeal to the many years that had passed since the founding of the Ephesian church and how the subsequent generation of believers did not possess the same passion as the original converts. Hendriksen (1940: 61) explains the historical situation as follows:

> Thus it will be evident that the church at Ephesus was more than forty years old when Christ dictated this epistle. Another generation had arisen. The children did not experience that intense enthusiasm, that spontaneity and ardor which had been revealed by their parents when the latter first came into contact with the gospel. Not only this, but they lacked their former devotion to Christ. A similar condition occurred in Israel after the days of Joshua and the elders (Judg. 2:7, 10, 11). The church had departed from its first love.

Similar comments can be found in Thomas (1992: 141) and Kistemaker (2001: 115).

Some (Brighton 1999: 68n13) further argue that the reference to the "first" love recalls "the greatest and *first* commandment," which is to "love the Lord your God with all your heart and with all your soul and with all your mind" (Matt. 22:37–38).

Although the first option (loss of love for God and/or Christ) remains a possibility, there are compelling arguments in support of the second option (loss of love for others), leading us to conclude with a high degree of confidence that the actual problem in the Ephesian congregation was their lack of love for fellow church members.

First, there is the fulsome and strong character of the commendation (2:2–3, 6). It seems unlikely that Christ could so warmly praise the Ephesian church if it had lost its love for him or his Father. It also seems unlikely that the Ephesian church would have such strongly negative feelings toward wicked people—unable to put up with false apostles, hating the practices of the Nicolaitans—if it had abandoned its original devotion to God and/or Christ. Those whose love for God and/or Christ has waned are typically more tolerant or apathetic toward evil.

Second, the correction Christ offers (2:5a) seems more appropriate as an antidote to a lack of love for others than a lack of love for God and/or Christ. Although the first and second commands in the correction to "remember" and "repent" could fit either problem, the third command to "do the works you did at first" answers better the failure to love fellow believers. If the problem were failure to love God and/or Christ, the corrective command would more likely be something like "Believe in God!" or "Return to me!" The noun "works" earlier in the sermon (2:2) refers to the actions of the Ephesian believers toward other people rather than God, and the same object is likely in view here in the command to "do the works you did at first."

Third, love for others is a theme stressed in Johannine writings. It is not in the Gospels of Matthew, Mark, or Luke but only in John that we hear Jesus say: "A new command I give you: love one another. As I have loved you, so you must love one another. By this all people will know that you are my disciples, if you love one another" (John 13:34–35). The letter of 1 John repeatedly exhorts its readers to demonstrate love to fellow Christians, often doing so in strong language: "Whoever claims to love God yet hates a brother or sister is a liar. For whoever does not love their brother and sister, whom they have seen, cannot love God, whom they have not seen. And he has given us this command: Anyone who loves God must also love their brother and sister" (1 John 4:20–21; also 2:9–11; 3:11–14; 4:16). The brevity of 2 John does not prevent this letter from affirming the same theme: "And now, dear lady, I am not writing you a new command but one we have had from the beginning. I ask that we love one another" (2 John 5). The equally brief letter of 3 John commends its recipient, Gaius, for his loving act of hospitality extended to faithful itinerant preachers: "Dear friend, you are faithful in what you are doing for the brothers and sisters, even though they are strangers to you. They have told the church about your love" (3 John 5–6a).

Fourth, the adjective "first" can refer either to time ("earlier, at first," BDAG 892.1) or to rank ("foremost, most important," BDAG 893.2). "Your first love," then, has two possible meanings: (1) the love that the Ephesians had at an earlier time ("the love that you had at first") or (2) the love that is most important, such as the Ephesians love for God and/or Jesus. The adjective "first" in the immediately following verse (2:5a, "Do the first things!") almost certainly refers to time ("Do the works you did *at first*"; so virtually all translations) rather than rank ("Do the most important works!"), and the close connection between these two verses ("first works" paralleling "first love") strongly suggests a temporal meaning for the adjective "first" in both places.

Fifth and most significantly, the specific content of the commendation— not merely its length and warm tone—supports the second option. We have noted several times how the commendation reveals the passion of the Ephesian church for the truth. While its commitment to orthodoxy is a virtue for which the Ephesian church is praised by Christ, it was also apparently a vice of this congregation. What is true of people can also be true of churches: their greatest strength can paradoxically become their greatest weakness. The Ephesian church was so preoccupied with identifying wicked people, exposing false apostles, and rejecting the sinful practices of the Nicolaitans that a spirit of suspicion and mistrust permeated their fellowship, making it impossible for them to be the caring, compassionate community that they had been in the past. In short, they were a church of *loveless orthodoxy*. Caird (1966: 31) describes their situation like this:

> The one charge against the Ephesians is that their intolerance of imposture, their unflagging loyalty, and their hatred of heresy had bred an inquisitorial spirit which left no room for love. They had set out to be defenders of the faith, arming themselves with the heroic virtues of truth and courage, only to discover that in the battle they had lost the one quality without which all others are worthless.

Ladd (1972: 39) identifies the problem in Ephesus in the same way:

> The Lord had taught that mutual love was to be a hallmark of Christian fellowship (John 13:35). The Ephesian converts had known such a love in their early years; but their struggle with false teachers and their hatred of heretical teaching had apparently engendered hard feelings and harsh attitudes toward one another to such an extent that it amounted to a forsaking of the supreme Christian virtue of love. Doctrinal purity and loyalty can never be a substitute for love.

Love for fellow believers, of course, can never be completely disconnected from love for God. The intimate link between the vertical and horizontal dimensions of love is clear from the famous summary of the law (Matt. 22:37–39; Mark 12:29–31; Luke 10:27) and other key texts such as 1 John 4:20–21, cited above. Some commentators, therefore, argue that both dimensions of love are intended in Christ's complaint against the Ephesian church. Michaels (1997: 71), for example, interprets this verse as referring to "their love toward God and their generosity toward each other. . . . Here as everywhere in the Bible, love for God and love for one another are inseparable." Other exegetes similarly highlight both dimensions of love but rightly recognize that in this context love for others is primarily in view. Mounce (1977: 69–70) comments:

> The Ephesian church had forsaken its first love. The expression includes both love of God and love of humanity at large, but here it seems to refer mainly to the love that the Ephesian converts had for one another (as in 2 John 5). . . . Love for other believers was the distinctive badge of Christian discipleship, but at Ephesus hatred of heresy and extensive involvement in the works appropriate to faith had allowed the first fresh glow of love for God and one another to fade.

Jesus warned his followers about a coming time involving a twofold danger: a time when "many false prophets will appear and deceive many people" and that "the love of most will grow cold" (Matt. 24:11–12). The Ephesian church was commended for its faithful response to the first of these dangers but condemned for the way it fell victim to the second (Michaels 1997: 71). As important as orthodoxy may be to the overall mission of the church, it must never come at the expense of love for others.

The Correction (2:5a)

Christ does not merely rebuke the Ephesian church and then abandon them in their state of condemnation, leaving them to remedy their own sinful situation. Instead, he graciously provides a solution to their fundamental problem: "Therefore, remember from where you have fallen, repent, and do the works you did at first!" (2:5a)

The close connection between the correction and the complaint is signaled by the inferential particle "therefore" (*oun*): the three commands to "remember," "repent," and "do" all logically follow from the church's problem of failing to love others as they had done in the past. The first command in this three-step recovery program is to "remember." Remembering one's past can be a particularly powerful agent of moral change. For example, when the prodigal son was so hungry that he longed to eat the food he was feeding the pigs, he remembered his former life of abundance at home and then "came to his senses" and returned home, repentant and prepared to ask for his father's forgiveness (Luke 15:17–18). Paul, attempting the difficult task of unifying the church in Ephesus, which was seriously divided along ethnic lines over the issue of circumcision, commands his gentile readers to remember their former status: "At that time you were separate from Christ, excluded from citizenship in Israel and foreigners to the covenants of the promise, without hope and without God in the world" (Eph. 2:11–12). Some forty years later the Ephesian church is again commanded to remember its past. This time the challenge comes from Christ, who urges them to recall the concrete acts of love—kindness, compassion, empathy—that once characterized their fellowship.

The interrogative adverbial clause that follows the command to remember is rendered by most translations as "*how far* you have fallen," which highlights the great gap between the Ephesian church's past demonstrations of love and their current state. Some commentators further exaggerate this gap with poetic overstatement: "Pure love resided on the cliff high above, as it were, and they [the Ephesian church] had fallen deep into the valley below" (Thomas 1992: 142; see also Robertson 1933: 6.299). But though there was a significant difference between the church's past and present manifestations of mutual love, the interrogative adverbial clause more simply means "*from where* you have fallen" (BDAG 838.1). The use of the rarer perfect tense stresses the current condition of the church: their production of works of love had fallen off in the past and was still very much a present reality.

The second command of the correction is to "repent." This Greek verb (*metanoeō*) is made up of two parts and literally means "to change one's mind." In colloquial terms, it involves engaging in a mental U-turn—recognizing that one's old way of thinking is wrong and that a new perspective is needed. For the Ephesian church, repentance means realizing that their passion for the truth, though commendable, must not come at the expense of their passion for loving others. The importance of repentance, despite the natural human reluctance to admit error, must not be downplayed, since a change in thinking logically leads to a change in conduct. The Ephesians will not act in more loving ways until they first recognize the error of their old way of thinking and the need for change. The indispensability of repentance for initiating change is reflected in the fact that every one of the five problematic or unhealthy churches is called upon to repent: Ephesus (2:5 [2×]), Pergamum (2:16), Thyatira (2:21 [2×], 22), Sardis (3:3), and Laodicea (3:19). The specific complaint in each church varies, but the correction is the same: Repent!

The Ephesians' change in thinking ought to lead naturally to a change in conduct, and so the third command of the correction not surprisingly reads, "Do the works you did at first!" The fact that the climax of the three-step recovery program involves a call to "do" rather than "believe" or some other relational verb reinforces the conclusion that the complaint involves primarily a lack of love for others rather than a lack of love for God and/or Christ, even though these two aspects of love must not be too sharply distinguished. The Greek text places the direct object at the head of the sentence to stress the "first works" that the Ephesian church must do. The believers in Ephesus need to put love into action and demonstrate the kind of compassion and care for others that originally characterized their communal life and fellowship.

The Consequence (2:5b, 7b)

Each sermon closes with Christ spelling out the potential consequences that the church faces for its behavior. There are always two consequences: the first is normally negative, what punishment will ensue if the church fails to follow Christ's correction, and the second is always positive, what reward awaits the church if it repents and with Christ's help conquers its particular sin(s).

Negative Consequence (2:5b)

The negative consequence is presented as two conditional (if-then) clauses, with the second of the two appearing in reverse order, forming a chiasm:

A   But if not, (protasis)
    B   I am coming to you (apodosis)
    B′ and will remove your lampstand from its place (apodosis)
A′ if you do not repent. (protasis)

The payoff for recognizing this literary pattern is that the chiasm provides a clear answer to what verb is omitted and thus implied in the opening elliptical formula "But if not." This idiom, common in both Classical Greek and the NT, introduces an alternative possibility to something just said (BDF §376; BDAG 278.6, s.v. *ei*) and so could potentially refer to all three commands (remember, repent, and do) from the preceding correction. With its balancing clause (A′), however, the chiasm shows that it is the second of these three actions (repent) that is implied in the opening clause (A). The Pergamum sermon confirms this interpretation because its correction "Therefore repent!" is likewise immediately followed by the same elliptical formula "But if not" (2:16). Further corroboration is found in the Thyatira sermon, where the negative consequence is similarly stated as "If they do not repent" (2:22). The double reference to repentance in both the correction and the consequence (a triple reference, if one includes the implied verb) of 2:5a and 2:5b provides additional grounds for our assertion about the indispensability of repentance for correcting sinful conduct.

There are two key questions concerning the negative consequence: (1) What is the nature of the judgment threatened against the Ephesian church, and (2) what is the timing of that judgment?

THE NATURE OF THE THREATENED JUDGMENT

The first question deals with whether Christ's warning ("I will remove your lampstand from its place") refers to the destruction, loss of witness, or movement of the Ephesian church. In the opening chapter of Revelation, the seven lampstands are said to represent the seven churches (1:20), which leads most commentators to understand the removal of the lampstand as referring to the *destruction* of the Ephesian church. Beasley-Murray (1978: 75) states, "The bluntness of the words must be allowed full force; . . . that will mean the end of its existence as a church of Christ." Aune (1997: 75) similarly affirms, "This is nothing less than a threat to obliterate the Ephesian congregation as an empirical Christian community."

The book of Revelation later describes the two witnesses who will prophesy for 1,260 days as "the two lampstands" (11:4). This, along with the metaphor of a lampstand casting the light of testimony (Mark 4:21; Luke 8:16), has caused a few exegetes to argue that the negative consequence here for the Ephesian church is their *loss of witness* to the nations (Beale and Campbell 2015: 56; see also A. Johnson 1981: 434–35; Thomas 1992: 146–47). The destruction of the Ephesian church would obviously also result in the loss of their witness, but the evangelistic task of this congregation is not mentioned anywhere in the immediate context.

An alternative interpretation highlights the literal meaning of the verb *kineō* (2:5), which refers not to destruction but to *movement*: "to cause something to be moved from its customary or established place, *move away, remove*" (BDAG 545.1). This view was championed over a century ago by Ramsay (1904: 169–71, 184–86; 1994: 176–78), who argued that the background for this judgment against the Ephesian church was the three times this famous city and its strategic harbor had to relocate. Silting in the Cayster River was a constant problem for shipping, requiring the city's frequent relocation and leading ultimately to its abandonment. After reviewing this history of locational change, Ramsay (1994: 178) concludes:

> A threat of removing the church from its place would be inevitably understood by the Ephesians as a denunciation of another change in the site of the city, and must have been so intended by the writer. Ephesus and its church should be taken up, and moved away to a new spot, where it might begin afresh on a new career with a better spirit.

Others similarly appeal to the city's frequent locational changes but come to a more metaphorical interpretation of the threat to the Ephesian church. Hemer (1986: 53) argues, "The danger was that the great harbor-city and its vigorous church would be moved back under the deadening power of the [Artemis] temple." Wilson (2002: 262) asserts: "A less harsh, and perhaps better, reading is that Christ will move the Ephesian lampstand from its leadership position as an apostolic church among the Asian churches and pass its authority along to another congregation."

This softer judgment appeals to modern sensitivities, but it exaggerates the importance of the city's changes in location for citizens living at the end of the first century AD. The last major "movement" of Ephesus had been almost four hundred years earlier, under Alexander the Great's general Lysimachus, who relocated the city a short distance from one side of Mount Pion to the other. Even though the harbor continued to face the threat of silting in this new location, requiring dredging operations and other ultimately futile solutions, the location of this important port did not change during the late Hellenistic and Roman periods. Furthermore, the "movement" interpretation is undermined by Ramsay himself, who concedes that although the threat to "remove your lampstand from its place" was "natural and plain" in meaning to the Ephesians, "no other of the seven cities would have found those words so clear and significant" (1994: 178). Also, the verb *kineō* can have the meaning of eradication or destruction, as seen in Josephus's use of this word to describe critics of the Jewish faith who try to pressure Jews not to "move" their laws but to "remove" them (*Against Apion* 2.272). Finally, as R. H. Charles (1920: 52) observed a century ago: "That the threat in our text implies not degradation nor removal of the Church to another place, but destruction, seems obvious."

Though a severe judgment, Christ's destruction of the Ephesian church is no harsher than judgments found elsewhere in this sermon (e.g., his hatred of the works of the Nicolaitans) and in the messages to the other four unhealthy churches: he will make war against some in Pergamum with the sword of his mouth, will strike dead the children of Jezebel in Thyatira, declares the church in Sardis dead, and will vomit out the church in Laodicea. Instead of being offended at such a strong judgment, modern hearers should be sobered by this powerful reminder of the importance Christ places on the command to love others. If "the punishment fits the crime," then the potential destruction of the Ephesian church reveals how crucial it is for the body of Christ to be characterized by mutual love.

THE TIMING OF THE THREATENED JUDGMENT

We turn now to the second question raised by the threatened negative consequence, which asks how Christ's opening statement "I am coming to you" sheds light on the timing of his judgment against the Ephesian church. Does this refer to the parousia—the second coming of Christ at the end of time in order to inaugurate the final judgment of all people—or to an earlier, special coming of Christ to execute a preliminary judgment on the Ephesian church alone? Since virtually every sermon refers to the coming of Christ (2:5, 16, 25; 3:3, 11, 20), most often to punish a wayward church rather than to comfort a faithful one, this same question of timing is relevant for subsequent sermons as well. A compelling case for either position can be made, so it is not surprising that scholarly opinion is evenly divided, with a slight preference for a special coming of Christ distinct from his final parousia (so, e.g., Charles 1920: 52; Lenski 1935: 90; Caird 1966: 32; Ladd 1972: 39–40; Mounce

1977: 89; Beasley-Murray 1978: 75; Kistemaker 2001: 116; Beale and Campbell 2015: 56–57). In this debate, we should remember the important observation of Osborne (2002: 118): "Scholars often find too great a dichotomy between present and future judgment in the book. There is an inaugurated force in passages such as this one. Christ's coming in judgment in the present is a harbinger of his final coming. In this context, Christ's displeasure will be felt both in the present and at the final judgment."

Positive Consequence (2:7b)

Each sermon ends not with a negative tone of judgment but a positive note of victory, always expressed with the key verb *nikaō*, "to win in the face of obstacles, *be victor, conquer, overcome, prevail*" (BDAG 673.1). This word is important in John's writings, occurring some twenty-four times (Rev. 2:7b, 11b, 17b, 26a; 3:5, 12, 21 [2×]; 5:5; 6:2 [2×]; 11:7; 12:11; 13:7; 15:2; 17:14; 21:7; 1 John 2:13, 14; 4:4; 5:4 [2×], 5; John 16:33), with only four instances in the rest of the NT. This pattern of usage caused Swete (1911: 29) to observe, "The note of victory is dominant in St. John, as that of faith in St. Paul." The word "victory" (*nikē/nikaō*) is actually equated with "faith" (*pistis/pisteuō*) in 1 John 5:4–5: "And this is the *victory* that *conquers* the world—our *faith*. Who is the *victor* over the world but the one who *believes* that Jesus is the Son of God?" The description in Rev. 2:7b of "the one who is victorious," therefore, does not refer to a special class of Christians such as martyrs, believers who end up losing their life for following Jesus (so several commentators: e.g., Charles 1920: 54; Mounce 1977: 33; Harrington 1993: 57). Rather, it refers to all true Christians, not just those in Ephesus and in the other churches of Asia Minor. The plural in 2:7a makes this clear: this is what "the Spirit is saying to the church*es.*"

Nikaō can function as a metaphor for either athletic contests or military conflicts, and a form of the word is the name of the female deity "Nike," the goddess of victory, whose image is found widely in the ancient world. She is always portrayed holding a palm branch in one hand and having wings, which allow her to fly anywhere and give to the victorious athlete or conquering general the victory wreath, which she holds in her other outstretched hand (see fig. 1.3).

Although athletic contests were extremely popular in the ancient world, including in Asia Minor, the larger context of Revelation suggests that the military aspect is being evoked here (so also Aune 1997: 151; Osborne 2002: 122). The rest of the book depicts several battle scenes: the dragon against the child of the woman, two beasts out of the earth and sea against the Lamb, and

Figure 1.3. Marble relief of Nike, the winged goddess of victory, holding a wreath in her outstretched hand. Ephesus.

Babylon against the heavenly warrior. The struggle in the Ephesian church with the sin of loveless orthodoxy is but one manifestation of this larger spiritual battle. Charles (1920: 53) notes: "The word *nikaō* implies that the Christian life is a warfare from which there is no discharge." But though the metaphor of a military battle is sobering for the believers in Ephesus, they can be encouraged by the knowledge that they can emerge from this fight victorious.

Yet this victory is not so much something the Ephesian readers will accomplish as it is something Christ will graciously give them. This idea of victory as divine gift rather than human achievement is conveyed in two ways. First, it is explicitly stated in the phrase "I will give to that person." The victory that the Ephesians will ultimately enjoy is not the result of their giftedness or effort but of Christ's generosity. About "the one who is victorious," Lenski (1935: 95) rightly observes, "We may say that this reward is won by him, yet not as the spoils of victory from the enemy, but as a gift from the Lord, a gift of the Lord's abounding grace." Second, this idea is also implicitly conveyed by the subtle but significant difference between the "victory formula" found here in the sermon to the Ephesians and that found in the sermon to the Laodiceans. Although all seven messages refer to "the one who is victorious," only the final message includes the important addition "just as I was victorious" (3:21). In other words, the believer's victory is ultimately due not to one's own talents or persistence but to Christ's previous victory. It is only by virtue of their relationship to Christ and his empowering Spirit that believers can overcome sin and be victorious.

The reward that Christ will give to his victorious followers is "to eat from the tree of life." The OT background to the imagery evoked here would have been easily understood by the original hearers. It refers to one of the two special trees that God planted in the garden of Eden: the "tree of life" and the "tree of the knowledge of good and evil" (Gen. 2:9). Adam and Eve were permitted to eat fruit from the first tree but not from the second (Gen. 2:16–17). After they disobeyed God by eating fruit from the second tree, they were prohibited from eating any fruit from the first tree. God drove Adam and Eve out of the garden and placed angels and a flaming sword at its entrance to prevent them from eating from the tree of life and obtaining immortality (Gen. 3:24). In Jewish apocalyptic writings, the tree of life became a common symbol of the blessedness of eternal life given to God's people (1 En. 24.3–25.6; 2 En. 8.3; 2 Esd. [4 Ezra] 2:12; 8:50–52; T. Levi 18.9–11; T. Dan 5.12; 3 En. 23.18; Apoc. Elijah 5.6). This is what the tree of life represents at the end of the book of Revelation, where it is mentioned three times as part of the description of the new heaven and new earth (Rev. 22:2, 14, 19). Eating from the tree of life, therefore, represents more than having everlasting life; it represents participation forever in the blessedness of the end time when God and humankind and the whole creation again experience the perfect fellowship and peace that existed before the fall.

There is also a pagan background to the imagery of the tree of life that, though secondary, makes the text even more relevant to its Ephesian readers. The tree of life likely functions as a polemic against the local Artemis cult, which originally involved a tree shrine (see esp. Hemer 1986: 41–47). Before a temple was erected in honor of the goddess, the religious site was marked by a sacred tree. Callimachus (ca. 300–240 BC), a writer and librarian at Alexandria, describes how the Amazons set up an image to Artemis and worshiped her under an oak tree (*Hymn to Artemis* 237–39). Dionysius Periegetes, author of a 1,200-line poetical description of the then-known world that is variously dated between the second century BC and the second century AD, similarly refers to how the Amazons built a temple to Artemis at a site formerly marked by an elm tree (*Description of the Inhabited Earth*, lines 825–829). It is also significant that a date palm—along with a bee and a stag, other typical emblems of the goddess—appears on many coins from the pre-Roman period as a characteristic symbol of Ephesus and its patron deity Artemis (see fig. 1.4).

There is a strong likelihood, therefore, that the tree of life was intended to contrast sharply with the Artemis cult and so functioned as a reward that was

particularly relevant to the Ephesian
church (so also Osborne 2002:
124). In the other sermons, the
positive consequence is closely
linked to the specific, local situation of the church, making it
likely that this is also true here for
Ephesus. For example, the crown
of life is a fitting reward for those
in Smyrna who face death, and
manna is an appropriate reward

Figure 1.4. Tetradrachm coin from Ephesus (390–
380 BC) bearing symbols of Artemis: bee, palm
tree, and stag.

for those in Pergamum who resist the temptation to eat meat sacrificed to
idols. Beale (1999: 236) is correct but too tentative when he states, "Perhaps the
OT tree of life was chosen as emblematic of Christian reward because a tree
image was long associated either with the goddess Artemis or with Ephesus,
where the great Artemis temple flourished. What paganism promised only
Christianity as the fulfillment of OT hopes could deliver."

The final words of the sermon identify the location of the tree of life as
"the paradise of God." As was true of the tree-of-life image, here too the
OT background is primary, with possibly a secondary pagan background.
The word "paradise" is the term used in the Septuagint to refer to the garden of Eden. So this reference, like the tree of life, evokes a reversal of the
fall and a restoration of the blessedness that originally characterized the life
Adam and Eve enjoyed in the garden. And like the tree of life, the reference
to "the paradise of God" may also serve a polemical function against the
local Artemis cult. In the city of Ephesus, the goddess was first worshiped
around a tree shrine and then later at that same spot in a temple, but she was
also worshiped at a grove or garden near Ephesus called Ortygia, which was
believed to be the spot where Artemis was born. This sacred grove or garden
of Ortygia was called a "paradise." Not just Ephesians but people elsewhere
in the ancient world were familiar with this sacred grove as the birthplace of
Artemis. In the first century AD, an annual festival with great pageantry was
held here to honor the goddess, and the site drew pilgrims throughout the year
(Strabo, *Geography* 14.1.20). So the relative clause "which is in the paradise of
God" may be intended to intensify and sharpen the contrast with the Artemis
cult initiated by the reference to the tree of life. Modern readers inclined to
question any local allusion to the city's patron goddess must remember that
"Artemis permeated the consciousness of the Ephesians to the point that
it was a rock-bottom element in their collective and individual identities"
(Murphy-O'Connor 2008: 16). After noting the possible allusion to the sacred

grove of Artemis, Wilson (2002: 263) spells out the positive consequence for the Ephesian readers: "The paradise available to the worshippers of Artemis paled in comparison to the coming paradise of God."

The Contemporary Significance

Introduction

"Too much of a good thing." This well-known saying suggests that some things in life that are typically good can become not so good when taken to excess. For example, exercise is a good thing, and we should generally encourage each other to do it more. But if you overdo it and end up pulling a muscle or damaging some part of your body, exercise becomes not a good thing. Likewise, dessert is a good thing. In fact, some of us think that it's the best part of any meal! But if you eat too much dessert, it becomes not a good thing, and you have to think more seriously about doing the first good thing we mentioned—exercising!

The saying "Too much of a good thing" is a helpful way to think about the sermon to the Ephesians. The church in Ephesus is doing a good thing: they are commended for their *orthodoxy*. Don't be intimidated by this big word. "Orthodoxy" simply means "right belief" or "true teaching." Christ commends the Ephesian congregation for maintaining its orthodoxy in the face of false teachers with their misleading ideas and sinful actions. But the church became so obsessed with orthodoxy and so worried about the danger of false teachers negatively influencing their congregation that a climate of suspicion permeated their Christian community, and they were not able to be the loving church that they had been at first. And so in our message for today, I introduce you to the church of Ephesus, or as it can justly be called, "the church of loveless orthodoxy."

The Christ Title (2:1b)

If you compare all seven sermons side by side, it quickly becomes clear that they all follow the same structure or outline. The first item in each of the sermons is the Christ title. Before Jesus says anything to the church through John, there is first given to him a title. In fact, two titles are typically given to him. These titles are drawn from the vision of Christ given in the opening chapter of the book of Revelation (1:9–20). John reaches back to the earlier vision of Christ in chapter 1 and carefully selects two titles to describe Christ, titles with special relevance to the church being addressed.

The sermon to the Ephesian church starts off in an expected way with two Christ titles, the first of which goes like this: "These are the words of him who holds the seven stars in his right hand" (2:1b). If you lived in Ephesus or in any city in the first century AD and heard these words, you would recognize a claim to Christ's *power*. This claim to power would be understood from the fact that in the earlier vision, Christ simply "has" (1:16) the seven stars in his right hand, whereas here in the sermon to Ephesus Christ "holds" the seven stars in his right hand. What's the difference between "having" something and "holding" it? Actually, there is an important difference, since in the Greek language the verb "to hold" something means that you don't merely have it but you also control it and thus have power over it.

Jesus's power is further revealed by the fact that he holds the seven stars very specifically "in his right hand." Most of us are right-handed. Given a choice of which hand to use, we automatically choose our right hand, and as a result our right hand becomes stronger than our left. The Bible repeatedly refers to God's right hand to stress his power, and that's what is happening here in this reference to Christ's right hand.

Another way in which the first Christ title stresses his power involves a polemic against Rome and its power. For the original audience, the reference to Christ holding the seven stars would have brought to mind the image of seven stars that often appeared on Roman coins. The Roman emperors put an image of their face on one side of a coin and the image of seven stars on the other side. They wanted people to believe that they were demigods, men who were partly human but also partly divine, men whose power was so great that they could control the seven stars. If you lived in Ephesus or any other city within the Roman Empire in the first century, these coins signaled that Rome and its leaders were all-powerful, not only on earth but also in the heavens.

One day, however, a messenger arrives at the Ephesian church with a sermon from Jesus Christ given to John on the island of Patmos. Before he shares the sermon, however, he first describes Jesus as the one who doesn't merely "have" the seven stars but rather "holds" them in his powerful right hand. Jesus is the one whose power is greater than Rome's, the one who is all-powerful, not just on earth but also in the heavens. The Christ followers in ancient Ephesus as well as Christ followers today should pay careful attention to what their all-powerful Savior is about to say!

The second Christ title further identifies the one who is about to speak as "the one who walks in the middle of the seven golden lampstands." While the first title emphasizes Christ's *power*, the second title emphasizes Christ's *presence*. The earlier vision of Christ in chapter 1 makes clear that the seven lampstands are the seven churches (1:20). Thus the second Christ title portrays Jesus as being intimately present as he walks among the various churches in Asia Minor. Although Jesus is so powerful that he controls things not just on earth but also in the heavens, and although his power is greater than that of Rome and its emperors, he is not a distant and remote ruler. Quite the opposite: Jesus is very near his churches and present in their midst.

However, this presence is both comforting and challenging. On the one hand, it is comforting to the Ephesian believers and to us today to know that we are not alone but that the all-powerful Jesus Christ is present and *watches over* us. Jesus knows what we are going through; he knows our worries and fears. This is comforting! On the other hand, it is challenging to the Ephesian believers and to us today to know that the all-powerful Jesus Christ is present and *watches* us. Jesus knows our true spiritual condition, the ways in which we fail to live properly as his followers, especially the ways in which we "have abandoned the love we had at first." This is challenging!

The Commendation (2:2–3, 6)

The second item typically found in each of the seven sermons is the commendation. Long before the saying ever became popular, Jesus apparently knew the adage "If you don't have anything nice to say, don't say anything at all!" Jesus typically begins each sermon with something nice to say: he commends each church for what it is doing right.

What are the Christians in Ephesus doing right? What does Jesus commend them for? The short answer is that Jesus commends them for their *orthodoxy*. Jesus gives a thumbs-up to the Ephesian church when he says: "I love your passion for defending the truth, for rejecting the false teachings of wicked people, for exposing false apostles, and for hating the sinful practices of the Nicolaitans. Great job, Ephesian church!"

The main commendation is found in verses 2–3. The Ephesian church's passion for the truth is seen first of all in Christ's statement "You are not able to tolerate wicked people." Almost every church today has one or two members who live questionable lives and whom the church nevertheless tolerates. Because these questionable members typically don't come to the services every week and, when they do come, usually leave immediately after the service is over, it is often easier for a church simply to put up with such folks. But that's not how the Ephesian church handled this situation. This very conservative church took orthodoxy so seriously that it was "not able to tolerate wicked people."

Second, the Christians in Ephesus passionately guarded the truth by testing "those who call themselves apostles." Most churches today are so excited about anyone wanting to join their congregation that they eagerly and quickly welcome them as members. And if the person who wants to join is someone important, the congregation is usually even more eager to welcome them. But this was not the case in the

Ephesian church. Even when important Christian leaders claiming to be apostles visited them, the Ephesian church's first reaction was not to welcome them but to interrogate them. They said, "We have a few theological questions that we want you to answer first, and only if you pass our orthodoxy test will we let you be part of our fellowship."

Third, the Ephesian church's passionate defense of the truth is evident in an additional commendation that Christ gives them later in the sermon. In verse 6 Jesus says, "But you have this in your favor: you hate the practices of the Nicolaitans, which I also hate." It is not easy to determine with certainty who the Nicolaitans are and the nature of their practices. The little evidence we have suggests that they are "compromisers"—a group within the church that compromised the faith by engaging in pagan practices forbidden by Christ. The conservative Ephesian church, focused on orthodoxy, did not find the compromising theology of the Nicolaitans convincing and reacted very negatively to what they were doing. Our text clearly states that the Ephesian believers hate the practices of the Nicolaitans.

We contemporary Christ followers may wince at the strong language of "hate" and be uncomfortable at the Ephesian church's seemingly intolerant response. But we must not miss the fact that Christ is not rebuking the Ephesian congregation for this kind of hatred but is commending them! Orthodoxy, after all, is a good thing. Defending the truth rather than merely accepting what others, even leaders, are saying, putting their claims to the test, and guarding against false teaching that leads to sinful practices—this continues to be important to the mission of the church today.

The Complaint (2:4)

The third item that typically occurs in the outline of each sermon is the complaint. After commending a church for what it is doing right, Jesus normally follows with a complaint that spells out what they are doing wrong. In the sermon to Ephesus, the rather long and fulsome commendation is followed with a complaint that is short and not very sweet: "But I have this against you: you have abandoned the love you had at first" (2:4).

One possible way to interpret this verse is to see it as referring to the church's failure to love God and/or Christ. According to this view, the Ephesian church's current love for God and/or Christ was not as strong or deep as it had been in the past. Because this congregation was now forty to fifty years old, and the first generation of Christ followers had died and others had taken their place, some argue that their love for God and/or Christ was not as intense or enthusiastic as it had been when the congregation was founded.

Although this interpretation of the complaint is *possible*, it is not *probable*. In fact, several pieces of evidence suggest that the complaint deals with the Ephesian church's lack of love for one another: they have failed to be the loving, caring, and supportive community they were previously.

The first piece of evidence is that love for others is a theme stressed in the other writings attributed to the apostle John and thus is likely to be found also here in the sermon to Ephesus. It is not in the Gospels of Matthew, Mark, or Luke but only in John that we hear Jesus say: "A new command I give you: love one another. As I have loved you, so you must love one another. By this all people will know that you are my disciples, if you love one another" (John 13:34–35). The letter of 1 John repeatedly exhorts its readers to demonstrate love to fellow Christians, often doing so in strong language: "Whoever claims to love God yet hates a brother or sister is a liar. For whoever does not love their brother and sister, whom they have seen, cannot love God, whom they have not seen. And he has given us this command: Anyone who loves God must also love their brother and sister" (1 John 4:20–21; also 2:9–11; 3:11–14; 4:16). And both 2 John and 3 John, despite their short length, nevertheless also stress the importance of loving fellow brothers and sisters (2 John 5; 3 John 5–6).

The second and weightier piece of evidence is the especially long and fulsome character of the commendation (Rev. 2:2–3, 6). It is hard to believe that Christ would so warmly praise the Ephesian church if it had lost its love for God and/or Christ. It also seems unlikely that the Ephesian church would have such strong negative feelings toward wicked people or false apostles or the Nicolaitans if it had abandoned its devotion to God and/or Christ. As the intensity of a church's love for God and/or Christ begins to fade, the church generally grows more tolerant of those with whom it formerly disagreed or becomes more apathetic about them.

The third and final piece of evidence indicating that Christ is complaining about the Ephesian church's loss of love for others is the most important. We have already seen how the commendation reveals this congregation's concern for orthodoxy—its passion for defending the truth and its intolerance of wicked people and their sinful practices. But while orthodoxy is a good thing for which Christ commends the believers in Ephesus, "too much of a good thing" is not a good thing and can also be the reason why Christ criticizes the believers in Ephesus. What is true of people can also be true of congregations: their greatest strength can paradoxically become their greatest weakness. The Ephesian church was so preoccupied with identifying wicked people, exposing false apostles, and rejecting the sinful practices of the Nicolaitans that a spirit of suspicion and mistrust permeated their fellowship, making it impossible for them to be the caring, compassionate community they had been in the past. As our sermon title succinctly puts it, they were "the church of loveless orthodoxy."

Of course, love for fellow believers can never be completely disconnected from love for God and/or Christ. Our love for others is a natural consequence of our love for God and Christ, an expression of our gratitude for what God has done for us. But the emphasis in the sermon to Ephesus is on love for others—not the vertical dimension of our love for God and/or Christ but the horizontal dimension of our love for those around us, especially our spiritual brothers and sisters.

During his earthly ministry, Jesus warned about a coming time when his followers would face two dangers: first, "many false prophets will appear and deceive many people," and second, "the love of most will grow cold" (Matt. 24:11–12). Now many years later, Jesus commends the Ephesian congregation for how they are responding to the first of these dangers but also condemns them for how they are responding to the second of these dangers. As important as orthodoxy is to the overall mission of a church, it must never come at the expense of love for others.

The Correction (2:5a)

The fourth item found in the outline of each sermon is the correction. Christ does not rebuke a church for what they are doing wrong and then leave them to figure out how to fix their sinful situation on their own. Instead, he graciously provides a solution to his followers' spiritual problem. In the sermon to Ephesus, Christ's gracious correction goes like this: "Therefore, remember from where you have fallen, repent, and do the works you did at first!" (2:5a).

The first step in Christ's three-step recovery program is to "remember." Remembering something from the past can change how we act in the present. This can be seen in the well-known parable of the prodigal son (Luke 15:11–32). After partying hard and ultimately losing all his money and friends, the prodigal son finds himself so hungry that he is ready to eat pigs' food, but then his memory kicks in. He remembers the steak-and-caviar meals of his earlier life, the comfort of his home, and most of all, the love of his father. Because of these memories from his past, the son's actions in the present change. The Ephesian church similarly needs to have their memories kick in: they need to remember the concrete acts of love—the kindness, compassion, and empathy—that characterized their life together in the past and make sure that these same acts of love are evident in their life going forward.

The second step in their recovery program is to "repent." None of us likes to be told to repent because it implies that we have been doing something wrong. But if we don't first recognize how we are failing to love others truly and fully, then we will never live differently.

The third step is to "do." Christ commands "Do the works you did at first!" It isn't enough for the believers in Ephesus or for believers today merely to piously affirm the importance of love. No, Christ commands us to "do"—to put love into action and demonstrate in clear and tangible ways our compassion for others.

The Consequence (2:5b, 7b)

After the Christ title, the commendation, the complaint, and the correction, each sermon closes with the potential consequences that the church faces. There are always two consequences: the first is normally negative—what punishment the church faces if they fail to repent and follow Christ's correction; the second is always positive— what reward awaits the church if they repent and conquer their particular sin with Christ's help.

Negative Consequence (2:5b)

The negative consequence comes first and in the sermon to Ephesus goes like this: "But if not, I am coming to you and will remove your lampstand from its place, if you do not repent" (2:5b). In chapter 1 it is clearly stated that "the seven lampstands are the seven churches" (1:20). So when Jesus warns the Ephesians that he may remove their lampstand, it means that he may remove their church—that is, the church will die off and disappear. The reaction that most of us have to that negative consequence is "That's harsh!" And it is indeed a harsh punishment. But if the punishment fits the crime, then it reflects the importance Jesus attaches to love as the defining characteristic of his followers. We are not only to love God with all our heart, soul, mind, and strength but also to love our neighbor as much as we love ourselves. The continued existence of our church depends on our loving one another.

Positive Consequence (2:7b)

Thankfully, each sermon ends not with a negative tone of judgment but with a positive note of victory. The sermon to Ephesus thus comes to a close with this positive consequence: "To the one who is victorious, I will give the right to eat from the tree of life, which is in the paradise of God" (2:7b). The Greek verb for "victorious" here is a form of the word *nikē*, like the sporting goods company. Nike chose their name so that we would associate their products with victory, with winning, overcoming, and conquering. This same Greek verb is used at the end of each of the seven sermons, "To the one who is victorious [*nikōnti*]."

The important question that our text raises is this: "Are you a Nike Christian? In other words, are you a victorious Christian? Are you and I together as a church able to overcome the sin of loveless orthodoxy and be the caring, compassionate community that Christ has called us to be?" The good news of the gospel is that the answer to this important question can be a resounding "Yes!" You and I can be Nike Christians and win the victory over our sin—not because we are so talented or so hardworking but because Christ has already won the victory, and we who belong to Christ have his Spirit living in us. This divine Holy Spirit gives us the power to be loving Christians and to be a loving church.

What reward does Christ promise Nike Christians? Christ says that he will graciously give us "the right to eat from the tree of life." The book of Revelation, including the seven sermons in chapters 2–3, is saturated with allusions to the OT, and here we meet a clear reference to the Genesis story about the garden of Eden. God planted two special trees in the middle of that garden: the tree of life and the tree of the knowledge of good and evil (2:9). After Adam and Eve disobeyed God by eating from the tree of the knowledge of good and evil, they were driven out of the garden of Eden and prevented from eating from the tree of life. Fallen humanity continues to be prevented from eating from the tree of life until a special time in the future described at the very end of the book of Revelation, a time when Christ will return and establish a new heaven and new earth (Rev. 21:1; 22:1–2, 14, 19). The promise that the Ephesians will eat from the tree of life, therefore, offers a wonderful prospect for the future—a blessed time when Christ followers will enjoy the kind of paradise-like life that is barely imaginable now, a time when we will have perfect fellowship not only with God and Christ but also with each other in a new or restored creation.

The promise of eating from the tree of life would have been especially meaningful for the Ephesian Christians because it appears to allude to the local pagan cult of Artemis. Artemis was the patron goddess of the city of Ephesus, and worshipers from all over the world brought sacrifices to her famous temple in Ephesus. The Artemis temple was an architectural masterpiece, four times larger than the Parthenon in Athens, and considered one of the seven wonders of the ancient world. The citizens of Ephesus were so passionate in their devotion to Artemis that one day they sat in the city's 24,000-seat theater, shouting for two full hours: "Great is Artemis of the Ephesians!" (Acts 19:28). Many in that day believed that Artemis's temple was built on the exact spot where she had previously been worshiped around a sacred tree. People told stories of how worshipers originally honored Artemis at a tree shrine in this location. Old coins from Ephesus often depicted Artemis standing beside her holy tree and accompanied by a deer. The Ephesian Christians will be rewarded with access to a special tree—not the tree of the city's patron goddess, Artemis, but the tree of life of the one and only true God.

Conclusion

A thermometer can tell us whether we are *physically* healthy or sick, but how can we tell whether we are *spiritually* healthy or sick? Particularly, how can we determine the spiritual health of our local church? One effective measurement is the "truth test." If we are consistently learning the truth revealed in God's Word and are concerned about speaking the truth, teaching the truth, and defending the truth, it is a sign that we are spiritually healthy. Concern for the truth, for orthodoxy, is a good thing. It is an especially good thing because we live in a society saturated with untruth. The messages our culture gives us about what is important and where we should invest our time and effort are often false. In such a context, orthodoxy is a good thing. Christ commends the Ephesian church for its orthodoxy, and he is likewise calling us today to be passionate about the truth.

But "too much of a good thing" is not a good thing. There is the danger that our passion for the truth may come at the expense of our passion for loving others. And so there is a second way to determine whether we are spiritually healthy or sick, the "love test." Do we exhibit a pattern of loving those around us? Do we listen empathetically as others describe the hurt and pain in their life and then try to minister to them in their time of need? Is our congregation a caring and compassionate community? Do we readily accept repentant sinners and warmly welcome them fully into the fellowship of the church? Christ challenges the Ephesian church to be the loving community it had been in the past, and he is also calling us today to be passionate about demonstrating love toward others.

"Whoever has ears to hear, let them hear what the Spirit is saying to the churches!"—not only to the ancient church of Ephesus but also to the church of Jesus Christ today.

2

Smyrna

The Church of the Persevering Persecuted

The Christ Title (2:8b)

The two Christ titles in the sermon to Smyrna identify the one who is about to speak as "the First and the Last" and as the one "who became dead and lived." Virtually all the Christ titles are taken from the opening vision of Jesus in 1:9–20 and are selected by John because they are relevant for the specific church to whom the sermon is addressed. Both realities are evident here. The two titles originate from 1:17b–18 where Jesus says: "Do not be afraid. I am the First and the Last. I am the Living One; I was dead, and now look, I am alive for ever and ever!" The two titles also address the specific situation in Smyrna by stressing Christ's *sovereignty*—his control over everything that happens, including even the persecution and possible martyrdom of the Jesus followers in the church of Smyrna.

The first Christ title, "the First and the Last," appears two other times in the book of Revelation (at the book's opening [1:17] and closing [22:13]). It is a clear OT allusion to God's self-designation before his covenant people, Israel. In Isa. 41:4 God rhetorically asks and answers: "Who has done this and carried it through, calling forth the generations from the beginning? I, the LORD—with the first of them and with the last—I am he." The same divine title is repeated a few chapters later in Isaiah, where God states: "I am the first and the last; apart from me there is no God" (Isa. 44:6). And for yet a third time God prefaces his address to his people with the assertion: "I am he; I am the first and I am the last" (Isa. 48:12).

This OT allusion has both a general and specific meaning. In a general way, the first Christ title asserts the *deity* of Jesus. Since Christ shares the same title as the God of the OT, he also shares in his divine nature. This would be especially reassuring for the believers in Smyrna because their persecution originated primarily from Jews ("the synagogue of Satan") who denied the deity of Christ. Our conclusion that the choice of this Christ title was intentional is supported by the parallel with the sermon to Philadelphia, which begins with the Christ title "who is holy and true" (3:7) and likewise asserts the deity of Jesus as a polemic against the Jewish community in that city (also identified as "the synagogue of Satan"), who were the primary instigators of the persecution.

In a more specific way, the first Christ title also asserts the *sovereignty* of Jesus. The reference to "the First and the Last" involves the literary device *merismus*, which uses two extremes to describe the whole. The title claims that Jesus existed from the very beginning of time and will continue to exist until the end of time. In light of the allusion to Isa. 41:4, the title stresses that Jesus is with the Christians in Smyrna in exactly the same way that God was with the first generation of Israelites and would continue to be with his people down to the last generation at the end of time. In theological terms, Jesus is identical to the God of the OT in the way he exercises sovereignty over history and controls what his people experience within history. This, of course, means that nothing that happens to the church of Smyrna, neither the opposition they suffer nor the death they may face, is outside the sovereign control of Christ. Beale (1999: 213), a commentator who is especially attentive to the many OT allusions in the book of Revelation, notes:

> The expressions ["first" and "last"] refer to God's sovereignty over history, especially in fulfillment of prophecy and in bringing world affairs to a climax in salvation and judgment. God is transcendent over time and governs the way history proceeds because he is in control of its inception and conclusion. . . . As in Isaiah, the expression functions to assure John and his readers that Christ is in control of the vicissitudes of history, however bad they may seem.

The second Christ title, "who became dead and lived," expands on the first and makes a more direct connection to the specific situation in Smyrna. Christ's sovereignty is not limited to historical events experienced by the living; his control over history extends even to death. His supreme power over all historical events is so absolute that he even exercised authority over death by being killed and returning to life. The second title is clearly aimed at the particular concern facing the Christ followers in Smyrna, who are exhorted to endure persecution "even to the point of *death*" (2:10); if they do so, they will be rewarded with "the crown of *life*" (2:10), and they will certainly not be hurt by "the second *death*" (2:11). By this second title, Jesus is telling his listeners "Been there; done that!" To a church experiencing persecution and the possibility of martyrdom, it is wonderfully comforting to hear not only that Jesus experienced firsthand what they are facing but also that his control over historical events extends beyond this life even unto death.

The logical connection between these two Christ titles and the command later in the sermon, "Do not be afraid!" (2:10), should not be missed. It is precisely because Jesus has sovereignty over all events in history ("I am the First and the Last"), not just events pertaining to life but even those connected with death ("who became dead and lived"), that the Christians in Smyrna need not fear persecution or even possible martyrdom. This logical connection is found already in the opening vision of Christ in 1:9–20, with Jesus's beginning words to John: the command "Do not be afraid!" is immediately followed by the claim "I am the First and the Last. I am the Living One; I was dead, and now look, I am alive for ever and ever! And I hold the keys of death and Hades" (1:17b–18). The function of the two Christ titles is thus clear: to comfort the fearful believers in Smyrna.

In both Christ titles, some exegetes see allusions to the local setting. There are two possible connections, though neither is without problems. The city referred to itself on its coins as "First of Asia" and "First of Asia in beauty and size" as it competed with the nearby Asian cities of Ephesus and Pergamum for bragging rights (*British Museum Coins Ionia*, Sm. nos. 405, 413–14; Ramsay 1994: 185). A few commentators argue that the city of Smyrna's promotion of itself as "First" is the historical background for the first Christ title. For example, Osborne (2002: 128) states, "While Smyrna proudly called itself 'first' among the cities of Asia, it is Jesus alone who can validly be called 'first,' and that in a cosmic sense. This message was especially relevant to a church undergoing terrible opposition; they needed to hear that Jesus was still preeminent and watching over them" (so also D. Johnson 2004: 65). It is possible that the first Christ title has more than one background, alluding to both the OT and the local setting of Smyrna. Nevertheless, the secondary allusion is greatly weakened by the fact that this Christ title involves not just the word "First" but the word pair "the First and the Last." Furthermore, many ancient cities promoted themselves on their coins and inscriptions as "First" or "First of [a region]," so Smyrna's claim is not unique.

More commentators believe that there is a connection between the second Christ title and the local setting of Smyrna. The city had been destroyed by the Lydians in 600 BC and, after three centuries of relative abandonment, was rebuilt some two or three miles south of its original site in 290 BC by Antigonus and Lysimachus, generals of Alexander the Great (so Strabo, *Geography* 14.1.37; see also Pausanias, *Description of Greece* 7.5.1–3). A popular Roman orator who lived in Smyrna, Aelius Aristides (AD 117–181), compared the earlier destruction of Smyrna and its later restoration to the legendary phoenix, a bird that dies but magically returns to life (*Orations* 21). Perhaps the second Christ title, "who became dead and lived," alludes to this local tradition in Smyrna's history. Ramsay (1994: 196–97), who first proposed such an allusion, asserts, "All Smyrnaean readers would at once appreciate the striking analogy to the early history of their own city which lies in that form of address. . . . Like him who addresses it, Smyrna literally 'became dead and yet lived'" (see Hemer 1986: 60–65, who reexamines Ramsay's argument and tentatively accepts it; so also Morris 1969: 63; Osborne 2002: 128; D. Johnson 2004: 65). There is evidence, however, that despite its destruction in 600 BC, the city of Smyrna continued to maintain its identity and tradition, albeit with a greatly reduced population, and did not dramatically suffer a "death." Also, Smyrna was restored in 290 BC, nearly four centuries before the writing of the book of Revelation, making it unlikely that a first-century AD audience would have connected this Christ title with that past event. These two facts suggest that Ramsay may be overstating the claim that believers in Smyrna would "at once" hear, in the second Christ title, an allusion to the city's history. Nevertheless, Aristides's use of the phoenix analogy as late as the second century AD to describe Smyrna's history suggests that its citizens retained some memory of their city's destruction and rebirth. So a connection between these events and the second Christ title, though far from certain, is an intriguing possibility.

The Commendation (2:9)

The sermon to Smyrna transitions from the Christ title to the commendation, with the expected formula "I know." What is not expected, however, is what Christ knows about the church in Smyrna. Jesus typically refers to his knowledge of each church's "works" (2:2, 19; 3:1, 8, 15; but see an exception for Pergamum in 2:13), but here he is aware of Smyrna's "affliction." This change signals the fundamental theme of the sermon, reflected in our proposed title for this message: "Smyrna: The Church of the Persevering Persecuted."

Although "affliction" is the primary issue in this message, it is not the only object of the formula "I know." Christ is also aware that the church is experiencing "poverty" and "slander." These three nouns are not equal in importance and emphasis. Rather, "affliction" constitutes the general description and introduces the main commendation of the sermon, and "poverty" and "slander" describe the type of affliction and constitute the specific commendation. This repeats the commendation pattern we saw in the preceding sermon, to Ephesus (2:2), in which the first, general term ("works") is explained in more specific language by the second and third terms ("labor," "patience"). Here in 2:9, the conjunction (*kai*) that appears before the second term probably has an explanatory function (BDAG 495.1.c), so that the commendation should read "I know your affliction, *namely*, your poverty . . . and your slander from those who call themselves Jews." This understanding is adopted by several commentators. Thomas (1992: 162), for example, asserts, "The preferred relationship between the three [nouns] is to assign the first a general connotation and to make the second and third explanatory of it."

The two nouns ("poverty," "slander") that clarify in a specific way the meaning of the general commendation ("affliction") each have a parenthetical correction. The second term ("poverty") is immediately corrected with "but you are rich," and the third term ("slander from those who call themselves Jews") is immediately corrected with "and they are not but are a synagogue of Satan."

General Commendation: "Affliction"

Christ first commends the church in Smyrna for enduring persecution: "I know your affliction" (*thlipsis*). The word *thlipsis* can refer to the inward experience of anxiety that people have in times of crisis or difficulty (BDAG 457.2), but here it has the much more common meaning of an outward experience of "oppression, affliction, tribulation" (BDAG 457.1). In other words, the kind of affliction that the Jesus followers in Smyrna were enduring was not internal angst about their faith but some kind of outside pressure placed on them because they bore the name of Christ. In this context, then, *thlipsis* refers not to the kind of common suffering that can fall upon all humanity as a consequence of living in a fallen world but the specific kind of suffering that stems from identifying as a Christian.

No doubt the believers in Smyrna, at a basic human level, did not want "affliction" to be the key term used by Christ to commend them. Nevertheless, they could hardly be surprised that such persecution characterized their life as followers of Jesus. After all, he who is "the First and the Last" had clearly stated during his earthly ministry: "Everyone will hate you because of me" (Matt. 10:22). The apostle Paul states quite straightforwardly: "In fact, everyone who wants to live a godly life in Christ Jesus will be persecuted" (2 Tim. 3:12). Peter encourages his readers who are suffering for being Christians by writing: "Dear friends, do not be surprised at the fiery ordeal that has come on you to test you, as though something strange were happening to you" (1 Pet. 4:12). The author of Hebrews reminds his audience of the range of sufferings they endured for their faith, including social ostracism, imprisonment, and loss of property: "Remember those earlier days after you had received the light, when you endured in a great conflict full of suffering. Sometimes you were publicly exposed to insult and afflictions [*thlipsis*]; at other times you stood side by side with those who were so treated. You suffered along with those in prison and joyfully accepted the confiscation of your property" (Heb. 10:32–34). These and other NT texts make clear that a Christian's life may include affliction, and this truth was being faithfully lived out by the believers in Smyrna.

First Specific Commendation: "Poverty"

After the general commendation, the second specifies one way in which those in the Smyrna church were being afflicted for their faith: they were experiencing poverty (*ptōcheia*). Although some distinguish between this term and the related *penēs*, there is little justification for doing so. According to their view, *ptōcheia* refers to the complete lack of possessions (i.e., extreme poverty), while *penēs* refers to the lack of anything superfluous (i.e., moderate poverty; so Trench 1880: 128–29; Thomas 1992: 163; Mounce 1998: 74). Although such a distinction finds some support in secular Greek, the NT does not distinguish between the two terms (Osborne 2002: 129n2). To stress the severe poverty of the Macedonian believers, Paul does not use the word *ptōcheia* alone but adds the prepositional phrase *kata bathous*, "extreme poverty" (2 Cor. 8:2). Nevertheless, the poverty the Smyrnaean Christians endured because of their faith should not be downplayed. None of the other six churches are singled out for their economic suffering, which suggests that the poverty the Smyrna congregation endured was unusual, noteworthy, and probably severe.

Several possible causes for the Smyrnaean Christians' poverty have been suggested, some more plausible than others.

1. The majority of early Christians seemingly came from the lower class (1 Cor. 1:26; James 2:5), and so the believers in Smyrna may have already

been poor before they became followers of Christ. However, this view of the social makeup of the early church is too simplistic and fails to recognize the presence, though a minority, of those from the upper class. Furthermore, the poverty the Smyrnaean Christians endured was rooted not in their low social status but in their affliction as a negative consequence of their Christian faith.

2. Their neediness may have been caused by their giving excessively to other needy believers, following the example of the Macedonian Christians (2 Cor. 8:2–5; so Swete 1907: 32). Yet this explanation fails to appreciate the hyperbole Paul is using to shame his Corinthian readers, who thus far have not been giving financial help to other believers. And like the previous proposal, this explanation fails to link the Smyrnaeans' poverty with their affliction as the text does.

3. Their property was confiscated and their goods were stolen by hostile neighbors, either Jewish or pagan. The viability of this explanation is strengthened not only by texts such as Heb. 10:34 ("You joyfully accepted the plundering of your property") but also by examples throughout human history in which one marginalized group (whether Christian, Jewish, or other) is physically attacked by those in power.

4. It would be difficult for the uncompromising believers in Smyrna to succeed financially in a hostile, pagan environment (many commentators, e.g., Charles 1920: 56; Caird 1966: 35; Thomas 1992: 163; Aune 1997: 161; Fanning 2020: 127n6). In that day workers typically belonged to a trade guild, but membership in such associations required participation in various pagan religious ceremonies that would have been forbidden to Christians. The Jesus followers faced a hard choice: either compromise one's faith in order to retain membership in the guild and continue working or refuse to participate and risk unemployment and poverty (Schüssler Fiorenza 1991: 56; Witherington 2003: 98).

5. Some in the church were facing prison time and possible death (2:10), which would obviously bring severe financial consequences for believers and family members depending on them for support.

Although the fourth option seems the most plausible, it is impossible to know whether one or more of these options was the cause of the Smyrnaeans' poverty. Perhaps it was some combination of the last three proposals. What can be known with confidence, however, is that financial deprivation was one way these church members suffered for their faith. No health-and-wealth gospel was being experienced in Smyrna, and Jesus acknowledges this church's poverty.

The commendation is interrupted by a parenthetical correction: "but you are rich." This aside is introduced with the strong adversative "but" (Greek *alla*) and provides a powerful correction to the apparent poverty of the Christians in Smyrna. The world may see them as financially poor, but Jesus sees them as spiritually rich! This correction thus becomes a further commendation by Christ to encourage the afflicted Smyrnaean believers to persevere in their lowly status and in whatever other negative consequences have come from living out their Christian faith. This correction also prepares the reader for a sharp contrast in the seventh message, when the Laodicean church is described as financially rich but spiritually poor (3:17, "You say, 'I am rich; I have acquired wealth and do not need a thing.' But you do not realize that you are . . . poor").

Second Specific Commendation: "Slander"

The third commendation specifies the second way in which the Christ followers in Smyrna were being afflicted for their faith: "the slander from those who call themselves Jews." Elsewhere in the book of Revelation, the noun *blasphēmia*, along with the verbal form *blasphēmeō*, has its more basic NT sense of "blasphemy," that is, disrespectful and slanderous speech *against God* (13:1, 5, 6; 16:9, 11, 21; 17:3). In this verse, however, the noun refers to disrespectful and slanderous speech *against the Christ followers in Smyrna*. This slander can be understood in two ways: (1) in a broad sense, referring to the spreading of false rumors and malicious gossip about the Smyrnaean Christians; or (2) in a narrow sense, referring to denunciation, the act of bringing an official charge against these Christians before the city authorities (one of the few to distinguish clearly these two possibilities is Aune 1997: 162).

1. *Verbal slander.* The possibility that "slander" here refers in a broad sense to the Jews spreading false rumors about the Smyrnaean Christians is supported by the use of the verb *blasphēmeō* in two events recorded in the book of Acts. The first took place in Pisidian Antioch during Paul's first missionary journey: local Jews, after seeing the large crowds that had come to hear the apostle, "began to contradict what Paul was saying, and they *slandered* him" (Acts 13:45). The second event took place in Corinth during Paul's second missionary journey: the apostle was ministering in a synagogue there, which caused the Jews to "oppose and *slander* him" (18:6). A third relevant event took place in Iconium, although the key verb *blasphēmeō* is not used: unbelieving Jews "poisoned the minds" of the gentiles against Paul and Barnabas (14:2). Further support for the broad sense of slander lies in the testimony of the church fathers, who report that already in the early days of Christianity

Jews spread malicious gossip about Christians (Justin, *Dialogue with Trypho* 17.1; 108.2; 117.3; Tertullian, *To the Nations* 1.14; Origen, *Against Celsus* 6.27; see further Aune 1997: 162). Some of the slanderous lies raised against the Christ followers included the charge of cannibalism (eating the body and blood of the Lord), incest (demonstrating love to "brothers" and "sisters" and greeting them with a kiss), atheism (rejecting the worship of all gods except one), and treason (loyalty to Christ and his kingdom superseding loyalty to Caesar and the Roman Empire).

2. *Denunciation*. Alternatively, the slander the Smyrnaean church faced may refer more narrowly to denunciation, the bringing of an official charge against the Christians before the political leaders of the city. An example of denunciation occurred in Corinth during Paul's second missionary journey: the Jews brought the apostle to the "seat of judgment" (*bēma*) and formally charged him in the presence of Gallio, the governor of the province of Achaia (Acts 18:12–13). Another well-known example of Jews' denouncing Christians took place in Smyrna, resulting in the martyrdom of Polycarp in AD 155. Jews in the city denounced the eighty-six-year-old Polycarp publicly before the governor, saying: "This is the teacher of Asia, the father of the Christians, and the overthrower of our gods, he who has been teaching many not to sacrifice, or to worship the gods" (Martyrdom of Polycarp 12.2). Support for the narrow sense of denunciation is also found within the sermon to Smyrna: Christ tells believers that "the devil is about to put some of you in prison," and he commands them to be "faithful unto death" (2:10). Prison and the death penalty could only result from a specific charge being brought against Christians and not from mere malicious gossip or false rumors about them.

Additional support for the narrower sense of slander as denunciation is found in the correspondence between Pliny the Younger and the Emperor Trajan while Pliny was governor of Pontus and Bithynia in AD 111–112. This correspondence reveals that denunciation was a very real problem for Christians at a time and location quite close to the church of Smyrna. Pliny writes to Trajan to get the emperor's feedback on how he, Pliny, was conducting the trial of Christians and describes his procedure as follows:

> Meanwhile, in the case of those who were *denounced* to me as Christians, I have observed the following procedure: I interrogated these as to whether they were Christians; those who confessed I interrogated a second and a third time, threatening them with punishment; those who persisted I ordered executed. . . .
>
> Soon accusations spread, as usually happens, because of the proceedings going on, and several incidents occurred. An anonymous document was published containing the names of many persons. Those who denied that they were

or had been Christians, when they invoked the gods in words dictated by me, offered prayer with incense and wine to your image, which I had ordered to be brought for this purpose together with statues of the gods, and moreover cursed Christ—none of which those who are really Christians, it is said, can be forced to do—these I thought should be discharged. Others *named by the informer* declared that they were Christians, but then denied it, asserting that they had been but had ceased to be, some three years before, others many years, some as much as twenty-five years. They all worshipped your image and the statues of the gods, and cursed Christ. (*Letters* 10.96, emphasis added)

Trajan approves of how Governor Pliny has been dealing with the denouncement of Christians:

You observed proper procedure, my dear Pliny, in sifting the cases of those who had been *denounced* to you as Christians. For it is not possible to lay down any general rule to serve as a kind of fixed standard. They [Christians] are not to be sought out; if they are *denounced* and proved guilty, they are to be punished, with this reservation, that whoever denies that he is a Christian and really proves it—that is, by worshiping our gods—even though he was under suspicion in the past, shall obtain pardon through repentance. But anonymously posted *accusations* ought to have no place in any prosecution. For this is both a dangerous kind of precedent and out of keeping with the spirit of our age. (*Letters* 10.97)

Pliny mentions that Christians were "named by the informer," which refers to a snitch who did not merely spread malicious gossip about the Christ followers but brought a formal accusation against them before the governor. Keener (2000: 116) states: "This slander most likely refers to 'informers,' what the Romans called *delatores*. Roman officials normally depended on informers as accusers before they would prosecute a case, and this was true for prosecution of Christians in Asia in the decades immediately following Revelation's publication."

Although Pliny does not provide the identity of those informing on Christians, the sermon to Smyrna does, referring to "those who call themselves Jews." The political situation of the Jewish people at the time of the book of Revelation was vulnerable, which may have motivated them to denounce Christians before the Roman authorities. Rome not only recognized Judaism as a legitimate religion and permitted Jews to meet together, but it also granted them a special exemption from participating in the imperial cult and other pagan worship so that they could avoid the sin of idolatry. The First Jewish Revolt (AD 66–73), however, put these privileges in jeopardy. Jews were now forced to stop paying the annual temple tax to support the sanctuary in Jerusalem and instead to support the building of a new temple of Jupiter in Rome. In such a post-70 political situation, the Jews in Smyrna may have worried that the seemingly anti-Roman actions of Jewish Christians in their city might cause local authorities to take punitive action against their synagogue, and this fear may have driven the Jews to denounce the Christ followers in their community. As Witherington (2003: 99–100) observes: "It thus behooved Jews in Asia Minor and elsewhere to root out any messianic Jews or proselytes in their midst who might cause their own position in society to be further compromised." Keener (2000: 115) likewise notes that the Jews in Smyrna "could not afford to take chances," and "many Asian Jewish leaders were probably nervous about being associated with prophetic, messianic movements like Christianity" (so also Fanning 2020: 128).

The Jews may have been motivated by political realities to bring official charges against the Christ followers in Smyrna, but the city authorities were equally motivated for political reasons to take such charges seriously. Smyrna had a track record of loyalty to Rome. As early as 193 BC, before Rome's preeminence was guaranteed, Smyrna became the first city in Asia to erect a temple to the goddess Roma (Tacitus, *Annals* 4.56). Carthage, Rome's chief competitor, could have ultimately emerged victorious, and there were powerful kings nearby in Asia to which the city could have committed itself instead (e.g., the Attalid dynasty in Pergamum). In 84 BC, the Roman general Sulla and his troops were in Smyrna and facing the harsh winter weather without adequate clothing. Upon hearing of the situation, the local citizens spontaneously stripped off their outer garments and sent them to the desperate legions (Tacitus, *Annals* 4.56.3). Cicero (106–43 BC), the famous senator of Rome, called Smyrna "one of our most faithful and most ancient allies" (*Philippic Orations* 11.2.5). Livy (59 BC–AD 17) stated that Rome held Smyrna in honor because of that city's "extraordinary loyalty" (*History of Rome* 38.39.11). This long and strong relationship with Rome explains why Tiberius in AD 26 chose Smyrna over ten other Asian cities for the honor of building a second imperial temple (the first one was in Pergamum) in honor of the deceased emperor Augustus; his wife, Livia; and the Senate and to serve as its "temple keeper" (*neōkoros*). Additional evidence of Smyrna's loyalty to Rome includes a coin portraying Nero that was minted in the city; dedications to Titus and Domitian; and statues of Domitian, Trajan, and Hadrian (Yamauchi 1980: 58). Rome awarded Smyrna the title of "temple keeper" (*neōkoros*) two more times: once under Hadrian and then later under Caracalla.

All this suggests that civic authorities in Smyrna would have responded aggressively to the denunciation of Christians by local Jews. As Mounce

(1977: 93) notes, "In a city like Smyrna with its strong ties to Rome it would be a fairly simple matter to incite the authorities to action."

As was the case with the second commendation for enduring poverty, so also the third commendation of the church for enduring official denunciation is immediately followed by a correction. However, Christ does not correct the slander itself but identifies the source of the slander. "Those who call themselves Jews" is immediately qualified by the assertion "they are not but are a synagogue of Satan." The use of a negative clause ("they are not") balanced with the strong adversative clause ("but," *alla*) forms an emphatic antithetical statement. John stresses that the Jews who are bringing charges to the city authorities against Christians in Smyrna may be Jews by race and religion, but they are not true Jews. Their actions in persecuting the church reveal them to be a "synagogue of Satan." This striking phrase also occurs in the sermon to Philadelphia (3:9) and nowhere else in Scripture. The Philadelphian sermon displays several important similarities to the Smyrnaean sermon. In addition to the shared phrases "synagogue of Satan" and "those who call themselves Jews and are not," both sermons have no complaint section and occupy corresponding positions (the second, B, and sixth, B′) in the chiastic outline we examined in the introduction. "Synagogue of Satan" is an especially fitting name for those who were opposing the Smyrnaean church, because the name "Satan" (from Hebrew *śāṭān*) means "adversary" or "opponent." The name Satan appears later in the book of Revelation along with the label "the devil" (12:9), and this being is described as "the accuser of our brothers, who accuses them day and night before our God" (12:10). The Jews in Smyrna who were bringing official charges against the Christians before the Roman authorities proved by such actions that they were not really Jews, that is, members of God's covenant people, but human instruments in the hand of Satan, the ultimate source of slander and denouncement.

According to most commentators, by *explicitly* stating that the Jews in Smryna are not true Jews, John is *implicitly* stating who the true Jews are: the Christ followers in Smyrna—that is, the church. Hemer (1986: 67), for example, observes, "The writer [of Revelation] has his own usage of the term 'Jew.' He insists that the true people of God is a spiritual nation, not an ethnic group. The Christians were now the true Jews." Beale and Campbell (2015: 62) similarly assert, "That the Jewish community is identified as false Jews and a 'synagogue of Satan' confirms again that the church is seen by Christ as the true people of God, true Israel." The idea of the church being the true Israel is suggested already at the very beginning of the book of Revelation, where John identifies the seven churches as those made by Christ "a kingdom, priests to his God and Father" (1:6), which echoes God's call to Israel to be "a kingdom of priests and a holy nation" (Exod. 19:6). The idea is implied yet again in both 1:17 and in the immediate context of 2:8 and 2:10, where the language of "the first and the last" and "Do not fear" echoes God's words to the Israelites in Isaiah (41:4, 10; 44:2, 6, 8). The fact that God addresses the Christians in Smyrna with the same language he used to address Israel in the days of Isaiah suggests that the church now constitutes the true Israel (Beale and Campbell 2015: 62).

This important idea gains further support from Paul's letters. The apostle states in Rom. 2:28–29 that a true Jew is not identified by outward things like Jewish ethnicity and circumcision but by inward or spiritual things, such as belief in God and his Son. Later in the same letter, Paul portrays Israel as the natural branches of God's olive tree that have been broken off because of their unbelief, but the gentiles have been grafted in despite being a "wild olive shoot" (Rom. 11:17–21). That the gentiles (and thus the church) constitute the true Israel is further indicated in Philippians when, in contrast to those appealing to the Jewish practice of circumcision, Paul declares, "For it is we who are the circumcision, we who serve God by his Spirit, who boast in Christ Jesus" (Phil. 3:3). In his Letter to the Galatians, Paul argues at great length that his gentile readers are fully heirs of Abraham (3:6–9, 14, 15–18, 26–29; 4:21–31), and he identifies them in the closing (6:11–18) with the striking phrase "the Israel of God" (6:16), thereby implying that they already possess the status of the true Israel or the end-time people of God (for a fuller discussion of this controversial expression, see Weima 2016: 172–75).

The Complaint—None!

After commending a church for what it is doing right, Christ typically follows with a complaint that highlights what it is doing wrong. This shift from commendation to complaint is sometimes marked by the stereotyped phrase, "But I have [this] against you" (*alla echō kata sou*; so 2:4, Ephesus; 2:14, Pergamum; 2:20, Thyatira). At other times, the complaint formula is omitted because there is no commendation with which the complaint contrasts, and Christ proceeds directly to identifying his grievances against the church (so the sermons to Sardis and Laodicea). The omission of any complaint formula or complaint section here in the sermon to Smyrna is therefore noteworthy (the sixth sermon, to Philadelphia, also lacks a complaint). Normally the Bible is significant for what it says; in this rare instance, the Bible is significant for what it *does not* say. The complete absence of complaint, therefore, signals

how highly Christ regards the Christ followers in Smyrna and their perseverance in the face of persecution.

The Correction (2:10a)

It is not surprising that the absence of a complaint affects the content of the
correction. Since Christ does not point out any errors among the Smyrnaean
Christians, there is no command to repent and to live in a manner opposite
from what is specified in the complaint, unlike the sermons to Ephesus (2:5),
Pergamum (2:16), Thyatira (2:21), Sardis (3:3), and Laodicea (3:19; Philadelphia is similarly exempt from correction). Instead, this correction picks up
the preceding commendation of the Smyrnaean believers for their affliction
and commands them not to be afraid of any future affliction: "Don't ever
fear anything that you are about to suffer."

In the past, grammarians of the Greek language commonly claimed that
there was a difference between prohibitions (negative commands) expressed
with the aorist subjunctive and those expressed with the present imperative.
The former type was said to warn against an action not yet begun ("Don't
start to . . . !"), whereas the latter type warned against an action already in
progress ("Don't continue to . . . !"). Since the prohibition here in 2:10 uses
the present imperative, several commentators conclude that "the Christians
were *already* full of fear" and needed to stop fearing (Brighton 1999: 72; so
also Mounce 1977: 93n27; Thomas 1992: 166n37). Recent grammatical studies, however, have convincingly demonstrated that this claimed distinction
between the two forms of prohibition is not valid (Fanning 1990: 335–40;
Porter 1992: 220–29; Wallace 1996: 485, 714–17) and that the meaning can
be determined only on contextual grounds. Nevertheless, there does exist a
difference in meaning between the two forms: the present imperative is more
emphatic and highlights the ongoing nature of the action. This sense can
be somewhat captured with the translation: "Don't *ever* fear." Additional
emphasis is expressed through the use of the negative numerical *mēden* (not
one thing, nothing) instead of the simple negative *mē*. In 1:17 Christ commands John "Don't ever fear"; here he exhorts the believers in Smyrna more
emphatically "Don't ever fear *any of the things* you are about to suffer."

The phrase "any of the things you are about to suffer" must have initially
sounded ominous to the Christians in Smyrna. They were already suffering from poverty and accusations. What additional sufferings awaited them?
Christ prefaces his answer with the interjection "Behold" (*idou*), which draws
attention to what he says next. (*Idou* occurs 26 times in the book of Revelation,

6 of which are in the seven sermons: 2:10, 22; 3:8, 9 [2×], 20.) "The devil is about to throw some of you into prison in order that you may be tested." The additional suffering that some members of the church will bear is a more intense form of affliction: martyrdom. The Roman legal system did not normally impose imprisonment as a punishment because it required too much effort and cost to incarcerate individuals for lengthy periods of time (Ramsay 1994: 199; also Hemer 1986: 68). In support Aune (1997: 166) cites three passages from the Digest (48.8.9; 48.19.29; 48.19.35), a compendium of juristic writings on ancient Roman law. Prison was instead a preliminary and temporary stage while awaiting trial, whereas punishments could range from a fine or exile (only Roman citizens or powerful figures would be eligible for this) to death, the most common outcome. Other statements in this brief sermon make clear that martyrdom is the additional and more serious affliction that some believers in Smyrna will face: the references to "death" at the beginning (2:8, "who became dead") and the end (2:11, "second death") as well as the command to "be faithful to the point of death" (2:10b). Extrabiblical support is provided by the letter of Pliny the Younger to Emperor Trajan, which says that after Pliny interrogated three times those denounced to him as Christians, he had them executed (*Letters* 10.96).

Since the Christians in Smyrna are facing not just poverty and denouncement but also the possibility of death, how can Christ expect them to obey his command not to be afraid? Jesus has already given them one important reason why they need not fear an imprisonment that likely leads to martyrdom: his sovereign power over all historical events, so that even the affliction faced by believers in Smyrna is not outside his ultimate control—a control most significantly evident in Jesus's resurrection from death (see the earlier discussion of the two Christ titles in 2:8).

Jesus gives his followers two additional reasons why they ought not to be afraid, the first of which overlaps closely with the previous one. The reason for the affliction faced by the Smyrnaean church is implied in the purpose clause: "in order that you may be tested" (note the rare occurrence of the second-person plural, "you," both here and in the following verb ["you will have"], in contrast to the collective singular typically found throughout the seven sermons). The use of the passive voice with no explicit mention of the agent of the testing suggests that the primary actor behind the scene is God. The frequent use of the divine passive elsewhere in the book of Revelation makes its occurrence here likely (so also Osborne 2002: 133). Thomas (1992: 168) raises a few objections against this view, though he admits "a strong case to make God the agent exists." Additionally, the verb "about to" (*mellō*), which occurs twice in this verse, frequently introduces an action destined by

God (BDAG 628.2, "w. pres. inf. to denote an action that necessarily follows a divine decree"; see also Rev. 1:19; 12:5). This leads Caird (1966: 36) to state that for the Christians in Smyrna, "their ordeal will also be a divinely ordained test of their faith; for what Satan intends as a temptation, God uses as a test. Throughout his book, John is constantly trying to show how Satan's hand may be detected in the affairs of this world; he is equally insistent that Satan can do nothing except by permission of God, who uses Satan's grimmest machinations to further his own bright designs."

The final reason why the Smrynaean believers can fulfill Christ's command not to fear is that their persecution will be mercifully brief, and they will emerge from it victorious: "and you will have affliction for ten days" (the difference between the genitive of time used here, which normally expresses *time within which* something occurs ["during"], and the accusative, which states the *extent* of time ["for"], should not be stressed). Although the reference to ten days could be taken literally (Thomas 1992: 170), the symbolic use of numbers throughout Revelation, including the number ten (12:3; 13:1; 17:3, 7, 12, 16), strongly suggests a different meaning for this time reference. Most commentators understand "ten days" to refer to a brief period of time. Ladd (1972: 44) is representative of this majority opinion: "The number 'ten days' has no particular symbolic significance beyond that of indicating a relatively short period of persecution. . . . John does not expect an extensive universal persecution but a local one of short duration" (so also, e.g., Hendriksen 1940: 65; Caird 1966: 35; Beasley-Murray 1978: 82; Aune 1997: 166; Osborne 2002: 134; Witherington 2003: 101).

Additional support for this meaning of "ten days" comes from seeing it as an echo of the OT book of Daniel. This prophetic book opens with Daniel's request that he and his three friends not be forced to eat the Babylonian king's choice food because they do not want to defile themselves (Dan. 1:8–16). The trial period of their proposed alternative diet is ten days, and its importance is stressed by three references (Dan. 1:12, 14, 15). Their action of eating alternative food is twice identified as a test (*peirazō*: Dan. 1:12, 14 LXX), the same verb used here in Rev. 2:10. Furthermore, the book of Revelation makes frequent allusions to the prophecy of Daniel (27 times according to Charles 1920: lxviii–lxxxi), which suggests that John assumed his audience would be very familiar with this OT book (see also Beale 1984; Moyise 1995: 45–63) and would recognize these allusions. The believers in Smyrna would be encouraged by knowing that their coming, intense testing would be like that faced by Daniel and his three friends: a brief period during which their sovereign God would protect them. As Wilson (2002: 263) observes, "Ten days is symbolic for a brief period of time. Daniel and his friends refused to eat the defiled Babylonian food and were tested for ten days. When the period was over, they emerged vindicated (Dan. 1:12–15), as those in Smyrna are expected to be" (see also Keener 2000: 116; Osborne 2002: 134; Fanning 2020: 129).

The allusion to Dan. 1 may also have been chosen because of its connection between food and idolatry, which parallels the powerful temptation faced by the church of Smyrna and all the original readers of the book of Revelation to eat food sacrificed to idols. The defilement that Daniel wanted to avoid was likely the idolatry involved in eating the food of King Nebuchadnezzar, which had been devoted to the gods of Babylon (the verb "defile" [*alisgeō*] used in Dan. 1:8 LXX is connected with idolatry; see Acts 15:20). This OT story, then, would have served as a powerful example to the churches of Asia Minor who were likewise being tested to compromise their faith by participating in cultic meals, where they would be guilty of eating food sacrificed to idols—the specific charge that Christ brings against the next two churches (Pergamum, 2:14; Thyatira, 2:20). Beale and Campbell (2015: 63) affirm that "ten days" alludes both to Dan. 1 and to the temptation of idolatry:

> The ten days persecution does not have to refer to a literal period of ten days because it is an allusion to the ten days when Daniel and his friends were "tested." Daniel was tempted to compromise with idolatry, which was likely the main reason he abstained from eating at the king's table, where the food was probably dedicated to idols (see Dan. 1:2; 5:1–4). Likewise, whether or not the ten days is literal, the point is that the Christians at Smyrna were also, like Daniel of old, not to compromise with idolatry.

The Consequence (2:10b, 11b)

The absence of a complaint in the expected structure of this sermon affects not just the correction but also the consequence. Each sermon closes with Christ identifying the two potential consequences the church faces: the first is normally negative, what punishment ensues if the church fails to follow Christ's correction; the second is always positive, what reward awaits the church if it repents and with Christ's help conquers its particular sin(s). Christ has no complaint against the church in Smyrna, so instead of warning them about a possible punishment, he comforts them with an additional reward. This sermon therefore ends with two positive consequences.

First Positive Consequence (2:10b)

The first consequence involves a paradox: if the Smyrnaean believers persevere in the face of persecution to the point of *death*, they will be rewarded with eternal *life*. Christ promises them, "Be faithful to the point of death, and I will give you the crown of life" (2:10b). The command "Be faithful!" (*ginou pistos*) shifts back to the collective singular after the unexpected plurals of the two preceding verbs ("in order that you may be tested and you will receive") so that the whole church is being addressed, not just those who will experience the additional persecution of prison and probable death. Although this first consequence would be especially encouraging to those facing martyrdom, Christ will give the crown of life not only to these heroes of the faith but to *all* his followers (James 1:12, "the crown of life that the Lord has promised to those who love him").

Some commentators see in the command to be faithful an allusion to the faithfulness that the city of Smyrna demonstrated toward Rome over the centuries (see esp. Hemer 1986: 70–71; Ramsay 1994: 200–202). Smyrna did indeed exhibit strong fidelity to Rome (see the discussion of 2:9b above), but "faithful" (*pistos*) is a common Christian word occurring frequently throughout the book of Revelation, making it unlikely that it was intended to allude to Smyrna's fidelity to Rome and unlikely that the Smyrnaeans, let alone those elsewhere in Asia Minor, would have recognized this special significance. The term is used to describe Jesus's faithfulness to his followers (1:5; 3:14; 19:11; possibly also 14:12) and the words of the Apocalypse itself (21:5; 22:6). When the term is applied to believers, as in the Smyrna sermon, it refers to their faithfulness to God, Christ, and the gospel in the face of great opposition and even death (2:10, 13; see also 17:14). In light of Pliny's letter to Trajan, the faithfulness of Smyrna's believers would have resulted in martyrdom for refusing to invoke the names of pagan gods, offering incense and wine to the image of the Roman emperor, and cursing Christ. The prepositional phrase "to the point of death" makes clear that there must be no limits to one's faithfulness (the preposition *achri* implies not just "up to" but also "including"; see BDAG 160.1.b; Acts 22:4; Hemer 1986: 71). The same point is made in the Gospels, where Christ calls believers to take up their cross and follow him (Matt. 10:38; 16:24; Mark 8:34; Luke 9:23; 14:27), which is not merely a metaphor for self-denial but a straightforward challenge to be faithful to him no matter the cost, even to the point of death (Osborne 2002: 135).

But although the cost of obedience may be great and possibly require death, the reward is even greater: Christ will give to the persevering persecuted in Smyrna "the crown of life" (either an appositional or epexegetical genitive: "the crown, namely, life"). This crown is not the royal tiara or diadem (*diadēma*) worn by kings and queens but the wreath (*stephanos*) worn by champion athletes and victorious generals. The book of Revelation refers to both types of headwear—using the word "diadem" to evoke the royal assertions of the seven-headed dragon (12:3), the ten-horned beast from the sea (13:1), and Christ (19:12)—but more frequently uses the word "wreath" for the spiritual reward given to faithful Christ followers (2:10; 3:11; 4:4, 10) as an athletic metaphor or a military image of what adorned the heads of those victorious in the spiritual contest/battle (6:2; 9:7; 12:1; 14:14). Wreaths were woven out of palm or other branches, flowers, or other forms of plant life (e.g., celery, parsley). Such crowns/wreaths would thus quickly deteriorate in contrast to the "imperishable" (1 Cor. 9:25) and "unfading" (1 Pet. 5:4) crown given to believers. The ancient world was as obsessed with sports as our modern age is, and athletic contests were held throughout the Roman Empire. There is evidence that games were held in each of the seven cities John addresses except for Thyatira (Wilson 2002: 265), and the Ionian games hosted by Smyrna are singled out for mention by Pausanias (*Description of Greece* 6.14.3). The victory wreath associated with these athletic contests, therefore, became a "familiar symbolic image to all adults and most children in Roman Asia" (Keener 2000: 117). This widespread familiarity means that the Christ followers in Smyrna would readily appreciate the metaphor of the victory wreath and its promise of eternal life. The parallel with the preceding sermon should not be missed: as the "tree of life" symbolizes the eschatological blessedness of the life that awaits the believers in Ephesus, so the "crown of life" signifies the same end-time reward for the believers in Smyrna.

This wreath metaphor may also have had an additional local allusion. A few ancient writers employ the metaphor of a wreath to describe the impressive buildings of Smyrna clustered in a circular manner on Mount Pagos, the location of the city's acropolis. Aelius Aristides, a Greek orator (AD 117–181) who lived

© Baker Publishing Group

Figure 2.1. Running athlete wearing the victory wreath. Life-size bronze statue recovered from Kyme, on the Aegean coast just north of Smyrna. Late Hellenistic Period (ca. 2nd–1st cent. BC). Archaeological Museum, Izmir, Turkey.

much of his life in Smyrna, uses the wreath metaphor to describe the restoration of this city after a devastating earthquake: "Ionia has had its crown saved" (*Orations* 22.443). In another passage, Aristides not only compares the beauty of Smyrna to the "crown of Ariadne" but also seemingly identifies the crown as the "emblem of the city" (*Orations* 15.374). Apollonius, a Greek philosopher (1st cent. AD), urges the citizens of Smyrna to take greater pride in themselves than in the beauty of their city "for it is a greater charm to wear a crown of men than a crown of porticoes [i.e., buildings]" (*Life of Apollonius* 4.7). These ancient voices lead Ramsay (1994: 186) to state, "'The crown of Smyrna' was a familiar phrase with the Smyrnaeans; and there can be no doubt that the phrase arose from the appearance of the hill Pagos, with the stately public buildings on its rounded top and the city spreading out down its rounded sloping sides." Further evidence that the crown functioned as a symbol of Smyrna comes from the many local inscriptions (nearly 20 percent of those uncovered) that contain the wreath emblem (Horsley 1983: 52, §17). The phrase "crown of life," therefore, may have been chosen not just for its common use as an athletic metaphor for victory but also because it had special relevance for the believers in Smyrna (Hemer 1986: 73–75; Keener 2000: 117; Wilson 2002: 264–65; Witherington 2003: 101). To those facing prison and probable death in a city whose emblem was a wreath, it would be particularly fitting to be promised the crown of life. The ubiquitous nature of the crown metaphor in the ancient world requires that conclusions about this secondary local allusion remain tentative rather than an established fact (see the critique of Aune 1997: 168). Nevertheless, the supporting evidence cited above suggests that just as the "tree of life" has a secondary background that makes this reward especially relevant to the Ephesian church, so also the "crown of life" was particularly appropriate for the persecuted believers in Smyrna.

Second Positive Consequence (2:11b)

Regardless of whether a church is spiritually healthy (as is Smyrna) or sick (as are most of the other churches), the sermon always ends with a promise to the victorious, and this sermon is no exception: "The one who is victorious will not be hurt at all by the second death." As elsewhere, this victory is a divine gift rather than the product of human achievement. (For a full explanation of the importance of the verb "to be victorious" in John's writings, see the comments above on 2:7b.) The reward that Christ will give his victorious followers is not something different from what he promised in the preceding verse but a mirror image of it. There it was expressed positively as receiving the "crown of life" (i.e., eternal life); here it is expressed negatively as avoiding the "second death" (i.e., eternal death).

Although the exact phrase "second death" is not found anywhere in the OT, it has roots in Judaism, occurring in the later targums (paraphrastic translations of the Hebrew Bible in Aramaic). A targum on Deut. 33:6 not only uses the phrase "second death" but also offers a helpful explanation: "May Reuben live in this world; and may he not die a second death, by which the wicked die in the world to come" (Tg. Onqelos Deut. 33:6; see also Tg. Isa. 22:14; 65:5–6, 15; Tg. Neofiti Deut. 33:6; Tg. Jer. 51:39, 57). Revelation 2:11b reflects this same idea of the "second death" as the spiritual punishment of the wicked after physical death (the "first death"). This is made even clearer by the three other occurrences of the phrase at the end of John's Apocalypse (20:6, 14; 21:8), the final two of which identify the "second death" as the "lake of fire," the final destination of the wicked: "But the cowardly, the unfaithful, the vile, the murderers, the sexually immoral, those who practice magic arts, the idolaters and all liars—they will be consigned to the lake of fire, which is the second death" (21:8).

Some speculate that John's choice of this uncommon phrase stems from his desire to answer the taunt of hostile local Jews who, in addition to denouncing Christians before the local authorities, were threatening them with an eternal punishment that takes place after their physical death (Hemer 1986: 76, 77). Rather than there being a polemical intent behind John's choice of the phrase "second death," however, it is more likely rooted in the desire to establish a contrast with the "crown of life," the reward for those facing martyrdom. The Christ followers in Smyrna are comforted with the promise that the second death will not harm them "at all." (The double negative construction *ou mē* with the aorist subjunctive is the strongest form of negation possible in Greek [BDF §365] and makes the promise emphatic.) In other words, these believers can face the physical suffering involved in their relatively quick "first death" in the sure and certain knowledge that they will in no way experience the much greater suffering of the spiritual and eternal "second death."

The Contemporary Significance

Introduction

The earliest story of a martyrdom outside the Bible involves a church leader named Polycarp. He was originally a disciple of the apostle John and, after the apostle's death, became bishop of the church of Smyrna, the same church to whom Jesus sent the sermon that we are looking at today. In the year AD 155 Polycarp was brought before the city officials and charged with being an atheist. You may well be puzzled at how a Christian could be accused of not believing in the existence of God, but the charge actually had some truth to it. Christians did not believe in the multiple gods and goddesses that the ancient Greeks and Romans worshiped, and so they were labeled as atheists. The worship of a different God is not what got Christians into trouble. Rather, what offended their pagan neighbors was the *exclusivity* of the Christians' faith in the one true God and their rejection of all other gods. And so it was that Polycarp, the bishop of the church of Smyrna and the leader of these offensive Christians, was about to be burned to death for being an atheist.

Polycarp was eighty-six when this tragic event took place. Seeing this elderly and frail Christian leader, the city official felt sympathy for him and tried to find a way for Polycarp to avoid this painful execution. He suggested to Polycarp, "Why don't you just say, 'Caesar is Lord,' put a bit of incense on this altar devoted to the image of the emperor, and then we can let you go?" In response Polycarp uttered the words that would make his martyrdom famous for all time: "Eighty-six years I have served Christ, and he never did me any harm. How then can I blaspheme my King, who saved me?"

The story of Polycarp's martyrdom is helpful for understanding the sermon to the second of the seven churches, the church of Smyrna. Like Polycarp, the believers in the church of Smyrna were persecuted for their Christian faith. Also like Polycarp, they did not renounce their Christian faith in the face of persecution but persevered even to the point of death. And so in our message today, I introduce you to the church of Smyrna, or as it can justly be called, "the church of the persevering persecuted."

The Christ Title (2:8b)

The first item in each of the seven sermons is the Christ title. Before Jesus says anything to the church of Smyrna, he is introduced by two titles. John goes back to the vision of Christ in the opening chapter of the book of Revelation (1:9–20) and chooses two descriptions of Jesus that are especially relevant to the situation in Smyrna.

The first Christ title identifies Jesus as "the First and the Last" (2:8b). In this title, the Christians in Smyrna would have heard a clear OT allusion. They would have said to themselves, "That's how God refers to himself! In the prophecy of Isaiah, God often says that he is the First and the Last" (Isa. 41:4; 44:6; 48:12). When a title referring to the God of the OT is now used to refer to Christ, it says something important about Jesus—that he too is God. This might not seem very important to contemporary Christians, who already believe in the deity of Christ, but it would have been extremely significant to the Christians in Smyrna. Later in this message we will learn that the Smyrnaean Christians were enduring persecution not just from their pagan neighbors but also from their Jewish neighbors, who were especially upset about the claim that Jesus Christ was not just a man but also God.

The first Christ title is more than just a claim about the deity of Jesus, however; it is also a claim about the *sovereignty* of Jesus. The title "the First and the Last" involves a special way of speaking called "merismus." That's when you refer to two extremes to describe the whole. For example, the OT psalmists often refer to the "morning" in one line and "the night" in the next line. These references to the two extreme times of the day are not intended to exclude the afternoon but rather include all the hours between morning and night—that is, the whole day. We still use this special way of speaking today. A car salesman might say to a prospective customer "This car has a bumper-to-bumper warranty," referring to the two extreme ends of the car to indicate that the warranty covers the entire car. Or you might say to someone "I ache from head to toe," referring to the two extreme ends of your body to say that your entire body hurts.

In a similar way, Jesus is described as "the First and the Last" to assert that he existed from the beginning of time and will continue to exist until the end of time. More specifically, the allusion to Isa. 41:4 stresses that Jesus will be with the believers in Smyrna from the beginning of time until the end of time and that Jesus has control and is sovereign over what is currently happening to the church of Smyrna, even with respect to their persecution and possible martyrdom. It would be comforting for the persecuted believers in Smyrna to be reminded that their Savior Jesus is "the First and the Last" and that nothing, including their difficult situation, is outside his control.

The second Christ title is even more directly relevant to the difficulties facing the church of Smyrna. Jesus is described as the one "who became dead and lived" (2:8b). If you are a follower of Christ living in Smyrna and being persecuted for your Christian faith by both pagan and Jewish neighbors, and if this persecution is so intense that it might even result in your arrest and death, it would be profoundly comforting to hear Jesus tell you at the beginning of his sermon "I am he who became dead and lived. I've been there and done that!" Jesus knows firsthand the kind of persecution that leads to death. More important, Jesus also knows firsthand what it's like to defeat death and come back to life, to have power over the grave. It is not only the persevering persecuted in ancient Smyrna but also the persevering persecuted in the church today who can be comforted that our Lord and Savior, Jesus Christ, has gone through exactly the same difficulties that we are going through. Even if our suffering leads to death, Christ's resurrection is a guarantee that we too will be restored to life.

The Commendation (2:9)

The second item typically found in each of the seven sermons is the commendation as Jesus praises the church of Smyrna for what they are doing right: "I know your affliction, namely, your poverty, yet you are rich; and I know the slander from those who call themselves Jews, yet they are not but are a synagogue of Satan" (2:9). There are three things for which Jesus commends the church of Smyrna: their affliction, their poverty, and their being slandered.

Jesus first commends their "affliction." This word refers to *Christian* suffering—that is, suffering for no reason other than being a follower of Jesus. It is not the same as *general* suffering, the kind of suffering that all people, regardless of their faith, endure from living in a sinful, fallen world. If you lose your job, you may well suffer, but that is not Christian suffering. If you visit the doctor and learn that you have cancer, you may well suffer, but that too is not Christian suffering. Jesus commends the church of Smyrna for their "affliction," for the suffering they are enduring for no reason other than that they bear the name of Christ.

Second, Jesus commends the church for their "poverty," which specifies one of the ways in which they are afflicted. It is not hard to envision how Christians in Smyrna might suffer financially for being Jesus's followers. Imagine that you are a farmer in Smyrna trying to sell your produce, but everyone in your community knows that you are a Jesus follower and therefore haven't offered a sacrifice to Demeter, the goddess of agriculture. Since your produce has not been blessed by Demeter, potential customers are worried that your food may rot before its due date or not taste good, and so they buy produce from a non-Christian farmer instead. Or imagine that you are a Jesus follower in Smyrna and visit other Jesus followers in the nearby city of Ephesus. When your pagan neighbors leave for a short visit, no one sneaks into their homes and steals anything, but when you as a Jesus follower return home, you find that your house has been ransacked (Heb. 10:34). These are just two of the many possible ways the church of Smyrna may have suffered financially for following Jesus. There is no support here or anywhere else in Scripture for a health-and-wealth gospel. Jesus does not promise that his followers in Smyrna will become rich but rather commends them for their poverty.

Third, Jesus commends the church of Smyrna for enduring "slander," more specifically, for enduring "slander from those who call themselves Jews" (2:9). "Slander" here can be understood in two different ways: in a broad way that refers to others spreading false rumors and malicious gossip about members of the church at Smyrna or, as is more likely the case, in a narrow way that refers to others bringing an official charge to the city authorities against these Christians. The difference between these two types of slander can be seen in an incident in the life of the apostle Paul that took place in Corinth. In the early days of Paul's eighteen-month ministry in Corinth, Jews from the local synagogue became angry at the apostle's theology and evangelistic success and "slandered" him (Acts 18:6); that is, they engaged in a smear campaign against Paul and spread nasty lies about him. Later these same Jews in Corinth engaged in a more aggressive form of slander by bringing an official charge against Paul to Gallio, the governor of the province of Achaia (Acts 18:12–13).

Which of these two types of slander was happening to the Christians in Smyrna? There is strong evidence in support of the second, more serious type. Later in this sermon, we will learn that the members of the church are facing both prison and death, two things that could happen only if an official charge had been brought against them. Earlier I mentioned how the charge of atheism resulted in the martyrdom of Polycarp in AD 155, several decades after the events described in Revelation. Important correspondence between Pliny the Younger, a governor of two nearby provinces in Asia Minor, and Emperor Trajan indicates that official charges were being brought against local Christians in AD 111–112, just a few years after the writing of the book of Revelation.

The situation of the church at Smyrna is therefore painfully clear. Not only are the Jesus followers there enduring affliction and financial poverty, but local Jews who rejected Jesus as God's Son are bringing official charges against them to the city authorities. These persecuted believers are facing prison and possible death, and yet they refuse to deny their Christian faith. They do indeed deserve to be named "the church of the persevering persecuted."

The Complaint—None!

The third item that typically occurs in each sermon is the complaint. After commending a church for what it is doing right, Jesus normally spells out what the church is doing wrong. That's why what comes next in the sermon to Smyrna—or more precisely, what does *not* come next—is so significant: the complaint is missing! Jesus utters no criticism at all about the church of Smyrna. Normally, the Bible is significant for what it says; here is a rare instance when the Bible is significant for what it *does not* say. Only two of the seven churches are so spiritually healthy and well that Jesus has no complaint. The majority of the churches are spiritually sick, with significant problems. The missing complaint shows that the church of Smyrna belongs to the rare group of healthy churches that we should try to emulate. We also are called to persevere in whatever persecution may come our way and live such faithful lives that Christ would have no complaint to bring against us.

The Correction (2:10a)

The absence of a complaint in this sermon affects the fourth thing typically found in each message: the correction. Since the church of Smyrna is not doing anything wrong, there is no need for Christ to command them to live differently. Instead, Christ commands them to keep doing the good for which he has already commended them, namely, persevering amid persecution. Christ gives them this command in verse 10a: "Don't ever fear anything that you are about to suffer. Behold, the devil is about to throw some of you into prison in order that you may be tested, and you will have affliction for ten days."

The church in Smyrna was already suffering for their Christian faith in two significant ways: they were suffering poverty (paying a price financially for following Christ), and they were being denounced (facing official charges before the city officials). As if this weren't bad enough, now Jesus tells them that some of their number are going to be thrown into prison! This is not just a bad thing but a deadly thing. Today we use imprisonment as a form of punishment, which can last many years. To avoid the expense of housing and feeding prisoners for long periods of time, ancient Rome imprisoned people only until their trial, which was usually a short time. Unless you were rich and powerful and thus able to bribe or pressure the judge, your brief stay in prison would be followed by an unfair trial in which you would likely be found guilty and sentenced to death. To a church not only suffering poverty and formal charges but also facing possible imprisonment and death, Jesus gives the corrective "Don't be afraid!"

At first blush, this seems like an impossible command to obey. How could any Christian, no matter how strong their faith, not be afraid in such a situation? Actually, Jesus has already given two reasons why this is possible. In the Christ titles given at the start of this sermon, Jesus reminds the church of Smyrna and the church today of two important things. First, he is "the First and the Last" and so has sovereign control over everything that happens, even the persecution that his followers must sometimes endure. Second, he "became dead and lived"; even if his followers are persecuted to the point of death, Jesus has "been there and done that," and his resurrection is a guarantee of our own resurrection.

In verse 10a Jesus gives the church of Smyrna an additional reason why they should not be afraid in the face of opposition: their persecution will be mercifully brief, and they will emerge victorious from it. This is expressed in the words "in order that you may be tested, and you will have affliction for ten days." The references to being tested for ten days most likely allude to a story from the book of Daniel. In the opening scene, Daniel and his three friends living in the palace of the Babylonian king refuse to eat the royal food in order to avoid defilement from eating anything offered to a pagan god. Their choice of an alternative diet is twice described as a test (Dan.

1:12, 14), and three times we are told that the test lasted ten days (Dan. 1:12, 14, 15). The Greek translation of this OT passage uses the same words for "test" and "ten days" found here in the sermon to Smyrna. What happened to Daniel and his three friends after ten days? Did they emerge from this period of testing as scrawny weaklings who nearly died from hunger? Not at all! In fact, they not only survived this period of testing but thrived, coming out far healthier than all the other young men in the courts of the king. Jesus's followers in Smyrna, therefore, need not be afraid, since their anticipated, more intense persecution will be like the testing faced by Daniel and his three friends: it will be brief, and their sovereign Master will watch over them so that they emerge victorious.

The Consequence (2:10b, 11b)

Each sermon closes with the potential consequences that the church faces. There are always two consequences: the first is normally negative—what punishment the church faces if they fail to repent and follow Christ's correction; the second is always positive—what reward awaits the church if they do repent and with Christ's help conquer their particular sin. As we have already seen, however, the sermon to Smyrna has no complaint: this church is not doing anything wrong. It is hardly surprising, then, that Christ does not warn them with a possible punishment but instead comforts them with an additional reward so that this sermon ends with two positive consequences.

First Positive Consequence (2:10b)

The first consequence involves the metaphor of a crown: "Be faithful to the point of death, and I will give you the crown of life" (2:10b). This crown metaphor can be easily misunderstood by modern hearers. We hear the word "crown" and immediately think of what kings and queens wear: a crown made of gold and precious jewels. Greek has a specific word for this kind of royal crown, from which we get our English word "diadem." But this is not the word found in our text. Here a different Greek word is used—one that refers to what champion athletes and victorious military leaders wear, a victory wreath woven out of palm branches or other plant life. People in the ancient world were as obsessed with sports as we are today. Athletic games were held in most major cities, including the city of Smyrna. This means that the Jesus followers in Smyrna, as well as the other believers in Asia Minor listening in, would have easily understood and appreciated the metaphor of "the crown of life," that is, the victory wreath and its promise of eternal life. Those who suffer poverty, slander, imprisonment, and even death for no reason other than that they bear the name of Christ are given the wonderful promise that, if they persevere in their persecution, they will be given the victory wreath of eternal life!

Second Positive Consequence (2:11b)

Each of the seven sermons concludes with a promise "to the one who is victorious," and the sermon to the church of Smyrna ends in the expected way by giving the positive consequence of persevering in the face of persecution: "The one who is victorious will not be hurt at all by the second death" (2:11b). Hopefully you remember that the Greek word for "victorious" is related to the name of a popular sporting goods company, Nike. The implication is that if you are using Nike sports equipment or wearing Nike clothes, you will be victorious; you will win!

The important question that our text raises is this: "Are you a Nike Christian?" In other words, are you a victorious Christian? Are you able to persevere amid whatever persecutions come your way? The good news of the gospel is that the answer to this important question can be a resounding "Yes!" You and I can be Nike Christians and win the victory, not because we are so talented or so hard working but because Christ has already won the victory, and we who belong to Christ have his Spirit living in us. It is this divine Holy Spirit who gives us the power not to be intimidated or afraid to live out our faith, no matter what kind of pushback comes our way.

What is the reward of the Nike Christian? Christ graciously promises to preserve you so that you "will not be hurt at all by the second death." There is not one but two deaths that all people potentially face. The first death is your physical death, the moment when you stop breathing and your body dies. But there is also a second death that is much worse than the first, a second death that the book of Revelation twice calls "the lake of fire" (20:14; 21:8), which is the final destination of the wicked. But the good news is that Nike Christians will in no way be hurt by this second death. Followers of Jesus who persevere in the face of persecution will not only be given the wreath crown of life but will be kept from the horror of the second death.

Conclusion

What is God saying to us Christians today through the sermon to the ancient church of Smyrna? In answering this question, it is helpful to distinguish between "major-league" persecution and "minor-league" persecution.

Most of us Western Christians thankfully do not have to worry about major-league persecution. We rarely, if ever, suffer in dramatic ways simply because we bear the name of Christ. We are not poor, slandered, thrown into prison, or killed for our Christian faith. But sadly, these things are experienced by many Jesus followers in the global church. In some countries, Christianity may be officially tolerated but in everyday life it is not. You might not be arrested for being a Christian, but your neighbors will look down on you, you will be rejected by family members, and your church will be a target for vandalism. In some countries, you are required to list your religion on a job application and, if you identify yourself as a Christian, you won't be hired. Local government officials might force you to take down the cross on your building, or the owners of the rental space your church uses for worship might not let you renew the lease, or your pastor might be threatened with arrest if he is not careful about what he says in his sermons. This is just a sample of the many ways our Christian brothers and sisters around the world suffer every day for their faith.

Even though we rarely hear about such things in our Western news media, we do bear an important responsibility to our persecuted fellow believers. The writer of Hebrews gives this clear command: "Continue to remember . . . those who are persecuted as if you yourselves were being persecuted" (Heb. 13:3). We are called to remember, pray for, and support our brothers and sisters in the global church who are going through major-league persecution.

But what about life closer to home? What we face in the Western church by comparison may be minor-league persecution, but it still qualifies as suffering for our faith. As Christians, by refusing to engage in unethical practices in our work and business, we may suffer financially, we may not be promoted as quickly as others, or we may find it hard to compete with businesses that don't follow the same moral standards. As Christians, we may be attacked for our beliefs and thus suffer socially. We may be mocked for our supposedly discriminatory attitudes toward human sexuality and increasingly portrayed in television and film as self-righteous, bigoted, and hypocritical. The sobering reality is that we live in a society that is rapidly becoming not just less Christian but anti-Christian.

When our faith is tested and persecution comes our way, how are we going to respond? By the power of Christ and his Spirit, let us be like the church of Smyrna, the church of the persevering persecuted. Let us repeat the last words of Polycarp, which he made famous at his martyrdom: "For _____ years I have served Christ, and he never did me any harm. How then can I blaspheme my King, who saved me?"

"Whoever has ears to hear, let them hear what the Spirit is saying to the churches!"—not only to the ancient church of Smyrna but also to the church of Jesus Christ today.

3

Pergamum

The Church of Idolatrous Compromise

The Christ Title (2:12b)

The six other sermons open with two or more descriptions of the Jesus who is about to speak. The message addressed to Pergamum, by contrast, has only one depiction of Jesus, making it the briefest Christ title among the seven sermons. But though short, it is by no means sweet: "These are the words of him who has the sharp, double-edged sword" (2:12b). This description, like virtually all of the Christ titles, comes from the opening vision of Jesus in 1:9–20, which provides a more complete picture of where this sword is located: "and coming out of his mouth was a sharp, double-edged sword" (1:16). The church of Pergamum, therefore, is presented immediately with an intimidating image of Jesus, who does not merely hold a deadly weapon in his hand but has one coming out of his mouth, which is confirmed later in the sermon (2:16b, "I will fight against them with the sword of my mouth") and stressed by this second mention of the sword.

The meaning of this Christ title is determined first of all by its clear allusion to two OT texts, both of which come from the prophet Isaiah and both of which deal with the "servant of the Lord," the coming messiah: "He made my mouth like a sharp sword" (Isa. 49:2) and "He will strike the earth with the rod of his mouth; with the breath of his lips he will slay the wicked" (Isa. 11:4). That John does indeed have these two Isaiah texts in mind becomes clear from his later words in the book of Revelation, where the thought of the sharp sword from the mouth (Isa. 49:2) of the warrior messiah who defeats the beast is combined with his act of slaying the wicked (Isa. 11:4): "Coming out of his mouth is a sharp sword with which to strike down the nations" (Rev. 19:15). What, then, does the image found in the Christ title of the sermon to Pergamum mean? Not just the general truth that Jesus is the promised messiah but more specifically that he is the eschatological judge. In the context of this sermon as a whole, the OT allusions present Jesus as the end-time judge who will justly punish both the wicked in the world (those in the city of Pergamum who have already killed Antipas, Christ's faithful witness, and who continue to persecute other Christ followers) and also the wicked in the church (those who follow the teachings of Balaam and of the Nicolaitans).

As is often the case in the book of Revelation, the image has not only an OT background but also a local pagan setting. In explaining the meaning of the sharp, double-edged sword, Thomas (1992: 181) observes, "Apparently the manner of Christ's appearance to John in the vision of chapter 1 was prompted by the specific situations in which these churches found themselves as well as by the OT expressions that are the source of the figures by which He is described in the vision." The sword is a weapon capable of inflicting death and so naturally functioned as a symbol of power. Roman emperors regularly carried a sword or dagger as a public sign of their power to rule and to judge (Tacitus, *History* 3.68; Suetonius, *Galba* 11; Cassius Dio, *Roman History* 42.37). Pergamum, as the capital city of the Roman province of Asia (see the evidence cited in Hemer 1986: 82–84), was where the governor (proconsul) resided and from where he exercised the "right of the sword" (Latin *ius gladii*), the power to rule over every area of life, including the right to execute enemies of the Roman Empire. Paul recognizes the power symbolized in the sword, writing to the Christians in Rome, "The ruler does not bear the sword for no reason; he is the servant of God, an agent of wrath, to bring punishment on the wrongdoer" (Rom. 13:4).

This Christ title involving the sharp, double-edged sword, therefore, is especially appropriate for the Jesus followers living in Pergamum under the direct power of Rome's representative and facing not only outside opposition to their faith but also internal pressure from false teachers within the church to compromise their distinctly Christian lifestyle. The Jesus who will soon speak a word to them of both commendation and complaint is first introduced as the one who has the sharp, double-edged sword: Jesus—not Rome—is the one who truly has the ultimate power over life and death. Ramsay (1994:

213) highlights the appropriateness of this Christ title for the Pergamum church as follows:

> In this letter the intimate connection between the church and the city, and the appropriateness . . . of the opening address to the church are even more obvious than in the two previous letters. "These are the words of him who has the sharp, double-edged sword." The writer is uttering the words of him who wears the symbol of absolute authority, and is invested with the power of life and death. This is the aspect in which he addresses himself to the official capital of the province, the seat of authority in the ancient kingdom and in the Roman administration. To no other of the seven cities could this exordium have been used appropriately. To Pergamum it is entirely suitable. He that has the absolute and universal authority speaks to the church situated in the city where official authority dwells.

Figure 3.1. Relief on a panel from Trajan's victory column (erected AD 113) depicting an enemy soldier holding the special *rhomphaia* sword.

The image of power and authority to judge conveyed by the sharp, double-edged sword is intensified by the specific type of sword that Jesus has coming out of his mouth. Two types of swords are mentioned in the book of Revelation. One is the *machaira*—a short sword or dagger about eighteen inches long, which was commonly carried by Roman soldiers (see Rev. 6:4; 13:10, 14). The other is the *rhomphaia*—a much longer sword associated with the Thracian fighters who lived in what is today the region of northeast Greece (see Rev. 1:16; 2:12, 16; 6:8; 19:15, 21). The *rhomphaia* sword had a two-foot-long wooden handle attached to a three-foot-long, slightly curved blade to enable its use as both a thrusting and slashing weapon. Its long handle and overall length required two hands to wield, and it was capable of cutting an opponent's shield in half with one strong blow. These features explain why the *rhomphaia* sword developed a reputation as a particularly fearsome weapon.

It is significant, then, that the type of sword that Jesus has is not the *machaira* but the *rhomphaia*. The image that Christ presents of himself through John to the Pergamum church is nothing like the tender depictions of him typically found in modern church-school material, where Jesus is holding little children in his lap, while surrounded by a few lambs. Here he is the end-time judge who comes with the full power and authority represented by the sword. Although the Pergamum church has some positive features (see the commendation below), the single Christ title with its threatening image of the deadly *rhomphaia* sword coming out of his mouth—an image repeated in the sermon's closing—reveals Christ's overall negative judgment about this church because of its sin of idolatrous compromise.

A sword figures prominently in the OT story of Balaam cited later in this sermon. Balaam's donkey sees an angel of the Lord standing in the middle of the road with "the sword [*rhomphaia*] drawn in his hand" and so turns off the road into a field (Num. 22:23 LXX). A short time later, when the donkey's path is again blocked by the angel and the beast refuses to go any further, Balaam gets so angry that he exclaims to the animal, "If only I had a sword [*machaira*] in my hand, I would kill you right now" (22:29 LXX). God then opens Balaam's eyes, and "he saw the angel of the Lord standing in the road with his sword [*machaira*] drawn" (22:31 LXX). After the Israelites later fall into the sin of idolatry and sexual immorality due to the plan advised by Balaam, this pagan diviner is justly killed "with the sword [*rhomphaia*]" for his actions (Num. 31:8). There may well be a logical link in the mind of John between the *rhomphaia* sword as a Christ title and his later reference to the OT story of Balaam.

The Commendation (2:13)

The shift from the Christ title to the commendation is signaled, as it is in all seven sermons, with the expected formula, "I know." This second section in the sermon, containing Christ's praise of his followers in Pergamum, is structured as an *inclusio*. Three key words compose the boundaries of this literary unit: the adverb "where," the verb "lives," and the proper noun "Satan."

> Opening: "I know *where* you *live*, where the throne of *Satan* is"
> Closing: ". . . *where Satan lives*"

Sandwiched within this *inclusio* are two verbal clauses that affirm in both a positive ("but you hold fast my name") and negative ("and you did not deny faith in me") way the faithfulness of the Pergamum church despite living in an idolatrous city where Satan dwells. The intensity of the satanic opposition they have faithfully endured is illustrated by an explanatory clause that highlights the martyrdom of one of their church members: "even in the days of Antipas, my faithful witness, who was killed among you." By arranging the commendation in this way, John draws attention to the two main clauses at the center of the *inclusio* and thus stresses Christ's praise for the faithfulness of the Pergamum church despite intense persecution.

The opening statement reveals the problem that the Pergamum church faces: it lives where Satan has his throne. "I know where you live, where the throne of Satan is." The verb "you live" (*katoikeis*) denotes not a temporary residence but a permanent dwelling. Jesus is speaking to those who have established roots in Pergamum and are not able to remove themselves from the potentially deadly environment of living in a city where Satan has his throne. A throne is occupied by rulers and people with authority and so, like the sharp, double-edged sword, is an image of power. The "throne of Satan," therefore, refers metaphorically to the power that Satan has and uses in a malevolent manner to oppose Christ and his followers. As with the phrase "synagogue of Satan" in the sermon to Smyrna, so here the mention of Satan by name reveals the true enemy of Christians. The martyrdom of Antipas and the persecution that the believers in Pergamum currently endure may outwardly be the actions of local city officials and hostile pagan neighbors, but they are ultimately the actions of Satan, who is working behind the scenes, using political institutions and human individuals to harm the followers of Christ. The "throne of Satan" is a metaphor that expresses the truth of Paul's words that "our struggle is not against flesh and blood but . . . against the powers of this dark world and against the spiritual forces of evil in the heavenly realms," and this disguised hostile activity is all part of "the devil's schemes" (Eph. 6:11–12).

The metaphor "throne of Satan" likely has a specific connection to the city of Pergamum, especially when we note the reference to "*the* throne of Satan." As Aune (1997: 182) observes, "The fact that *thronos* is articular suggests that that the author is alluding to a specific throne (either literally or figuratively), which he expects the readers to recognize." Several proposals have been put forward as to the precise identity of "the throne of Satan" (see the helpful surveys of Hemer 1986: 84–85; Thomas 1992: 182–85; Aune 1997: 182–84), five of which are discussed below.

1. *The acropolis of Pergamum.* Approaching Pergamum from the south, as one would naturally do if coming from Smyrna, the acropolis looks like a giant throne on which Satan could sit and from which he could control the city below (so Wood 1961–62: 264). However, unlike Mount Pagos at Smyrna, which was referred to as a "crown" by some ancient sources, there is no evidence that any writer referred to the Pergamum acropolis as a "throne." Additionally, the acropolis at Pergamum, though steep and striking, is not unique, since most major cities were situated on and around a high hill.

Figure 3.2. Sacred road to the Asclepius healing center, with the Pergamum acropolis in the background.

2. *The great altar of Zeus Savior.* A massive U-shaped altar dedicated to Zeus Savior (*zeus sōtēr*) was built on the acropolis during the reign of one of Pergamum's most important kings, Eumenes II (197–159 BC), to commemorate his victory over the marauding Gauls in 190 BC. This enormous altar, which measured 120 feet wide and 112 feet deep (front to back), was decorated with an impressive frieze depicting the traditional battle between the Olympian gods (representing order) and the giants (representing chaos), who have serpent tails instead of legs. Several facts have led many commentators to believe that John had this altar in mind as the "throne of Satan": the U-shape of this altar resembles a throne; an altar was often equated with a throne in the ancient world; the giants' serpent tails would remind Christian readers of Satan's portrayal as a snake (Rev. 12:9, 14, 15; 20:2); and the title "Savior" (*sōtēr*) being ascribed to Zeus would be offensive to Christians, who understood this to be a title appropriate only for God and/or Christ. However, other cults in Pergamum were also associated with serpent imagery and with the title "Savior" (see "The Asclepius Healing Center" below), which weakens the case for seeing the Zeus altar as "the throne of Satan."

3. *The Asclepius healing center.* After Epidauros in the Peloponnesus and the island of Kos, Pergamum was the third most important center in the ancient world for Asclepius, the god of healing. As was typically the case for

© Baker Publishing Group

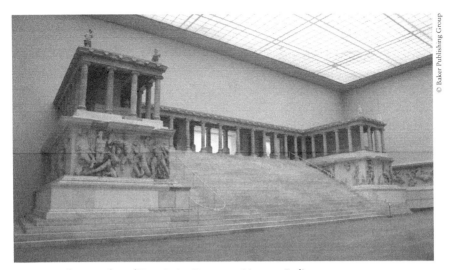

Figure 3.3. The great altar of Zeus Savior. Pergamum Museum, Berlin.

cultic sites associated with this deity, this healing center (the ancient equivalent of the Mayo Clinic) was located on the outskirts of the city and was approached by the "Via Tecta," a sacred road 2,700 feet long and 60 feet wide. The site contained multiple buildings: a forecourt; a large main courtyard surrounded on three sides with covered columned walkways (stoas); a library; a theater seating 3,500; a 262-foot underground tunnel connecting the sacred pools to the healing center; and a temple to Asclepius. Asclepius was typically portrayed with a snake coiled around the god's walking stick, and the forecourt in Pergamum had an altar in its center showing a relief of snakes. The temple in Pergamum was dedicated to Asclepius Soter (Savior), and a gold votive offering of an ear was discovered at the site with the inscription "To Asclepius Soter." The connection of Asclepius to the image of a snake and to the title "Savior" as well as the renown of this site in the ancient world have led some to see this healing center as Revelation's "throne of Satan." Yet as noted above, the great altar of Zeus shares these same two connections as well as its fame, which weakens the uniqueness of this identification.

Giovanni Dall'Orto / Wikimedia Commons

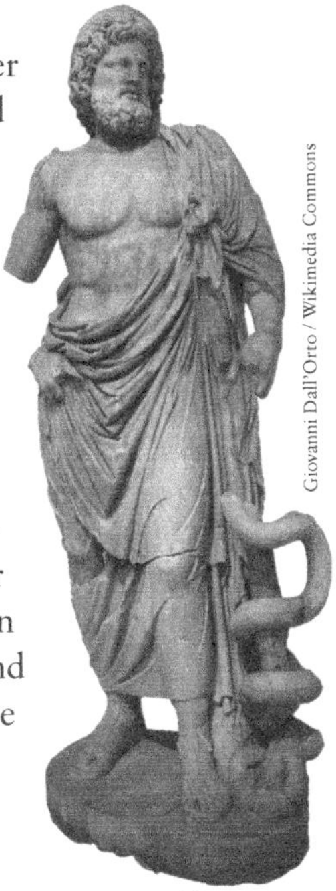

Figure 3.4. Marble statue of Asclepius, god of healing, with a snake wrapped around his walking stick. National Archaeological Museum, Athens.

4. *The imperial cult.* Pergamum was an important
city for the imperial cult, the
worship of the Roman state
and individual Roman em-
perors. The people of Asia
petitioned Augustus to allow
them to consecrate a tem-
ple in his honor, and he
acceded to their request in
29 BC, requiring it to be

Figure 3.5. *Left*: Caesar Augustus. *Right*: Temple of Roma
at Pergamum. Coin of the Commune (Provincial League) of
Asia.

built in Pergamum, the capital city. The exact location of this temple has not
yet been discovered, but it is portrayed on many coins of the city and of the
Commune (Provincial League) of Asia. Further evidence that Pergamum functioned as a major center of the imperial cult lies in the fact that it was granted
the privileged status of *neōkoros* (temple keeper) yet again shortly after the
time when the book of Revelation was written: a second imperial temple was
erected in AD 114 on the acropolis in honor of Trajan. The majority of modern
exegetes share the logic expressed by Ladd (1972: 46): "John used the phrase
['the throne of Satan'] because Pergamum was the center of the imperial cult
with its worship of the emperor, which was becoming the greatest danger to
the Christian Church" (so also, e.g., Charles 1920: 61; Mounce 1977: 96–97;
Hemer 1986: 82–87; Keener 2000: 123; Kistemaker 2001: 128–29; Osborne
2002: 141; Witherington 2003: 102). The strength of this option, however, is
weakened by three factors. First, a temple to the goddess Roma was built by
Smyrna already in 196 BC, many years before Pergamum erected its temple to
Augustus. Second, in AD 26 Pergamum competed with eleven other cities in
Asia for permission from Tiberius to build an imperial temple and lost out to
Smyrna because of that city's long-standing relationship with Rome. Third,
at the time that Revelation was likely written, other cities in Asia were also
granted the right to build an imperial temple, including two of the seven ad-
dressed in the sermons (Smyrna and Ephesus), which casts doubt on whether
Pergamum can be uniquely identified as the "throne of Satan."

5. *Pergamum as the center of Christian persecution.* In these seven sermons, Pergamum is the only city explicitly mentioned as a place where
someone was martyred for faith in Christ (Antipas, Rev. 2:13b) and where
the "throne of Satan," meaning his power, was especially felt by the Jesus
followers. Since only the proconsul (governor), who resided in the capital
city of Pergamum, had the "right of the sword" (*ius gladii*) on behalf of
the Roman state, he may well have been involved in some capacity with the

death of Antipas. This would explain the fittingness of the single Christ title in this sermon, since the *rhomphaia* sword would effectively position the power of Jesus over the local Roman representative's "right of the sword." This view also potentially overlaps with the other main proposals: the refusal of some Christians in Pergamum to participate in the many pagan temples in the city (the great altar of Zeus Savior, the cult of Asclepius Savior, and the worship of the many other pagan gods, including the imperial cult) naturally led to charges of atheism and treason and to other acts of opposition, making Pergamum the Asian center of Christian persecution and thus the "throne of Satan." Aune (1997: 183–84) states, "It appears that the 'throne of Satan' should be identified not with a specific architectural feature of Roman Pergamon . . . but rather with *Roman opposition* to early Christianity, which the author of Rev 2–3 perceived as particularly malevolent in that city" (emphasis original).

Figure 3.6. Antipas being martyred in the "brazen bull."

Although the precise identification of the "throne of Satan" must remain tentative, there is no uncertainty about how this striking phrase functions in the commendation: it makes Christ's praise of the Pergamum congregation all the more impressive. These church members reside in a city where "the throne of Satan" is located, a city "where Satan lives," and yet as the double verbal clause at the center of the *inclusio* stresses, "You hold fast my name, and you did not deny faith in me."

The first and positive half of this double clause employs the verb *krateō*, a word whose "primary signification is the exercise of power" (BDAG 564), "to grasp forcibly, seize." Since the object of this verb is the name of Christ, it here has the figurative sense of "remain firm" or "hold fast." Despite living in a city where Satan's throne, or power, is putting great pressure on the believers in Pergamum, causing some to compromise their faith by engaging in idolatrous and sexually immoral practices (see the complaint at 2:14), most in the church are "holding fast" and living in a manner consistent with their new identity as those who bear the name of Christ. The exhortative function of this commendation should not be missed. People typically want to live up to the praise they receive from others. By praising the Christians in

Pergamum for holding fast Christ's name amid persecution, John puts pressure on them to continue this commendatory behavior as they face ongoing opposition to their faith.

The second and negative half of the double clause gives a parallel and similar commendation to the Pergamum church, with the notable difference that it shifts the time perspective from the present to the past: "and you did not deny faith in me" (the genitive *mou* is not possessive ["my faith," i.e., the Christian faith] but objective ["faith in me"]; so also possibly Rev. 14:12). The opposition that they are currently enduring was also a reality in their recent past. Although the details of this previous persecution cannot be known, the praise that Jesus gives his followers in Pergamum suggests that they had been pressured to deny their faith in Christ. The letter of Pliny the Younger to Emperor Trajan and the ruler's response (for the text of these two important letters, see the comments on Rev. 2:9) as well as the story of Polycarp's martyrdom in Smyrna make clear that in some places formal charges were being brought against Christians. The Christ followers who were "outed" in this way were then challenged to deny their faith and to prove their sincerity by offering a sacrifice to the emperor and by cursing Christ; those who refused to do so were put to death.

This is what apparently happened to one member of the Pergamum church. Jesus praises this congregation for not denying his name "even in the days of Antipas, my faithful witness, who was killed among you." Almost nothing is known about this important person, the only martyr mentioned by name in the entire book of Revelation. Some commentators have wrongly claimed that his name means "against all" and that this reflected his heroic stand against all evil (so, e.g., Walvoord 1966: 67). The less idealized truth is that Antipas is a shortened form of the common Greek name Antipatros (see Josephus, *Ant.* 14.1.3). Other exegetes note that Antipas is never listed among the martyrs of the first two centuries who are connected with Pergamum (so, e.g., Thomas 1992: 186). This fact, however, is insignificant, since these other martyrs number only three and are all related to the same event that took place a century or more after the death of Antipas (see Eusebius, *Church History* 4.15.48). More worthy of note is that Antipas is identified by Christ as "my faithful witness," the same title ascribed to Jesus at the very beginning of the book of Revelation (1:5). Therefore, Antipas shares with Jesus a very important connection: both have been faithful in testifying to the truth of the gospel to the point of death.

Jesus died on a cross, but Antipas appears to have suffered a different yet equally gruesome death. According to the Byzantine hagiographers, Antipas was killed in a "brazen bull," a torture and execution device designed in ancient Greece and later also used by the Romans. In this method, the condemned was placed in a hollow, life-sized brass bull, and a fire was started underneath, which slowly roasted the person to death. The horror of this death was compounded by the creation of a complex system of tubes and stops in the brass bull so that the prisoner's screams of pain were converted into sounds like the bellowing of an infuriated bull, thereby amusing those watching the ghastly spectacle. Whether this is the way Antipas was killed cannot be known with certainty. What is beyond dispute, however, is that Christ has memorialized the name of Antipas for eternity by identifying him as "my faithful witness" and holding him up to the church in Pergamum as one whose perseverance to the point of death should be emulated as they live in the city where Satan lives.

The Complaint (2:14–15)

The shift from the commendation to the complaint section is signaled by the stereotyped phrase "But I have against you a few things" (cf. 2:4, Ephesus; 2:20, Thyatira). The "few things" (*oliga*) refers to the *number* and not the *relative importance* of the complaint that Jesus makes (contra Aune 1997: 185, who translates this phrase as "But I hold a *minor matter* against you"). The rest of the sermon makes clear the seriousness of the situation, for the church's failure to repent and correct the situation will result in Christ coming to make war against them with the sharp, double-edged *rhomphaia* sword coming out of his mouth (2:16; cf. the Christ title in 2:12). The Greek adjective *oligos* is used only once elsewhere in the seven sermons (3:4, "But you have a few names"); in both cases the focus is on number, not relative importance (so also in the rest of book of Revelation: 12:12; 17:10). Rather than taking the plural number to be a generic reference to one thing (so Charles 1920: 62), it is better to take it literally, especially when the rest of this unit lists more than one complaint. The "few things" are two charges that Jesus ultimately makes against some in Pergamum: they are "eating food sacrificed to idols" (i.e., the sin of idolatry) and "committing sexual immorality."

John uses the OT story of the false prophet Balaam to make these two complaints: "There are some among you who hold to the teaching of Balaam, who was teaching Balak to place a stumbling block before the sons of Israel: to eat food sacrificed to idols and to commit sexual immorality" (2:14). John's many OT references and allusions in the seven sermons presuppose that second- and third-generation Christian readers in Asia Minor would know these stories well enough not to need him to spell out the details. Many contemporary readers, however, do not have such knowledge and thus need to have the story of Balaam explained so that its relevance to the Pergamum situation can be fully appreciated.

Near the end of their forty-year period of wandering in the wilderness, the Israelite people came to the plains of Moab, where they could look west across the Jordan and see the promised land of Canaan. Balak, the king of Moab, was terrified of the threat posed by this foreign nation and promised to pay Balaam, a pagan diviner, a large sum of money to place a curse on the Israelites. At first the plan fails miserably. A series of humbling and even humorous events involving a donkey who speaks results in Balaam blessing Israel numerous times (Num. 22–24). Nevertheless, despite these blessings from Balaam, the Israelites fall into sexual immorality and idolatry: "The men [of Israel] began to indulge in sexual immorality with Moabite women, who invited them to the sacrifices to their gods. The people ate the sacrificial meal and bowed down before these gods" (Num. 25:1–2). God punishes his chosen people for their immoral and idolatrous actions by sending a plague that kills 24,000. Balaam's involvement in this shameful incident in Israelite history is later revealed: the sinful actions of God's people happened because of "the advice of Balaam" (Num. 31:16). Later Jewish writers confirm the widespread belief that Balaam advised Balak to tempt the men of Israel with the most beautiful women of Moab so that they would commit sexual immorality with these foreigners and join them in idolatrous worship of the Moabite gods (Philo, *Life of Moses* 294–96; Josephus, *Ant.* 4.6.6). In NT times, Balaam became the prototypical false prophet (2 Pet. 2:15–16; Jude 11).

When Jesus complains in Rev. 2:14 that some in the Pergamum church "hold to the teaching of Balaam," he is referring to those who, like this OT diviner, are giving false teaching or advice and causing God's people to compromise their faithfulness to him and ultimately to engage in the sins of idolatry and sexual immorality. Since Balaam had such a notorious reputation, it is clear that the group being rebuked by Jesus did not themselves claim to be followers of Balaam and would certainly have been offended at such a label. Rather, the name "Balaam," like "Jezebel" in Thyatira (2:20), is chosen partly to signify the false and deceptive character of the teaching associated with this group. The Balaam label was primarily chosen, however, because of the parallel between the two sins that this OT character tricked God's people into committing and the same two sins that some in the Pergamum church have been deceived into committing: eating food sacrificed to idols and committing sexual immorality.

First Complaint: Eating Food Sacrificed to Idols

It is hard for the modern reader to appreciate fully how powerful a temptation the first of these two sins was for the early Christians. Cultic meals played a crucial role in the worship experience of the ancient world. The Greek word John uses (*eidōlothyton*) refers to some form of food that is sacrificed to a pagan god: grain, wine, or meat. Only a small portion of the meat was sacrificed to the deity; holocaust offerings in which all the meat was consumed by fire were rare. The remaining portions of meat were handled in two possible ways. The meat might be sold in the marketplace, with the proceeds going for the upkeep of the pagan sanctuary from which it came (Pliny the Younger, *Letters* 10.96.10, notes that "the meat of sacrificial victims is on sale everywhere"). This type of meat is referred to in the NT as *makellon*, "marketplace meat" (1 Cor. 10:25), and was considered acceptable for Christians to eat (1 Cor. 10:23–30). Alternatively, worshipers could eat the leftover meat in a dining room at the same temple or in a building associated with the deity. The NT refers to this type of meat as *eidōlothyton*, "food sacrificed to an idol" (Acts 15:29; 21:25; 1 Cor. 8:1, 4, 7, 10; 10:19, 28 [var.]; Rev. 2:14, 20), which was judged to be unacceptable for Christians to eat since it would make them guilty of idolatry. The key difference was whether the eating of such food took place within a religious context so that this was no longer a regular meal but a *cultic* meal. The connection between food sacrificed to idols and the sin of idolatry is spelled out in the Didache, an early Christian treatise (1st or early 2nd. cent. AD): "Keep strictly away from food sacrificed to idols, for it involves the worship of dead gods" (6.3).

The cultic meal was just as important to the worship experience as the offering of the sacrifice itself. This was the case not only throughout the different regions of the ancient world but also throughout the different centuries. Kane (1975: 321, cited by Willis 1985: 15) helpfully summarizes the situation:

> Some form of the cult meal was one of the *fundamental* features of Greek religious festivities, and took the form of a meal devoted to, presided over, or shared with the gods. Usually meat or other food was offered to the god and then—apart from reserved portions—consumed by the participants. This was so at the public festivals organized by the City State, and in smaller political and social groups, whether public or private. This was so in the pre-Classical, the Classical, the Hellenistic, and the Roman periods. (emphasis added)

Very brief papyrus invitations to these religious or cultic meals have been discovered in Egypt. Although only twenty of these dinner invitations have been found thus far, the highly consistent form followed in all of them (see

Kim 1975) suggests that they are typical of what was a common piece of writing in the ancient world, which implies that participation in cultic meals was very common. Sixteen of the invitations are connected with the cult of Sarapis, an Egyptian chief male deity, and the remaining four involve Isis, the divine twin sister of Sarapis. One papyrus (P.Oxy. 2791) serves as a good representative of the brief length and consistent form of these dinner invitations: "Diogenes invites you to dinner for the first birthday of his daughter in the Serapaeum [the temple of Serapis] tomorrow, which is Pachon 26, from the 8th hour onward" (Coles 1970).

Since a couple of these dinner invitations identify the occasion as a birthday or coming-of-age celebration, a few scholars have claimed that, from the participants' perspective, these meals did not have a religious function but merely served a social purpose. Willis (1985: 44–45), for example, stresses that "the meals mentioned in the papyri [dinner invitations] were predominantly social occasions of co-religionists" and consisted of "pleasant intercourse and conviviality." This purely social interpretation of the meal's function, however, must be rejected in light of the universal truth concerning the three most important factors about real estate, whether ancient or modern: "Location, location, location!" That the dining rooms were often located within the precincts of a pagan temple would naturally link the food eaten there with the worship of that deity, especially if a portion of the same food had been sacrificed to the deity. As Murphy-O'Connor (1983: 172) observes, "The location of the dining rooms inevitably conferred a religious character on the parties held there." It is also striking that one of the dinner invitations identifies the host of the meal not as any human person but as the god himself: "The god invites you to dine at the table, which will take place tomorrow in the temple of Thoeris from the 9th hour" (P.Colon. 2555). Horsley (1981: 6) cites this papyrus invitation as "the most clear-cut evidence that these banquets had a fundamentally religious character." Paul's overall comments in 1 Cor. 8:1–11:1 reveal that this apostle clearly considered meals eaten in a temple's dining room to have a religious function, and he also worried that some in the Corinthian church would think this as well: "Some people are still so accustomed to idols that when they eat food sacrificed to an idol, they think of it as having been sacrificed to a god" (1 Cor. 8:7).

The discovery of a cultic dining room in Pergamum's middle acropolis (see Radt 1988: 307–13) is especially relevant to the situation in that city and Christ's specific complaint that some church members are "eating food sacrificed to idols." This uniquely structured building consists of a single room with a three-foot-high podium (leading the archaeologists to name it the "Podium Hall"), seven feet deep and running along the outside walls of the

J. A. D. Weima

Figure 3.7. Cultic dining room (Podium Hall) in Pergamum.

building. This construction allowed up to seventy people to climb up onto the podium by way of steps and then recline—the traditional position for eating in the Greco-Roman world (1 Cor. 8:10, *katakeimai*)—on the raised podium with their feet toward the outside wall and their heads toward the inside. The inside edge of the podium is slightly lower than the rest of the podium, covered in marble, and roughly one foot wide; it functioned as a shelf on which food could be placed and eaten by those reclining on the podium. Standing in the center of the room are two altars—one for the imperial cult of Augustus and the other for the cult of Dionysus—on which food was sacrificed as part of the cultic meal. Murals on the walls portrayed vine branches, leaves, and grape clusters—all images associated with Dionysus.

This highlights the crucial role that cultic meals played in the religious experience of the ancient world and reveals why these dinners became such a powerful temptation for the early Christians. Garland (2003: 347–48) notes:

> Occasions for eating in connection with an idol or on the premises of an idol's temple were numerous. The celebrations of many cults were closely bound up with civic and social life because religion and politics were indivisible in ancient Hellenistic city life. If Christians took part in civic life, they would have been expected to participate in a festival's sacrificial meals in some form or another.

Gentile Christians, no doubt, had participated in cultic meals throughout their lives before they became followers of Jesus, and it is not surprising that many of them wanted to continue this practice even after becoming Christians. Evidence that this is exactly what happened can be seen in several key NT texts where the problem of eating food sacrificed to idols is addressed. The Jewish Christian leaders who gathered in Jerusalem to consider the issue of circumcision felt the need to write a separate letter to their gentile brothers and sisters (the so-called Apostolic Decree), exhorting them not to engage in the kind of activities that they knew were typical for gentiles, and the first item in this list is "abstain from food sacrificed to idols" (Acts 15:29). The temptation of participating in cultic meals was such a great problem for the believers in Corinth that the apostle Paul devotes three complete chapters to the topic (1 Cor. 8:1–11:1). Jesus's complaints against the church in Pergamum (Rev. 2:14) and the church in Thyatira (Rev. 2:20) reveal that the temptation of eating food sacrificed to idols continued to plague the church even at the end of the first century.

What argument or logic did those in Pergamum who bought into "the teaching of Balaam" (2:14) use to justify participating in cultic meals? Neither this sermon nor the one to Thyatira gives us the answer to this question. Judging by the situation in Corinth, where the same problem was occurring, a plausible answer is this: some believers were appealing to "knowledge," specifically the knowledge that there is only one God and that idols do not really exist. A Christian armed with this knowledge can eat either in a temple dining room or in another building devoted to a pagan deity and not become guilty of idolatry (note the multiple occurrences of "knowledge" and the key role this word plays in 1 Cor. 8:1–13). Some believers in Pergamum were likely saying to themselves and to other church members, "Isn't there only one true God? And Athena, Zeus, Dionysus, and Asclepius—the four major deities worshiped in our city—are they not all merely pretend gods, who do not really exist? Since I know this important truth, why can't I participate in cultic meals? These deities mean nothing to me!"

Second Complaint: Committing Sexual Immorality

The second complaint that Jesus brings against some in the Pergamum church is that they are "committing sexual immorality." A number of commentators argue that this does not literally refer to actual sexual sins but is rather a metaphor for idolatry and that, consequently, the church is not guilty of two sins but one—idolatry (so, e.g., Caird 1966: 39; Beale 1999: 250; Keener 2000: 124; Koester 2014: 288–89; Beale and Campbell 2015: 67; Fanning 2020: 138,

140). In support of this interpretation, they typically appeal to three things. First, the metaphor of Israel as an unfaithful wife, prostituting herself with other gods, is an extremely common trope in the OT (e.g., 2 Kings 9:22; Isa. 57:3, 8; Jer. 3:9; 13:27; Ezek. 16:15–36; 23:7–35; Hosea 1:2; 2:2–13; 4:12; 5:4; Nah. 3:4; note also the reference to "prostitute" in Rev. 17:1, 15–16). Second, the word used here for committing sexual immorality (verb *porneuō*; cognate noun *porneia*) occurs elsewhere in the book of Revelation with a metaphorical meaning (14:8; 17:2, 4; 18:3, 9). Third, the same charge of "committing sexual immorality" is found in the Thyatira sermon (2:20) in conjunction with the OT story of Jezebel, and she is always associated with the sin of idolatry, never with sexual immorality (or so they argue).

While the metaphorical sense of "committing sexual immorality" is certainly a possible interpretation, there are more compelling reasons for understanding this second complaint literally. First, despite at times having a metaphorical sense in the book of Revelation, the word used here (and its cognates) is also used literally (9:21; 21:8; 22:15), and so it clearly could refer to actual sexual misconduct here in 2:14. Second, the context includes a reference to the OT story of Balaam, who was ultimately responsible for causing God's people to commit not just the sin of idolatry but also the sin of sexual immorality. As Num. 25:1–2 makes clear: "The men [of Israel] began to indulge in sexual immorality with Moabite women, who invited them to the sacrifices to their gods. The people ate the sacrificial meal and bowed down before these gods." Third, it would be redundant and not rhetorically effective to list two actions back-to-back ("eating food sacrificed to idols and committing sexual immorality") in which the first action is meant literally and the second action metaphorically. Fourth, as noted above, the reference to the plural "few things" which Jesus has against the Pergamum church most naturally refers not to a single complaint of idolatry but the two complaints of idolatry and sexual immorality. Fifth, the word "sexual immorality" is paired with "food sacrificed to idols" in three other places in the NT outside the book of Revelation (Acts 15:29; 21:25; 1 Cor. 10:7–8), and in those places the context shows that it has an obviously literal meaning.

Sixth, sexual activity was frequently connected with banquets or formal meals in the ancient world, including apparently also cultic meals. Seneca refers to "luckless slave boys" serving at official meals who are sexually assaulted by those dining (*Epistles* 95.24). In another letter, Seneca refers to those serving wine who are at the mercy of the sexual advances of their master: "The wine-server has to dress like a woman and to wrestle with his advancing years. . . . He is kept awake all night, dividing his time between his master's drunkenness and his lust" (*Epistles* 47.7). Quintilian denounces inappropriate conduct at meals where children see "our female lovers and our male concubines; every dinner party is loud with foul songs and things are presented to their [children's] eyes about which we should blush to speak" (*Institutes of Oratory* 1.2.6–8). Prostitutes (*hetairai*) were frequently present at banquets and formal dinners, as were women playing flute and harp, who typically pleased guests with more than just their music (Juvenal, *Satires* 11.162–70; Cicero, *For Murena* 13; Plutarch, *Table Talk* 613C). On the basis of these and other ancient texts, Fotopoulos (2003: 149) states, "One regular feature of formal Greco-Roman meals, whether occurring in private homes or in a pagan temple, was entertainment that frequently included sexual relations."

The complaint that Jesus brings against the church at Pergamum, therefore, is twofold: it involves both the sin of idolatry and the sin of sexual immorality. Although some congregational members were faithfully "holding on to" the name of Jesus despite the challenges of living in a place where satanic pressures were prevalent, others in the church were "holding on to" the misleading teaching of Balaam. This teaching, which likely involved an appeal to the knowledge that idol gods do not really exist since there is only one true God, became a stumbling block to other members of the church, causing them to compromise their faith and participate in cultic meals, where they were not only guilty of idolatry but also put themselves in a setting that often involved sexual immorality.

One Group or Two? Before the complaint section comes to an end, Jesus names another group within the Pergamum church besides those who hold to the teaching of Balaam: "Thus you also have those who similarly hold to the teaching of the Nicolaitans" (2:15). Was this group similar to but separate from the Balaamites so that the Pergamum church had two distinct groups within it—the Balaamites and the Nicolaitans—or were these two groups the same, so that there was only one group within the church? The matter is complicated by the fact that the grammar of this verse is awkward and confusing because of three expressions: the opening "thus" (*houtōs*), the middle "you also" (*kai sy*), and the concluding "similarly" (*homoiōs*).

The opening "thus" most naturally refers to the immediately preceding statement (BDAG 741.1) and explains that statement such that "the teaching of Balaam" is the same as "the teaching of the Nicolaitans" (so most commentators; contra MacKay 1973; Thomas 1992: 193; Coutsoumpos 1997: 24). That these two groups are, in fact, one and the same is strengthened by the use of the same verb to describe advocates of both groups: those who "hold to" (*krateō*) the teaching of Balaam and those who "hold to" (*krateō*) the teaching of the Nicolaitans. The two groups are further united by the fact that their names mean essentially the same thing: Balaam in Hebrew means "one who consumes or rules over the people," and Nicolaus in Greek means "one who conquers the people" (Hemer 1986: 89; Michaels 1997: 76; Beale and Campbell 2015: 67). Osborne (2002: 145) concludes that "the best solution is to take this not as a comparison between two similar movements but as a comparison between a single movement (the Nicolaitans) and the Jewish tradition about Balaam: 'In the same way that Balaam subverted the Israelites, these false teachers are trying to subvert you.'" Caird (1966: 38–39) states more succinctly: "There were not two types of errors in Pergamum, only one: 'the teaching of Balaam' is merely John's opprobrious name for 'the teaching of the Nicolaitans.'" The middle adverb "you also" refers to the Ephesian congregation who, as it is clear from Jesus's earlier sermon to them, "also" faced the challenge of the Nicolaitans (see 2:6). The concluding adverb "similarly" likewise has the situation of the Ephesian church in view: some in Pergamum are holding to the idolatry-inducing teaching of the Nicolaitans in a way that is similar to some in Ephesus who are affirming the false teaching of this same group.

In our study of the sermon to Ephesus, we examined at some length the identity and teachings of the Nicolaitans, and so the reader is directed to that earlier discussion. Here we simply repeat the conclusion reached there: the Nicolaitans advocated teachings that caused believers to compromise their faith and participate in pagan activities, making them guilty of idolatry and sexual immorality.

The Correction (2:16a)

The shift from the complaint to the correction is signaled by the command "Repent therefore!" (2:16a), using the same key verb found in the correction section of all the other sermons to unhealthy churches (Ephesus, 2:5a, 5b; Thyatira, 2:21a, 21b; Sardis, 3:3; Laodicea, 3:19b). The verb "repent" is missing from the sermons to Smyrna and Philadelphia because these were healthy churches that did not require complaint or correction. Although Jesus does not spell out the specific sins from which the Pergamum church must repent, the inferential particle "therefore" (*oun*) closely connects the correction with the preceding complaint, making clear that the church must repent from the compromising theology of the Nicolaitans, who justified participating in cultic meals and thereby made believers vulnerable to the closely connected sins of idolatry and sexual immorality. The verb "repent" (*metanoeō*) literally means "to change one's mind" (BDAG 650.1). Jesus, therefore, is not merely challenging the Pergamum church to regret or feel bad about what they have done. Instead, he is commanding them to adopt a new way of thinking that recognizes the false nature of the teaching of the Nicolaitans and how their misleading arguments have caused believers to commit the serious sins of idolatry and sexual immorality.

Jesus issues the command to repent not just to the proponents of the teaching of the Nicolaitans but to the whole congregation, even those who were earlier commended for holding on to the name of Christ and not denying him despite satanic pressures within the city of Pergamum (2:13). Although only a portion of the Pergamum congregation has bought into the false, Balaam-like teaching of the Nicolaitans, all members are guilty of tolerating this group's idolatrous and immorality-inducing claims. The situation, then, is the opposite of that in Ephesus. The Ephesian church rightly rejected the teaching of the Nicolaitans and hated their evil works but are rebuked by Jesus for not demonstrating love to fellow members. The Pergamum church, by contrast, wrongly tolerates the teaching of the Nicolaitans and are rebuked by Jesus for not preventing fellow members from participating in cultic meals and making themselves guilty of idolatry and sexual immorality.

The Consequence (2:16b, 17b)

In typical fashion, the sermon to Pergamum closes with Christ giving the two potential consequences depending on how this church responds to his call to repentance. The first consequence is negative, what punishment will ensue if the Pergamum congregation fails to follow Christ's correction; the second is positive, what reward awaits if this congregation repents and with Christ's help conquers its particular sins.

Negative Consequence (2:16b)

The negative consequence repeats the image of Jesus as the eschatological judge raised in the opening Christ title: "But if not, I am coming to you soon and will make war against them with the sword of my mouth" (2:16b). In this conditional clause, the first half (the protasis) consists of the idiomatic phrase "But if not," which is an abbreviated expression for the fuller phrase "But if you do not repent." This is not only implied from the context where the immediately preceding command is "Repent therefore" but also explicitly stated in the earlier sermon to Ephesus, where the abbreviated expression "But if not" is repeated and stated more fully later in the same verse as "if you do not repent" (2:5).

The second half of the conditional clause (the apodosis) refers to the coming of Christ: "I am coming to you." The presence of such a comment is hardly surprising, given that the consequence section of virtually every sermon includes a reference to the coming of Christ (2:5, 16, 25; 3:3, 11, 20), most often to punish a wayward church, as is the case here, but also to comfort a faithful one. The addition of the adverb "soon" stresses the imminence of Christ's coming. As noted in discussing the reference to Christ's coming in 2:5, here we again face the question of whether this coming refers to the second coming of Christ at the end of time to inaugurate the final judgment of all people or to a special coming of Christ to execute a preliminary judgment on the Pergamum church alone. A sharp distinction between these two options should be avoided since a preliminary judgment, though more likely in view here, functions also as an important harbinger of the final judgment to take place at Christ's parousia.

The threatening nature of Christ's coming as the eschatological judge is emphasized with the second clause of the apodosis: "and I will make war against them with the sword of my mouth." The verb "make war" (*polemeō*) refers to aggressive, violent action (Rev. 12:7 [2×]; 13:4; 17:14; 19:11) and, with one exception (James 4:2), is not found in any other NT writing. This intimidating image of Christ coming as the end-time warrior in order to fight against those who refuse to repent of their evil ways is intensified by the weapon he uses to wage war: "with the sword of my mouth." As in the opening Christ title, here too the sword is not the *machaira*—the short sword or dagger about eighteen inches long commonly used by Roman soldiers—but the *rhomphaia*—the much longer, slightly curved sword of the Thracian fighters. The Christ title highlights the "sharp, double-edged" feature of this sword, but here that weapon is also described as "of my mouth"—echoing the image of Jesus in the opening of the book (Rev. 1:9–20), where he is portrayed with "a sharp double-edged sword *coming out of his mouth*" (1:16b). The sword, therefore, is a metaphor for the tongue and the word of just judgment that Jesus as the eschatological judge will speak. The reference to the *rhomphaia* sword rather than the *machaira* sword creates a "grotesque imagery of so huge a 'tongue' flowing out of the mouth" (Osborne 2002: 92n10), which is intended to stress the threatening nature of Christ's just judgment.

Who is the recipient of this word of just judgment? The shift from the second person ("I will come to *you* soon") to the third person ("I will make war against *them*") might suggest that Jesus's word of judgment is directed only to the Nicolaitans and to those in the Pergamum congregation who embrace their teaching. Against this conclusion, however, is the fact that the command to repent was given to the whole church, and so it is more likely that the threat of Christ's coming to proclaim judgment is similarly directed at all members of the church in Pergamum. The threatening nature of Christ's coming may seem heavy-handed and condemnatory in our contemporary nonjudgmental culture, but it reveals how seriously Jesus judges the situation to be—not just the closely connected sins of idolatry and sexual immorality committed by some members of the Pergamum church but also the inappropriately tolerant stance of the rest of the church toward this false teaching.

Positive Consequence (2:17b)

The sermon to Pergamum comes to a close in the same way that all the seven sermons do—with the "victory formula" that employs the key verb *nikaō*, meaning "to win in the face of obstacles, *be victor, conquer, overcome, prevail*" (BDAG 673.1). Although this point has already been mentioned in our examination of the sermons to both Ephesus and Smyrna, it is important enough to bear repeating: the victory is not a human achievement but a divine gift. This significant theological point is conveyed explicitly here in 2:17b with the twofold occurrence of the statement "I will give to that person . . ." The possession of hidden manna and the white stone ought not to be viewed as the spoils of victory from the enemy but as gracious gifts from Christ. The same point is made implicitly by contrasting the victor formula here with its occurrence in the final sermon to Laodicea, which includes a second reference to the key verb *nikaō*: "To the one who is victorious . . . , *just as I was victorious*" (3:21). What is stated in a climatic way to the seventh and least healthy of the churches is also true for the church of Pergamum: their ability to overcome the danger of accepting or tolerating the false teaching of the Nicolaitans ultimately rests not on their own unique talents or persistent efforts but on Christ's previous victory. Only through one's relationship to Christ and the empowering presence of his Spirit can the Jesus followers overcome their sin and be victorious.

Hidden Manna

The first of the two gifts that Christ will graciously give to victorious believers is "hidden manna": "To the one who is victorious, I will give to that person some of the hidden manna" (2:17b). Manna, of course, refers to God's miraculous provision of food to his people during their forty-year period of wandering in the wilderness (Exod. 16:1–36). Shortly after their exodus from Egypt, the people of Israel grumbled about the lack of food and pined for their old life in Egypt, where they claimed to have sat around pots of meat and eaten all the food that they wanted. God graciously responded to their complaints not by punishing his distrusting people but by sending them bread from heaven in the form of thin flakes on the ground. The word "manna" comes from the Hebrew expression *mān hû'*, which means, "What is it?": "When the Israelites saw it [manna on the ground], they said to each other, 'What is it?'" (Exod. 16:15; so also Josephus, *Ant.* 3.32).

For Jews in NT times, this OT story of God's miraculous provision of food became a sign or metaphor of the future messianic age. There was a wide-spread Jewish expectation that God would once again miraculously provide food for his people when his future kingdom was inaugurated. For example, 2 Baruch states: "And it will happen at that time that the treasury of manna will come down again from on high, and they will eat of it in those years because these are the ones who have arrived at the consummation of time" (29.8). According to the Sibylline Oracles, one of the blessings enjoyed by God's people in the future kingdom is "they will eat the dewy manna with white teeth" (7.149). Genesis Rabbah, a religious text from Judaism's classical period (AD 300–500), refers to manna as "the bread of the age to come" (82.8). This widespread Jewish expectation for God to provide manna or food in the messianic age explains the reaction of the crowd to Jesus's miracle of feeding the five thousand: "After the people saw the sign that Jesus performed, they began to say, 'Surely this is the Prophet [i.e., the Messiah] who is to come into the world'" (John 6:14–15).

The gift of manna to the Christians in Pergamum who are victorious, therefore, is a way of promising them their share in the blessing of the messianic age. Just as eating from the tree of life is a powerful metaphor for the Ephesian church's participation in the blessing of paradise, so also eating from manna is a compelling symbol for the Pergamum church's participation in the blessed age to come. The gift of manna fits naturally with the previous reference to Balaam and the forty-year wilderness wanderings, the period when both the incident with Balaam and the gift of manna occurred. Yet the gift of manna seems even more fitting because of the particular complaint that Christ brings against the Pergamum church: if they overcome the temptation to eat food sacrificed to idols, they will be rewarded with something better to eat.

The manna that victorious believers in Pergamum will be given is described as "hidden." The use of the rare perfect tense (*kekrymmenou*) indicates that the hidden quality of this eschatological food is not a minor point but is stressed: it refers to manna that was hidden at some point in the past but continues to exist in the present in a state of hiddenness. The significance of this "hiddenness" has been variously explained. A few scholars, on the basis of Jesus's claim in John 6:35 (and 6:48) that he is "the bread of life," take the manna to be Christ—a truth that is "hidden" from unbelievers (Hendriksen

1940: 67; Vincent 1924: 450; Wong 1998: 348–49). Others appeal to the wide-spread Jewish expectation, already observed above, that manna would again be provided by God in the messianic age. They point out that this end-time food will be available only to victorious believers and will be "hidden" or kept from the rest of humankind (e.g., Walvoord 1966: 70; Morris 1969: 68).

The majority of commentators, however, rightly explain the description "hidden" in light of a Jewish tradition concerning the jar of manna that was preserved in the ark of the covenant. God gave instructions to Moses and Aaron to place one day's ration of manna in a golden jar and to keep it with the two tables of the law "before the LORD," in the ark of the covenant (Exod. 16:32–34; see also Heb. 9:4), to be a memorial for future generations. Many years later, the Babylonian king Nebuchadnezzar captured the city of Jerusalem and destroyed not only the temple but also, one would naturally assume, the items within it, including the ark of the covenant, which contained the golden jar of manna. Jewish tradition, however, claims that the ark and its contents were removed from the temple just before the capture of the capital city and the destruction of its most holy building and that the ark is now safely hidden and will continue that way until the coming of the messiah, when it will be restored to the new temple in Jerusalem. One version of this tradition explains that the prophet Jeremiah hid the ark in a cave on Mount Nebo (2 Macc. 2:4–6). A second version, dating to the time of the book of Revelation, claims that an angel took the ark and other sacred items stored in the temple and that they were swallowed up by the earth and thus hidden in an undisclosed location (2 Bar. 6.7–10). A third version, dating to the second century AD, describes how God commanded Jeremiah and his secretary Baruch to take the holy vessels of the temple away for safekeeping and that the earth was ordered by its Creator to swallow and hide them until the return of the exiles in the messianic age (4 Bar. 3.10–19). Although none of these versions explicitly refers to the golden jar of manna, its inclusion in this Jewish tradition is implied in Heb. 9:4 and is stated in the later rabbinic sources (Hemer 1986: 95). This explanation thus confirms the eschatological meaning of the metaphor of manna: to eat of hidden manna can only mean that the messiah has come and that the blessings of the end-time age, which his arrival ushers in, will now be enjoyed by those who are victorious in overcoming the idolatrous temptation to eat meat sacrificed to idols.

WHITE STONE

The second of the two gifts that Christ will graciously give to victorious believers is a white stone: "And I will give to that person a white stone, and on the stone is written a new name that no one knows except the one who receives it" (2:17c). The precise meaning of this metaphor may be the most difficult item to determine among all the many exegetical issues one faces in the seven sermons of Rev. 2–3. The interpretive difficulty is illustrated by the fact that at least ten different meanings have been proposed (see the extensive survey by Hemer, who examines seven of these meanings in the main text [1986: 96–104] and another three in an endnote [1986: 242n85]).

The meaning of the "white stone" depends primarily on how one answers the related question: To whom does the new name refer? Does it apply to the victorious Christian or to God or Christ? Before reviewing the four most commonly held interpretations of the white stone, we first consider the referent of the new name. In the sermon to Philadelphia, Christ says "I will write on them the name of my God, . . . and I will also write on them my new name"(3:12). Later in the book of Revelation, Jesus is described as follows: "He has a name written on him that no one knows but he himself" (19:12). This suggests that the "new name" in the sermon to Pergamum similarly refers to the name of God or, more likely, the name of Christ. Yet this interpretation does not agree well with the added description: it is a name "that no one knows except the one who receives it." As Hemer (1986: 102) observes, "That name [in 3:12] is promised to all victors, but this name [in 2:17] is the peculiar possession of each individual." Osborne (2002: 149) likewise notes, "It is hard to see how the name of God or Christ would be known only by the overcomer; more likely it is a 'new name' given to the overcomer by Christ." This interpretation receives further support from OT parallels where God promises that his people in the messianic age will be given a "new" or "another" name that will last eternally: "I will give them an everlasting name that will endure forever" (Isa. 56:5). "You will be called by a new name that the mouth of the LORD will bestow" (Isa. 62:2). "You [the wicked] will leave your name for my chosen ones to use in their curses; the Sovereign LORD will put you to death, but to his servants he will give another name" (Isa. 65:15).

Having examined interpretations of the new name, we will now try to identify the white stone.

1. *A jewel.* Three closely related proposals identify the "white stone" as a jewel. The first appeals to later Jewish writings claiming that in the messianic age precious stones or jewels would fall down from heaven along with the manna (Midrash Ps. 78.4; b. Yoma 75a). The second and third proposals connect the white stone to the vestments of the Jewish high priest: either the two onyx stones on the shoulder strap of the high priest's ephod (a sleeveless garment) bearing the names of the twelve tribes, six on each stone (Exod. 28:9–12; so Stuart 1843: 472–73; Chilton 1987: 110), or the Urim

(Exod. 28:30), which is claimed to be a diamond inscribed with the name of God (so Trench 1867: 135–38).

All three of these proposals pair nicely with the hidden manna, for along with the golden jar of manna in the ark, the vestments of the high priest were believed to be hidden and would reappear in the messianic age. The tradition behind the first proposal, however, is not widespread and thus not well known, describes not one jewel but many, and does not involve any name inscribed on the jewels. The second proposal fails because it involves not one stone but two, neither stone is white, and the names inscribed on them are well-known ones of the twelve tribes. The third proposal involves a highly questionable identification of the Urim as a diamond, the absence of any evidence that the Urim had a name inscribed on it, and the difficulty of explaining how such a high-priestly symbol would function as a reward for a victorious Christian.

2. *An amulet*. The white stone may refer to an amulet engraved with a magical formula or the name of a god in order to bring the wearer good luck and protection from evil (so, e.g., Moffatt 1910: 358; Beckwith 1919: 461–63; Charles 1920: 66–67; Lohmeyer 1970: 27; Lohse 1976: 29; Aune 1997: 190–91). Amulets would typically have an image on one side and a magical formula on the other. They were worn in a way that made the image readily visible to others, but the formula would remain hidden from view. In the worldview of that day, it was widely believed that supernatural forces were largely harmful to humanity but that their detrimental effects could be controlled and so minimized through the right incantations or magical sayings. Such amulets were popular not only with pagans but also with Jews and, in later times, even with Christians (see the sources cited by Aune 1997: 191). A possible parallel use of the word found in 2:17 for "stone" (*psēphos*) as referring to an amulet is found in the second-century-AD writing of Artemidorus, a professional diviner from Ephesus, who describes a plate of bronze on which is written the name of the Egyptian god Sarapis and which is hung around a person's neck (*Onirocritica* 5.26). The knowledge of a god's name was commonly believed to give one the right to call upon that deity for help. Thus, in this interpretation, the "new name" written on the white stone or amulet is the name of God or Christ, who has power to protect and save the wearer from pagan enemies and their pagan gods. This name is "new" because it is "probably in contrast to the great variety of *old* pagan names for various supernatural beings found on amulets and magical gems" (Aune 1997: 191).

Some commentators reject this interpretation: "It is doubtful that the Lord would look to a pagan source for His symbolism in the same message where he has warned so strongly against worldly relations" (Thomas 1992: 199; see also Hendriksen 1940: 68; Worth 1999: 148: "Why would John so blatantly seem to violate the theological demands of his own faith to make his point?"). Against this objection are the many other places where the book of Revelation uses pagan symbols. Furthermore, this interpretation could be viewed as a polemic *against* the use of magical amulets since they do not contain the "new" name of the one and only true God. The weakness of this view rests instead on the likelihood that, as we observed above, the "new name that no one knows except the one who receives it" refers not to God or Christ but to the victorious Christian.

3. *A vote of acquittal*. The white stone may refer to a "voting-pebble" (BDAG 1098.1): jurors in ancient courtrooms would commonly vote for acquittal with a white stone and for conviction with a black one (Aeschylus [5th cent. BC], *Eumenides* 737–56; Ovid [1st cent. AD], *Metamorphoses* 15.41–42; Plutarch [AD 46–120], *Alcibiades* 22.2; Plutarch, *Moralia* 186e). The same word for "stone/pebble" (*psēphos*) has this meaning in Acts 26:10. When Paul meets with King Agrippa during his two-year house arrest in Caesarea Maritima, he refers to his earlier persecution of Christians as throwing "a stone/pebble against them," meaning "casting my vote against them." This meaning would be especially relevant if a denunciation, an official charge, were brought against any Christians with the likelihood of a guilty judgment.

Although this explanation is supported by the same use of the word "stone/pebble" elsewhere in Scripture and the widespread familiarity in the ancient world with the white voting pebble, it suffers from a few problems. The voting pebble is typically thrown into an urn and not given to the person facing a court case. The image here involves only one voting pebble, but such a procedure for determining someone's innocence or guilt is not required for a one-person jury consisting of either God or Jesus. Most problematic is the inability to account for the presence of a new name that no one knows, since the exoneration of the accused believer would require a public disclosure of this person's name.

4. *An admission token*. A small stone or pebble or a small piece of wood or bone was commonly used in the Greco-Roman world as a token (*tessera*) of recognition, a voucher, or a ticket of admission (see esp. Hemer 1986: 98–99). A token was sometimes broken into two pieces and each half given to two parties in a friendship or contract so that they or their descendants could later show the complementary half and thus force the other person to recognize the relationship. In other circumstances a token was given to victors at athletic games as a voucher, enabling the winners to receive certain rewards at public expense. More commonly a token functioned as an admission ticket to public assemblies or festivals. This has led some commentators to view the white stone as an admission token to the messianic banquet and thus, along with hidden manna, a blessing that victorious Christians enjoy in the eschatological age. Caird (1966: 42), for example, states: "The 'white stone'

is probably the Conqueror's ticket of admission to the heavenly banquet, a very permanent ticket to an eternal feast" (so also Ladd 1972: 49; Ford 1975: 399–400; Beasley-Murray 1978: 88; Efird 1989: 57).

The strength of this proposal is that it explains well the pairing of the two gifts of the hidden manna and the white stone: both are symbols connected with the blessed end-time age when believers will enjoy the provision of heavenly food and entrance into the messianic banquet. Although tokens were not necessarily white or always inscribed, these features of the pebble or small stone can be readily explained. "White" is commonly used in the book of Revelation to symbolize eternal life or purity from sin (Rev. 3:4–5, 18; 4:4; 6:11; 7:9, 13–14). The inscribed name personalizes the admission token and ensures that it cannot be used by anyone other than the one bearing that name.

The difficulty in reaching a definitive conclusion about the proper interpretation of the "white stone" drives home the important principle that we should shout when Scripture demands it but also whisper when Scripture demands it. In other words, there are many subjects that the Bible addresses frequently and with great clarity: about these, the preacher and teacher ought to shout. But there are some subjects that the Bible addresses infrequently and with less clarity: about these, the exegete ought to whisper. It may well be that one ought to whisper about the precise meaning of the white stone. In this situation, whispering is not a sign of treating God's Word in a wimpy or wishy-washy manner; rather, it is evidence of having such a high respect for the biblical text that one dares not speak more definitively than the text allows. Nevertheless, on the basis of our careful study of 2:17b, it can be confidently stated that the hidden manna and white stone are both end-time symbols of the blessings that await victorious followers of Jesus. This is the positive consequence that ought to be boldly "shouted" by preachers and teachers to the church today.

The Contemporary Significance

Introduction

Compromise is almost always needed to get a positive result. Take, for example, marriage. If a husband and wife are each always insisting on getting their own way and refusing to make any concessions to the wishes of their partner, then the result is constant conflict and an unhappy marriage. Compromise is essential to a good marriage. Or consider politics. If politicians are always shouting the party line and refusing to make any concessions to members of an opposing political party, then the result is gridlock, and nothing ever gets done. Compromise is essential to good politics.

In some situations, however, compromise brings not a positive result but a disastrous one. Some issues are so important that even a small concession ought to be unthinkable. This is the situation facing the Christians in Pergamum. Many Jesus followers in Pergamum wanted to do something that was popular in their day, something that all their pagan neighbors were doing but that was clearly wrong for Christians to do. Yet many of these Jesus followers wanted so badly to do this popular thing that they compromised their faith, which then brought a disastrous result: they became guilty of idolatry. And so, in our message for today, I introduce to you the church of Pergamum, or, as it can be justly called, "the church of idolatrous compromise."

The Christ Title (2:12b)

The first item in each of the sermons to the seven churches is the Christ title. In the sermon to Pergamum, his title is short but by no means sweet: "These are the words of him who has the sharp, double-edged sword" (2:12b). Before Jesus says anything to the church at Pergamum, he portrays himself in this threatening way. Imagine a preacher walking up to the pulpit and, before uttering one word, pulling out a gun. The congregation would gasp in fear, since like a sword, a gun is a deadly weapon. Likewise, the congregation in Pergamum would have gasped in fear at this threatening image of Jesus with a sharp, double-edged sword, wondering what it means. In this Christ title, some would have heard an allusion to words used in the prophecy of Isaiah to describe the servant of the LORD (Isa. 11:4; 49:2)—the messiah who was coming with the sword of his mouth to judge the wicked. Did this mean that Jesus was coming to judge them? What were they doing wrong to deserve such judgment?

This threatening image of a Jesus who is coming in judgment with a sword is made even more intimidating, however, because of the type of sword that he has. Two types of swords are mentioned in the book of Revelation. The *machaira*, a short dagger about eighteen inches long, was commonly carried by Roman soldiers. The second type, the *rhomphaia,* was a much longer sword used specifically by fearsome fighters from the region of Thrace in northeastern Greece. The *rhomphaia* was five feet long, having a two-foot long handle and a three-foot long, slightly curved blade. Its long handle and long overall length enabled its user to wield it with two hands and swing it hard enough to cut an enemy's shield in half with a single strong stroke. It is this second, more deadly sword that is specifically mentioned in the Christ title. In our modern analogy, it would be like the preacher in the pulpit pulling out a submachine gun instead of a pistol!

Dear friends, the Jesus who is about to speak not only to the Christians in Pergamum but also to you and me is not your Sunday-school Jesus, the kind of romanticized Jesus who has little children serenely sitting in his lap while baby lambs are frolicking all around. This Jesus is instead a figure who judges, the servant of the LORD, whose coming to execute judgment was described long ago by the prophet Isaiah. Jesus is the end-time judge with the full power and authority represented by the sword, not a regular sword but a deadly *rhomphaia*. What will Jesus Christ's judgment be of the church of Pergamum? What will his judgment be of us?

The Commendation (2:13)

The second item typically found in each of the seven sermons is the commendation. Here Jesus praises the church of Pergamum for what they are doing right: "I know where you live, where the throne of Satan is, but you hold fast my name, and you did not deny faith in me, even in the days of Antipas, my faithful witness, who was killed among you, where Satan lives" (2:13).

The threatening image of a *rhomphaia* in the Christ title is followed with another threatening image mentioned twice in the commendation: "the throne of Satan." Pergamum is a city where Satan exercises the kind of control and influence wielded by a king, as someone powerful who sits on a throne. Satan is working hard through both institutions and individuals in Pergamum to put pressure on the Jesus followers and destroy their Christian faith. This satanic pressure is so great, in fact, that there is one member of the church, Antipas, who has been martyred. There are others like him who continue to follow Christ faithfully. To these members of the Pergamum church, Jesus gives the thumbs-up sign and says, "Great job, church of Pergamum! You are faithful despite living in a city where Satan has his throne!"

Does "the throne of Satan" refer to something specific in the city of Pergamum, and if so, what might that specific thing be? Although the precise identification of "the throne of Satan" would have been clear to the Christians living in Pergamum at that time, it is not so clear to us today. There are some intriguing options, but it is impossible to be certain. Don't let that fact disappoint you. The more important point of this threatening and twice-occurring image is clear: the Christians in Pergamum lived in a place where it was hard to be a follower of Jesus. It would be like a Christian today moving into a new neighborhood that proudly advertised itself on the entrance sign as "The Subdivision of Satan." Yet despite living in such a satanic or hostile environment, some in the church of Pergamum remained faithful, and so Jesus commends them for this: "You hold fast my name, and you did not deny faith in me."

The Complaint (2:14–15)

After the good news (the commendation), there typically comes, as the third item in the structure of each sermon, the bad news (the complaint). Sadly, Jesus does have a significant complaint to bring against the church of Pergamum: "But I have a few things against you. There are some among you who hold to the teaching of Balaam, who was teaching Balak to place a stumbling block before the sons of Israel: to eat food sacrificed to idols and to commit sexual immorality. Thus you also have those who similarly hold to the teaching of the Nicolaitans" (2:14–15).

There is a lot here, but don't miss the core of the complaint: "eating food sacrificed to idols." Christians today may find it hard to understand what's implied in the phrase "eating food sacrificed to idols" or to appreciate how popular this practice was in the ancient world and what a powerful temptation it was for the early Christians. When people went to a pagan temple, as they regularly did, they would bring a gift: some kind of food to sacrifice to the god or goddess honored in that pagan temple. This sacrificial food could be something simple like grain or wine but preferably would be some kind of meat. Only a small portion of this meat would be sacrificed on the altar, so most of the raw meat remained.

This leftover meat would be handled in one of two ways. (1) The priest could sell the leftover meat in the marketplace and then use the money to pay for the upkeep of the temple building and its operations, or (2) the offerer could take the meat to the temple dining area and eat it in a meal with family and friends. It is this second option that Christ is addressing in the sermon to the church at Pergamum because this meal had religious significance. Such dinners were a regular, popular part of pagan life but were forbidden to Christians. Jesus followers who participated in a religious meal held in a temple dedicated to a pagan god were establishing a level of intimacy with that pagan god that made them guilty of idolatry. That's the heart of Christ's complaint against some in the Pergamum church: they are eating meat sacrificed to idols and thus guilty of the sin of idolatry.

The rest of the NT shows that those in Pergamum were not the only Christians who struggled with the temptation to join these popular religious meals. In fact, "eating meat sacrificed to idols" was a widespread problem in the early church. You are probably aware that the Jerusalem Council described in Acts 15 dealt with the controversial issue of circumcision, but did you know that this same council of Jewish Christian leaders also sent a letter to all the gentile churches, warning them against eating meat sacrificed to idols (Acts 15:29; 21:25)? Did you know that the Christians in Corinth so desperately wanted to participate in these religious meals that the apostle Paul needed three whole chapters to stop them from this form of idolatry (1 Cor. 8:1–11:1)? And did you know that Christ's complaint in his fourth sermon, to the nearby church of Thyatira, was also about eating meat sacrificed to idols (Rev.

2:20)? The Jesus followers in Pergamum were by no means alone in struggling with the temptation to join the popular practice of eating meat sacrificed to idols and becoming guilty of the sin of idolatry.

If Christians were not allowed to participate in these religious meals, why did some in the Pergamum church do it? How did they justify doing something that was clearly forbidden? The text here does not give an answer to this question, but it is likely that they used the same excuse the Corinthian Christians were using to justify participating in these idolatrous meals: they appealed to their supposedly superior knowledge (1 Cor. 8:1–13). They cleverly reasoned like this: "We Jesus followers recognize only one true God. We know that Athena, Zeus, Dionysus, Asclepius, and all the other gods worshiped in our city are only pretend gods and don't really exist. Since we know this important truth, we can participate in the religious meals, and they won't impact us at all!"

It is bad enough that Christ's complaint involves the charge that some in the Pergamum church are compromising their faith in order to attend pagan religious meals and so making themselves guilty of idolatry. But there is also a second, closely related complaint that Christ brings against them: they are also committing sexual immorality. These religious dinners often involved more than just eating food: they also involved sex. Women were brought to these meals to provide entertainment, and this often led to sexual activity. There is therefore a close connection between the twin sins of "eating food sacrificed to idols" and "committing sexual immorality." In fact, every time the Bible mentions the first sin of "eating food sacrificed to idols," it always mentions the second sin of "committing sexual immorality" (Acts 15:29; 21:25; 1 Cor. 10:7–8; Rev. 2:20).

These two sins are also linked in the OT story of Balaam, which is used here to introduce Christ's complaint. The story of Balaam would be funny if it hadn't turned out to be fatal for some of God's people. The Israelites were near the end of their forty years of wandering in the wilderness when they came to the plains of Moab. The king of Moab, Balak, panicked at the presence of this huge foreign nation on his land, and so he sought help from a false prophet named Balaam. The king promised to pay Balaam lots of gold and silver if he would put a curse on the people of Israel. At first the plan fails miserably. After a series of humbling and humorous events involving a donkey who speaks, Balaam ends up not cursing the Israelites but blessing them! But Balaam gets the last laugh. He advises the king to tempt the men of Israel with beautiful women from Moab, and this alternate plan is a huge success. In one of the most shameful events in Israelite history, many men from Israel join women from Moab in doing the same two things that some in the Pergamum church are doing: they eat food sacrificed to the pagan gods of Moab and so are guilty of idolatry, and then they have sex with the women of Moab and so are guilty of sexual immorality (Num. 25:1–2).

Therefore the complaint that Christ makes against the church of Pergamum is serious, involving two closely connected sins. The first and primary sin is that they have compromised their faith by eating food sacrificed to idols and so are guilty of idolatry. The second closely related sin is that they are committing sexual immorality. To use the words of our sermon title, Pergamum is "the church of idolatrous compromise."

The Correction (2:16a)

Christ, however, does not give up on the church of Pergamum. He doesn't abandon them to their just punishment but instead graciously reminds them that it's not too late to correct their sin of idolatry. Jesus gives them this crucial command: "Repent therefore!" (2:16a).

The word "repent" literally means to "change your mind"—to adopt a radically new way of thinking. The Jesus followers in Pergamum need to say to themselves and to others in their congregation: "I was wrong. I was wrong to claim that going to pagan temples and having a meal there was no big deal since all these gods are fake and don't really exist. I now admit that I was compromising my Christian faith just to do something that everyone else was doing. I now recognize that what I was doing actually made me guilty of idolatry. I now publicly state that I have no business being part of these religious meals and the sex that often is connected with these dinners. I repent of it all!"

The Consequence (2:16b, 17b)

The sermon to Pergamum comes to an end in the same way all the sermons do: Christ spells out the two consequences that this idolatrous church now faces.

Negative Consequence (2:16b)

The first consequence is negative and goes like this: "But if not, I am coming to you soon and will make war with them with the sword of my mouth" (2:16b). The threatening image of Christ with a sword given at the beginning of the sermon is repeated here at the end. Good speakers never say the same thing twice . . . unless they want to emphasize what they are saying! This second reference to the "sword" emphasizes the threatening nature of the Jesus who will fight against those in the church of Pergamum who continue in their idolatrous and sexually immoral ways. The threatening nature of this Jesus is emphasized even more by the type of sword that he will use in this fight—not the wimpy Roman dagger but the frightening five-foot-long *rhomphaia*. What's more, we are told that this deadly sword is coming out of Christ's mouth! The sword, then, is a metaphor for the tongue and the word of judgment that Jesus will speak against those in the Pergamum church who refuse to repent of their sinful ways.

To many in our contemporary, open-minded and tolerant culture, this threatening image of Jesus may seem to be far too judgmental. Perhaps you are uneasy with this picture of Jesus with a five-foot-long deadly weapon coming out of his mouth. You may well prefer the Sunday-school Jesus, who warmly welcomes little children on his lap and who would never raise his voice in anger against anyone. But instead of being uncomfortable with the Jesus we meet in the sermon to Pergamum, we should be uncomfortable with the sins that cause Jesus to speak a word of judgment. Idolatry and sexual immorality are serious sins that will indeed be judged by Jesus. The worship of false gods and the misuse of sex ought to have no place at all in the life of a Christ follower, whether they live in the first or the twenty-first century.

Positive Consequence (2:17b)

The last word in each sermon, however, is not about judgment for sin but victory over sin. The sermon to the church of Pergamum thus ends, as expected, with the victory formula: "To the one who is victorious" (2:17b). You likely remember that the Greek word used for "victorious" here is also the name of a popular sporting goods company, Nike. The company chose this name so that we would associate their products with being victorious, with winning. This Greek word is used at the end of each of the seven sermons, including this sermon to the church of Pergamum: "To the one who is victorious."

The important question that our text raises is this: Are you a Nike Christian? In other words, are you a victorious Christian? Are you able to overcome the sin of idolatry? The good news of the gospel enables us to answer this important question with a resounding "Yes!" You and I can be Nike Christians and win the victory—not because we are so talented or so hard working, but because Christ has already won the victory so that we who belong to Christ have his Spirit living in us. It is this divine Holy Spirit who gives us the power we need to resist compromising our faith and falling into the sin of idolatry.

What reward does Christ give to the Nike Christian? The first of the two gifts that Christ offers is something to eat: "To the one who is victorious, I will give that person some of the hidden manna." Manna, of course, refers to the food that God miraculously provided for the Israelites every morning during their forty-year wanderings in the wilderness. In NT times this OT story of God's miraculous provision became associated with the future messianic age. There was widespread expectation that with the coming of the messiah and the inauguration of the messianic age God would again provide food for his people. This expectation was evident in how people responded to Jesus's miracle of feeding the five thousand: the people interpreted

Jesus's miraculous provision of food as a clear sign that he was the messiah and that the blessed messianic age was starting (John 6:14–15). The gift of manna to the victorious Christians in Pergamum, therefore, is a powerful sign that they will enjoy life in the blessed messianic age. If they are Nike Christians, who by the power of Christ's Spirit are victorious over the temptation to eat meat sacrificed to idols, they will be fittingly rewarded with something to eat in the blessed messianic age.

Yet these victorious Christians will be given not just manna but more precisely *hidden* manna. God told Moses and Aaron to place one day's ration of manna in a golden jar and to put that jar into the ark of the covenant so that future generations would be reminded of how God miraculously provided food for his people. Many years later, the Babylonian king Nebuchadnezzar destroyed the temple and, one would naturally assume, all the items in it, including the ark of the covenant with the golden jar of manna. Jewish tradition, however, claims that the ark and its contents, including the jar of manna, were secretly removed from the temple just before Nebuchadnezzar destroyed it and that these sacred items are now safely hidden and will remain so until the messiah comes and ushers in the blessed messianic kingdom. If the Christians in Pergamum will be given "hidden" manna, this can mean only one thing: the messiah has come, and Nike Christians will enjoy life with him in the blessed messianic kingdom.

The second of the two gifts that Christ offers the victorious believers in Pergamum is a white stone: "And I will give that person a white stone, on which is written a new name that no one knows except the one who receives it" (2:17c). It is difficult to determine the precise meaning of this "white stone." In fact, it is probably the most difficult interpretive issue found in the seven sermons of Rev. 2–3. Ten different meanings of the white stone have been proposed, but as with the reference to the throne of Satan, which proved challenging to interpret, we shouldn't get too frustrated at not knowing the exact meaning of the white stone. What can be confidently stated is that the white stone, like the hidden manna, is a sign of the end-time blessing that awaits Nike Christians who by Christ's Spirit overcome the temptations of idolatry and sexual immorality.

Conclusion

The sermon to the church of Pergamum might seem irrelevant to us twenty-first-century Christians. We never eat religious meals in a pagan temple and so perhaps can't see how the complaint that Christ brings against the believers in Pergamum has any important implications for us today. But nothing could be further from the truth.

The sermon to the church of Pergamum is directly relevant to millions of Asian Christians around the world. A big part of their family culture involves ancestor worship: the belief that dead family members continue to exist and that their spirits have the ability to bring about good fortune to family members who are still alive. There are certain religious days when Asian Christians visit their pagan relatives or friends, and a table is set up in the home containing not only pictures of dead parents and grandparents but also specially prepared food. Like the ancient Jesus followers in Pergamum, these Asian Christians are tempted to compromise their faith so that they can do something popular in their culture and join in these religious meals. And like the ancient Jesus followers in Pergamum, these Asian Christians may also try to justify what they are doing by saying to themselves: "I know that these dead ancestors are not really alive and present with us. So what's the problem with eating?" The problem, however, is that they potentially become guilty of idolatry by venerating or worshiping someone other than the one true God.

The sermon to the church of Pergamum is additionally relevant to any Christian who, though not tempted to eat food as part of a pagan religious meal, is tempted to become obsessed with the many gods of our age and so likewise become guilty of idolatry. For example, there is the "god" of money. We may not bow down and pray to money, but money may nevertheless be the most important thing in our lives. Each decision may be based on whether it brings us more or less money, and the amount of money we have may determine whether we are happy or sad. Some even use a divine name to refer to money, calling it the "almighty dollar." Like the ancient Jesus followers in Pergamum, we may try to justify our love of money by saying, "Actually, the Bible says not that money is the root of all evil but that the *love* of money is the root of all evil. So there is nothing evil or bad about money itself. What's more, I use my money to support our church and all kinds of kingdom causes!" Yet despite such self-justifying logic, the question remains: Have we developed such an obsession with money that we have become guilty of idolatry?

There is the "god" of work. Some of us use our job to bring us power and prestige. Some of us become so preoccupied with our work that we have little or no time left for our relationship with God—we never seem to have enough time to pray to God or listen to him speak in his Word or to serve God by serving others. Some of us are so devoted to our work that we have little or no time left for a spouse or children. Work has become the most important thing in life. Like the ancient Jesus followers in Pergamum, we try to justify our obsession with work by saying: "I need to provide for myself, don't I? And shouldn't I use my God-given talents to the best of my ability in my job? What's more, I try to show through my work that I am a Christian, that I serve Jesus not just in my home life but also in my work life!" Yet despite such self-justifying logic, the question remains: Have we developed such an obsession with work that we have become guilty of idolatry?

There is also the "god" of sports. Our devotion to a particular team or athlete is so passionate that it borders on being religious. Our free time during each weekend is completely taken up by high school sports on Friday, college sports on Saturday, and professional sports on Sunday. We gladly spend a lot of money on a hat, shirt, or jacket with the name and/or number of our sports idol on it. Sports is such a priority in our lives that on any given Sunday, some of us will skip church because we've decided that it is more important to take our son to his baseball game or our daughter to her basketball tournament. Like the ancient Jesus followers in Pergamum, we try to justify our obsession with sports by saying: "Doesn't Paul say in 1 Tim. 4:8 that 'physical training is of some value'? Besides, playing sports teaches our children the importance of discipline, training, and teamwork!" Yet despite such self-justifying logic, the question remains: Have we developed such an obsession with sports that we have become guilty of idolatry?

Time does not allow us to explore the many other potential "gods" that steal our time and devotion; false "gods" that distract us from our exclusive commitment to the one and only true God. Christ's sermon to Pergamum is a strong warning not just to his followers then and there but also to his followers here and now to beware of the sin of idolatry. We are challenged instead to be Nike Christians, who by the power of the Holy Spirit repent of our idolatrous ways and make God and his Son, Jesus Christ, not merely number one in our lives but the *only one* in our lives!

"Whoever has ears to hear, let them hear what the Spirit is saying to the churches!"—not only to the ancient church of Pergamum but also to the church of Jesus Christ today.

4

Thyatira

The Church of Idolatrous Compromise

The Christ Title (2:18)

Each of the seven sermons typically opens with two descriptions of Jesus before he addresses the church. The sermon to Thyatira differs from this pattern by adding to this double description of Jesus an opening title: "These are the words of *the Son of God*, whose eyes are like a flame of fire and whose feet are like burnished bronze." The title "the Son of God" is emphasized in four ways. First, emphasis is given to this title by its mere presence: the speaker in every other sermon is left unidentified ("These are the words of *him who* . . ."), but here he is explicitly named as the Son of God (the only other exception is Laodicea: "These are the words of *the Amen*," 3:14). Second, the following two descriptions of Jesus—"whose eyes are like a flame of fire, and whose feet are like burnished bronze"—are borrowed, as are nearly all the Christ titles in the sermons, from the opening image of Jesus in 1:9–20 (see 1:14b, 15a). Yet the title "the Son of God" is not borrowed from 1:9–20, which suggests that it was added by the author in order to emphasize a point not sufficiently stressed by the usual double description of Jesus. Third, the title is further emphasized by its uniqueness in the book of Revelation: the title "the Son of God," despite being widely used elsewhere in the NT (46×), occurs nowhere

129

else in Revelation (although God is called the Father of Christ in 1:6; 2:28; 3:5, 21; 14:1). Fourth, the title "the Son of God" is placed in the emphatic position ahead of the other two descriptions of Jesus.

What point or message, then, is being stressed by the title "the Son of God"? The answer lies in its clear allusion to Ps. 2:7, "I will proclaim the Lord's decree: He said to me, 'You are my son; today I have become your father.'" That this title does indeed allude to Ps. 2:7 is confirmed by the fact that the end of the Thyatira sermon (2:27, "and he will destroy them with an iron rod, as ceramic pots are shattered") quotes explicitly from Ps. 2:9. The title "the Son of God" stresses Christ's role as *judge*, since this is the primary function of God's son in Ps. 2: he will come to judge the kings and rulers of the world who conspire and plot against God and his anointed one. The emphasis on Christ's role as judge is also seen in the subsequent description of him: "whose eyes are like a flame of fire and whose feet are like burnished bronze." This description comes from Dan. 10:6, where the heavenly man in the prophet's vision reveals the judgment that the enemies of God's people, Israel, will surely face (Dan. 10:1–12:13).

Often in the book of Revelation, an image, title, or expression not only has an OT background but also alludes to the local pagan setting, and this appears to be the case here with the opening Christ title "the Son of God." This title likely reflects a polemic against the patron god of Thyatira, Apollo Tyrimnos, and against the imperial cult. Tyrimnos was an ancient Lydian sun god (Thyatira is located in the region of what was formerly Lydia), who was later assimilated to the Greek god Apollo. Although he is never named on surviving coins from Thyatira, his image appears frequently: Tyrimnos is typically depicted naked (symbolizing his divine status), except for a cloak (a chlamys) fastened with a brooch around his neck, and holding the double-headed battle ax (the *bipennis*, a fitting symbol for a military outpost like Thyatira) poised to cut his en-emies to pieces. Since Apollo is widely known as the son of Zeus, the reference to Christ at the beginning of the letter as "the Son of God" may function as a polemic against the local god Apollo Tyrimnos. The plausibility of this connec-tion gains strength from the description of Christ

Figure 4.1. Coin from Thyatira. *Left*: Laureate head of Trajan (AD 98–117); right facing, slight drapery. *Right*: Apollo Tyrimnos, wreathed and naked but for chlamys cloak, holding a laurel branch and double-headed ax.

as one "whose feet are like burnished bronze." This image likely refers to a unique local product of bronze produced in Thyatira by a trade guild whose patron god was Apollo Tyrimnos (Hemer 1986: 116; also see below the further explanation of the unique term "burnished bronze").

The opening Christ title "the Son of God" may also be set in opposition to the imperial cult, with its worship of the Roman state (personified as a woman, "Roma") and of individual emperors deified after death. Roman emperors typically identified themselves as "son of god" in their letters and decrees. Augustus, for example, opens his letter to the city of Ephesus: "Emperor Caesar, son of the god Julius" (Aune 1997: 202). Thus, as Keener (2000: 133) observes: "The Asian churches may well hear in Jesus's biblical title 'Son of God' a direct challenge to the imperial cult" (see also Fanning 2020: 148). The fact that many of the first-century emperors highlighted their connections with the god Apollo, sometimes identifying themselves as descendants of Apollo, meant that Apollo worship—including the worship of Apollo Tyrimnos in Thyatira—was closely tied with emperor worship (Schüssler Fiorenza 1991: 54). In fact, it appears that the imperial cult in Thyatira became assimilated with the cult of Apollo Tyrimnos. The annual festival to honor Apollo Tyrimnos was broadened to include the deified emperors by adding the imperial title "Sebasta" ("revered"; Worth 1999: 158). On one occasion in Thyatira, prayers and sacrifices were offered to both Apollo Tyrimnos and the deified emperors (Price 1980: 32). Although the evidence dates from over a century after the book of Revelation, Ramsay (1994: 235–36) appeals to coins from Thyatira published under the emperor Caracalla (AD 198–217) that show the close relationship between the imperial cult and the local worship of Apollo Tyrimnos.

This historical background reveals the polemical aspect that is likely at work in the opening Christ title "the Son of God," in addition to the OT allusion to Jesus as judge. As Mounce (1977: 102) observes, this title "stands in strong contrast to the local cultic worship of Apollo Tyrimnos, which was merged with that of the emperor (identified as Apollo incarnate) so that both were acclaimed as sons of Zeus. Thus it is not the emperor or the guardian deity of Thyatira, but the resurrected Christ, who is the true son of God." Beale (1999: 259) similarly notes: "This title is also an intended contrast with the local deity Apollo Tyrimnaeus and the divine emperor, both of whom were referred to as sons of the god Zeus. The readers must give their exclusive adoration to Jesus and trust him for their economic welfare, since he alone is the true Son of God."

As noted above, the description of Jesus as one "whose eyes are like a flame of fire, and whose feet are like burnished bronze" is borrowed from the opening image of Jesus in 1:9–20 (see 1:14b–15a) but ultimately comes from the vision in Dan. 10:1–12:13. In Dan. 10:6 the man from heaven is said to have "eyes like torches of fire and . . . legs like the gleam of burnished bronze." This OT allusion is important for further emphasizing the role of Jesus as *judge*, since in its original context the heavenly man reveals to the prophet Daniel the judgment that God will surely bring on those who oppose him and his chosen people. The fiery eyes of Jesus further stress his perceptive and penetrating eyesight, which sees through the deceptive arguments of Jezebel, who was misleading some in the Thyatiran church. This foreshadows his words later in the sermon: "I am he who searches minds and hearts" (2:23). The burnished bronze feet of Jesus further stress his power to stamp and crush any opposition he may face from Jezebel and those in the Thyatiran church who have come under her deceptive influence.

The image of feet of burnished bronze may well reflect a local connection. The Greek word used here, *chalkolibanos*, is rare, occurring only here and in 1:15 and nowhere else in the Bible or any other surviving Greek text. Consequently, it is not clear precisely what type of metal is in view, whether brass (an alloy of copper and zinc) or bronze (an alloy of copper and tin; see Hemer 1986: 111–17; Aune 1997: 96). We know that (1) John did not choose to use the term *chalkos*, found in Dan. 10:6 LXX, but the rare compound term *chalkolibanos*; and (2) John would not use a term that was unknown to his readers. This leads us to conclude that the word refers to a unique type of metal produced in Thyatira and was a technical term connected with a local trade guild (so Kiddle 1940: 37; Caird 1966: 43; Hemer 1986: 111–17; Osborne 2002: 153; Fanning 2020: 148). If this is correct, it further highlights the polemical intent in the opening Christ title, pitting the Son of God against the son of Zeus, Apollo Tyrimnos, the patron god of many local trade guilds. Hemer (1986: 116–17) concludes his extended discussion of the unique term *chalkolibanos* as follows:

> If then the context is of local industry, it seems likely that the local patron-god Apollo Tyrimnaeus is in John's mind. . . . The designation ["Son of God"] may be set against opposing religious claims or against a syncretistic attempt to equate the person of Christ with deities recognized by the city. . . . The Thyatiran Christians were subject to organized paganism, but the realities of the case were those of Ps. 2, where the Lord was the master of oppressive earthly powers. In the "Son of God" the church had her true champion, irresistibly arrayed in armour flashing like the refined metal from the furnaces of the city.

The image that Jesus presents of himself in the Christ title is sobering for the church in Thyatira. As the Son of God, he comes to them first and foremost as judge, the role ascribed to God's son in Ps. 2. This title further asserts the preeminence of Christ over all other competing sons of gods, whether they be the local patron deity, Apollo Tyrimnos, or a Roman emperor. Christ's role as judge is further stressed by his fiery eyes, which can see clearly into the hidden intentions of people's minds and hearts, including those of Jezebel and all her deceived followers in Thyatira. Christ's role as judge is emphasized yet again by his burnished bronze feet, which can easily stamp out all opposition to his rule. Although the Thyatiran church has some positive features (see the commendation below), the Christ title at the beginning of this sermon foreshadows Christ's overall negative judgment about this church, a negative judgment because of its sin of idolatrous compromise.

The Commendation (2:19)

Before the "bad news" of Christ's complaint against the Thyatiran church, however, comes some "good news" of commendation introduced by the expected formula "I know." What Jesus knows about the church in Thyatira is the same thing that he knows about four other churches to whom the book of Revelation is addressed: "your works" (so also 2:2, Ephesus; 3:1, Sardis; 3:8, Philadelphia; 3:15, Laodicea). In all but one case (3:8 is an exception), this general reference to "your works" is immediately clarified in the next clause, introduced with either an explanatory *hoti* (3:1, 15) or, as is the case here and in 2:2, an explanatory *kai* (BDAG 495.1.c). The commendation of Thyatira, therefore, does not consist of five positive attributes but four: "I know your deeds, *namely*, your love and faith and service and perseverance." This understanding of the grammar is confirmed by the fact that the possessive "your" comes after "perseverance" but applies to all four preceding nouns, signaling that they all belong together as a single unit. Consequently, it would be wrong to divide these four nouns into two pairs, with the first two items (love, faith) providing the inner motivation of the "works" and the second two items (service, perseverance) providing the external actions that spring from this motivation (so, e.g., Charles 1920: 68; Mounce 1977: 102; Thomas 1992: 211; Kistemaker 2001: 137). All four nouns are instead presented as a group of equal members in which each one provides clarification of the general works that Christ's commendation has in view.

The first virtue, love (*agapē*), occurs nowhere else in the book of Revelation except in the sermon to Ephesus (2:4; the related verb appears 4 times). This is surprising given the constant mention of this virtue elsewhere in the NT. It is unclear whether the love at work in the Thyatiran church is directed toward

God or fellow believers or both, but the contrast with the Ephesian church, where the lack of love for other Christians is emphasized, is suggestive. To the Ephesians, Christ complains "you have abandoned the love you had at first" (2:4) and commands them to "do the works you did at first" (2:5). By contrast, Christ commends the Thyatirans by saying "your last works," including works of love, "are greater than the first." The second virtue, faith (*pistis*), has two distinct but closely related meanings: (1) the "faith" or trust that believers place in God and/or Christ; (2) the believer's perseverance or "faithfulness" in the face of temptation and opposition. Both meanings are found elsewhere in the book of Revelation (2:13; 13:10; 14:12), so it is unnecessary to single out one aspect here. The third virtue, service (*diakonia*), occurs only here in Revelation but is common elsewhere in the NT (33 times; the related verb appears 37 times). It refers generally to the help and assistance one gives to others, often in a voluntary or self-sacrificial manner (BDAG 230). The fourth and final virtue, perseverance (*hypomonē*), occurs often in Revelation (1:9; 2:2, 3, 19; 3:10; 13:10; 14:12), suggesting its importance, and refers to maintaining one's faith in the face of strong opposition or outright persecution.

The use of not one or two or even three virtues but four positive attributes to commend the church in Thyatira suggests that this congregation is healthy and one with whom Christ is well pleased. This positive evaluation of the church is supported by Christ's follow-up observation that "your last works are greater than the first." In other words, the Thyatiran believers are not content with the status quo, a maintenance ministry mentality, but are increasing quantitatively and perhaps also qualitatively in their commendatory works. Many modern commentators are impressed with Christ's commendation of the church in Thyatira, referring to it as "high praise" (Lenski 1935: 116; Osborne 2002: 155) and asserting that the church is "highly commended" (Witherington 2003: 104) and "could receive no higher praise" (Kistemaker 2001: 137).

However, there is a generic quality to the commendation that must temper our assessment. Christ's commendations of other churches are much more specific and allow one to get a clearer understanding of precisely what the congregation is doing well. Christ's praise of the Thyatiran church, though real, is general and does not reveal anything distinctive or unique about the good things this congregation is doing. This stands in contrast to the rest of the sermon, which is quite specific about the bad things taking place in this church. In any case, if any in Thyatira were sticking their chests out in pride at Jesus's words of commendation, their feelings of vanity would be short-lived as the Son of God, whose fiery eyes pierce the hidden motives of people's hearts, presents his complaint against them.

The Complaint (2:20)

The shift from commendation to complaint is signaled by the stereotyped phrase, "But I have this against you" (so also 2:4, Ephesus; 2:14, Pergamum). After the fourfold commendation of the immediately preceding verse, a few have found this shift "sudden and abrupt" (Kistemaker 2001: 137). However, in light of the judgment foreshadowed in the Christ title, the generic character of the commendation, and especially the pattern established in the preceding sermons to Ephesus and Pergamum, this shift is expected and not at all awkward.

Jesus brings this specific complaint against the church in Thyatira: "You tolerate the woman Jezebel, who calls herself a prophetess and teaches and deceives my servants to commit sexual immorality and to eat food sacrificed to idols." The fundamental problem at Thyatira is the same as that at Pergamum: the sin of idolatry ("to eat food sacrificed to idols") and its closely related sin of sexual immorality. The two problems are presented in reverse order to that of Pergamum; the potential significance of this is explored below.

In the Pergamum sermon, the complaint was illustrated with an OT reference to the false prophet Balaam. Here at Thyatira the complaint is illustrated with an OT reference to the evil queen Jezebel. Jezebel may have been born a princess, but her life turned out to be anything but a fairy tale. Though Phoenician, she became the wife of Israel's king Ahab (reigned 869–850 BC), and her wicked character is revealed in several infamous episodes: her campaign to kill all the prophets of Yahweh (1 Kings 18:4, 13); her support of 450 prophets of Baal and 400 prophets of Asherah (18:19); her attempt to kill Elijah (19:1–3); and her devious framing of Naboth, which resulted in his death by stoning and allowed Ahab to obtain the victim's vineyard (21:1–16). Jezebel is especially known and condemned in both the OT and later Jewish writings for introducing the Northern Kingdom of Israel to Baal worship (1 Kings 16:31–34; 21:25–26; 2 Kings 9:22; Josephus, *Ant.* 8.317) and thus inciting the sin of idolatry. This makes Jezebel an appropriate and particularly effective OT figure to express the fundamental complaint Christ has against the Thyatiran church.

It is implausible that the name of the prophetess in Thyatira was the same as this notorious OT figure; Jezebel is almost certainly a nickname given by John to characterize and condemn her idolatrous actions. Various attempts to identify her are summarized below.

1. *Lydia.* Based on her hometown connection with Thyatira, a few commentators have suggested that Jezebel might be Lydia, the seller of purple cloth, who became a Christ follower through Paul's ministry in Philippi (Acts

16:14–15, 40). This, however, is mere conjecture, with nothing concrete to link these two individuals beyond the hometown connection. Also, the chronology doesn't really line up: Lydia's conversion took place around AD 50, but Jezebel of Thyatira was active forty years later, since the book of Revelation is traditionally dated to the mid-90s.

2. *Wife of a church leader in Thyatira.* A few manuscripts add the possessive "your" after "woman" so that the complaint reads: "You tolerate that woman *of yours.*" Since the word "woman" in Greek is commonly used for "wife," the person in view could be the spouse of the leader or bishop of the Thyatiran church (so, e.g., Beckwith 1919: 466; Alford 1976: 573). However, the textual evidence—both external and internal—significantly undermines this possibility: more weighty manuscripts omit the possessive "your," and its presence in some manuscripts can be explained as scribal confusion due to the presence of four other occurrences of exactly the same word in this and the immediately preceding verse (Metzger 1994: 664). This possibility also requires that "angel" in the opening of this sermon (2:18) refer to the human leader of the church, which is questionable. Furthermore, even if the possessive "your" were included here, the four preceding instances of this same word refer to the corporate church, and so it should have the same sense here; thus it could not refer just to the leader of the congregation.

3. *Local sibyl.* Some scholars have proposed that Jezebel was a local sibyl, a woman who prophesied in the name of a god or goddess while in an ecstatic state. It is more specifically asserted that Jezebel is a "Sibyl [named] Sambathe," a prophetess or priestess of a deity whose sanctuary was located just outside the city of Thyatira (so Schürer 1893; Court 1979: 34; Keener 2000: 134; see also Hemer 1986: 117–19). It is highly unlikely, however, that such an obviously pagan figure would be accepted and followed by those in a Christian church, which the sermon claims is happening in Thyatira. Proponents of this identification counter that syncretistic tendencies in the Thyatiran church allowed this local sibyl to influence that congregation. Nevertheless, there remain significant uncertainties about the identity and even the existence of the Sambathe sanctuary as well as any proposed link between this cult and the Jezebel mentioned here.

4. *Symbolic representative of Thyatiran church.* A few commentators have interpreted the name Jezebel as a symbol representing the church in Thyatira, conveying its character, rather than as a specific historical figure. Support for this view may come from the similarity between the reference to "the woman" (2:20) and "her children" (2:23) and the phrase "to the chosen lady and her children" in 2 John 1, where it almost certainly refers to the congregation as a whole ("chosen lady") and its individual members ("her children";

Beale 1999: 260–61). However, the five references to Jezebel in the immediately following verses using the third-person singular pronoun "her" (Rev. 2:21 [2×], 22 [2×], 23) strongly imply that a particular individual is in view.

5. *Prominent woman.* The traditional identification of Jezebel is the most likely explanation: she was a prominent woman in the Thyatiran church who, like her OT namesake, was persuading believers to compromise their faith and become guilty of idolatry and sexual immorality. She may have possessed wealth and

Figure 4.2. Fresco of a banqueting scene from Herculaneum (AD 50–79) reflecting the common link between formal meals and sexual activity.

upper-class status so that she was a patroness of one of the local house churches (so Aune 1997: 203; deSilva 1992: 294 claims that she opened her home to the Nicolaitan prophets and supported them), but her prominence was primarily because she claimed to be a prophetess. Although the feminine form of the word "prophetess" occurs only twice in the NT (by contrast the masculine form "prophet" occurs 144 times), women with oracular abilities were a widespread phenomenon in the ancient world (see the comment above concerning the possibility of Jezebel being a local sibyl) and in the early church. Elderly Anna was labeled a prophetess (Luke 2:36), and Philip the evangelist, one of the Seven, had four unmarried daughters who were known for their prophetic abilities (Acts 21:8–9). Female believers in Corinth prophesied (1 Cor. 11:5), and a woman named Ammia in the nearby church of Philadelphia is identified as a first-century prophetess (Eusebius, *Church History* 5.17.3–4). By calling herself a prophetess, Jezebel was claiming that her teaching not only contained divine revelation but also possessed divine authority.

Christ, whose fiery eyes are able to see through Jezebel's false claims, asserts that her teaching—rather than being divine in origin and authority— "misleads my servants." The verb "misleads" (*planaō*) occurs elsewhere in the book of Revelation to describe the deceiving actions of the false prophet (13:14; 19:20), the harlot Babylon (18:23), and Satan (12:9; 20:3, 8, 10). The use of this verb to describe the deceptive nature of Jezebel's teaching links her to this terrible trio of deceivers and reveals the seriousness of Jesus's complaint against this woman and her misguided followers.

One Complaint or Two?

After raising the general problem that the Thyatiran church is tolerating an influential woman and self-proclaimed prophetess in their community, Jesus expresses his specific complaint against this congregation: they are being led "to commit sexual immorality and to eat food sacrificed to idols." These are the same two complaints that Jesus brings against the Pergamum church, though expressed in reverse order, so both sermons address the same issue. This raises the same question discussed in the previous chapter: Is Jesus making one complaint against Thyatira or two?

If the reference to "committing sexual immorality" is taken literally, there are two complaints, one dealing with sexual sin and the other with "food sacrificed to idols" (i.e., the sin of idolatry). If "committing sexual immorality" is a metaphor for spiritual infidelity, there is only one complaint, that of idolatry. The evidence for each position was carefully examined in the chapter on the Pergamum sermon and can be reviewed there. In that discussion I concluded that there were compelling grounds for seeing two complaints rather than one.

Besides the six pieces of evidence examined in the previous chapter, there are a few additional points found in the Thyatira sermon that support this conclusion. First, although OT Jezebel is primarily connected with the sin of idolatry, she is also accused in one text of "sexual immoralities" (2 Kings 9:22 LXX: the plural *porneiai*). Second, Baal worship, which Jezebel introduced to Israel, was associated with inappropriate sexual conduct. Beale and Campbell (2015: 72), who argue that idolatry is the primary complaint, nevertheless concede that "sexual immorality could be secondarily in mind since this was often part of Baal worship." Third, the combination of "sexual immorality" and "food sacrificed to idols" is also found in the Apostolic Decree in Acts 15 and reflects language similar to what Jesus uses here ("I will not impose any other burden on you," Rev. 2:24; cf. "not to burden you with anything beyond the following requirements," Acts 15:28). Since the Apostolic Decree clearly refers to actual sexual misconduct, it is plausible to interpret the phrase "to commit sexual immorality" in the Thyatira sermon as literal rather than metaphorical.

Ranking the Two Complaints

Assuming that Christ's complaint against the church in Thyatira does involve the two sins of sexual immorality and idolatry, are they both equal problems in this congregation, or should one be ranked higher than the other? The order of these two complaints is the reverse of that found in the Pergamum sermon, suggesting that the first-mentioned sin, sexual immorality, may have been a greater problem in Thyatira. Charles (1920: 71) comments, "It will be observed that the order of the words here differs from that in ii.14. Here it is probably intended to mean that the primary object of the prophetess was sexual immorality" (so also Hemer 1986: 120). If this conclusion is correct, a better title for this sermon would be "Thyatira: The Church of Sinful Sex." Against this conclusion, however, is that the two references in the immediately following verses to Jezebel's "sexual immorality" (2:21, *porneia*) and "those who commit adultery with her" (2:22) are both metaphorical, expressing in traditional OT language how God's people are "prostituting" themselves with false gods and being unfaithful to their covenant relationship with the one true God. In other words, they are guilty of idolatry. So although sexual misconduct was part of the problem at Thyatira, the fundamental concern is the sin of idolatry. The situation, therefore, parallels Pergamum in the immediately preceding sermon. The Thyatiran church is similarly compromising its faith through idolatry and the closely connected sin of sexual immorality.

Trade Guilds

Most commentators interpret Christ's complaint to Thyatira as a specific problem related to believers' membership and participation in trade guilds (the earliest scholars to make this connection appear to be Ramsay 1904: 324–26, 329–30, 346–53; Swete 1907: lxiii–lxiv; and Charles 1920: 69–70). These trade guilds were somewhat like modern unions in that they consisted of workers engaged in a similar trade or occupation. Other guilds or "voluntary associations" (the designation given to such groups by modern scholars such as Kloppenborg and Wilson 1996) were formed not on the basis of a common trade but a collective purpose such as ensuring the proper burial of its members. These clubs or associations, which were extremely popular in the Roman world, typically involved members sharing a common meal—a

Photo by Philip Harland

Figure 4.3. Relief of Nike, goddess of victory (2nd–3rd cent. AD), holding a palm branch in her left hand and a wreath in her right hand, located at the entrance to the theater in Philippi. The inscription indicates that this relief was dedicated on behalf of the association of gladiators.

meal that not only was dedicated to the guild's patron deity but also at times offered sexual entertainment. Any Christ follower who belonged to such a voluntary association, therefore, would naturally be tempted to eat food sacrificed to idols and commit sexual immorality. Osborne (2002: 156–67) summarizes the situation this way:

> One thing we can state with a sense of confidence: the problem in Thyatira centered on the guilds. For persons to maintain their livelihood, some connection, indeed membership, in the guilds was a virtual necessity. For Christians the problem was that this mandated participation in the guild feasts, which themselves involved 'meat offered to idols,' since the patron gods of the guilds were always worshiped at the feasts. . . . At times this could also involve immorality.

It should be acknowledged—especially since no commentators seem to do so—that there is nothing explicitly stated in the sermon to Thyatira that links the complaint against this church directly with trade guilds or other voluntary associations. Nevertheless, such a link is highly plausible and indeed probable. The few inscriptions from Thyatira that have been discovered reveal that "more trade guilds are known in Thyatira than in any other Asian city" (Ramsay 1994: 238). Hemer (1986: 107–8) notes that "the city's most obvious peculiarity was then its unusually large number of influential tradeguilds. Associations of this kind were an ancient feature of community life in Asia, especially in Lydia. . . . Their prominence at Thyatira, however, is quite exceptional." Inscriptions from Thyatira reveal the following types of trade guilds: wool workers, linen workers, makers of outer garments, tanners, leather workers, potters, bakers, shoemakers, slave traders, and, noteworthy in light of the rare term used in the Christ title, bronze workers. Voluntary associations in Thyatira formed not on the basis of a common trade but for a collective purpose included those that promoted the interests of Romans and those that honored sports heroes at the local games. There was even a club identified as "men in the prime of life" (Hemer 1986: 108).

The fact that the economic and social aspects of the guilds were intimately linked with their religious aspect created a serious challenge for Christians: How could they survive financially in their profession without belonging to the local trade guilds and exposing themselves to the twin sins of idolatry and sexual immorality? How could they demonstrate solidarity with their pagan neighbors without putting themselves in a vulnerable situation involving idolatry and sexual immorality? How could they avoid being rejected by their social circles without maintaining their membership in these other types of voluntary associations? Of course, this dilemma was not unique to the church in Thyatira; it would have been a major challenge faced by most Jesus followers throughout Asia Minor as well as by Christians throughout the ancient world.

In this difficult situation, Jezebel, the self-proclaimed prophetess in the church of Thyatira, had a teaching that some congregational members accepted. John does not reveal the content of the teaching other than referring to it later in the sermon as "the deep things of Satan" (2:24) but mentions only its idolatrous and sexually immoral results. Yet, on the basis of the situation in Corinth, where believers were similarly tempted to eat food sacrificed to idols, it seems probable that Jezebel was appealing to "knowledge"—specifically, the knowledge that there is only one God and that idols do not really exist, so the Christian who has this knowledge can join in guild banquets and eat food devoted to the patron deity without becoming guilty of idolatry (note the frequent occurrence of "knowledge" and the key role this word plays in 1 Cor. 8:1–13). Jezebel was likely teaching something close to this: "You believe, don't you, that there is only one true God? You know, don't you, that Apollo Tyrimnos and all the other deities are merely made-up gods, who do not really exist? Armed with this important knowledge, you are free to participate in the guild banquets!"

The Correction: For Jezebel and Her Followers (2:21)

The structure of the Thyatira sermon differs slightly at this point: in other sermons the correction and consequence are directed at the *whole* church, but here in the Thyatira sermon *two different groups* are addressed. The first group consists of Jezebel and her followers, for whom the expected correction (2:21) and consequence (2:22–23) are negative. The second group consists of the rest of the Thyatiran church, for whom the expected correction (2:24–25) and consequence (2:26–28) are positive.

The shift from the complaint to the correction is signaled by the twofold occurrence (2:21) of the key verb "repent," used in the correction section of all the sermons directed to unhealthy churches (Ephesus, 2:5a, 5b; Pergamum, 2:16a; Sardis, 3:3; Laodicea, 3:19b). The verb "repent" is understandably missing from the sermons to Smyrna and Philadelphia since they are healthy churches whose sermons have no complaint section. But instead of the expected command dealing with the *present-time* need for repentance, as in the other occurrences, here the corrective action of repentance is referred to as a *past* event: "I gave her time to repent, but she is not willing to repent of her immorality." The clear implication of Christ's statement is that the misleading teaching of Jezebel has already been tested, as all prophetic utterances need to be (1 Cor. 14:29, 32; 1 Thess. 5:19–22; 1 John 4:1), and has been found to be false. It is unclear whether this negative judgment about her teaching comes directly from John himself (see 3 John 10) or indirectly from another leader at the apostle's direction. What is clear, however, is that this negative judgment comes ultimately from Christ and so has the full weight of his authority. The use of the past tense ("I gave her time to repent") also means that Jezebel and her followers (although she alone is mentioned here, those in the Thyatiran church who accept her teaching are explicitly identified in the immediately following verse and so are also clearly in view) cannot plead ignorance as an excuse, saying, "We didn't know that what we were saying and doing was wrong!"

But instead of responding to Christ's patient offer of grace in giving her time to repent, Jezebel was not willing. The sobering truth is that sin can have such a powerful hold over people that they stubbornly hang on to their rebellious ways. This is also seen later in the book of Revelation when those not killed by the terrible plagues of the sixth trumpet still "did not repent of the works of their hands" (9:20a), works identified as "worshiping demons and idols of gold and silver and bronze and stone and wood" (9:20b) as well as "sexual immorality" (9:21). The specific thing that Jezebel and others in the Thyatiran church need to repent of is "her immorality." The noun found here (*porneia*) is related to the first of the two verbal forms used in the complaint (2:20), which again raises the issue of whether it ought to be understood literally or figuratively. In this case, there is near universal agreement among commentators in support of the figurative reading, since the metaphor of Israel as an unfaithful wife prostituting herself with other gods is common in the OT (e.g., 2 Kings 9:22; Isa. 57:3, 8; Jer. 3:9; 13:27; Ezek. 16:15–36; 23:7–35; Hosea 1:2; 2:2–13; 4:12; 5:4; Nah. 3:4). In the present context, however, sexual immorality is intimately connected with idolatry (not only in the immediately preceding verse [2:20] but also in the immediately preceding complaint against the Pergamum church [2:14]). In our study of the Pergamum sermon, we noted that sexual activity frequently occurred during banquets or formal meals in the ancient world, including cultic meals and guild feasts. It is better, therefore, to view the single reference to immorality here as a "summary term reflecting both sins of verse 20" (Osborne 2002: 158). One way to capture this double meaning of the summary term is to translate the noun *porneia* in this instance not narrowly as "sexual immorality" (as with the verbal form in 2:20) but more broadly as "immorality," so that it can refer to both the sin of idolatry and the sin of sexual misconduct (similarly the NIV).

The Consequence (Negative): For Jezebel and Her Followers (2:22–23)

The sermon continues its focus on the first of the two groups in the Thyatiran church—Jezebel and her followers—by following the structure of the other messages and proceeding to the negative consequence that this group is facing because it refuses to repent and correct its idolatrous and sexually immoral ways. The consequence section is set apart from the preceding correction by the interjection "Behold!" which is meant to draw attention to what Jesus is about to say. The opening words of Jesus's judgment are given in the form of two clauses that are parallel with each other, as is evident from the fact that the one verb ("I will throw") does double duty for both clauses and that the object in each clause is followed by the same prepositional phrase:

I will throw	her	into a sickbed
and	those who commit adultery with her	into great suffering.

The first clause, which literally means, "I will throw her into a *bed* [*klinē*]," is a Hebrew idiom (see esp. Charles 1920: 71, who cites 1 Macc. 1:5; Jdt. 8:3; also, e.g., Beasley-Murray 1978: 91; Aune 1997: 205; Beale 1999: 263n125) meaning to send someone a sickness as a form of divine punishment (BDAG 549.1, "*lay someone on a sickbed*, i.e., strike her w. an illness"). The parallel structure of the two clauses means that "bed" is matched with "great suffering," and so a few translations render the first term more fully as a "bed *of suffering*" (NIV, NLT). Although there are dangers in linking sickness and sin too closely (e.g., the disciples' wrong interpretation for why a man was born blind: John 9:1–3), it nevertheless is also true that disease and even death are at times a divine punishment for sin (e.g., some in Corinth became sick and died due to their sinful celebration of the Lord's Supper: 1 Cor. 11:27–30). Here Jesus spells out the negative consequence of Jezebel's sin of misleading others into committing sexual immorality and idolatry: he will send her a life-threatening illness.

The reference to a "bed," however, evokes not only the image of a sickbed but also almost certainly that of a dining couch, where the closely related sins of sexual immorality and idolatry take place (so Ramsay 1904: 351–52; Beale 1999: 263n125; Hemer 1986: 121, 252; Wilson 2002: 269). The word for bed (*klinē*) is the same word used for dining couches, on which participants in guild feasts and cultic meals would recline. Among the papyrus invitations to religious meals that have been discovered in Egypt, we read the following: "Ammonios asks you to dine at the couch [*klinē*] of the lord Sarapis in the dining hall of the Sarapeion [i.e., temple to the Egyptian god Sarapis/Sera-pis] on the 9th, beginning from the 9th hour" (P.Oxy. 62.4339). Such dining couches at guild feasts and cultic meals were also commonly used for female entertainment, which included sex (see fig. 4.2 above, the fresco of the ban-queting scene from Herculaneum). Since Jezebel reclines on a couch to eat food sacrificed to idols and to engage in sexual immorality, God will cause her couch of sinful pleasure to become a bed of suffering. The punishment fits the crime as the "party couch" at guild feasts will be turned into a sickbed.

The second of the two parallel clauses reveals the negative consequence that will come upon not only Jezebel but also "those who commit adultery with her." Just as the single word "immorality" in 2:21 is a "summary term" for the two sins of 2:20 (committing sexual immorality and eating food sacrificed to idols, i.e., idolatry), here too the single reference to "committing adultery" ought to be interpreted as a reference to both these closely connected sins. As Hemer (1986: 121) observes, this reference "may be understood figuratively of those in the church who had been led astray by Jezebel into idolatry, though incidental reference to its immoral character is not excluded." The negative consequence for Jezebel involves being thrown "into a sickbed"; the parallel punishment for her followers involves being thrown "into great suffering" (*eis thlipsin megalēn*). It is not clear whether this refers narrowly to "the great tribulation" (7:14), a period of specific trials that will immediately precede the end of time (see also Matt. 24:21), "the hour of testing" (3:10); or gener-ally to a time of suffering and affliction (NIV, "suffer intensely"). The former interpretation is supported by the only other combined occurrence of the two terms in the book of Revelation in 7:14 (*ek tēs thlipseōs tēs megalēs*), though the weight of this parallel may be undermined by the notable absence of the article here in 2:22. The latter interpretation is strengthened by the remain-ing instances of *thlipsis* in the book of Revelation (1:9; 2:9, 10), which refer generically to affliction. This ambiguity, however, should not prevent one from clearly hearing the very serious consequences that Jezebel and her fol-lowers face "if they do not repent of her [idolatrous and sexually immoral] works" (2:22c).

The intense suffering into which Christ will throw Jezebel and her follow-ers is described further in the following clause: "And I will kill her children with disease" (2:23a). These are not Jezebel's physical children born from her idolatry (contra Beckwith 1919: 467) but her spiritual children, those who embrace her misleading teaching and engage in idolatry and sexual sin. This metaphorical meaning of "children" is found elsewhere in Johannine writ-ings (1 John 3:1, 2, 10 [2×]; 5:2; 2 John 1, 4, 13; 3 John 4) and was commonly used to refer to followers of a particular spiritual leader (e.g., Isa. 8:18; 1 Cor.

4:14, 17; Gal. 4:19; 1 Tim. 1:2, 18; 2 Tim. 1:2; 2:1; Titus 1:4; Philem. 10; 1 Pet. 1:14). A local example of this practice can be seen in the case of Papylus, a Christian from Thyatira, who was brought before the Roman proconsul in Pergamum; when asked whether he had any children, he replied: "I have children in the Lord in every province and city" (Martyrdom of Carpus, Papylus, and Agathonice 24–34; cited by Aune 1997: 206).

The judgment that Christ brings against the "children" or followers of Jezebel literally states: "I will kill with death." One possibility is that the prepositional phrase "with death" (*en thanatō*) is a Hebraism that intensifies the verb: "I will *surely* kill." Many leading translations follow this sense, rendering the clause as "I will strike her children dead" (NIV, NRSV, ESV, NLT). However, since the Greek word "death" is regularly used in the LXX to translate the Hebrew word for "plague, pestilence," another possibility is that the prepositional phrase "with death" means "I will kill *with the plague*." This second meaning is strongly supported by Rev. 6:8, where the verb "to kill" is paired again with the same prepositional phrase "with death": "to kill with sword and with famine and with plague [*en thanatō*]" (see also Rev. 18:8). Further support lies in a likely allusion here to Ezek. 33:27 LXX, where the same combination of the verb "to kill" and the dative noun "death" means not literally "to kill with death" but "to kill with [the] plague." The likelihood of this allusion is increased by the fact that the declaration following in Ezek. 33:29, "And they will know that I am the LORD," is seemingly echoed in the next words here in Rev. 2:23, "And all the churches will know that I am the one who . . ."

Hemer (1986: 121) mistakenly sees a problem here, saying, "The judgment upon the children seems more severe than that upon Jezebel herself." But this is not actually the case. Although 2:22 lacks any explicit reference to the death of Jezebel, this is the well-known penalty that her OT namesake paid: she was thrown from an upper window, her blood was splattered on the building's wall, the horses trampled her underfoot, and the dogs devoured her flesh so that there was nothing left of her body to bury (2 Kings 9:30–37). The Jezebel in the Thyatiran church will be thrown into a sickbed, which will similarly lead to her ultimate death; so also her spiritual children will die by means of plague and pestilence. The reference to their death likely involves another well-known allusion to the OT Jezebel and her children, killed because of her sin. Seventy princes, sons of the wicked Ahab, were decapitated; their heads were placed in baskets, sent to Jezreel, and placed in two piles at the entrance to the city gate. In this way Jehu brought the greatest dishonor to the wicked house of Ahab and wiped it out (2 Kings 10:1–11).

The negative consequence for Jezebel and her followers in Thyatira is indeed severe, but it sends a powerful message: "And all the churches will know that I am the one who searches hearts and minds, and I will give to each one according to your works." The fact that this is the only use of the plural "churches" in all seven sermons apart from the stereotyped "hearing" formula ("Whoever has ears, let them hear what the Spirit is saying to the churches") is not likely to be accidental or insignificant. Instead, this lone plural reference to the "churches" strategically located in the exact center of the middle sermon highlights the speaker's expectation that each church is to hear and heed the sermons addressed to the other churches. Although the looming judgment of death is especially relevant for the church in Thyatira, where one group has been misled into engaging in idolatrous and sexually immoral practices, all the churches of Asia Minor are similarly warned of the fatal negative consequence of engaging in such sinful activity.

This negative consequence also reaffirms the divine nature of Christ, already asserted in the opening title "the Son of God" (2:18). His just decree of death makes known to all the churches that "I am the one who searches *hearts and minds*." The Greek text actually refers to "kidneys and hearts," since it was believed that these two parts of the human body were the location of a person's true feelings, inner desires, and hidden motives. Although the OT much more commonly refers to God's knowledge of "the hearts" of individuals, there are at least five occurrences where God tests both "the hearts" and "the kidneys" of people (see NASB notes for Pss. 7:9; 26:2; Jer. 11:20; 17:10; 20:12). The same word pair here in Rev. 2:23 alludes specifically to Jer. 17:10, since this OT text refers to God, who not only "tests hearts and examines kidneys" but who also "gives to each one according to his ways." The idea of recompense for one's works is found in the immediately following statement by Christ: "I will give to each of you according to your works." This OT allusion is important in revealing the deity of Christ: the original speaker in Jeremiah 17:10 identified himself as "I the LORD," but now it is the exalted Christ who possesses the same divine ability to perceive the true beliefs and hidden motives of Jezebel and her followers and to issue a just judgment of death against them. It is possible but less certain that the divine nature of Christ is further implied by the presence of the statement "I am" (*egō eimi*; so Thomas 1992: 223–24). This OT allusion also looks back to and explains the opening Christ title, where Jesus identifies himself as one "whose eyes are like a flame of fire," namely, his perceptive and penetrating eyesight by which he searches "hearts and minds" (the modern equivalent of the OT expression "kidneys and hearts") and sees through the deceptive arguments of Jezebel, which are misleading some in the Thyatiran church.

The negative consequence to Jezebel and her followers finally concludes with a statement of recompense for their evil works: "I will give to each of you according to your works." Although this statement continues, as noted above, the allusion to Jeremiah 17:10, it also echoes more generally the OT principle of retribution—the *lex talionis*—found throughout Scripture. As Osborne (2002: 161–62) observes, this principle of retribution "is a critical biblical theme, beginning with the OT (Ps. 62:12; Prov. 24:12; Hos. 12:2) and reiterated by Christ (Matt. 16:27), Paul (Rom. 2:6; 14:12; 2 Cor. 11:15; 2 Tim. 4:14) and Peter (1 Pet. 1:17)." The theme of retributive justice plays a significant role in the book of Revelation, occurring not just here but also in several later passages (14:13; 18:6; 20:12, 13; 22:12). Any benefit or pleasure that Jezebel and her followers may be enjoying now from their participation in guild feasts will be short-lived: Christ the judge will justly repay them according to their idolatrous and sexually immoral works. The shift from the singular "her works" in the previous verse to the plural "your works" here makes clear that those who follow the misleading instruction of Jezebel cannot avoid punishment by blaming their teacher but will justly be held accountable for their own culpable activity.

The Correction: For the Rest of the Thyatiran Church (2:24–25)

After finishing his words of correction and consequence directed to the first group in the Thyatiran church—Jezebel and her followers—Christ turns his attention to the second group in the church and his words of correction and consequence for them. This important shift in audience is signaled in four ways. First, the contrast with the preceding verses is introduced with the adversative particle "but" (*de*). Second, the change in audience is indicated by the second-person plural personal pronoun "to you" (*hymin*), which is located for emphasis at the head of the sentence. Third, the second group is distinguished from the first group by the phrase "the rest, the ones in Thyatira." Fourth, a parallel use of the verb "to throw" (*ballō*), clear in the original Greek, contrasts the two sets of members in the church: "I will throw" introduced the preceding section (2:22–23) to describe what Christ will do to the first group ("*I will throw* her into a sickbed and those who commit adultery with her into great suffering"), and the same verb introduces 2:24–25 to describe what Christ *will not* do to the second group ("*I will not throw* on you another burden").

The second group, identified as "the rest, the ones in Thyatira," is described by two relative clauses that further distinguish them from the first group: the rest of the Thyatiran church consists of those "who do not have this teaching, who do not know 'the deep things of Satan,' as they say." The first relative clause shows that, though the whole congregation is guilty of tolerating Jezebel (see the complaint in 2:20), not everyone has accepted her teaching. The first group went beyond the sin of tolerating this false prophetess; they increased their guilt by accepting her misleading instruction and joining in her immorality. The second group did not do any of this: they "do not have this teaching." What the specific *content* of this teaching was is not clearly stated anywhere in this sermon; only its *results* are described. As noted above, the situation in Corinth, where believers were similarly tempted to eat food sacrificed to idols, makes it probable that Jezebel was appealing to knowledge—specifically, the knowledge that there is only one God and that idols do not have any real existence (see 1 Cor. 8:4–6). According to her, Christians armed with this knowledge can join in guild banquets and eat food devoted to the patron deity and yet not become guilty of idolatry.

Unfortunately, this reconstructed situation cannot be confirmed by the second relative clause, which refers to Jezebel's false teaching with the enigmatic phrase "the deep things of Satan." Should this phrase be understood literally or sarcastically, and what does it refer to? If we take the phrase at face value, it means that Jezebel's teaching involves "deep" or profound things (BDAG 162.2: "pertaining to something nonphysical perceived to be so remote that it is difficult to assess") revealed to her either from or more likely about Satan that would allow those with such knowledge to participate in guild feasts or cultic meals without any idolatrous consequences. But there is no evidence for a literal reading that asserts that Jezebel taught her followers to participate in satanic activities in order "to appreciate fully the grace of God" (Mounce 1977: 105) or "to show their mastery over it" (Osborne 2002: 163). One might therefore assume that Jezebel presented her teaching as "the deep things of God" (see 1 Cor. 2:10), which John (or Christ) sarcastically describes as "the deep things of Satan." This would be somewhat similar to the two descriptions of what Jews undoubtedly called "the synagogue of God" as "the synagogue of Satan" (Rev. 2:9; 3:9). The fundamental weakness with this reading, however, is that John explicitly attributes the enigmatic phrase to Jezebel and her followers: "as they say" (it is very unlikely that this parenthetical clause looks ahead to "another burden" instead of back to "the deep things of Satan").

The most plausible view is that Jezebel claimed divine revelation from God about profound things pertaining to Satan and that such knowledge would prevent her followers from falling into the twin dangers of idolatry and sexual immorality while attending guild feasts and cultic meals. Since the temptation to participate in these pagan gatherings was great, it no doubt took little effort on Jezebel's part to convince many in the Thyatiran church to embrace her teaching.

The second group in that congregation, however, did not accept her teaching and did not embrace "the deep things of Satan." To them Christ states what he will *not* "throw" their way: "I will not impose [lit., "throw"] any other burden on you." There are at least three proposals identifying the nature of this "burden" (*baros*; BDAG 167.1: "experience of something that is particularly oppressive"). (1) It refers to additional punishment: although Christ will "throw" Jezebel and her followers into the punishment of sickness and ultimately death, he will "not throw" the rest of the Thyatiran church into any other punishment (Roloff 1993: 55). (2) It refers to the command in the immediately following verse: Christ will not impose any burden or responsibility other than their need to "hold fast" and resist the false teaching and evil practices of Jezebel and her followers (so, e.g., Lenski 1935: 122; Thomas 1992: 230; Osborne 2002: 164). (3) It refers to the Apostolic Decree, a letter sent from the Jewish leaders at the Jerusalem Synod of AD 49 to the gentile churches "not to impose an additional burden on you except these essentials" (Acts 15:28; so, e.g., Charles 1920: 74; Zahn 1924: 292–93; Ladd 1972: 53; Hemer 1986: 123; Beale 1999: 266; Kistemaker 2001: 140–41; Fanning 2020: 155n41).

The strength of the third proposal is twofold. First, there are a number of verbal parallels between Christ's statement here and Acts 15:28: in addition to the key and relatively infrequent word "burden" (*baros*; elsewhere in the NT only in Matt. 20:12; 2 Cor. 4:17; Gal. 6:2; 1 Thess. 2:7), both texts include the preposition "on" (*epi*), the second-person plural personal pronoun "you," and the adverb "except" (*plēn*, Rev. 2:25). Second, the content of the Apostolic Decree, which prohibits eating food sacrificed to idols and committing sexual immorality (Acts 15:29; see also 15:20), matches up with the twofold complaint that Christ brings against the Thyatiran church in Rev. 2:20. Thus, Christ is not imposing any additional burden on this congregation other than the obligation for all gentile believers not to participate in guild feasts and cultic meals, which would expose them to the sins of idolatry and sexual immorality.

The correction section in each of the seven sermons features the use of the imperative mood as Christ typically commands the unhealthy churches to repent (Ephesus, 2:5; Pergamum, 2:16; Sardis, 3:3; Laodicea, 3:19b) and the healthy churches to other appropriate action (Smyrna, 2:10; Philadelphia, 3:11). The correction section in the Thyatira sermon also contains Christ's imperatival call to action: "But hold on to what you have until I come!" The adverb *plēn*, when found at the beginning of a sentence or clause, functions as "a marker of something that is contrastingly added for consideration" (BDAG 826.1). To his preceding statement about not imposing any other burden on the rest of the Thyatiran church, Christ adds the command that they "hold on to what you have." The same combination of the verb "hold on to" (*krateō*) and the relative clause "what you have" occurs later, in the sermon to Philadelphia (3:11). In both places, the referent of "what you have" is not spelled out but implied from the context. Here it likely looks back to the "burden" just mentioned: the true teaching of the apostles concerning the need to abstain from food sacrificed to idols and from committing sexual immorality in contrast to the false teaching of Jezebel. The rest in the Thyatira congregation are commanded by Christ to "hold on," or persevere, in the face of the temptation to participate in the guild feasts and cultic meals, and to continue such faithfulness "until I come." Christ's reference to his coming should be recognized as a threat to the Thyatiran church, urging them to obey his corrective command: he will come and personally see how each congregational member responds to his words of correction.

The Consequence (Positive): For the Rest of the Thyatiran Church (2:26–28)

The sermon continues to distinguish two groups in the Thyatiran church: Jezebel and her followers in contrast to the remaining members of the congregation. The consequence for Jezebel and her followers—which is justly negative in light of their idolatrous and sexually immoral works—has already been given earlier in the sermon (2:22–23). As we have come to expect, the message now shifts from the correction to the positive consequence for the rest of the Thyatiran church. This shift is signaled by the presence of the victory formula, which employs the key verb *nikaō*, meaning "to win in the face of obstacles, *be victor, conquer, overcome, prevail*" (BDAG 673.1). That this victory is not a human achievement but a divine gift is made clear by Christ's twice-stated assertion: "I will give to that person" (2:26b, 28b). The possession of "authority over the nations" and "the morning star" should not be viewed as earned rewards for one's spiritual victory but as gracious gifts from Christ. This important theological point gains further support from the victory formula in the seventh and final sermon to Laodicea, which highlights how the believer's victory is linked to and thus dependent on Christ's victory: "To the one who is victorious . . . , just as I was victorious" (3:21). What is true for the Laodicean church is also true for the Thyatiran church: its ability to overcome the misleading teaching of Jezebel and the evil works of both her and her followers rests not on its members' individual efforts but on Christ's previous victory.

The victory formula here is unique: whereas the other six sermons simply identify the conquering Christian with the single participle "the one who is victorious," the Thyatira sermon adds a second participle: "the one who is victorious and the one who keeps my works until the end" (2:26a). Aune (1997: 209) finds this addition "extremely problematic" on the grounds that "one 'keeps' or 'obeys' not *works* but instructions or commands." It is true that the verb "keep" (*tēreō*) elsewhere in the book of Revelation frequently takes as its object these and other nouns (1:3; 3:3, 8, 10; 12:17; 14:12; 16:15; 22:7, 9) and that the object "works" with this verb is rare. However, far from being "extremely problematic," the unique phrase "the one who keeps my works" skillfully forms a striking contrast with the preceding references to "her works" (2:22, i.e., the works of Jezebel) and "your works" (2:23, i.e., the works of Jezebel's followers; so also Thomas 1992: 232; Osborne 2002: 165). There is likely also an intended allusion to the beginning of this sermon, where Christ commends the church as a whole for "your works"—their four "later works" of love, faith, service, and perseverance, which are greater than their first works (2:19). These are identical with "my works," the works of Christ that the Thyatiran church must "keep" and do "until the end," that is, up to the time when Christ returns (2:25, "until I come").

Authority over the Nations (2:26b–27)

Those who, with Christ's help, conquer the temptation to engage in idolatrous and sexually immoral behavior and who instead do the works of Christ will receive two blessings or rewards. The first positive consequence is introduced with the main verb "I will give," which will ultimately be paired with a comparative clause "just as also I have received." Sandwiched between these two clauses is a close paraphrase of Ps. 2:9. The resulting structure can be visually represented as follows:

> I will give to him authority over the nations—
>> and he will destroy them with an iron rod,
>>> as ceramic pots are shattered—
> just as also I have received authority from my Father.

The first reward is that victorious believers will share in Christ's authority and kingly rule (2:26b). The central idea here is not God's delegating to all humanity rulership over the earth (Gen. 1:26–27; Ps. 8:6; so Keener 2000: 136) but God's delegating to his chosen people rulership over the rest of humanity in the messianic age. Several OT texts created the expectation that God's people would enjoy privileged positions of power during that future kingdom (e.g., Ps. 149:4–9; Isa. 60:14; Dan. 7:14, 18, 27). Not surprisingly, the same expectation is alive and strong in the NT. Jesus promised his disciples: "Truly I tell you, at the renewal of all things, when the Son of Man sits on his glorious throne, you who have followed me will also sit on twelve thrones, judging the twelve tribes of Israel" (Matt. 19:28; see Luke 22:29–30). Paul rebuked the Corinthians for going to the secular law courts to bring a dispute against a fellow congregational member, arguing: "You know, don't you, that the Lord's people will judge the world?" (1 Cor. 6:2). Paul encouraged persecuted believers with a trustworthy saying: "If we endure, we will also reign with him" (2 Tim. 2:12). The believers in Laodicea are similarly rewarded with sharing in the messianic rule of Christ: "To the one who is victorious, I will give the right to sit with me on my throne" (Rev. 3:21). The book of Revelation, in fact, frequently highlights how faithful Christ followers will share in his reign (Rev. 1:6; 2:26; 3:21; 5:10; 20:4, 6; 22:5).

This first positive consequence of having "authority over the nations" is further explained by means of a close paraphrase of Ps. 2:9: "and he will destroy them with an iron rod, as ceramic pots are shattered" (2:27). A reference to this particular OT text was foreshadowed already in the opening Christ title, the Son of God, which echoes Ps. 2:7. Here at the end of the sermon the OT reference to Ps. 2:9 is much more exact, not merely an echo but a "free rendering" (Charles 1920: 74, 77; Mounce 1977: 106; Hemer 1986: 124) or "incredible paraphrase" (Osborne 2002: 166), if not an explicit quotation (several translations put this verse in quotation marks or separate it from the surrounding text by means of indention: NIV, NKJV, NET, NRSV, NLT, LEB). The paraphrase may actually include the preceding clause of 2:26b as well, though its parallels with Ps. 2:8 are not as close as with Ps. 2:9.

Revelation 2:26b–27	Psalm 2:8–9 LXX
I will give to him	And I will give to you
authority over the nations,	nations as your inheritance,
	and as your possession
	the ends of the earth.
and he will rule/destroy them	You will rule/destroy them
with an iron rod,	with an iron rod;
as ceramic pots	as a pot of ceramic,
are shattered.	you will shatter them.

Psalm 2:9 had been read messianically for at least a century before the writing of the book of Revelation (Pss. Sol. 17.23–24), and it is interpreted

that way in its two other appearances in Revelation: "And she gave birth to a son, a male child, who is to rule all the nations with an iron rod" (Rev. 12:5); "and he will rule them with an iron rod" (19:15). Here in 2:27 it is applied both to Christ and to the victorious believer who shares in Christ's authority over the nations.

There is much debate among commentators about whether this first reward of authority consists of sharing in Christ's domination over the nations ("he will rule") or his destruction of the nations ("he will destroy"). The issue centers on the meaning of the verb *poimainō*, taken from the LXX translation of Ps. 2:9. The verb literally refers to a person who tends sheep, "to shepherd," and so could have here the metaphorical and positive sense of protecting, caring for, nurturing (Rev. 7:17, Christ "will shepherd" those who survive the great tribulation). The context, however, is quite negative, since "the activity of 'shepherd' has destructive results" (BDAG 842.2.γ): shepherding with an iron rod is compared to ceramic pots being broken into pieces. The two references to Ps. 2:9 later in the book of Revelation make this clear. The context of 12:5 is similarly negative, and, more significantly, in 19:15 the verb *poimainō* is paralleled by the verb *patassō*, meaning "to inflict something disastrous, strike" (BDAG 786.2).

Also relevant to this debate, though adding to its complexity, is the fact that the Hebrew text of Ps. 2:9 has the verb רעע (*rʿʿ*), meaning "to strike, break." If the consonants of the word in the original Hebrew text are given different vowels, the verb could instead be derived from רעה (*rʿh*), meaning "to shepherd." This difference in vowels may be why the Septuagint translators used the Greek verb *poimainō* to render the original Hebrew word, which John then included in his paraphrase of this verse. It is also possible that John may have been aware of a secondary and more negative meaning of *poimainō*: in at least three OT LXX texts, it has the sense "to lay waste, destroy" (Ps. 49:15 [48:15 LXX]; Jer. 6:3; Mic. 5:6 [5:5 MT, LXX]). If this is so, then John used the primary and positive sense of "to shepherd" in Rev. 7:17 and the secondary and negative sense of "to destroy" here in Rev. 2:27 as well as in 12:5 and 19:15 (so Charles 1920: 76; Thomas 1992: 233n91; Aune 1997: 210–11; Osborne 2002: 166–67; note also Beale 1999: 267, who argues that John has both meanings in view in 2:27 so that it refers not only to the negative judgment of unbelievers but also to the positive, salvific protection of believers).

The vast majority of translations and commentators, influenced by the negative context but aware of the primary, positive sense of "shepherd," render *poimainō* more neutrally as "rule." Despite the widespread acceptance of this view, it ought to be rejected in favor of the alternative meaning of "destroy."

There are three reasons for this. First, the immediate context of 2:27 should be given full consideration. As Osborne (2002: 166–67) plainly puts it: "The violence connoted in the 'rod of iron' and the 'shattering' of the pottery is simply too strong for 'rule.'" Second, John's citation of Ps. 2:9 elsewhere in the book of Revelation, where it has not the sense of "rule" but the stronger meaning of "destroy" (12:5; 19:15), ought to be followed also in 2:27. Third, John was undoubtedly aware of the larger context of Ps. 2, to which he alludes in the opening Christ title in Rev. 2:18 (Ps. 2:7) and closely paraphrases here in 2:26b–27 (Ps. 2:8–9). This psalm concludes with a warning to the kings and rulers of the earth that their refusal to submit to God's son will result in their destruction (Ps. 2:12). The reward that Christ will give to victorious believers, therefore, is truly impressive: this gift of authority over the nations involves nothing less than the full authority given to Christ by his Father to judge and justly destroy those engaged in idolatrous and sexually immoral acts.

Two images clarify even further the gift of authority over the nations. The first is the "iron rod," which could refer either to a *kingly* iron scepter or a *shepherding* iron club—a wood club capped with iron for beating back and killing wild animals that threaten the sheep. The latter option is more likely in light of the reference to Ps. 2:9 in 19:15, where the iron rod is paralleled with the "sharp sword"—the long and deadly *rhomphaia* used by the rider on the white horse "to strike down the nations" (see the fuller description of this sword in the discussion of 2:12 in the chapter on Pergamum).

The second image illustrating the kind of authority given to believers over the nations involves broken pieces of pottery: "as ceramic pots are shattered." The meaning of this image is best seen in Jeremiah 18:1–19:15, which contains a lengthy depiction of a potter and his pottery: just as the potter has the power and right either to reshape (Jer. 18:1–23) or break (Jer. 19:1–15) any piece of pottery that displeases him, so God has the power and right to deal with his wayward people whom he has created. The ancient pagan world also had a ritual in which ceramic pots were inscribed with the name of a nation's enemy and then broken into pieces to symbolize the total destruction of that nation (Krodel 1989: 129). The image of ceramic pots being shattered is especially appropriate for the Thyatiran church, given the known existence of a potters' guild in their city (*CIG* 3485 = *IGRR* 4.1244; Hemer 1986: 125, 246n10; Ramsay 1994: 238). Therefore both images—the shepherding iron club and the broken pieces of pottery—depict Christ's absolute authority, which he shares with his victorious followers, an authority not just to control but even to destroy.

The opening clause of the first positive consequence for the rest of the Thyatiran church ("I will give to him authority over the nations") is finally concluded with the comparative clause "just as I also have received [authority] from my Father" (2:28a). Although the object of what Christ has received is not explicitly stated in the Greek text, the word "authority" is clearly assumed from the parallel with the opening clause. The use of the perfect tense "I have received" emphasizes that this absolute authority was not only given to Christ from his Father at some point in the past (Matt. 29:18, "All authority on heaven and earth has been given to me") but also that Christ still possesses it, and this present possession allows him in turn to give such authority to his faithful followers.

The Morning Star (2:28b)

In contrast to the first reward given to the victorious members of the Thyatiran church, the second is stated briefly and without any clarifying comments: "And I will give to him the morning star" (2:28b). The meaning of this metaphor is difficult to determine with certainty. A century ago, Charles (1920: 77) observed: "No satisfactory explanation has as yet been discovered of these words." In more recent times, Hemer (1986: 126) likewise acknowledges that "the precise point of this promise is lost and any attempt to assign it a firm *Sitz im Leben* [life setting] is necessarily speculative." But though determining the meaning of "the morning star" has proved problematic, it is not as hopeless as these quotes suggest.

The plausibility of an OT background for the metaphor of the morning star is increased not just by the use of Ps. 2:9 to clarify the first reward but also by the widespread allusions to the OT found throughout the book of Revelation. The close paraphrase of Ps. 2:9 and particularly its reference to the image of the "iron rod" may have caused John to think of Balaam's fourth oracle, where the words "rod" (or "scepter") and "star" are combined in synonymous parallelism: "A star will come out of Jacob; a rod/scepter will arise out of Israel" (Num. 24:17). That John knows this OT text is clear from his words later in the book of Revelation, where he applies Num. 24:17 to Christ: "I [Jesus] am the root and the offspring of David, the bright morning star" (22:16). That John would use the star metaphor based on this OT text as a second reward for the Thyatiran church is hardly surprising, since he had just finished using the OT story of Balaam in the immediately preceding Pergamum sermon, and that church shares in common with Thyatira the same two complaints about eating food sacrificed to idols and committing sexual immorality.

Balaam's prophecy about the star coming from Jacob was widely interpreted within Judaism as a reference to the messiah. In fact, the star metaphor

originating from Num. 24:17 became a stock messianic expression in many
Jewish writings (T. Levi 18.3; T. Jud. 24.1; CD 7.18–21; 1QM 11.6–7; 4QTesti-
monia 9–13). The messianic leader of the second Jewish revolt (AD 132–135)
was given the name "Bar Kokhba," meaning "Son of the Star." Christians
too interpreted the "star" from Balaam's prophecy as a messianic promise
that had been fulfilled in Christ. As noted above, John affirms this at the end
of the book of Revelation (22:16). The messianic understanding of the star
metaphor is also found in 2 Pet. 1:19, where not only is there an allusion to
Num. 24:17 ("until the day dawns and the morning star rises in your hearts"),
but also the allusion follows Peter's quotation two verses earlier of Ps. 2:7
and thus uses the same combination of OT texts as the sermon to Thyatira.
The early church fathers similarly interpreted the star in Balaam's prophecy
as a messianic prediction of the coming of Christ (Justin, *Dialogue with Trypho* 106.4; Hippolytus, *Commentary on Daniel* 1.9; Origen, *Against Celsus*
1.59–60). The messianic interpretation of Num. 24:17 appears to have been
well-known in both Jewish and Christian communities, and this likely serves
as the background for understanding John's use of the star metaphor. The
additional description of this star as a "morning" star may also stem from
Num. 24:17: it states that a star "will rise" (*anatelei*) from the house of Jacob,
and the cognate noun of this verb (*anatolē*) can have the meaning of "sunrise"
or "dawn" (BDAG 74.3; see Beale 1999: 269).

In light of these observations, the meaning of the second reward, being
given "the morning star," becomes clearer: the victorious ones in the Thyatiran church will share in the messianic rule of Christ. As Aune (1997: 212)
states: "The gift of the morning star must refer to the fact that the exalted
Christ shares his messianic status with the believer who conquers." Beale and
Campbell (2015: 75) likewise assert: "Therefore, the 'morning star' is a symbol associated with the messianic reign which has commenced with Christ's
resurrection. The application of this emblem to believers indicates that they
will participate in this reign if they overcome" (so also with varying degrees
of certainty: Mounce 1977: 107; Hemer 1986: 125, 128; Beale 1999: 268–69;
Kistemaker 2001: 142; Osborne 2002: 168; Wilson 2002: 270). This interpretation is supported by the parallel formed with the first reward: what is stated
literally as being given authority over the nations is also stated metaphorically
as being given the morning star.

Although the OT background of Balaam's prophecy in Num. 24:17 is
primary for understanding the meaning of "the morning star," this metaphor may also have some connection with the pagan context of that day. The
"morning star" in the Roman world was the planet Venus, which ancient writers considered to be a star (e.g., Pliny the Elder, *Natural History* 2; Cicero, *On*

the Nature of the Gods 2.53). Since Venus can be seen at dawn just before the rising of the sun, it became known as the "morning star"—the star that appears in the morning. Ever since Babylonian times, the star Venus was widely regarded as a symbol of victory and sovereignty and this was still true in the Roman period. All the emperors in the Julio-Claudian line followed the lead of Julius Caesar in claiming to be a descendant of the goddess Venus. The Roman legions carried her zodiac sign, the bull, on their standards. Since the Romans viewed the planet Venus, the "morning star," as a symbol of Rome's conquest and control over other nations, the gift of this symbol to victorious Christians involves a powerful polemic: the authority over the nations and a symbol of that authority, the morning star, belong not to Rome but to Christ, who shares his limitless rule with his faithful followers. After observing that the morning star "was a symbol of sovereignty in the ancient world and especially in Rome," Beale (1999: 269) similarly asserts that "the allusion to Numbers has been called forth in order to emphasize that Christ is the true world sovereign in contrast to the claims of evil world empires like Rome" (see also Beasley-Murray 1978: 93–94; Osborne 2002: 168; Wilson 2002: 270).

The Contemporary Significance

Introduction

There are several women in the Bible whose bad behavior warrants putting them in the notorious category of "bad girls of the Bible." But the "baddest" of these "bad girls" was a woman named Jezebel. Jezebel grew up as a princess, but her life was anything but a fairy tale. She was bad because she was married to a bad king—King Ahab of the Northern Kingdom of Israel. Jezebel was bad because she almost singlehandedly killed every prophet of Yahweh, the one true God. She was bad because she supported 450 prophets of the false god Baal and another 400 prophets of the false goddess Asherah. Jezebel was bad because she repeatedly tried to get rid of a pesky prophet of the Lord named Elijah. She was bad because she deviously had Naboth framed and executed, and then she seized control of Naboth's vineyard for her husband. But Jezebel was the "baddest" of the "bad girls of the Bible" because she introduced God's people to the worship of Baal and thus caused them to be guilty of idolatry.

What does Jezebel, the baddest girl of the Bible, have to do with the church of Thyatira? This congregation had a charismatic female teacher who was guilty of doing the same thing that Jezebel did: she was spreading a compromising theology that led some in the church of Thyatira to commit idolatry. John gives this false, self-proclaimed prophet the fitting nickname "Jezebel." And so, in our message today, I introduce you to the church of Thyatira, or, as it can be justly called, "the church of idolatrous compromise."

The Christ Title (2:18)

The first item in each of the sermons to the seven churches is the Christ title. Before Jesus directly addresses each church, he introduces himself with titles (normally two but in this sermon three) that foreshadow something important about the message he is about to give to each church. To understand the three Christ titles given to the church in Thyatira, you need to know the OT very well, and John clearly assumes that his ancient readers did.

The first Christ title is "the Son of God." Do you hear in this title the words of Ps. 2, where a descendant of David is identified as the son of God (Ps. 2:7)? Psalm 2 was well-known by the earliest Christians and cited repeatedly throughout the NT. John cites Ps. 2 here at the beginning of this sermon and at the end (2:27). The Jesus followers in Thyatira would know that the primary task of God's son in Ps. 2 is to judge all those who plot against God and his people. So they would recognize that this first title stresses Christ's role as *judge*.

The second and third titles also stress Christ's role as judge, because he is described as one "whose eyes are like a flame of fire and whose feet are like burnished bronze." Do you hear in these titles the words of Dan. 10? That's where one of the better-known visions of the prophet Daniel is found: the vision of a man from heaven whose outward appearance caused Daniel to be filled with terror, a man whose eyes were flaming like a fire and whose feet were shining like polished bronze. The primary task of this man from heaven in Dan. 10 is the same as the primary task of God's son in Ps. 2: to judge all those who plot against God and his people. The Christians in Thyatira would therefore know that these second and third titles also stress Christ's role as judge.

This image of Jesus as judge is sobering not only for the church in Thyatira but also for the church today. The one who is about to speak is the Son of God, whose primary task is to judge all those who plot against God and his people, whether they be a charismatic female teacher with the nickname Jezebel and her deceived followers or any other spiritual leader in the twenty-first century who similarly misleads God's people into committing idolatry. The one who is about to speak has "eyes like a flame of fire" that can see clearly into people's hidden motives and know whether their intentions are good or evil. The one who is about to speak has "feet like burnished bronze," which can easily stamp out any kind of opposition to his rule. This Jesus is not your Sunday-school Jesus, the kind of romanticized Jesus who has little children serenely sitting in his lap while baby lambs are frolicking all around. Instead, this Jesus is a judging ruler: the Son of God who speaks with divine authority and power. What will his judgment be concerning the church of Thyatira? What will his judgment be toward us?

The Commendation (2:19)

Before Jesus the judge brings a complaint against the church of Thyatira for what they are doing wrong, he commends this congregation for what they are doing right: "I know your deeds, namely, your love and faith and service and perseverance, and that your last deeds are greater than the first" (2:19). Jesus gives the thumbs-up sign as he says, "Great job, church of Thyatira! You've got not one, not two, not three, but four things for which I can commend you. What's more, you've managed to avoid the 'maintenance ministry mentality' that so many churches fall into. Instead of being satisfied with the status quo or simply resting on your laurels, you are doing even greater deeds than you did at first!"

The Complaint (2:20)

But any members of the church in Thyatira who might begin to stick their chests out in pride at Jesus's words of commendation would find such feelings short-lived. Jesus the judge immediately proceeds with his complaint: "But I have this against you: You tolerate the woman Jezebel, who calls herself a prophetess, and who teaches and deceives my servants to commit sexual immorality and to eat food sacrificed to idols" (2:20). Jesus uses his fiery eyes to see through the misleading teaching of Jezebel and her followers, and he identifies the true problem at work in the church: some congregational members are "eating food sacrificed to idols" and thus are guilty of idolatry. The false teaching of this charismatic female teacher is causing many to compromise their faith by participating in religious meals, with the result that the congregation in Thyatira can be called "the church of idolatrous compromise."

You likely remember, from the previous sermon to Pergamum, the important details about these religious meals. We learned that, when people brought a gift of meat to be sacrificed at a pagan temple, only a small portion of the meat would actually be sacrificed on the altar. The leftover meat was often taken by the worshipers to a dining room located within the pagan temple and then eaten as part of a meal. This was not a normal meal but a religious meal, and it was a popular part of pagan life. For Christians, however, these religious meals were strictly forbidden. If you as a Jesus follower participated in one of these religious meals, you would be participating in the worship of that pagan god on a level of intimacy that would make you guilty of idolatry. That's the heart of Christ's complaint against some in the Thyatiran church: they are "eating meat sacrificed to idols"; they are guilty of idolatry.

But Christ brings a second, closely connected complaint against the church in Thyatira: they are also "committing sexual immorality." From the previous sermon to Pergamum we learned that women were brought into these religious meals in order to provide entertainment, and this often led to sexual activity. So there was a close connection between the twin sins of eating food sacrificed to idols and committing sexual immorality.

These two sins are also linked in the account of the OT character of Jezebel, who is mentioned in Christ's complaint. Jezebel is first and foremost connected with the sin of idolatry. As we have already seen, Jezebel is the baddest of the bad girls of the Bible because she introduced God's people to the worship of Baal and therefore caused them to be guilty of idolatry. But she is also connected with the sin of sexual immorality. Although this sin is not highlighted as much as idolatry in the account of her life, the OT does refer to her sexual immoralities (2 Kings 9:22 LXX). What's more, Baal worship, which Jezebel introduced to Israel, was associated with sinful sexual conduct. As he did the church of Pergamum, Jesus the judge charges the church of Thyatira with the sin of idolatry and its closely related sin of sexual immorality.

There is another aspect to these religious meals, however, that we did not consider in the previous sermon to Pergamum. These meals took place not only as part of the worship in pagan temples but also as part of the social gatherings of *trade guilds*. Trade guilds were similar to modern-day unions, organizations formed by workers of a similar trade. Some of the many different trade guilds that we know existed in Thyatira included wool workers, leather workers, potters, bakers, shoemakers, and bronze workers. These trade guilds gathered regularly to share a common meal, which, in addition to the meal, involved a sacrifice of food to their patron god or goddess and often included sexual entertainment.

These trade guilds, and particularly the religious meals they hosted, posed a very serious dilemma for the Jesus followers in Thyatira and elsewhere by creating a conflict between religious commitment and economic survival. Christians probably reasoned something like this: "If we join the trade guilds and participate in their religious meals, then we'll be guilty of idolatry and sexual immorality. But if we don't join the trade guilds and don't participate in their religious meals, then we're committing economic suicide. How will we survive financially?!"

Addressing this situation, Jezebel, the charismatic female teacher and self-proclaimed prophet, probably said something like this: "I've got good news for you! You know something very important that most people do not. You know that there is only one true God—the God and Father of the Lord Jesus Christ. You know that all the different gods and goddesses worshiped in these religious meals don't really exist.

Since you have this important knowledge, there is no danger in your participating in these religious meals. You can be a Jesus follower *and* a member of these trade guilds!"

Sadly, many in the church of Thyatira found Jezebel's teaching convincing. Perhaps it was not even that hard for her to convince them. After all, many of us are simply looking for any reason at all, no matter how weak or lame it may be, to justify doing something that we want to do, even though deep down we know it is wrong. But for the church of Thyatira, Jesus the judge looks at the situation with his fiery eyes, sees what is really going on, and brings a just complaint against them: they have compromised their faith and are guilty first and foremost of idolatry.

The Correction for Jezebel and Her Followers (2:21)

The sermon to Thyatira has thus far followed the same outline found in all the other sermons: the Christ title, the commendation, and the complaint. The two remaining sections, the correction and the consequence, follow with a slight change: they address two different groups in the church. The correction and consequence for Jezebel and her followers comes first, followed by the correction and consequence for the rest of the church in Thyatira.

The correction directed to Jezebel and her followers goes like this: "I gave her time to repent, but she is not willing to repent of her immorality" (2:21). Every correction in the sermons to the seven churches involves a command to repent, so we are not surprised to find a reference to repentance here. But what is different and striking is that the reference to repentance occurs not in the present tense but in the *past* tense: at some earlier point, Jesus judged the teaching of Jezebel and her followers to be false and gave them time to repent. In other words, Jezebel and her followers cannot plead ignorance and say: "We didn't know that what we were saying and doing was wrong! We didn't know that it was sinful for us to attend these religious meals!" Jesus graciously gave them time to repent of their idolatry and sexual immorality, but they were "not willing."

Don't miss the significance of the little phrase "not willing." At the end of this message, we will be reflecting on the various idols in our own lives today—things that are interfering with our exclusive devotion to God. As we think about these contemporary idols and are challenged to repent of loving them too much, will we be like Jezebel and her followers, who were not willing to change? What makes an idol an idol in our lives is that we love it, it brings us happiness or comfort or meaning. Don't be naive about the powerful allure of our idols or about the control they can exert over our lives. Jezebel and her followers were graciously given the opportunity to repent, but they were "not willing." What about us? Christ is graciously giving us time to repent, give up our infatuation with worldly idols, and make God not merely the number one God in our lives but, more crucially, the *only* God in our lives. Are we willing to do this?

The Consequence (Negative) for Jezebel and Her Followers (2:22–23)

The sin of idolatry is serious, so it is not surprising that there is a very serious negative consequence for Jezebel and her followers who are participating in religious meals. Jesus the judge says: "I will throw her into a sickbed and those who commit adultery with her into great suffering" (2:22).

This verse contains a clever wordplay that you can't see in the English translation. The word "sickbed" in Greek literally refers to a couch—something on which people in the ancient world would recline. These couches were used during the religious meals, since people did not sit upright on a chair when they ate but reclined on a couch. These couches would also be used for sexual acts at these religious meals. Jesus says: "If you, Jezebel and others in the church, continue to lie on these couches for your idolatrous meals and your acts of sexual immorality, then I am going to take your 'party couch' and turn it into a 'sickbed'!"

But Jesus the judge will do even more: "And I will kill her children with disease" (2:23a). There will be a parallel between what happened to the OT Jezebel and her children and the NT Jezebel and her spiritual children in Thyatira. What ultimately happened to the baddest of the bad girls of the Bible? The OT Jezebel was pushed out of an upper-story window and landed on the road below like an overripe watermelon. Horses came along and trampled her underfoot; then dogs devoured her flesh so that there was nothing left of her body to bury (2 Kings 9:30–37). All of Jezebel's children—along with the other sons of her wicked husband, King Ahab—were decapitated; their heads were placed in baskets and stacked in two piles at the entrance to the city of Jezreel.

This negative consequence is indeed severe. Yet it sends a powerful message not only to the NT Jezebel and her followers in Thyatira but also to all those who take the sin of idolatry lightly. Jesus the judge continues: "And all the churches will know that I am the one who searches hearts and minds, and I will give to each one according to your works" (2:23b). Jesus is not only a judge but a *just* judge. His fiery eyes allow him to see what others cannot, to see what is hidden in our hearts and minds. Jesus knows whether our motives are true or false, and this allows him to give to each one of us what we justly deserve.

The Correction for the Rest of the Thyatiran Church (2:24–25)

After finishing his words of correction and consequence aimed at Jezebel and her followers, Jesus spells out the correction and consequence for the rest of the Thyatiran church: "But I say to you—to the rest, the ones in Thyatira who do not have this teaching, who do not know 'the deep things of Satan,' as they say—I will not impose any other burden on you. But hold on to what you have, until I come!" (2:24–25).

The key word in this correction is "burden." It occurs only a few times in the NT and reminds us of another place where this word occurs: the Apostolic Decree of Acts 15. You likely already know that Acts 15 describes the important meeting of the Jewish Christian leaders in Jerusalem, where they made a momentous decision: they decided that gentile Christians did not need to be circumcised. You perhaps do not know, however, that these Jewish Christian leaders in Jerusalem also made another momentous decision in their meeting: they decided to write a letter to gentile Christians everywhere saying that they did not want to impose any additional "burden" on them except for four things, and two of those four things were the sins of which the church of Thyatira was guilty: eating food sacrificed to idols and committing sexual immorality.

So when Jesus says to the rest of the Thyatiran church, "I will not impose any other *burden* on you," Jesus means, "I'm not asking you to do something unreasonable. The burden you are being asked to bear is what all my followers bear. All Christians must not eat food sacrificed to idols and so become guilty of idolatry. All Christians must not commit sexual immorality. I'm not putting on you any burden other than what all my followers willingly bear. Like you, they are commanded to 'hold on' and persevere in the face of the temptation to participate in the religious meals hosted by the trade guilds."

The Consequence (Positive) for the Rest of the Thyatiran Church (2:26–28)

As we would expect, the sermon to the church of Thyatira ends with the victory formula. Since this is now the fourth sermon containing a reference to the one who is "victorious," you likely remember that the Greek word for "victorious" is also the name of a popular sporting goods company, Nike. The idea is that, if we are using Nike sports equipment or wearing Nike clothes, we will be victorious—we will win!

The important question that our text raises is this: Are you a Nike Christian, that is, a victorious Christian? Are you able to overcome the sin of idolatry? The good news of the gospel is that the answer to that important question can be a resounding "Yes!" Yes, you and I can be Nike Christians and win the victory—not because we are so talented or so hard working, but because Christ has already won the victory and those who belong to Christ have his Spirit living in us. This divine Holy Spirit gives us the power to avoid the sin of idolatry and to not compromise our faith.

What is the reward of the Nike Christian? The positive consequence is described like this: "The one who is victorious and who keeps my works until the end, I will give to that one authority over the nations—and he will destroy them with an iron rod as ceramic pots are shattered—just as also I have received authority from my Father. And I will give to that one the morning star" (2:26–28). Two rewards are mentioned here. The first reward is described with many words while the second one is described with only a few, and the first reward alludes to Ps. 2:9 while the second reward alludes to Num. 24:17. But both rewards ultimately refer to the same thing: Nike Christians share in the messianic rule of Christ. God the Father has given Jesus authority over the nations, and here Jesus says to Nike Christians that they will share in this authority. Although they may now suffer from refusing to participate in idolatrous and sexually immoral meals, they will one day receive what God has already given to Christ, authority over the nations: they will share in the messianic rule of Christ!

Conclusion

In his book *Counterfeit Gods*, Tim Keller (2009: xiv) defines idolatry this way: "Idolatry means turning a good thing into an ultimate thing." It is a mistake to think that an idol is only something that is totally bad. The sin of idolatry is much more subtle than this. An idol is more often something that is good, but if that good thing becomes more important to our happiness, meaning in life, and identity than God, then we've turned that "good thing into an ultimate thing" and are guilty of idolatry. Again, an idol is more often something that is good, but if we pursue that good thing with a passion and devotion that ought to be reserved for God alone, then we've promoted that good thing into an ultimate thing and are guilty of idolatry.

Take, for example, sex. Sex is one of God's creational gifts and so is good. More precisely, sexual relations are good when they take place between a husband and a wife within the covenantal relationship of marriage. But if we use sex merely to satisfy our own selfish desires instead of as an expression of intimate love for our spouse, if we visit porn sites online and think that it's not a problem because no one is getting hurt, or if we are obsessed with having a certain kind of sexual experience or having sex with someone who is not our spouse, then we've turned a good thing into an ultimate thing and have become guilty of idolatry.

Work is a good thing. Adam and Eve worked in the garden before the fall, and work is one of God's good creational gifts. Work is a good way to use the talents that God has entrusted into our care, it is a good way to provide for ourselves and our families, and it is a good way for us to show in our public life that we are followers of Christ. But if we are obsessed with our job because we want it to bring us power, prestige, or money; if we work so hard that we don't spend time with God in prayer or in his Word; or if we pour so much energy and emotion into our job that we don't have any energy or emotion left for our spouse or children or others, then we've turned a good thing into an ultimate thing and are guilty of idolatry.

Under certain conditions, alcohol can be a good thing. A glass of fine wine to accompany a special meal or a cold refreshing beer on a hot summer day can be a good thing. But if we believe that it's impossible to have a fun time without including booze, if we use alcohol to help us get through the hard times of life (they don't call it "Southern Comfort" for nothing), or if we can't control how much we drink, then we've turned a good thing into an ultimate thing and have become guilty of idolatry.

Self-esteem or self-worth is a good thing. Each of us bears God's image and has value and importance, and having a healthy sense of self-worth is a good thing. But if we go through life with an exaggerated sense of our own importance; if the three most important people in our lives are "Me, Myself, and I"; or if we go into any situation with the mentality that "It's all about me," then we've turned a good thing into an ultimate thing and have become guilty of idolatry.

Family is a good thing. God has created us as social beings who need the presence and support of others, and so it is wonderful to be part of a family, to enjoy the love and support of a spouse or parent or children. But if we let our family relationships become more important than our relationship with God and what he has called us to believe and do, if we view singles as being second-class citizens compared to us who are married, or if we put the commitment to our genetic family members above our commitment to our spiritual family members, the church, then we've turned a good thing into an ultimate thing and have become guilty of idolatry.

Dear friends: Have you turned a good thing in your life into an ultimate thing? Is there something in your life that has become more important to your happiness, your sense of meaning in life, or your identity than God? Are you pursuing something with the passion and devotion that ought to be reserved for God alone? In contrast to Jezebel and her followers, who were unwilling to repent, are you willing to repent and identify the thing that has become an idol in your life? Pray that Christ will send his Spirit so that you can become a Nike Christian and overcome the sin of idolatry.

"Whoever has ears to hear, let them hear what the Spirit is saying to the churches!"—not only to the ancient church of Thyatira but also to the church of Jesus Christ today.

5

Sardis

The Church of Deadly Complacency

The Christ Title (3:1a)

The sermon to Sardis contains two Christ titles: it identifies Jesus as "the one who has the seven spirits of God and the seven stars." The phrase "the seven spirits of God" occurs nowhere else in the Bible except for three additional times in the book of Revelation: 1:4 (but without the possessive "of God"), 4:5, and 5:6. The cryptic nature of this uncommon phrase has caused some debate over its intended meaning.

The two main proposals are that "the seven spirits of God" refer either (1) to seven angels or (2) to the Holy Spirit. The first proposal identifies the seven spirits with the seven angels referred to later in the book of Revelation (seven angels are connected with the seven bowls, trumpets, and plagues: 8:2; 15:1, 6–8; 16:1) or with the seven (arch)angels referred to in some Jewish writings (1 En. 20.1–8; 2 En. 19.1–3; Tob. 12:15; 2 Esd. [4 Ezra] 4:1; so, e.g., Charles 1920: 12–13; Krodel 1989: 83; Aune 1997: 34–36). According to this view, the main idea of the first Christ title is that Christ "has" these spirits in the sense not merely of possession but rather of authority/control over them. Against this view, however, is the fact that nowhere else in the book of Revelation is "spirit" used as a clear reference to "angel," and there is no compelling explanation for why John would do so here, especially since the word "angel" appears frequently (67×) throughout the book.

A few advocates of this "seven spirits = seven angels" proposal have further defended their view by claiming that there are not two Christ titles but one: the "and" located between the two titles is not conjunctive but explanatory, so that the Christ title should read: "the seven spirits of God, *namely*, the seven stars" (see, e.g., the NEB translation; Caird 1966: 48; Aune 1997: 215). Furthermore, since 1:20 informs us that the seven stars are the seven angels of the seven churches, "the seven spirits of God" must ultimately refer to the seven angels of the seven churches. But though the explanatory use of "and" does occur with some frequency in the seven sermons, it never does so elsewhere among the Christ titles. Even more persuasive is the fact that in the Ephesus sermon "the seven stars" is used as a distinct Christ title separate from and not explained by "the seven golden lampstands" (2:1), and this is most likely the way it functions in the Sardis sermon as well.

The second proposal identifies "the seven spirits" with the Holy Spirit, and the strongest support for this view is the previous use of this phrase in the opening greeting of the book of Revelation: "Grace and peace to you from him who is and who was and who is to come, and *from the seven spirits who are before his throne*, and from Jesus Christ, the faithful witness, the firstborn of the dead, and the ruler of the kings of the earth" (1:4). The reference to "the seven spirits" between the mention of God the Father and God the Son requires that the expression be understood to refer to God the Holy Spirit. Some have tried to minimize this evidence by citing two texts where the Father and Son are mentioned in the same breath in connection with angels rather than the Holy Spirit: "in the presence of God and of Christ and of the elect angels" (1 Tim. 5:21); "when he [Christ] comes in his glory and the glory of the Father and of the holy angels" (Luke 9:26). However, these parallels are not exact; their force is weakened by at least two differences. First, angels clearly rank below God and Jesus in terms of authority, so angels are appropriately mentioned last in the texts from Paul and Luke, whereas "the seven spirits" stands between the mention of God and Jesus. Second, Rev. 1:4 speaks not just of the seven spirits being present with God and Jesus (1 Tim. 5:21) or of participating in their glory (Luke 9:26) but of giving grace and peace, divine gifts that only a full member of the Trinity can give.

The earlier use of the uncommon phrase "the seven spirits" in 1:4, therefore, allows us to say with confidence that also in 3:1 this same phrase refers to the Holy Spirit. As Sweet (1979: 98) states, "'The seven spirits' are functionally the same as 'the Holy Spirit.'" It is less certain, however, *why* John refers to the Holy Spirit in this cryptic way. Why not simply use the word

"Spirit," as he does elsewhere (14×) in the book of Revelation? (The terms "Spirit of God" and "Holy Spirit" never occur in this document.) Some take the number seven literally so that "the seven spirits" refers to the one Holy Spirit who is at work in each of the seven churches (Swete 1911: 5–6; Allo 1933: 9; see also Beale 1999: 189). Others take the number seven symbolically as a reference to completeness so that "the seven spirits" refers to the fullness and perfection of the work of the Holy Spirit (Seiss 1909: 1.45; Cowley 1983: 186; Kistemaker 2001: 150).

However, most commentators see an OT allusion in the reference to "the seven spirits." The LXX translation of Isa. 11:2–3 describes seven spirits of God that will be evident in the future king who comes from the branch of Jesse: "And the Spirit of God will rest on him—the Spirit of wisdom and of understanding, the Spirit of counsel and of might, the Spirit of knowledge and of godliness will fill him, the Spirit of the fear of God." The likelihood of this connection is weakened by the fact that only six spirits are mentioned in all the Hebrew versions of Isa. 11:2–3 (i.e., the MT, the Qumran Isaiah scroll, and rabbinic literature). Also, the LXX version breaks the poetic parallelism of three couplets by adding "of godliness" to the third couplet, thus providing additional evidence that it does not reflect the original form of this important messianic text. Yet throughout the book of Revelation, John's OT allusions frequently reflect the LXX text, so it is plausible that he is also doing so here. Furthermore, the LXX version of Isa. 11:2–3, with its seven spirits rather than six, was known in both early Judaism (1 En. 61.11) and early Christianity (see the texts cited by Aune 1997: 33), making it likely that John also knew of the seven-spirits version of this OT text and alluded to it here in the first Christ title. John's reference to the "root of David" in Rev. 5:5 is an allusion to Isa. 11:1, so clearly he was familiar with the text of Isa. 11, making it more probable that he was also thinking of it in the Christ title of 3:1.

Another less obvious but possible OT origin for John's use of the phrase "the seven spirits of God" is Zech. 4:1–14. In the remaining two places in Revelation where the phrase "the seven spirits of God" occurs, the seven spirits are equated with "the seven lamps of fire" (4:5) and with "the seven eyes" that are "sent out into all the earth" (5:6). These same two items—seven lamps and seven eyes—are mentioned together in Zech. 4:1–14 (4:2, 10) along with the idea that the seven eyes "look upon all the earth" (4:10 LXX). Between the references to the seven lamps and the seven eyes is this statement about the Spirit: "This is the word of the LORD to Zerubbabel: 'Not by might, nor by power, but by my Spirit,' says the LORD Almighty" (Zech. 4:6). God is asserting that the Jerusalem temple will be rebuilt not merely through human agency but through divine help, through the power of God's Spirit. Although several commentators find the proposed allusion to Zechariah in the first Christ title compelling (so, e.g., Caird 1966: 15; Ladd 1972: 25; Beasley-Murray 1978: 55; Hemer 1986: 142; Thomas 1992: 68), others believe that these claimed parallels are "artificial and unconvincing" (Aune 1997: 34). Admittedly, the proposed links to Zech. 4:1–14 are less clear than the allusion to Isa. 11:2–3, making the Isaiah text the more likely origin of the reference to "the seven spirits of God" (some allow for the possibility that both OT texts are in view: Beale 1999: 189–90; Osborne 2002: 61; Fanning 2020: 161).

What does it mean, then, for Christ to identify himself first to the church in Sardis as "the one who has the seven spirits of God"? Based on the earlier use of this uncommon phrase in 1:4, it means that Christ has the Holy Spirit. Since the two main workings of the Spirit in contemporary Judaism were to inspire prophecy and to give life to what is dead, Christ is saying that the dying or dead church in Sardis needs to hear and heed the prophetic warning in this sermon (note the concluding refrain in this and every sermon: "Let the one who has ears hear what the Spirit is saying to the churches") and seek from him the life-giving power of the Holy Spirit (Beasley-Murray 1978: 94–95; see also Thomas 1992: 246). If "the seven spirits of God" involves an allusion to Isa. 11:2–3, Christ is also asserting his status as the promised messianic king, who has seven spirits or qualities that are divine in origin and a source of blessing to God's people. For the church in Sardis, this means that Christ as the messianic king offers to this dying or dead congregation the reviving presence of the Holy Spirit, which it desperately needs in order to live again.

Christ further identifies himself as "the one who has . . . the seven stars." This Christ title repeats one found in the sermon to Ephesus, but it lacks two features of the earlier message that emphasized Christ's power: (1) here we find the softer verb "he has" (as also is the case in the opening vision of Christ in 1:9–20) rather than the stronger expression "he holds"; and (2) the seven stars are not said to be "in his right hand." This is the only place where a Christ title is repeated. Some titles from the vision of Christ in 1:9–20 never appear in any of the sermons (e.g., "a robe reaching down to his feet," "a golden sash around his chest," "hair as white as snow-white wool," "a voice like the sound of rushing waters"), which suggests that this repetition of "the seven stars" is deliberate and especially relevant to the situation in Sardis.

We examined the meaning of "the seven stars" in detail in the Ephesian sermon (see chap. 1, "The Christ Title [2:1b]"), so here we can simply review our earlier conclusions. The "seven stars" are "the angels of the seven churches" (1:20), most likely referring to the guardian angel of each congregation. By asserting his control over the guardian angel of the church of Sardis, Christ asserts his sovereignty over the Sardis church itself. As Osborne (2002: 173) puts it: "Christ's controlling the seven stars (angels) suggests that through their angel Christ controls the church, and it must answer to him alone."

The authority of Christ that is spotlighted in this second Christ title likely also involves a polemic against Rome and its assertion of power. The Roman emperors frequently depicted themselves and their family members on coinage as demigods whose power extended beyond earth to control the planets and the stars (see figs. 1.1 and 1.2 in the Ephesus sermon). This repeated mention of Christ holding "the seven stars" represents a challenge to Roman power and "the pretensions of Roman emperors who asserted their cosmic rule with symbols of planets surrounding them" (Krodel 1989: 95).

The Commendation—None!

In each of the four preceding sermons, the Christ title is immediately followed by the commendation, the unit where Christ praises the church for what they are doing well. In every case the transition to this new unit is signaled by the simple formula, "I know." Thus it is no surprise to hear Christ say to the believers in Sardis and any others who are listening "I know your works." However, what comes next is surprising and significant, since the words that follow are not a commendation but a complaint: "I know your works, namely, you have a reputation of being alive, but you are dead" (3:1b). The situation in the Sardis church is so serious that Christ is not able to give any words of commendation about them. Just as the omission of the complaint section in the Smyrna sermon highlights how *positively* Christ regarded that congregation, so here the omission of the commendation section in the Sardis sermon highlights how *negatively* Christ regards this congregation. Paul's Letter to the Galatians provides a literary parallel to the Sardis sermon: Paul is so concerned about the spiritual health of the Galatian believers that he omits his usual thanksgiving section and replaces it with a rebuke section (Gal. 1:6–10).

The omission of the commendation section as well as Christ's description of the Sardis church as "dead" might lead to the conclusion that it is the worst of the seven churches. Mounce (1977: 109), for example, states, "The church at Sardis comes under the most severe denunciation of the seven." Witherington (2003: 105) similarly claims, "This message is the most strongly negative of the seven." But though the sermon to Sardis involves the harshest judgment of the seven messages thus far, the "honor" of being the worst church belongs to Laodicea, the only other congregation not to receive any words of commendation. In addition to Christ declaring the Laodiceans to be "wretched, pitiable, poor, blind, and naked" (3:17), he says they make him want to throw up (3:16). The placement of Laodicea in the seventh and climactic position confirms its status as the worst of the seven churches.

Another reason Sardis does not qualify as the worst church is that, though it fails to earn any *commendation* from Christ, it does receive from him an important *concession*: "But you have a few people in Sardis who have not soiled their clothes, and they will walk with me in white, because they are worthy" (3:4). Within this dying or dead church exist a "few people"—an important minority—who do not come under the harsh judgment that Christ has for the congregation as a whole. The Greek text actually does not use the phrase "a few people" but "a few names." This is noteworthy because the word "name" (*onoma*) occurs four times within this brief, six-verse sermon:

3:1b   "You have a *name* [i.e., reputation] of being alive, but you are dead."

3:4a   "You have a few *names* [persons] in Sardis who have not soiled their clothes."

3:5b   "I will never erase the *name* of that person from the book of life."

3:5c   "I will confess the *name* of that person before my Father and before his angels."

The repetition of this Greek word not only gives lexical coherence to the literary unit of 3:1–6 but also functions as an important thread, tying together its central message. Only those who do not complacently base their salvation on the "name" (the past reputation of the church) and who are counted among the "few names" who have lived distinctively moral lives will have their name written in the book of life and be named by Christ, who advocates their case before his Father, the heavenly judge.

In contrast to the majority of the congregation, this minority within the Sardis church is identified as having "not soiled their clothes." Clothes were a common metaphor in the ancient world for one's moral and spiritual condition: white or clean clothes symbolized ethical and religious purity, whereas soiled clothes signified immoral and irreligious conduct. All participants in pagan cultic activity wore white, not just the priests, and worshipers would not dare to come into the temple and the presence of their god in soiled clothes (so Keener 2000: 144n15, who cites Josephus, *Jewish War* 2.1; Josephus, *Ant.* 11.327; Philo, *Contemplative Life* 66; Euripides, *Bacchanals* 112; Pausanias, *Description of Greece* 2.35.5; 6.20.3; Diogenes Laertius, *Lives* 8.1.33). Roman political candidates wore a *toga candida*, a "whitened toga" bleached dazzling white with chalk to signify their virtue and honesty. The Bible also frequently uses white apparel with positive connotations: martyrs in heaven are given "white robes" (Rev. 6:11; 7:9, 13–14), God on his throne wears white (Dan. 7:9), Jesus's clothes become white at his transfiguration (Matt. 17:2), and heavenly messengers often appear in white garments (Matt.

28:3; John 20:12; Acts 1:10; Rev. 4:4; 19:14). The Bible conversely uses dirty apparel with negative connotations: the prophet Zechariah has a vision of Joshua the priest dressed in filthy clothes, symbolizing the sins of both the priest and the people (Zech. 3:1–5).

It is difficult to determine the specific immoral or irreligious conduct that the few members of the Sardis church avoided in order not to dirty their clothes. The verb "soil" (*molynō*) is used only three times in the NT: once here to refer literally to the staining or soiling of clothes (though the resulting phrase "they have not stained their clothes" involves a metaphor) and twice elsewhere with the figurative sense of "to cause something to be ritually impure, *defile*" (BDAG 657.2). This figurative sense is found in Rev. 14:4, where the 144,000 "did not defile themselves with women" (i.e., the sin of sexual immorality with the possible metaphorical meaning of idolatry), and in 1 Cor. 8:7, where the conscience of the one eating meat sacrificed to idols (i.e., the sin of idolatry) "is defiled." Since both these sins are explicitly identified in the immediately preceding sermons of Pergamum and Thyatira, it is tempting to see sexual immorality and idolatry as the source of defilement among most members of the Sardis church, in contrast to the few who avoided it (see Charles 1920: 81; Beale 1999: 276). Nevertheless, neither sin is explicitly mentioned, and both the complaint (3:1b) and the correction (3:2–3a) are vague in identifying the "works" that Christ finds inadequate, so this interpretation cannot be asserted with confidence.

The clothing metaphor used in the first half of the concession (3:4a) is continued and combined with a "walking" metaphor in the second half (3:4b): "and they will walk with me in white." Some (e.g., Aune 1997: 222) have seen an allusion to Enoch and Noah; during their long earthly lives both "walked with God" (Gen. 5:22; 6:9), which seems to refer to an intimate, unmediated, and thus blessed relationship to God. The Septuagint translation of these two OT texts, however, refers to their pleasing God and so removes the metaphor of walking, making it unlikely that John has this idea in view. Others (e.g., Swete 1911: 51; Mounce 1977: 112; Kistemaker 2001: 153) claim an allusion to the itinerant ministry of Jesus throughout Galilee and Judea, where walking with Jesus conveys the idea of not just fellowship with him but also discipleship (see John 6:66; 8:12). More find compelling the proposal of Ramsay (1904: 386–87) that "walking with me" is intended to evoke the image of a Roman triumph parade celebrating an important military victory. The emperor was accompanied by a procession of leading Roman citizens wearing pure white togas (so also, e.g., Ford 1975: 413; Hemer 1986: 147; Worth 1999: 190–91; Osborne 2002: 179). Although believers in Sardis and Asia Minor would not have witnessed such triumphs firsthand, since they took place only in Rome, they would likely know of them through either eyewitnesses or written accounts. Juvenal (*Satires* 10.45), for example, describes a triumphal procession to Rome's Circus Maximus: "Trumpets before, and on the left and the right; a cavalcade of nobles, all in white." Local processions in Asia were likely modeled on Roman triumphs. Paul was confident that his readers in Corinth and Colossae were sufficiently familiar with a triumphal procession because he evokes it as a metaphor in his letters to them (2 Cor. 2:14; Col. 2:15). The minority of church members in Sardis who had not compromised their faith were, therefore, worthy to be the white-clothed attendants of the victorious Christ, walking with him in his triumphal procession.

The Complaint (3:1b)

Christ's concession that there are a few in Sardis who have not soiled their clothes and so are worthy to walk with him in his triumphal procession does not come, however, until near the end of the sermon. What the original readers are instead confronted with immediately after the opening Christ title is not the expected commendation, which is here strikingly absent, but the complaint. Christ's words begin promisingly enough in the main clause, "I know your works," which is how all the previous commendations began (2:2, 19; see also 3:8, 15; cf. 2:9, 13, which have "I know" with a different object). In the subsequent explanatory clause, however, things take an unanticipated turn: "namely, you have a reputation of being alive, but you are dead" (3:1b).

This complaint, which is shorter and blunter than any other in the sermons, distinguishes between reputation and reality: the Sardis church has a reputation for being alive, but in reality it has become so complacent about its faith that Christ judges it to be spiritually dead. In this first of four occurrences of the word "name," which plays a key role in the sermon, it has the rarer sense of "reputation" (BDAG 714.4: "recognition accorded a person on the basis of performance, *[well known] name, reputation, fame*"; see also 1 Chron. 14:17 LXX; 1 Macc. 8:12; Mark 6:14). It is clear, then, that the Sardis church in the past gave evidence of their faith in such obvious ways that they earned the respect of the surrounding churches and developed a reputation for being a healthy, vibrant congregation. Sadly, however, this reputation no longer matches reality, as Christ succinctly and straightforwardly states: "but you are dead."

Christ provides no further explanation for his sobering assessment and so leaves unanswered the question of what specifically the believers in Sardis were doing wrong. The problem, however, can be inferred from the correction in 3:2–3a and concession in 3:4, though the general nature of these comments requires that any reconstruction of the situation remain tentative. The first command, "Be watchful!"—emphasized by its location, its grammatical construction (see comment on 3:2a), and its repetition later in the sermon (cf. 3:2a and 3:3b)—suggests that the Sardis church is complacent about their Christian faith and not alert to the dangers of living in a pagan culture hostile to the exclusive claims of the gospel. Christ's explanatory statement, "For I have not found your works complete in the presence of my God," implies that the conduct of the Sardis church is clearly not appropriate, though it remains unclear what kind of sinful conduct is in view. The concession that a few congregational members have not "soiled their clothes" (3:4) means that the majority of the church has engaged in immoral behavior. Elsewhere in Scripture, the rare verb "soiled" (*molynō*; see the previous section) refers to the sins of sexual immorality and idolatry (eating food sacrificed to idols), the two sins explicitly identified in Christ's complaint against the churches of Pergamum and Thyatira. Although the pagan culture of that day meant that the believers in Sardis would surely also face these same two common issues, neither one is explicitly mentioned, and so the problem should be identified more broadly as one of complacency—a seemingly innocuous problem yet in reality so dangerous that, in Christ's judgment, it has led to spiritual death.

In the complaint that the church of Sardis had a reputation for being alive but in reality was now dead, Ramsay (1904: 365–77) saw an allusion to the history of the city. Sardis was widely recognized as a once-powerful city, whose glory days were now well in the past and whose prestige had declined dramatically. Beale (1999: 272–73) is one of several later commentators who also see this allusion: "Just as the city in general was living off a former but no longer existing fame, so the same attitude had infected the church" (see also, e.g., Moffatt 1910: 364; Peake 1919: 249; Charles 1920: 78; A. Johnson 1981: 448; Hemer 1986: 143). Of the seven cities addressed in Revelation, Sardis was the oldest and most famous. In AD 26, when the eleven cities of Asia Minor were competing for the privilege of being designated *neōkoros* and host of the imperial cult, the delegation from Sardis appealed to its noble history (Tacitus, *Annals* 4.55.7–8). Sardis remained an important city in NT times, but among the seven cities of Revelation, it was the one that had fallen farthest from its former glory, offering a fitting comparison to the situation of the church in Sardis. Seeing an allusion here to the city's history and its decline from its previous prestige gains further support from another historical allusion found in this sermon: the famous capture of its supposedly unconquerable acropolis (see "The Correction" below for further details).

The Correction (3:2–3a)

Christ's serious complaint against the Sardis church might lead us to conclude that there is no hope that this spiritually complacent congregation will recover. However, the fact that this sermon includes a correction suggests that it is not too late for grace to have a life-changing effect. Christ has not given up on the church in Sardis and offers words of correction so that this dying congregation may yet be restored to life. We must regard the verdict that this church is dead as "a figurative overstatement (hyperbole) intended to emphasize the church's precarious spiritual state and the imminent danger of its genuine death" (Beale 1999: 273).

Christ's correction consists of five imperatives. The first imperative is the most important because it heads the list. Its grammatical construction (a periphrastic expression using the supplementary verb *ginomai* instead of the expected *eimi*) expresses a greater emphasis than the simple imperative forms found in the four subsequent commands (see Porter 1992: 46; Fanning 2020: 163n10). Also, it is the only one of the five imperatives that is repeated later in the sermon (3:3b). This first command is commonly translated "Wake up!" It rarely has the literal sense of waking from sleep, however, but usually bears the figurative meaning of being "in constant readiness, *be on the alert*" (BDAG 208.2) and so is better rendered "Be watchful!" The verb *grēgoreō* often occurs in the context of end-time discussions to stress the need for believers to be vigilant and prepared for the return of Christ (Matt. 24:42; 25:13; Mark 13:35, 37; Luke 12:37; 1 Thess. 5:6; Rev. 16:15). Its present-tense form here stresses the ongoing nature of the action and so emphasizes the need for the Sardis church to live in a state of constant watchfulness. The stress on this opening command implies that the fundamental problem facing this congregation was complacency, not being vigilant about the all-too-real dangers threatening the church's life.

In the emphatic double reference to being "watchful" (3:2, 3a) and the upcoming reference to Christ's coming "like a thief" (3:3b), most commentators see a clear allusion to a tradition about Croesus, king of Lydia (560–547 BC), and the capture of the acropolis at his capital Sardis. Croesus became legendary for several reasons. First, he was famous for his wealth, particularly the vast amount of gold he mined from the sands of the nearby Pactolus River, where the mythical king Midas washed his hands to rid himself of the "Midas Touch." Croesus's renowned wealth is evident in his funding of the Artemis temple construction in Ephesus, one of the seven wonders of the ancient world. Well after NT times, the church father Clement of Alexandria (AD ca. 150–ca. 212) alludes to Croesus's riches in his claim that it was impossible to

Figure 5.1. Artemis temple in Sardis, with the city's acropolis in the background.

buy eternal salvation even with all the gold of the Pactolus River (*Exhortation to the Greeks* 9.71).

Another reason Croesus's life was universally known and repeatedly recounted was his arrogance and complacency, which led to the capture of his supposedly impregnable acropolis at Sardis. When Croesus asked the Delphic oracle whether he should wage war against the Persian king Cyrus, he received this answer: "On the day you cross the River Halys [into Persian territory], you will surely destroy a great empire." Mistakenly concluding that the oracle was guaranteeing his victory, Croesus attacked the Persians, which did indeed lead to his destroying a great empire, his own. After an initial battle with Cyrus ended in a draw, Croesus withdrew for the winter season to his 1,500-foot-high acropolis at Sardis, which was widely believed to be unconquerable. Even centuries later, "to capture the acropolis of Sardis" was proverbially "to do the impossible" (Hemer 1986: 133).

Cyrus surprised Croesus by disregarding military convention and not withdrawing for the winter season. Instead, Cyrus went to Sardis and besieged the city. Croesus demonstrated his arrogance by naively trusting in his supposedly unconquerable acropolis to protect him. He was so confident in the safety of his acropolis that he did not even bother posting guards on its steepest section. The ancient historian Herodotus informs us that a Persian soldier managed to scale the cliff of the acropolis "where there was no guard stationed, for there was no fear that it would ever be captured at that place, for the acropolis is sheer and impregnable there" (*Histories* 1.84). The Persian soldier and others who followed him then opened the city gates from the inside, and Sardis was captured after a mere fourteen-day siege. Thus the complacency of Croesus led to the destruction of his kingdom.

The story of how the acropolis at Sardis was conquered and other details of Croesus's life became so well-known in the ancient world that there developed what can justly be called a "Croesus tradition," stories repeatedly retold not merely for entertainment but also for education. Teachers warned their students to avoid his example of pride and complacency. Aune (1997: 220) observes: "The moral lessons derived from this series of events [in the Croesus tradition] (one must avoid pride, arrogance and over-confidence and be prepared for unexpected reversals of fortune) became a *topos* for later historians and moralists."

The second capture of the Sardis acropolis increased the notoriety of these events. Three centuries after the Persians did what was believed to be impossible in fourteen days, Antiochus III (the Great) and his army besieged the city in 215 BC for over a year without success. As the attacking army was losing hope of success, a soldier named Lagoras, from the island of Crete, took advantage of Sardis's overconfidence and complacency. According to ancient historian Polybius, Lagoras "had considerable experience in war and had learned that as a rule cities fall into the hands of their enemies most easily from some neglect on the part of their inhabitants, when, trusting to the natural or artificial strength of their defenses, they neglect to keep proper guard and become thoroughly careless" (*Histories* 7.15.2). Noticing that birds were regularly resting on one section of the city wall, Lagoras concluded that this section must be unguarded. After waiting for a moonless night, he climbed the cliff of the acropolis at the unguarded spot, accompanied by fifteen select men, entered the fortress, and opened the gates from the inside, allowing two thousand soldiers to enter the city and capture Sardis a second time by a sneak attack.

The story of the double capture of the acropolis at Sardis due to the city's complacency and lack of vigilance was so

Figure 5.2. *Left*: Wreathed head of Antiochus III (223–187 BC). *Right*: Inscription "King Antiochus" with an image of the god Apollo testing an arrow in his right hand and holding a bow in his left hand. He is sitting on the Delphi omphalos, or navel, marking Delphi as the center of the world.

well-known in the ancient world that many commentators believe it is behind Christ's warning to the church at Sardis to "Be watchful!" Ladd (1972: 56), for example, states, "This admonition was particularly relevant in Sardis, for in the city was an impregnable acropolis which had never been seized by frontal attack; twice, however, in the history of the city, the acropolis had been taken by stealth because of lack of vigilance on the part of its defenders." Mounce (1977: 110–11) similarly asserts, "The exhortations to watchfulness would carry special weight in Sardis because twice in its history the acropolis had fallen to the enemy due to a lack of vigilance on the part of the defenders. . . . As in history, so in life, to consider oneself secure and fail to remain alert is to court disaster."

A few scholars have questioned whether the fall of Sardis's acropolis is being alluded to here. Wood (1961–62: 264) states, "Perhaps the Christians in Sardis would have found the words under consideration a less obvious reference to historical disasters, from three to five hundred years previous, than we now suppose. It is extremely doubtful if the defeat of Napoleon, so used, would cut much ice with the French Church today!" Ramsey Michaels (1997: 82) asserts that this allusion is "unlikely because (1) these incidents were centuries earlier; (2) the message is to the Christian congregation, not the city of Sardis; (3) the image of the thief in connection with a command to 'watch' or 'stay awake' was common in early Christianity, based on the well-known sayings of Jesus (see Matt. 24:43–44 par. Luke 12:39–40; 1 Thess. 5:2). The warning could as easily have been directed to Ephesus or Laodicea, or to the unfaithful in any congregation."

Responding to such challenges, Hemer (1972–73) cataloged the abundant references to the Croesus tradition in the ancient world, including references to his wealth, his misinterpretation of the Delphic oracle, his battle with Cyrus, his mounting the funeral pyre, and especially the fall of his supposedly unconquerable acropolis. These ancient references date to the first and second century AD (and thus overlap with the date of the book of Revelation) and are found in Christian and Jewish writings as well as pagan sources. Furthermore, these references are so numerous that one can justly refer to the Croesus tradition and its proverbial character. As Hemer (1986: 133) puts it: "The case for seeing historical allusion in the letter to Sardis is related to an appreciation of the formative and proverbial character of the [Croesus] event. It is impracticable to reproduce the literary evidence in the present study: there is far too much of it."

The second of the five commands that make up the sermon's correction section consists of the following exhortation: "Strengthen what remains and is about to die." The verb used here (*stērizō*) literally refers to putting something firmly in place but in the NT normally has the figurative sense of being emotionally or spiritually strong in the face of some internal struggle or external obstacle (BDAG 945.2: "to cause to be inwardly firm or committed"; see Luke 22:32; Acts 18:23 [where the compound form *epistērizō* occurs]; Rom. 1:11; 16:25; 1 Thess. 3:2, 13; 2 Thess. 2:17; 3:3; James 5:8; 1 Pet. 5:10; 2 Pet. 1:12). There is uncertainty about what the Sardis church needs to strengthen. The neuter form of the direct object *ta loipa* suggests that it refers not to people but to things, specifically, the works that Jesus finds to be deficient, mentioned in the immediately following clause. However, the relative clause describing these remaining things as "which are about to die" suggests that it refers to people (since it is people, not works, who typically die), specifically the few names of the congregation "who have not soiled their clothes" (3:4a). According to Aune (1997: 216), the assumption that neuter adjectives refer only to nonliving things is incorrect, and he cites 1 Cor. 1:27–28 and Heb. 7:7 in support. Perhaps there is justification, then, in following those commentators who argue that the neuter object refers to both people and works: the Sardis church is commanded to strengthen both the minority within their congregation who are dying but not yet dead and the works that ought to accompany a healthy, living church (so, e.g., Charles 1920: 79; Thomas 1992: 249; Kistemaker 2001: 151; Osborne 2002: 174–75).

The reason for issuing the first two commands is spelled out in an explanatory clause: "For I have not found your works complete in the presence of my God." In the book of Revelation and throughout the NT, the verb "to find" (*heuriskō*) often has a juridical meaning in which someone is "found" to be either guilty or innocent (Rev. 2:2; 5:4; 12:8; 14:5; 20:15; Acts 5:39; 23:9; 1 Cor. 15:15; 2 Cor. 5:3; 1 Pet. 1:7; 2 Pet. 3:14). The image evoked with this verb and emphasized with the use of the perfect tense, therefore, is of the members of the Sardis church standing in the divine courtroom before God, the ultimate judge, and hearing Christ, as God's prosecuting attorney, bring a damning charge against them: their works are not complete. (This legal scene is recalled later in the sermon, in 3:5c: "I will acknowledge the name of that person before my Father and before his angels.") It is not stated what kind of works are in view, but the later references to soiled versus white clothing (3:4a, 4b, 5a)—a common metaphor in the ancient world for one's moral and spiritual condition—strongly suggest that Christ is referring to the ethical and religious conduct of the Sardis church. The overall problem of complacency that characterizes this congregation is revealing itself concretely in works that, despite being sufficient to garner them a positive reputation among fellow believers, are judged to be deficient before God and Christ.

The third, fourth, and fifth commands are set apart from the previous two by the inferential particle "therefore" (*oun*), showing that these imperatives come as a result of the preceding commands: if the believers in Sardis are to be watchful and to strengthen what remains, then they must do these three things. The third command that Christ gives the complacent Sardis church is "Remember, therefore, what you have received and heard." Memory about one's own past can be a powerful agent for moral change. For example, when the prodigal son was so hungry that he longed to eat the food he was feeding the pigs, he remembered his former life of abundance at home, "came to his senses," and returned home repentant and prepared to ask for his father's forgiveness (Luke 15:17–18). In an effort to help unify the Ephesian church, which was badly divided along ethnic lines over the issue of circumcision, Paul commands his gentile readers to "remember" their former status of being "separate from Christ, excluded from citizenship in Israel and foreigners to the covenants of the promise, without hope and without God in the world" (Eph. 2:11–12). The church in Sardis is called upon to remember specifically "what you have received and heard." In other words, they must go back to the basics and recall the gospel message that was first shared with them when their congregation was founded.

The verb "received" likely functions here as a technical term for the reception (and passing on) of confessional or traditional material. Paul, for example, introduces what is likely a confession about Christ's death and resurrection in 1 Cor. 15:3b–5 with the words "For I passed on to you as of first importance what I also *received*" (15:3a). This verb choice signals that the apostle did not produce the words about Christ's death and resurrection himself but rather "received" them as a confessional formula sometime after his conversion to Christ and later "passed on" this confession to the Corinthian church during his eighteen-month ministry there (see also 1 Cor. 11:23, where Paul "received" and then "passed on" a quotation from the Lord's Supper tradition). The church of Sardis, then, is commanded to remember what they have received: the important confessions of the Christian gospel that were passed on to them when they first came to faith. The additional comment that they must also remember what they have "heard" expresses the necessity of not merely hearing these important confessions but also obeying them by responding with works that are judged to be complete.

The fourth command makes explicit the obedient response of the Sardis church to the gospel that was implicit in the preceding reference to what they have heard. Here the verb *tēreō* has the sense of "to persist in obedience" (BDAG 1002.3); this command is rendered in most translations as "Obey!" The same verb was used with this sense in the previous sermon to Thyatira when speaking of "the one who obeys my works to the end" (2:26). Although the object of what the Sardis church must obey is not stated, it is easily supplied from the context: the confessions about the Christian gospel referred to in the previous command that they have received and heard. Remembering these foundational truths is important but not enough: they must also be obeyed.

The fifth and final command—"Repent!"—brings the correction section to a close and is found in every sermon that contains this literary unit (Ephesus, 2:5 [2×]; Pergamum, 2:16; Thyatira, 2:21 [2×], 22; Laodicea, 3:19). Elsewhere the call to repentance occurs at or near the beginning of the correction, but here it stands in the final position. Repentance logically needs to occur before obedience, which makes its location at the end of the commands puzzling. This unusual order may be an example of a literary device called "latter-former," the placing of two events in reverse order, a phenomenon that occurs several times in the book of Revelation (3:17; 5:5; 6:4; 10:4, 9; 20:4–5, 12–13; 22:14). This device is used to highlight the more important element in the pair (Aune 1997: 221; Mathewson 2016: 41). If this is being done here, then it puts greater emphasis on the need for the Sardis church to obey the important confessions of the gospel that were originally passed on to them.

The Consequence (3:3b, 5)

The Sardis sermon closes with the usual pattern of Christ giving the two consequences that this congregation faces. The first consequence is negative: what punishment the Sardis church will receive if it fails to heed the corrective commands to be watchful and to strengthen both its dying members and the works that ought to accompany a healthy, living congregation. The second consequence is positive: what blessings the Sardis church will receive if it repents and with Christ's help conquers its sin of complacency.

Negative Consequence (3:3b)

The negative consequence (3:3b) is set apart from the preceding correction (3:2–3a) by means of the inferential particle "therefore" (*oun*), which highlights the logical connection between these two sections. Christ warns the Sardis church of the negative consequences if they fail to carry out the five commanded corrections: "Therefore, if you are not watchful, I will come like a thief." The idea of Christ coming to the Sardis church to exact punishment is not in itself notable, since this warning appears in six of the seven sermons (2:5, 16, 25; 3:3, 11, 20), but describing the unexpected nature of his arrival as "like a thief" is unique.

The simile comparing the coming of Christ to an unanticipated break-in by a thief has both a NT background and a local historical background. During his earthly ministry, Jesus urges his followers to watch for his return and uses the same metaphor of the unexpected arrival of a thief: "Therefore, be watchful [*grēgoreite*], because you do not know on what day your Lord will come. But understand this: If the owner of the house had known at what time of night the thief was coming, he would have kept watch and would not have let his house be broken into" (Matt. 24:42–43; see also Luke 12:39–40). Paul also uses this simile in describing the sudden arrival of "the day of the Lord," his favorite expression for referring to end-time events that include the coming of Christ: "For yourselves know very well that the day of the Lord will come like a thief in the night" (1 Thess. 5:2). Paul stresses that this eschatological event will surprise only unbelievers and not followers of Christ who are watchful and ready for his return: "But you, brothers and sisters, are not in darkness, for that day to surprise you like a thief" (1 Thess. 5:4). Peter also employs the simile in his response to scoffers who cynically ask, "Where is the promise of his coming?" He asserts that "the day of the Lord will come like a thief" (2 Pet. 3:10). This same simile stressing the need to be vigilant appears again later in the book of Revelation, where Jesus says: "See, I am coming like a thief. Blessed is the one who keeps watch [*ho grēgorōn*]" (Rev. 16:15).

None of these other uses of the simile or metaphor of a thief's unexpected arrival, however, are expressed in the conditional form found in the Sardis sermon: "If you are not watchful . . ." This marks the second time in this brief message that Christ refers to the church's need for vigilance, thereby stressing even further the first of the five commands in the correction: "Be watchful." This twofold call to vigilance, along with the reference to Christ's coming like a thief, has been widely seen as an allusion to the two times Sardis's supposedly impregnable acropolis was taken by surprise and captured. For example, Beale (1999: 276) observes: "If they do not repent and become watchful, Christ's coming will catch them by surprise, just as years before Cyrus's attack . . . , and then later that of Antiochus the Great . . . , caught the city off guard because of its lack of vigilance." Keener (2000: 144) similarly states: "But this warning [that Christ will come like a thief] would also prove especially alarming to proud Sardians schooled from youth in the history of their city. Conquerors had never overtaken Sardis by conventional war, but had twice conquered it unexpectedly because Sardians had failed to watch adequately."

The threatening image of Christ coming like a thief is made more ominous in three ways. First, there is the addition of an explanatory comment: "and you will certainly not know at what hour I will come against you." The unexpected timing of Christ's coming in judgment, which has already been implicitly asserted in the simile of a thief (since the victim typically does not know when such a crime will take place), is now stated explicitly. Second, the use of the emphatic future negation (the double negative with the aorist subjunctive; see BDF §365) stresses that those facing judgment at Christ's coming will *certainly* not know the timing of that event: it will catch them completely by surprise. Third, the future of the Sardis church is made more bleak by the prepositional phrase that Christ employs: he warns the church that he will come not merely "to you" but in a more menacing manner "against you" (the preposition *epi* is likely "a marker of hostile opposition, *against*" (BDAG 366.12; so Mathewson 2016: 42).

Positive Consequence (3:5)

Thankfully, each sermon ends not with a negative tone of judgment but on a positive note of victory, and this is true even for Christ's strongly critical message to the dying church in Sardis. The positive consequence is signaled in 3:5 in typical fashion by the presence of the "victory formula" that employs the key verb *nikaō*. For observations about how important this verb is within John's writings, how it functions as a metaphor for military conflicts, and how the victory is not a human achievement but a divine gift, the modern reader is encouraged to (re)read the extended discussion of the victory formula in the first sermon, the one to Ephesus (see chap. 1, "Positive Consequence [2:7b]").

The "one who is victorious" over the deadly sin of complacency will be graciously given three blessings. The first is that such a person "will thus be dressed in white clothes" (3:5a). This initial blessing is closely linked with the immediately preceding concession (3:4) in a couple of ways. The adverb "thus" (*houtōs*) functions inferentially: it looks back to Christ's concession that there are "a few people in Sardis who have not soiled their clothes" (3:4a), and this provides the reason why their reward will involve being clothed in white. Also, the content of both the promise of the preceding concession and also that of the initial blessing is essentially the same: to "walk with me in white" (3:4b) involves being "dressed in white clothes" (3:5a).

We have already observed (see discussion of 3:4 under "Commendation" above) that clothes are a common metaphor in the ancient world for one's moral and spiritual condition: white or clean clothes symbolize ethical and religious purity, whereas soiled clothes or no clothing at all signifies immoral and irreligious conduct. The positive and negative connotations of this metaphor can be seen elsewhere in the book of Revelation: the Laodicean church, which is the worst of the seven congregations, is judged to be naked (3:17). The twenty-four elders seated on thrones are dressed in white robes (4:4).

Believers who have been martyred for their faith are given white robes (6:11). The great multitude of peoples that no one could count are standing before the throne and the Lamb, wearing white robes, having washed them in the blood of the Lamb and made them white (7:9, 14). Jesus declares that the one who "keeps watch and remains clothed, so as not to go naked and be shamefully exposed" (16:15), is blessed. In 3:4 (as observed earlier), the combining of the clothing metaphor with a walking metaphor ("and they will walk with me in white") may be intended to evoke the image of a Roman triumph celebrating an important military victory, in which a procession of leading Roman citizens wearing pure white togas accompanied the victor. If so, the first blessing of being "dressed in white clothes" may also continue the metaphor of the Roman triumph of the preceding verse. Osborne (2002: 98) states: "As victorious conquerors, they will participate in Christ's triumphant procession at the eschaton, wearing the 'white' of 3:4."

There is a second blessing for the one who is victorious over the sin of deadly complacency: "and I will certainly not erase the name of that person from the book of life" (3:5b). The metaphor of white clothing, or more specifically of a Roman triumph, is replaced with another metaphor frequently found in OT and early Jewish writings: the book of life, in which the names of the saved are written and from which the names of the wicked are blotted out. This image first emerges after Israel's idolatrous worship of the golden calf at Mount Sinai, when Moses intercedes for his people before God: "Please forgive their sin—but if not, then blot me out of the book you have written" (Exod. 32:32–33). Some OT texts depict God as recording the names of the elect in a registry (Ps. 87:6; Isa. 4:3; Dan. 12:1). Other OT texts that form the background to Christ's words in this second blessing to the Sardis church refer to erasing names from the book of life (Exod. 32:32–33; Ps. 69:28). The OT metaphor of a divine registry and of erasing names from this book continues to be found in early Jewish writings. First Enoch, for example, exhorts the righteous to endure the days of wickedness patiently in the knowledge that "the names of the sinners shall be blotted out from the book of life" (108.3; see also 1 En. 47.3; 104.1; Jub. 19.9; 30.19–20; 36.10; 1QM 12.3). Given its widespread use in the OT and early Jewish writings, the metaphor not surprisingly also occurs in several NT documents. Jesus urges the seventy-two he sends out not to be discouraged by the opposition they will face but instead to "rejoice that your names are written in heaven" (Luke 10:20). The writer of Hebrews refers to the worldwide body of believers as those "whose names are written in heaven" (Heb. 12:23). The apostle Paul identifies Euodia, Syntyche, Clement, and the rest of his coworkers as those "whose names are in the book of life" (Phil. 4:3). John, however, makes the greatest use of this metaphor in the NT; the book of life mentioned here in the second blessing is the first of six such references in the book of Revelation (see 13:8; 17:8; 20:12, 15; 21:27).

Although the metaphor of erasing someone's name from the book of life ought to be understood primarily against the backdrop of OT and Jewish writings, it also mirrored a widespread ancient practice in the Greco-Roman world. Cities maintained a list of citizens in a public registry, and individuals convicted of a serious crime would have their names blotted out. In Athens, for example, citizens who were sentenced to death had their names erased from the list of citizens before their execution (Dio Chrysostom, *Orations* 31.84). One specific instance of this practice involved Theramenes (died 404 BC), a controversial Athenian statesman, whose name was erased from the roll of citizens so that he could then be executed without a trial (Xenophon, *Hellenica* 2.3.51–53). Significantly, both Dio Chrysostom and Xenophon, who mention this practice of erasing names from the city registry, use the same verb for "erase" (*exaleiphō*) found in the promise to the Sardis church that their name will not be "erased" from the book of life. In fact, the frequency with which this verb is used in this context suggests that it may well be "a technical term for erasing the names of citizens from the registry" (Aune 1997: 225). This metaphor may have been especially familiar to the Sardis church, since its city, as the western capital of the former Persian and Seleucid Empires, was a repository of such citizen-registers (Hemer 1986: 148).

In light of the OT, early Jewish, and the Greco-Roman backgrounds to the practice of erasing names from the book of life or an official city registry, the significance of the second blessing promised to the Sardis church comes clearly into view. Any person from the *dying* church of Sardis who overcomes the *deadly* sin of complacency is assured that their name will not be erased from the book of *life*, nor will they lose their status as citizens of Christ's kingdom. This good news is made even better by being strongly emphasized: just as the negative consequence was stressed grammatically by means of the emphatic future negation ("You will *certainly* not know at what hour I will come against you"), so this same grammatical construction (the double negative followed by either the aorist subjunctive or future indicative: see BDF §365) underscores the positive consequence: "I will *certainly* not erase your name from the book of life."

The third blessing for those in Sardis who overcome the deadly sin of complacency is that Christ will be their advocate at the final judgment: "and I will acknowledge the name of that person before my Father and before his angels" (3:5c). The image of a heavenly courtroom scene is evoked in three ways. First, the previous metaphor of the book of life commonly occurs in a divine judgment scene: God sits on a throne, surrounded by heavenly courtiers (Dan.

7:9–10; 1 En. 47.3; 90.20; Rev. 20:11–12). In fact, the origin of the book-of-life metaphor is "that of the ancient Near Eastern royal court, where records were made available to the king for dispensing justice (Ezra 4:15; Esther 6:1)" (Aune 1997: 223). Caird's claim (1966: 50) that with the third blessing "the scene changes from City Hall to lawcourt," therefore, is misleading, since the law court is already envisioned in the second blessing with its metaphor of the book of life. Second, Christ's promise here to his victorious followers in Sardis echoes the promise he gave to the disciples during his earthly ministry: "Whoever acknowledges me before others, I will also acknowledge before my Father in heaven" (Matt. 10:32). The parallel version in Luke replaces the final prepositional phrase "before my Father in heaven" with "before the angels of God" (Luke 12:8). The form of the saying here in the Sardis sermon combines these two versions of Jesus's words. This echo of Jesus material also conjures up a law-court scene, since, as Wilson (2002: 273) rightly reasons, "a public forensic context is indicated in the earthly acknowledgment, some kind of heavenly courtroom scene is undoubtedly envisioned for the divine acknowledgment." Third, the legal setting is further called to mind by the verb choice "I will acknowledge" (*homologeō*), which in this context has a strong juridical force. The picture that emerges in the third blessing, therefore, is reassuring: when the "few names" in Sardis—those who overcome the deadly sin of complacency—appear in the heavenly courtroom before God, the divine judge, Christ will be their advocate and acknowledge their name before his Father and the angels, and they will receive a verdict of not guilty.

The Contemporary Significance

Introduction

On August 11, 1974, a truly amazing event took place. After six years of careful planning, a French high-wire walker named Philippe Petit managed, with the help of a number of friends, to put a cable between the Twin Towers of New York's World Trade Center 1,362 feet in the air. Over the next 45 minutes, he walked eight times back and forth between the two buildings, which were 200 feet apart. But he did not just walk on the cable; he danced, knelt, and even lay down as he saluted the police officers on either end who were waiting to arrest him when he stepped off the cable. Petit's accomplishment garnered worldwide attention; as a result of his newfound fame, he was hired by the Ringling Brothers to perform in their circus act. On the day of his inaugural performance, however, during a practice session where he was walking on a cable about 40 feet in the air, Philippe Petit fell! Although he broke a few bones, more than anything he was upset with himself. He said, "I can't believe it! I don't ever fall!"

How could this happen? How could someone successfully walk a cable 1,362 feet in the air while buffeted by gusty winds and then a short time later fall from a cable 40 feet in the air under perfect conditions? The answer lies in one word: *complacency*. When you are walking on a wire 1,362 feet in the air, with gusty winds buffeting your body, you are very much aware that your life could be over at any second. Your nerves are on edge. Your faculties are on high alert. You are paying razor-sharp attention to what you are doing and are well aware of what a dangerous situation you are in. But when it is merely a practice session, and you are walking only 40 feet in the air with no one watching, then you drop your guard. Then you become complacent.

Complacency is not a good thing. If someone calls you complacent, you are rightly offended. But we need to recognize how dangerous complacency is. It is not merely a bad thing; as we learn from our text, it is a *deadly* thing. And so in our message for today, I introduce you to the church of Sardis, or as it can be justly called, "the church of deadly complacency."

The Christ Title (3:1a)

The first item in the outline of every sermon is the Christ title. Before Jesus says anything, we are given two descriptions of him. This pattern is followed in the opening of the sermon to the church in Sardis: "These are the words of the one who has the seven spirits of God and the seven stars" (3:1a).

The first Christ title identifies Jesus as one "who has the seven spirits of God." This unusual phrase is found nowhere else in the Bible except in the book of Revelation, but its use at the beginning of this book shows that "the seven spirits of God" is another way of referring to the Holy Spirit. The book of Revelation opens with a trinitarian greeting identifying each of the three persons of the Trinity: "Grace and peace to you from him who is and who was and who is to come, and from the seven spirits who are before his throne, and from Jesus Christ, the faithful witness, the firstborn of the dead, and the ruler of the kings of the earth" (1:4). The person of the Trinity mentioned first in this greeting is God the Father; the person of the Trinity mentioned last in this greeting is Jesus Christ; and in between references to God the Father and Jesus Christ comes the reference to "the seven spirits"—in other words, the Holy Spirit.

But if "the seven spirits" refers to the Holy Spirit, why didn't John simply say when addressing the church in Sardis that Jesus has the Holy Spirit? The answer seems to be that "the seven spirits" is an allusion to the ancient Greek (LXX) translation of Isa. 11:2–3. There the future king who is to come from the branch of Jesse (that is, the messiah) will have the sevenfold Spirit of God: one spirit of wisdom, one of understanding, one of counsel, one of might, one of knowledge, one of godliness, and one of the fear of God. This means that the Jesus who is about to speak is that future king, the messiah, who has seven spirits, or divine qualities, that will equip him to bless God's people. The complacent church of Sardis, dying and almost dead, must recognize Jesus as the messianic king who has the life-giving Spirit of God, which they desperately need in order to live once again.

Jesus not only has the life-giving Spirit of God, but in the second Christ title we also learn that he holds "the seven stars." The book of Revelation clearly states that the seven stars are "the angels of the seven churches" (1:20), presumably the guardian angels of each congregation. That Jesus "has" or controls the guardian angel of the church of Sardis means that he controls the church of Sardis; he has authority over them, and they must heed what he is about to say.

The authority of Jesus highlighted in the second Christ title likely also involves a polemic against Rome and its rival claim to authority. The reference to "seven stars" would have brought to people's minds the image of seven stars that often appeared on Roman coins, with the Roman emperor's image on the other side of the coin. The emperors wanted people to believe that they were demigods: men who were partly human but also partly divine, with power great enough to control the seven stars. These coins claimed that Rome and its leaders were all-powerful, not only on earth but also in the heavens.

One day, however, a messenger arrives in the Sardis church with a sermon from Jesus Christ revealed to John on the island of Patmos. Before Jesus says anything to them, they hear that he is the one who has "the seven stars." Jesus is the one whose authority is greater than Rome, the one who is all-powerful not just on earth but also in the heavens. The Christ followers in Sardis and Christ followers today must recognize that Jesus has authority over them and that they must heed what he is about to say!

The Commendation—None!

The second item that every sermon typically has is the commendation. Jesus usually says something positive about what the church is doing right. This sermon to Sardis is number five of the seven, which means that the Christians in Sardis have already heard Jesus's commendation to the believers in Ephesus, Smyrna, Pergamum, and Thyatira. It is now finally their turn, and they are eagerly waiting for Jesus's words of commendation to them. But what do they hear him say? "I know your works, namely, you have a reputation of being alive, but you are dead" (3:1b).

Notice not what the biblical text says but instead what it does *not* say. The commendation is missing in this sermon. The situation is so bad at Sardis that Jesus cannot say anything positive about them. The situation is the reverse of what we discovered in the sermon to Smyrna: Jesus evaluates the church in Smyrna so positively that he doesn't have any words of complaint to bring against them, but Jesus evaluates the church in Sardis so negatively that he doesn't have any words of commendation to say about them.

There is, however, a bit of a silver lining for the Sardis church. Jesus may not be able to give a *commendation* to them, but he is able to make a *concession* about them. A few verses later Jesus concedes, "You have a few in Sardis who have not soiled their clothes" (3:4). There is a small group within the congregation with whom Jesus does not find fault or blame. Nevertheless, this concession cannot hide the harsh reality that Jesus's overall assessment of the Sardis church is negative: they are a dying or dead church, for which Jesus has no words of commendation. This harsh reality should be a wake-up call, not just for the church of Sardis but also for the church today; believers must realize how deadly the problem of complacency really is.

The Complaint (3:1b)

The third item in every sermon is typically the complaint. After Jesus commends a church for what they are doing right, he spells out for them what they are doing wrong. For the Christians in Sardis, however, Jesus disappointingly skips the commendation and moves directly to the complaint: "I know your works, namely, you have a reputation of being alive, but you are dead" (3:1b).

Jesus's complaint indicates that churches have a reputation. Just as people develop a reputation over time, so also churches develop a reputation. This reputation may be good or bad, and it may involve the church's size or its style of worship or its theology or its hospitality or its ministry to those in need. This raises an important question: What kind of reputation does our church have? If a news reporter went to people in our community and asked them about our church, what would those people say? If a journalist went around to our coworkers or neighbors and asked them about us, what would those people say? What kind of reputation do we as Jesus followers have?

Surprisingly, the church in Sardis had a positive reputation. Jesus says, "You have a reputation of being alive." This means that the Sardis church was not always in a state of complacency. At one time they were a healthy church. So what happened to them? How can a church with a reputation for being alive get to the point that Jesus has nothing good to say about them and instead labels them dying or dead?

The answer is found in the next words of Jesus; he tells the Sardis church what they must do to correct the situation. We are not quite there yet in our study of this sermon, but we can use that part of Jesus's message to understand the problem. Jesus commands this church: "Be watchful!" (3:2a). What kind of people need to be commanded to be watchful? Those who are not paying attention, those who, spiritually speaking, are asleep rather than awake. Those who are not alert to the dangers of living in a pagan culture that is hostile to the exclusive claims of the gospel. To use the key word in our sermon title, those who are complacent.

Jesus also later says about the Sardis church, "For I have not found your works complete in the presence of my God" (3:2b). Jesus complains that their conduct is not satisfactory. Their lifestyle does not reflect a healthy and vibrant relationship with Christ. That's the problem with the church of Sardis: they are not spiritually alert and seeking to live a distinctly Christian life but are complacent and willfully ignorant of the deadly dangers that threaten their very existence.

The Correction (3:2–3a)

The fourth item typically found in Jesus's sermons to the seven churches is the correction. Jesus has just told the Sardis church what they are doing wrong, and so he naturally goes on to explain how the church can fix their deadly dilemma: "Be watchful! Strengthen what remains and is about to die! For I have not found your works complete in the presence of my God. Remember, therefore, what you have received and heard! Obey and repent!" (3:2–3a).

Five commands are found here, but the command at the top of the list is the most important because it occurs in the first position, is worded emphatically in the original Greek, and is the only one of the five commands to be repeated later in the sermon. This first and most important command is the one we have already talked about, the command "Be watchful!"

The command to be watchful or spiritually alert would have been especially relevant for the Christians in Sardis because there was a very famous story about the capture of the Sardis acropolis, which resulted from the city's lack of vigilance. Sardis had an acropolis (the high part of their city) that was supposedly unconquerable. In fact, there was a saying in the ancient world, "To conquer the acropolis at Sardis," which was another way of saying "To do the impossible." A couple of generations ago, the expression "To go to the moon" was another way of saying "To do the impossible." But Sardis, which was famous in the ancient world for having an acropolis that was impossible to conquer, was conquered, not once, but twice! Two times the ruler of Sardis was so sure that the city was safe and that it was impossible for any enemy to enter the acropolis and conquer the city that he became complacent and did not post guards at its steepest sides. And because of the complacency of these rulers, the city of Sardis was captured. People in the ancient world loved to repeat the story about the conquest of the supposedly unconquerable acropolis of Sardis, which fell because of its complacency.

Jesus is warning not only the Christians in Sardis but believers today as well: "Be watchful!" We need to be much more aware of the danger of complacency, much more alert to the spiritual dangers that surround us, and much more vigilant in our dependence on Jesus, the one who has the life-giving Spirit whom we desperately need to live faithfully as God's people in this fallen world.

The Consequence (3:3b, 5)

The fifth and final item in the outline of each of the seven sermons is the consequence. There are usually two consequences: first, a negative consequence if the church does not change its sinful ways; second, a positive consequence if the church does change its sinful ways. Both of these consequences are found in the sermon to the church in Sardis.

Negative Consequence (3:3b)

First, the negative consequence. Jesus says: "Therefore, if you are not watchful, I will come like a thief, and you will certainly not know at what hour I will come against you" (3:3b). This marks the second time that Jesus tells the Sardis church to "be watchful." Jesus is thus emphasizing the deadly danger of complacency. He says, "Wake up, you Christians in Sardis! Beware of the complacency that characterizes your spiritual life—a complacency that shows itself in deeds that are not pleasing in the sight of God, deeds that are not distinctly Christian, deeds that fail to demonstrate my grace working in your life. Wake up, or else I will come against you like a thief!"

Jesus's coming is almost always described in the NT as a good thing. Jesus's return to earth as a victorious king is something that gives believers wonderful comfort for the present and powerful hope for the future (1 Thess. 4:17–18; 5:9–11). But not everyone will experience Jesus's second coming as a wonderful comfort and powerful hope. As an old hymn by John Newton (1774) puts it, Christ's coming will be a "Day of Judgment" as well as a "Day of Wonders." And so this verse warns not only the believers in Sardis but us too about the deadly danger of complacency, about the need to anticipate and prepare for Jesus's glorious return so that it will be for us not a day of judgment but a day of wonders.

Positive Consequence (3:5)

Jesus's last word to the Christians in Sardis, however, is not a negative warning of judgment but a positive promise of victory. This sermon ends in the same way that all the sermons thus far have ended: with the victory formula. Since this is now the fifth time that we have heard Jesus refer to "the one who is victorious," you no doubt remember that the Greek word used here is the name of a popular sporting goods company, Nike. The message is that if you are using Nike sports equipment or wearing Nike clothes, you will be victorious, you will win!

The important question that our text raises is this: Are you a Nike Christian, a victorious Christian? Are you able to overcome the sin of complacency? The good news of the gospel is that the answer to this important question can be a resounding "Yes!" You and I can be Nike Christians and win the victory, not because we are so talented or so hard working, but because Christ has already won the victory. We who belong to Christ have his Spirit living in us, and this divine Holy Spirit gives us the power to be spiritually alert and vigilant in our faith.

What reward awaits the Nike Christian? There are three positive consequences, and the first one is this: "The one who is victorious will thus be dressed in white" (3:5a). Clothes were a common metaphor in the ancient world for one's moral condition: white clothes symbolized ethical purity, and dirty clothes symbolized immoral conduct. That white clothes are a positive symbol of ethical purity is clear from the rest of the book of Revelation: the twenty-four elders seated on thrones are dressed in white robes (4:4), believers who are martyred for their faith are given white robes (6:11), and the great multitude whose number no one can count and who are standing before the throne and the Lamb are wearing white robes (7:9, 13). White clothing as a symbol of ethical purity is also seen in the ancient Roman practice of citizens running for political office bleaching their togas to a dazzling white to symbolize the genuineness of their motives.

White clothing is still a positive symbol of ethical purity today. Brides may spend much time and energy deciding whom to invite to their wedding, where to have the reception, what kind of flowers to get, which photographer to use, and so on. But one decision they don't spend time on is the color of the wedding dress. The dress will be white because white still symbolizes ethical purity. If we, through Christ, are Nike Christians who conquer the sin of complacency, then we will be dressed in white; that is, our lives will be characterized by purity and holiness, having shed the dirty clothes of sinful living.

Jesus's second reward for the Nike Christian is as follows: "And I will certainly not erase the name of that person from the book of life" (3:5b). The metaphor of the book of life, into which the names of the saved are written and from which the names of the wicked are rubbed out, is widespread in the OT. Not surprisingly, this metaphor is continued in the NT, including some six references in the book of Revelation. This explains why, in the iconography of the early church, Jesus is frequently depicted holding a book in his lap—not the Bible but the book of life. Jesus promises us that if we, by his power, are Nike Christians who overcome our complacency and vigilantly live out our faith, our name will never be erased from the book of life. What a comfort to know that we do not need to fear the final judgment, that moment when Jesus comes back and opens the book of life. We have a wonderful promise that our name is now in that book and will never be rubbed out!

There is yet a third reward for the Nike Christian. Jesus also says, "And I will acknowledge the name of that person before my Father and before his angels" (3:5c). This third reward should be understood as part of a heavenly courtroom scene, where we have been charged with breaking God's holy law and now find ourselves standing before the divine judge. God is about to pronounce us guilty because we deserve judgment, but just before the official sentence of "Guilty" is pronounced, Jesus interrupts the court proceeding by declaring, "Stop! Throughout their lives, these faithful people acknowledged me before others, and so I now acknowledge them before you, Father, and before all your angels." If you are a Nike Christian who overcomes the deadly danger of complacency and vigilantly lives out your faith, you can be confident that Jesus will acknowledge you before his Father in the final judgment as someone who ought to be declared "Not guilty" because Jesus has already paid the penalty in full for all your sins.

Conclusion

It is impossible for anyone to repeat what the French high-wire walker Philippe Petit did in 1974. It is impossible not because another person could not physically perform such a feat but because of the sobering reality that the Twin Towers of the World Trade Center no longer exist. Those two buildings were destroyed by terrorism; to be more precise, they were destroyed by terrorism made possible by American complacency. At the time, the United States naively thought it was safe and secure from the problem of terrorism and was complacent about the potential dangers that threatened its very existence. But on September 11, 2001, America discovered the hard way that complacency is not just a bad thing but a deadly thing.

Complacency is deadly, not just for nations, but also for churches. Congregations need to be aware of how deadly the danger of complacency can be. Today we hear Jesus giving us a gracious command, "Be watchful! Don't be blind to the spiritual battle taking place between my kingdom and that of the evil one! Live distinctly Christian lives, lives that demonstrate the transforming power of grace! Rededicate yourselves to me because I alone have the life-giving Spirit of God, whom you need to be a Nike Christian and overcome the sin of complacency."

"Whoever has ears to hear, let them hear what the Spirit is saying to the churches!"—not only the ancient church of Sardis but also the church of Jesus Christ today.

6

Philadelphia

The Church of the Persevering Persecuted

The Christ Title (3:7b)

In each of the sermons reviewed thus far, a common feature of the Christ titles is their relevance for the specific church to whom the sermon is addressed. This feature is especially evident in the three Christ titles in the sermon to Philadelphia: "These are the words of the Holy One, the True/Trustworthy One, the one who holds the key of David: what he opens no one can shut, and what he shuts no one can open" (3:7b). All three Christ titles involve either an allusion to or a close citation of the OT and serve as an especially appropriate polemic against the local Jewish community, which was strongly opposing the Philadelphian church. This congregation was, as Osborne (2002: 186) notes, "under severe threat from a powerful Jewish presence in the city. Therefore, the names of Christ chosen here reflect that situation and reassure the beleaguered Philadelphia Christians that the Messiah is indeed on their side, not on the side of the 'synagogue of Satan' (3:9)."

The first Christ title, "the Holy One," is used to describe God in several OT texts (e.g., 2 Kings 19:22; Job 6:10; Pss. 78:41; 89:18; Prov. 9:10; Jer. 50:29; 51:5; Hab. 3:3). It is an especially common designation for God in Isaiah, where the full title "the Holy One of Israel" occurs some twenty-five times

(Isa. 1:4; 5:19, 24; 10:20; 12:6; 17:7; 29:19; 30:11, 12, 15; 31:1; 37:23; 41:14, 16, 20; 43:3, 14; 45:11; 47:4; 48:17; 49:7; 54:5; 55:5; 60:9, 14). The multiple connections to the book of Isaiah found elsewhere in the sermon make it the likely source of this first Christ title as well. John (1) explicitly cites from Isa. 22:22 in the third Christ title, (2) alludes to this same text in 3:8 ("no one can shut"), (3) seems to allude to Isa. 45:1 in 3:8 ("open door"), (4) strongly echoes Isa. 60:14 in 3:9 ("I will make them come and fall down at your feet"), and (5) may allude to Isa. 43:4 in 3:9 ("and acknowledge that I loved you"). It is also clear from Rev. 6:10 ("How long, Sovereign Lord, holy and true . . . ?") that John understands "holy" as a title for God.

John's use of this divine title to describe Jesus in the Philadelphia sermon asserts the deity of the one who is about to speak despite the denial of his divine status by the local Jewish community. This polemical purpose is strengthened by the close parallel with the Christ title in the Smyrna sermon. The Smyrna congregation was similarly persecuted by "the synagogue of Satan," and the message to them opens with a Christ title that uses another of Isaiah's designations for God, "the first and the last," to emphasize the deity of Christ in contrast to local Jewish opponents, who denied Jesus's divine status. The message to Philadelphia begins with a Christ title that likewise echoes one of Isaiah's titles for God, "the Holy One," and stresses Jesus's deity despite opposition from the resident Jewish community.

Determining the meaning and function of the second Christ title is complicated by the fact that the adjective used (*alēthinos*) can have the sense of something that is either "true" or "trustworthy" (BDAG 43.1). In a Greek context, this adjective refers to what is true or genuine in contrast to what is false or fictitious. This meaning allows the second Christ title to have a polemical function, just like the first and third titles. "The True One" Christ title establishes a general polemic, emphasizing that Jesus is the one who speaks the truth to the Philadelphian church, in contrast to their Jewish opponents, who falsely "claim to be Jews though they are not, but are liars" (3:9a). This Christ title also creates a specific polemic, presenting Jesus as the true or genuine Messiah despite the rejection of his messianic status by the Jewish community in Philadelphia. This latter polemic is recognized by Beale (1999: 283), who states, "The idea of 'true' carries connotations of Jesus being the true Messiah, who has begun to fulfill messianic prophecy . . . , though he is rejected by the Jews as a false messianic pretender."

In a Hebrew context, however, the adjective *alēthinos* refers to what is "trustworthy" or "faithful" (see 3:14; 19:11; 21:5; 22:6 for examples of *alēthinos* coupled with *pistos*). Jesus is "the Trustworthy One," whom the Philadelphian church can confidently count on to vindicate them in the face

Figure 6.1. The Shebna Inscription (7th cent. BC). A three-line Hebrew funerary inscription from the entrance of a limestone tomb that may have contained the remains of Shebna, the royal administrator for King Hezekiah. British Museum.

of persecution they are enduring at the hands of the local Jewish community. Since the two qualities, true and trustworthy, are combined in the Christ title of the immediately following sermon to Laodicea (3:14, "the faithful and true witness"), both ideas may be intended here as well. As Osborne (2002: 187) concludes: "It is likely that neither possibility should be excluded: Christ is both the 'real' Messiah and the 'faithful' one."

The third Christ title, "the one who has the key of David," must be understood along with the immediately following clauses: "what he opens no one can shut, and what he shuts no one can open." This latter expression does not contain a separate fourth appellation of Christ but rather is part of the third Christ title, and together they originate from Isa. 22:22: "I will place on his shoulder the key to the house of David; what he opens no one can shut, and what he shuts no one can open." The backstory to this not-so-well-known OT text involves a person named Shebna, who held a position in the court of Hezekiah, king of Judah. He was no minor administrator (as the translation "palace administrator" might suggest; 22:15 NIV, NLT) but a powerful person who controlled access to the king and the running of his administration ("master of the household"; NRSV), much like the White House chief-of-staff functions for an American president. Shebna reveals his vanity and selfish ambition by having a grave carved for himself out of solid rock in a prominent place among the tombs of Israel's kings (Isa. 22:15–16). Isaiah the prophet informed Shebna that God was greatly displeased with his arrogant act and was going to send him to a far country, where he would have no need for his elaborate tomb and would die in disgrace (22:17–19). Isaiah also prophesied that God would depose Shebna from his prominent position and replace him with Eliakim, son of Hilkiah. Not only would God clothe Eliakim with the robe and sash of Shebna (22:20–21), but he would give him an even more powerful symbol of his new authority: "the key to the house of David" (22:22).

A key in the ancient world differed from its contemporary counterpart in ways that accentuate its function as a metaphor for power and authority. First, unlike a modern key, which is small and easily portable, an ancient key was large and awkward to carry. This explains why God promised not simply to hand Eliakim the key to the house of David but to place it "on his shoulder" (Isa. 22:22). Second, unlike a modern key, which can be copied and given to several people, there was typically only one key for an ancient door, which meant that the person who possessed this key wielded unique authority (Keener 2000: 150n1). The authority that Christ enjoys as the one who alone has the key of David is stressed by the following explanatory phrase: "What he opens no one can shut, and what he shuts no one can open." In the original context of Isa. 22:22, this refers to the absolute authority that Eliakim, the new master of the household, would wield to control access to the palace and the king. In the context of Rev. 3:7, this now refers to the absolute authority that Jesus, the true and trustworthy Messiah, possesses to control access to "the city of my God, the new Jerusalem" (3:12), that is, the kingdom of God.

The third Christ title functions as yet another polemic against the Jewish community in Philadelphia. The key of David as a metaphor for Christ's absolute authority to control access to God and membership in his kingdom is in direct response to the claim of the local synagogue that only those on its membership rolls could legitimately consider themselves to be God's chosen people. As Beasley-Murray (1978: 59) observes,

> The immediate background of the phrase ["who has the key of David"] was the claim of the Jews in Philadelphia that they were the true people of God who held the key to the Kingdom of God. John contradicts this claim by asserting that the key to the kingdom which had belonged to Israel really belongs to Jesus as the Davidic Messiah (5:5; 22:16) and had been forfeited by Israel because she had rejected her Messiah. It is Christ alone and no longer Israel who can give [people] entrance into the messianic Kingdom.

The polemic in the third Christ title, especially the explanatory comment about opening and shutting, may be responding specifically to the local synagogue's recent act of excommunicating Christian Jews from its membership and thus from the religious protection that the Jewish community had secured from Rome (this historical situation is discussed more fully below; see

"The First Interjection [3:8b]"). Mounce (1977: 116) reflects the opinion of many commentators: "The language of Isaiah is used to present Christ as the Davidic Messiah with absolute power to control entrance to the heavenly kingdom. It may be an intentional contrast with the practice of the local synagogue in excommunicating Christian Jews" (so also, e.g., Hemer 1986: 161; Beale 1999: 284; Keener 2000: 150; Osborne 2002: 187–88). Thus, even before offering any specific words of comfort to the persecuted Philadelphian church, Christ's self-identification in the third title would be profoundly reassuring to his Jewish followers, who had recently endured or were currently facing expulsion from the synagogue.

The Commendation (3:8–11a)

The sermon to Philadelphia follows the expected pattern in moving from the Christ title to the commendation, a shift signaled by the recurring formula "I know," the object of which is usually "your works" (missing only for Smyrna [2:9] and Pergamum [2:13]). There is, however, a unique feature about this commendation: Christ interrupts his praise of the Philadelphian church three times to describe blessings that he either has already given or will yet give to this congregation. Instead of the second-person pronoun in which Christ acknowledges the good things that "you" (the Philadelphian church) have done, this commendation contains more first-person statements of what "I" (Christ) have done or will do for the congregation. The first two of these statements begin with the particle "See!" (*idou*, 3:9) and function as parenthetical statements of reward in contrast to words of commendation. The third of these first-person statements is linked to the immediately preceding commendation by repeating the same verb: "Because you have *kept* . . . I will also *keep* you" (3:10). The syntax of 3:8–10 is admittedly "unclear" (Mathewson 2016: 45) and so open to debate. Nevertheless, as we work through these verses, it is important to distinguish between the commendation proper—the praiseworthy things that the Philadelphian church has done—and the three interjected statements of blessings that Christ has done or will do for this congregation. These two types of material, which are mixed together in the commendation, can be visually distinguished as follows:

> I know your works (*See, I have set before you an open door, which no one is able to shut*), namely, you have little power, yet you have kept my word and have not denied my name. (*See, I will make those from the synagogue of Satan, the ones who call themselves Jews though they are not but are false—see, I will*

make them come and fall down at your feet and acknowledge that I loved you.)
Because you kept my word to endure patiently, *I will also keep you from the
hour of trial that is going to come on the whole world to test the inhabitants
of the earth.* (Rev. 3:8–10)

The unique occurrence and extended nature of these first-person statements
emphasize how pleased Christ is with the Philadelphian church and why
this congregation and the one in Smyrna represent the two healthy churches
among the seven addressed in Revelation.

The Start of the Commendation (3:8a)

The commendation begins with the formulaic statement "I know your
works." In every other sermon that includes this statement (2:2, 19; 3:1, 15),
the object "works" is clarified by the following clause, introduced with the
conjunctions *kai* or *hoti,* both of which have an explanatory function (BDAG
495.1.c; 732.2). That pattern in the other sermons strongly suggests that here
too "works" is explained by the subsequent *hoti* clause, even though it occurs
later in the verse: "I know your works . . . , *namely,* you have little power, yet
you have kept my word and have not denied my name."

The First Interjection (3:8b)

This interpretation of the grammar requires that the intervening clause
("See, I have set before you an open door, which no one is able to shut") is
a parenthetical insertion into the commendation (so, e.g., Swete 1911: 54;
Charles 1920: 86–87; Mounce 1977: 117; Beale 1999: 286; Osborne 2002:
188–89; Smalley 2005: 89). This interjection within the commendation suggests that Christ cannot wait to finish describing the works for which he is
commending the Philadelphian church and instead interrupts that thought
to remind the congregation of his own actions on their behalf rather than
focusing on their actions. The Message translation puts it: "I see what you've
done. Now see what *I've* done." The importance of this parenthetical remark
is underlined by the introductory particle "See!" (*idou*), which draws attention
to what follows. Christ stresses that he has "set before you an open door that
no one is able to shut." The metaphor of an open door that Christ prevents
anyone from closing originates naturally from the citation of Isa. 22:22 in the
immediately preceding third Christ title: "the key of David" evokes the image
of a door about which it is similarly stated, "What he opens no one shuts."
This metaphor may also stem from yet another Isaiah text. In Isa. 45:1 the
Lord states his intention to "open doors" before the Persian king Cyrus, that

is, to break down the gates of cities he besieges so that he will be victorious (Beale 1999: 289).

More important and thus more controversial than the origin of the open door metaphor, however, is its meaning. Paul uses this image three times in his letters, always to refer to an opportunity for evangelism (1 Cor. 16:9; 2 Cor. 2:12; Col. 4:3). The metaphor also occurs in Acts 14:27, though in this instance the door is open not to those proclaiming the gospel but to those receiving it. These texts have led some to conclude that the evangelistic meaning for the metaphor of an open door had become fixed by the time the book of Revelation was written and that this is why the metaphor appears in the Philadelphia sermon with no accompanying words of explanation (Ramsay 1904: 404). Several commentators have found this argument convincing and believe that Christ is highlighting the rich evangelistic opportunity that he is giving the church in Philadelphia to spread the gospel (so, e.g., Charles 1920: 87; Hendriksen 1940: 75; Caird 1966: 51–53; Beale 1999: 286; Keener 2000: 150; Kistemaker 2001: 159).

Three contextual reasons, however, have caused the majority of commentators to reject an evangelistic meaning for the open door metaphor, instead understanding it to refer to entrance into the kingdom of God (e.g., Ladd 1972: 59; Mounce 1977: 117; Beasley-Murray 1978: 100; Thomas 1992: 277–78; Aune 1997: 236; Michaels 1997: 84; Osborne 2002: 188–89; Witherington 2003: 106; Fanning 2020: 173). First, missionary activity is not highlighted in any of the seven sermons or in the rest of the book of Revelation. Second, the commendation, which usually offers praise for a church's previous works, is an unlikely place to challenge the Philadelphian church to perform new good works such as increased evangelistic activity. Third, the book of Revelation, rather than Paul's letters, provides a more immediate context for the open door metaphor, for the same wording is used in 4:1–2 to describe entrance into heaven, or what Christ calls "the city of my God, the new Jerusalem" (3:12)—that is, the kingdom of God.

The door is identified not merely as being "open" but also as one "that no one is able to shut," repeating and thus emphasizing a point already made in the preceding verse (3:7, "what he opens no one shuts") about the excommunication of Jewish Christians from the local synagogue in Philadelphia. In the early days of Christianity, Jewish Christians continued to worship in their local synagogue, which allowed them to enjoy the protection Rome had given Judaism as an officially recognized religion. Over time, however, the division between the two groups became more pronounced, and some synagogues began to excommunicate Jewish Christians from their fellowship. This practice is mentioned in the Gospel of John: "For already the Jews had decided that anyone who acknowledged that Jesus was the Christ would be put out of the synagogue" (John 9:22; see also John 12:42; 16:2). This local practice became official at the Council of Jamnia in AD 90 with the addition of the twelfth benediction to the prayer regularly used in synagogue liturgies: "Let the Nazarenes [Christians] and Minim [heretics] be destroyed in a moment, and let them be blotted out of the book of life and not be inscribed with the righteous."

Against this historical backdrop and coming on the heels of the third Christ title, this parenthetical interjection of Christ (3:8a) would have been profoundly comforting to the persecuted church of Philadelphia. Although Jesus followers may have been excommunicated from the synagogue, Christ has the key of David, which guarantees them entry into the messianic kingdom, and what Christ opens, not even the "synagogue of Satan" can close. Although the door to the synagogue may be closed to them, Christ has set before them an open door into the kingdom of God, a door that the local Jewish community cannot shut.

The Resumption of the Commendation (3:8c)

The commendation, which began with the formulaic expression "I know your works" and was then interrupted with the parenthetical comment of 3:8b, now continues with the explanatory statement of 3:8c: "namely, you have little power, yet you have kept my word and have not denied my name." These words are also paralleled in the sermon to Smyrna. There Christ's commendation of the vulnerable position of that persecuted congregation ("I know . . . your poverty") intensified the word of encouragement that follows ("yet you are rich"). Here Christ's similar commendation of the weakness of the Philadelphian church ("You have little power") makes their praiseworthy conduct even more impressive ("yet you have kept my word and have not denied my name"). The word order of the first clause emphasizes the adjective "little": it is placed at the head of the clause and separated from its modifying noun by the verb. Christ thus stresses how little power the Philadelphian church has, referring not so much to the small size of the congregation as to its lack of influence within the local community. Since the social or political power of any group is typically linked to both the number and social status of its members, it can be assumed that the Christians in Philadelphia were few and came mostly from the lower class (see 1 Cor. 1:26–27).

The second and third clauses in this part of the commendation (3:8c) form a parallel structure in which the opening half is stated positively ("yet you have kept my word") and the closing half is stated negatively ("and have not denied my name"). Thus the second and third clauses should not be distinguished too sharply from each other, as if each were making an independent point, but should instead be interpreted as one literary unit, with both clauses expressing the same basic truth. The opening positive half commends the Philadelphian church because "you have kept my word." As in its earlier uses in two preceding sermons (2:26; 3:3a), the verb *tēreō* here has the sense of "to persist in obedience" (BDAG 1002.3) and so could be rendered, "You have *obeyed* my word" (so some translations: TLB, NCV; see also the discussion in Aune 1997: 237). The singular form of the object of what the church has obeyed, "my word," occurs also later in the commendation with the same verb and with a noun that clarifies the content of that word: "You have kept [obeyed] my word about *perseverance*" (3:10a). This implies that the believers in Philadelphia faced opposition to their faith; here Christ is praising them for obeying his command to persevere despite such persecution.

The closing half of the parallelism supports this reconstruction of the historical situation. The additional commendation, "You have not denied my name," suggests that believers in Philadelphia were pressured publicly to renounce their faith in Christ. In the immediately following verse, "those who call themselves Jews" makes clear that the local Jewish community played a key role in the persecution the Philadelphian church endured. Perhaps the Jewish community brought an official charge—a denunciation—against Christians before the local leaders of the city, similar to what they did against Paul in Corinth (Acts 18:12–13) and what was later done against Polycarp in Smyrna (Martyrdom of Polycarp 12.2). Despite these adverse circumstances, the believers in Philadelphia did not deny the name of Christ. They were not like the later Christians in Asia Minor who were denounced to Pliny the Younger during his time as governor of Pontus and Bithynia in AD 111–112. Pliny informs Emperor Trajan about this situation:

> Those who *denied* that they were or had been Christians, when they invoked the gods in words dictated by me, offered prayer with incense and wine to your image, which I had ordered to be brought for this purpose together with the statues of the gods, and moreover cursed Christ—none of which those who are really Christians, it is said, can be forced to do—these I thought should be discharged. Others named by the informer declared that they were Christians, but then *denied* it, asserting that they had been but had ceased to be. . . . They all worshiped your image and the statues of the gods, and cursed Christ. (*Letters* 10.96, emphasis added)

The Second Interjection (3:9)

Christ interrupts his commendation of the Philadelphian church a second time with another first-person statement of what he will do for this congregation (3:9). Like the earlier one in 3:8b, this interjection is introduced with the Greek particle for "See!" (*idou*) to draw attention to what follows. The statement that follows begins by clarifying the identity of those who are persecuting the Philadelphian church: "I will make those who are of the synagogue of Satan, who call themselves Jews, yet are not, but are lying . . ." (3:9a). The wording of this description is identical to what was said about those persecuting the Smyrna church, except here the word order is changed slightly and Christ adds the final negative judgment, "but they are lying." Jews in Philadelphia who have acted to put pressure on the Christians in the city to disobey the word of Christ and deny his name may be Jews by race and religion, but they are not true Jews. If they were genuine Jews, they would acknowledge Jesus as divine ("the Holy One"), the Messiah ("the True One"), and the sole means of entrance into the kingdom of God ("the one who has the key of David"). Instead, their actions in persecuting the church reveal their real identity as "the synagogue of Satan." This striking phrase occurs only here and in the sermon to Smyrna (2:9), thereby forming yet another important parallel between these two messages. The identification fits those who are persecuting the church and perhaps also denouncing believers before local city officials, since the name "Satan" (from Hebrew *sāṭān*) means "adversary" or "opponent." Later in the book of Revelation, Satan (also called "the devil"; 12:9) is described as "the accuser of our brothers, . . . who accuses them day and night before our God" (12:10). The Jews in Philadelphia who were pressuring church members to publicly deny the name of Christ were proving by their actions that they were in reality not "Jews"—that is, members of God's covenant people—but human instruments in the hand of Satan, who is the ultimate source of the persecution endured by the church.

The second part of the interjection describes what Christ will do to reward the Philadelphian church for persevering in their faith: he will vindicate them before the very same people who persecuted them. "See, I will make them come and fall down at your feet and acknowledge that I have loved you" (3:9b). The first part of the interjection opens with the Greek particle for "See!" and the verb "I will make" (the verb *didōmi*, which normally means "to give," here has the sense of "to cause something to happen"; BDAG 242.4). This first part contains so many clauses clarifying the identity of those opposing the Philadelphian church that it does not finish stating exactly what Christ will make "the synagogue of Satan" do. The second part of the interjection, therefore, resumes the assertion of the first part by similarly opening with the particle "See!" and the verb "I will make" (though this time the verb *poieō* is used) and proceeds to state that Christ will make the Jewish persecutors "come and fall down at your feet."

There are many OT and early Jewish texts predicting that in the last days gentiles who oppressed Jews will fall down in submission before Israel and Israel's God (Ps. 86:9; Isa. 2:3; 14:2; 45:14; 49:23; Ezek. 36:23; Zech. 8:20–23; 1 En. 10.21. Sib. Or. 3.716–20, 725–31). Christ's promise here to the Philadelphian church could be a "collective allusion" (Beale 1999: 287) to some of these texts. It is more likely, however, that Christ's promise echoes Isa. 60:14: "The sons of your oppressors will come bowing before you; all who despise you will bow down at your feet."

The likelihood that Rev. 3:9 refers specifically to Isa. 60:14 increases when we consider a further allusion to this same verse further on in the sermon to Philadelphia. In 3:12, the positive consequence is that Christ will write on victorious believers in Philadelphia "the name of my God, and the name of the city of my God, the new Jerusalem." This description may reflect the closing words of Isa. 60:14, where the oppressors of God's people will not only come and bow down before them but will also call them "the City of the Lord, the Zion of the Holy One of Israel" (so Aune 1997: 238). Christ's second interjection comforts the Philadelphian church by telling them that this OT expectation will be "turned on its head" (Osborne 2002: 191) in what one commentator has called "the grim irony of providence" (Moffatt 1910: 367): instead of gentile oppressors paying homage to the Jews, it is the Jews who will pay homage to the predominantly gentile church in Philadelphia.

There is much debate about whether the reference to Jews coming and bowing at the feet of the gentile church in Philadelphia refers to their submission or to their conversion. Those who interpret the earlier reference to the open door as an evangelistic opportunity typically understand this as the *conversion* of the Jewish people. They also appeal to the verb "bow" (*proskyneō*), which normally means "worship": "Worship denotes abject submission and homage before the glory of the church and can hardly be practiced by anyone who has not become Christ's follower" (Thomas 1992: 282). However, there are compelling reasons for seeing this as referring to Jewish *submission*. First, as was demonstrated above, the open door metaphor does not refer to an opportunity for evangelism. Second, the verb "worship" in this context refers to a common Middle Eastern act of showing deference and respect to others and is thus better translated as "kneel" or "bow" (so virtually all major translations). As Aune (1997: 238) notes: "This prostration has no religious significance but is simply the traditional (oriental) expression of homage and honor." Third and most significant, Christ states that the Jews will bow not "at my feet" but "at *your* feet," bowing in submission to the church rather than in worship of Christ. Finally, in this context the emphasis lies more on what these words mean for the persecuted Philadelphian church than for their Jewish oppressors, and so this verse should be seen as stressing not Jewish conversion or even Jewish submission but rather Christian vindication.

This vindication will not just consist of Jews coming and honoring the Philadelphian church but also of Christ making these oppressors "know that I have loved you." This may involve yet another echo from Isaiah (so, e.g., Charles 1920: 89; Hemer 1986: 164; Beale 1999: 288; Osborne 2002: 191), where the reason God promises to deliver captive Israel from their Persian enemy is "because I have loved you" (Isa. 43:4). But even if this specific text is not in view, it is clear from several other statements in Isaiah (41:8; 44:2; 60:10; 63:9) and elsewhere in the OT that Israel enjoys a unique position among all the nations as the people whom God loves. The final words of Christ's second interjection into the commendation are therefore another instance of turning an OT truth on its head: the Jews persecuting the believers in Philadelphia will be forced to acknowledge that it is the predominantly gentile church in their city and not themselves as ethnic Jews who now enjoy the privileged status of being the object of divine love.

Both implicitly and explicitly, 3:9 asserts that the church now constitutes the true Israel. It does so *implicitly* in the statement that the Jews in Philadelphia, despite calling themselves Jews, "are not but are liars." As Beale and Campbell (2015: 62) observe: "That the Jewish community is identified as false Jews and a 'synagogue of Satan' confirms again that the church is seen by Christ as the true people of God, true Israel." The same claim is asserted *explicitly* in the echo of Isa. 60:14 in the first part of 3:9b and the possible allusion to Isa. 43:4 in the last part of this verse. These two OT texts, which originally referred to Israel, are here applied to the predominantly gentile church of Philadelphia. It is not just an ironic reversal of what ethnic Jews were expecting but also an important theological assertion that the church now constitutes the true people of God, or what could be called the "new" or "true" Israel (see also the fuller discussion of 2:9c in chap. 2 above, in the final paragraphs of the section titled "Second Specific Commendation: 'Slander'"). We should also observe how the use of these two OT texts in 3:9 further stresses the deity of Jesus, which was asserted already in the opening Christ title "the Holy One." Jesus will do what Isaiah prophesied that Yahweh would do, thereby affirming his divine status: Jesus will cause the Jewish community which is currently persecuting the Philadelphian church to come and pay homage and recognize that these Christ followers are recipients of God's love and constitute the true Israel (so also Beale 1999: 288).

The Resumption of the Commendation (3:10a)

After his second interjection in 3:9, Christ resumes his commendation of the Philadelphian church in 3:10a. This resumption is indicated in two ways: the subject of the verb shifts from Christ's first-person voice saying what he will do to the second-person voice saying what "you," the Philadelphian church, have done. The statement "You have kept my word of perseverance" repeats exactly (though more fully with the addition of the noun "perseverance") the earlier clause "You have kept my word" in 3:8b, thereby continuing the idea expressed there. The commendation in 3:10a is introduced with the Greek conjunction *hoti*, which here functions as a marker of causality ("because, since") and clarifies the relationship between this dependent clause and the independent clause that follows (3:10b). This sequence is unusual, since dependent causal clauses like this typically stand in the last position, after the independent clause. The reversal of the normal order here creates emphasis: the Philadelphian church has done something commendatory, and this is why Christ will do something positive for them in the clause that follows.

What commendatory thing did the Philadelphian church do? They have obeyed Christ's teaching to persevere in the face of persecution (3:10a). As noted in the discussion of 3:8, the verb "you have kept" has the sense of "to persist in obedience" (BDAG 1002.3) and so could be rendered "you have obeyed." There is some uncertainty whether the believers in Philadelphia have kept (1) the word of Christ about perseverance, meaning Christ's teaching that they should persevere, or (2) the word about Christ's perseverance, meaning the example of Christ's own acts of perseverance. The first option views the personal pronoun "my" as modifying the entire preceding phrase so that it refers to "my word of patient endurance" (NRSV; NIV, "my command to endure patiently"; ESV, "my word about patient endurance"). The second option views the personal pronoun "my" as modifying only the immediately preceding noun "perseverance," so that it refers to "the endurance practiced by Christ" (Charles 1920: 89; Beale 1999: 290, "the model of Christ's own endurance"). Although the similar phrase earlier in the commendation, "You have kept my word" (3:8b), supports the first option, it must be conceded that the grammar allows for both interpretations. Furthermore, there is not much difference between obeying Christ's teaching about perseverance and obeying teaching about Christ's perseverance. The key idea in both interpretations is that believers in Philadelphia are being commended for their ability to persevere in their faith despite facing strong opposition.

The Third Interjection (3:10b)

The commendation is interrupted in 3:10b for a third time as Christ shifts again to the first-person voice and describes yet another blessing that he will give to the Philadelphian church. The earlier first-person interjections in 3:8b and 3:9 interrupt Christ's commendation of the church in a way that makes them parenthetical comments, but this interjection is intimately linked to the commendation. The close connection between the interjection of 3:10b and the preceding commendation of 3:10a is seen first in the opening Greek word *kagō* (an abbreviated form of *kai egō*), which means "I also." The "also" looks back to the previous clause: because the Philadelphian church has done something commendatory, Christ will "also" do something positive for them. The interjection of 3:10b is further linked to the preceding commendation of 3:10a by the use of the same Greek verb (*tēreō*, to keep): because the Philadelphian church "has kept" the word of Christ to persevere in the face of persecution, Christ will now "keep" them from the coming trial. Yet though the verb in each clause is the same, it is used with different meanings: whereas in the commendation of 3:10a the verb has the sense of "obey," in the interjection of 3:10b it has the sense of "protect." This verbal pun (the technical term is paronomasia, the deliberate use of words that sound the same or, as is the case here, are the same but have different meanings) draws the hearer's attention to the different nuances of the word and stresses the protective action of Christ.

Christ promises to keep, or protect, the Philadelphian church "from the hour of trial." The use of the Greek definite article in this phrase (lit., "*the* hour of *the* trial") suggests that a specific and well-known event is in view. The situation does not appear to be the same as that facing the Smyrna church, whose suffering would be local and limited (2:10, "you will have affliction for ten days"). "The hour of trial" for the Philadelphian church, by contrast, "is going to come upon the whole world." Although this description does not preclude a local trial in Philadelphia or Asia Minor, it clearly points to a global event. The universal scope is further suggested by the concluding clause: the trial is coming "to test those who live on the earth." The phrase "those who live on the earth" (*tous katoikountas epi tēs gēs*) is a technical expression in the book of Revelation (3:10; 6:10; 8:13; 11:10; 12:12 [var.]; 13:8, 12, 14; 17:2, 8) that always refers to unbelievers who worship the beast and persecute the Christ followers. The expectation of a worldwide period of tribulation that would occur just before God's final victory and the establishment of his eternal kingdom was widespread in both early Judaism (Dan. 12:1, 10; T. Mos. 8.1; Jub. 23.11–21; 2 Bar. 27.1–15) and Christianity (Matt. 24:3–31; Mark 13:7–20;

Luke 21:7–28; 2 Thess. 2:1–17), and this is almost certainly the event being referred to by the phrase "the hour of trial."

Some have claimed that Christ will protect believers from this universal, end-time trial by removing them physically from earth and bringing them to the safety of heaven. These commentators interpret Christ's interjection in 3:10b as his promise not to "protect you from" but rather to "remove you from" the hour of trial. In this verse, they see support for the idea that the church will be "raptured" from the earth to heaven before the seven-year period of the great tribulation (for an extended defense of this interpretation, see Thomas 1992: 286–88; also Fanning 2020: 177–78). Against this view, however, are a couple of important considerations. First, the only other occurrence in the NT of the verb "keep" (*tēreō*) with the preposition "from" (*ek*) is in another Johannine text, where the context makes the intended meaning of this construction clear. In John 17:15 Jesus prays to his Father, "I ask not that you take them out of the world, but that you *keep them from* the evil one." Here Jesus does not envision the physical removal of his followers from the trials of living in a world influenced by the evil one but instead asks for his Father's special protection of them as they go through these difficulties. So also Christ in Rev. 3:10 is promising the Philadelphian church not its removal but his protection from the end-time trials. Second, the book of Revelation elsewhere consistently depicts Christians not as physically escaping persecution, trouble, and martyrdom but as going through these trials (see 6:9–11; 11:7; 12:12–13, 17; 13:7; 16:6; 20:4). Mounce (1977: 103) is representative of most exegetes who see in 3:10b a promise not of exemption but of protection: "The hour of trial is directed toward the entire non-Christian world, but the believer will be kept from it, not by some previous appearance of Christ to remove the church bodily from the world, but by the spiritual protection he provides against the forces of evil" (for an evaluation of additional details related to this debate, see Beale 1999: 290–92).

Finding a statement about Christ's coming in 3:11a ("I am coming soon") is not at all surprising, since the book of Revelation opens with an affirmation of this truth (1:7, "See, he is coming . . . !"), and his advent is mentioned in six of the seven sermons (2:5, 16, 25; 3:3, 11, 20). The absence of any opening conjunction or particle (asyndeton), however, makes it unclear whether the statement of Christ's coming in 3:11a is connected to the preceding commendation or introduces a new unit in the sermon. That it looks *back* to what has just been stated is suggested by two factors. First, there is a verbal link with the previous verse: the "coming" of Christ (present indicative of *erchomai*) is connected lexically to the hour of trial that is "coming" (present infinitive of *erchomai*). Second, in contrast to the three previous references to the coming of Christ that have a punitive purpose (to remove Ephesus's lampstand, 2:5; to threaten Pergamum with the sword of his mouth, 2:16; to surprise and judge Sardis, 3:3), his advent here has a positive purpose related to the coming hour of trial described in the previous clause. As Hemer notes: "Verse 11, then, is to be taken closely with the preceding words. Christ's coming is here a comfort, as in 22.7, 20, not a threat (2.5, 16; 3.3)." Christ has just promised the Philadelphian church that he will protect them from the impending global tribulation, and his statement "I am coming soon" means that they will not face this trial alone but will have the presence and power of Christ, who will fulfill his promise of protection.

As with the other references to the coming of Christ in the sermons, here too there is ambiguity over the timing of this event: does it refer to a preliminary return of Christ before the parousia or to his definitive advent at the end of time? The reference to the worldwide tribulation that will occur just before God's end-time victory and the establishment of his eternal kingdom makes it more likely that Christ's final advent is in view. Yet the fact that Christ is coming "soon" also gives an inaugurated sense to this statement: he will shortly be present in their midst in a more powerful way than now, by the working of the Spirit, to protect the Philadelphian church in the trial that is about to come upon them and the whole world.

The Complaint—None!

The formal pattern found in the seven sermons overall is that the commendation is followed by the complaint: after praising a church for what it is doing right, Christ typically points out what it is doing wrong. This shift from commendation to complaint is sometimes marked by the formula "But I have [this] against you" (*alla echō kata sou*; so 2:4, Ephesus; 2:14, Pergamum; 2:20, Thyatira). In two sermons (Sardis and Laodicea) this formula is omitted because there is no preceding commendation with which the complaint contrasts. Instead, Christ proceeds directly to identifying the grievances he has against them. Here in the sermon to the Philadelphian church, the absence of the formula is noteworthy because there is no complaint (the same is true of the Smyrna sermon and serves as yet another link connecting these two messages). Normally the Bible is significant for what it says; here is a rare instance when the Bible is significant for what it *does not* say. So in addition to the fulsome character of the commendation section (3:8–11a), the lack of any complaint shows how positively Christ evaluates the church in Philadelphia and its perseverance in the face of persecution.

The Correction (3:11b)

The absence of any complaint naturally affects the content of the next literary unit that is typically found in each sermon, the correction. Since the Christians in Philadelphia are not said to be doing anything wrong, they are not commanded to "repent" as other churches are (2:5, Ephesus; 2:16, Pergamum; 2:21, Thyatira; 3:3, Sardis; 3:19, Laodicea) and are not urged to live in a manner opposite to the behavior identified in the complaint. Instead, this correction issues a command that they continue their commendatory conduct by persevering in the faith: "Hold fast to what you have."

This brief exhortation is the only command given to the Philadelphian church other than the formulaic opening exhortation to the angel of this church to "write" the sermon (3:7) and the typical closing exhortation to "hear" the sermon (3:13). This lone command (3:11b) is given in the present tense (in contrast to the same command given in the aorist tense in 2:25), which emphasizes the ongoing or continual need for the Philadelphian church to "hold fast." The verb *krateō* is a word whose "primary signification is the exercise of power" (BDAG 564), referring not merely to the action of "holding" something but of "holding fast" or "keeping firm hold" of it with all one's might. The command to the Philadelphia Christians to keep a strong grip suggests that they are experiencing stiff opposition to their faith. This is the historical context of the other two uses of the verb *krateō* in the sermons: the believers in Pergamum are commended for "holding fast" the name of Christ in the face of satanic opposition (2:13); the few faithful believers in Thyatira are commanded to "hold fast" in the face of Jezebel's false teaching and the common pagan temptation to engage in idolatry and sexual immorality (2:25). The believers in Philadelphia are similarly commanded to "hold fast" in the face of public attacks from the local Jewish community.

But to what must the Philadelphian church "hold fast"? The combination of the imperative "hold fast" and the relative clause "what you have" occurs here and in the Thyatira sermon (2:25), and in both places the content of "what you have" must be inferred from the context. What the Thyatiran church must hold fast to is described in 2:19, where Christ commends their works (see the discussion there), and the same is true for the Philadelphian church: they are to hold fast to the blessings described in Christ's three first-person interjections appearing within the commendation section.

What the Philadelphian church first and foremost has is what the "synagogue of Satan" denies that it has, membership in the kingdom of God. The local synagogue may have closed its door to the Philadelphian Christians and rejected their claim to being part of the people of God, but Christ has given these persecuted believers an "open door" into the kingdom that no one can shut (3:8a). Second, the church in Philadelphia has Christ's promise of vindication: their opponents will one day come, pay them homage, and acknowledge that they are the object of Christ's love (3:9). Third, they have Christ's promise of protection during the worldwide tribulation that will occur just before God's end-time victory and the establishment of his eternal kingdom (3:10b). The Philadelphian church must cling tenaciously to these three present and future blessings as they face strong opposition from the local Jewish community and others in the city who are trying to deny them these gracious gifts.

The Consequence (3:11c–12)

In the outline followed in all the sermons thus far, each message concludes with a double consequence: first, a negative consequence, which describes the punishment the church faces if it fails to follow Christ's correction; second, a positive consequence, which describes the reward Christ will give the church if it repents and with his help conquers its particular sin(s).

Negative Consequence (3:11c)

In the Smyrna sermon, the omission of a complaint results in the expected negative consequence becoming a positive one: they will receive "the crown of life" (2:10b). In this Philadelphia sermon, the metaphor of a crown is similarly used (thereby establishing yet another parallel with the Smyrna sermon), but the consequence retains its negative or warning character: "in order that no one may take your crown" (3:11c).

This crown is not a royal tiara or diadem (*diadēma*) worn by kings and queens but a wreath (*stephanos*) worn by champion athletes and victorious generals. The book of Revelation refers to both types of headwear, using the word "diadem" to evoke the royal assertions of the seven-headed dragon (12:3) and of the ten-horned beast from the sea (13:1) or to emphasize the exalted status of Christ (19:12). More frequently the book uses "crown" to refer to the "wreath" as an athletic metaphor for the spiritual reward given to faithful Christ followers (2:10b; 3:11c; 4:4, 10) or as a military image of what adorns the heads of victorious participants in the spiritual battle (cf. 6:2; 9:7; 12:1; 14:14). Wreaths were woven out of palm or other branches, flowers, or certain types of plants (e.g., celery, parsley). These wreath crowns would deteriorate quickly in contrast to the "imperishable" (1 Cor. 9:25) and "unfading"

(1 Pet. 5:4) crown given to believers. As is our modern age, the ancient world was obsessed with sports, and athletic contests were held throughout the Roman Empire. There is evidence that games were held in the cities of all seven churches except Thyatira (Wilson 2002:

Figure 6.2. *Left*: Wreathed head of Domitian. *Right*: Nike, goddess of victory, holding wreath and palm branch. The final words of the inscription read "Philadelphia Flavi."

265). The ruins of Philadelphia's stadium are still visible today, though this ancient athletic structure has not yet been excavated. A group of inscriptions from Philadelphia dealing with three different sets of games held there (*CIG* 3416, 3424, 3427, 3428) "exemplifies with unusual clarity the importance attached to athletic prowess" (Hemer 1986: 268). The victory wreath associated with these athletic contests, therefore, became a "familiar symbolic image to all adults and most children in Roman Asia" (Keener 2000: 117). This widespread familiarity means that the Christ followers in Philadelphia, as well as the other Asian believers listening in, would readily appreciate the metaphor of the victory wreath and heed the preceding command to "hold on to what you have" in the face of stiff opposition lest their persecutors rob them of their reward.

Positive Consequence (3:12)

The sermon to Philadelphia concludes with the expected victory formula employing the verb *nikaō*. For observations about how important this verb is within John's writings, how it functions as a metaphor for military conflicts, and how the victory is not a human achievement but a divine gift, the modern reader is encouraged to (re)read the extended discussion of the victory formula in the first sermon, the one to Ephesus (Rev. 2:7b). In three first-person interjections in the commendation (3:9–11a), Christ has already highlighted the three blessings that he either has already given (3:8a) or will yet give (3:9, 10b) to those in the Philadelphian church who keep his word and do not deny his name in the face of strong opposition from the local Jewish community and possibly also city leaders. The victory formula reveals two additional blessings that Christ will give to those who persevere amid persecution. Christ will (1) make his faithful followers pillars in God's temple and (2) write on them three names. These two acts, the first metaphorical and the second symbolic, reassure the oppressed believers in Philadelphia that they have both an honored and a guaranteed place in the kingdom of God.

The first, metaphorical act Christ promises involves a pillar or column: "As for the one who is victorious, I will make that person a pillar in the temple of my God, and they will never again leave it" (3:12a). The image of a pillar located in a temple would be readily understood in the ancient world, since even modest-sized cities had sanctuaries to various deities. Using the metaphor of a pillar to convey a person's importance and place of honor within the community was also well known. In his Letter to the Galatians, Paul refers to the early church leaders James, Peter, and John as "those esteemed as pillars" (Gal. 2:9), and in the First Letter to Timothy the church is described as "the pillar and foundation of the truth" (3:15). Clement of Rome (died AD 99) calls Peter and Paul "those greatest and most righteous pillars" (1 Clement 5.2). The metaphor is still common today: a respected figure in a church or city is sometimes referred to as "a pillar of the community." Victorious Christians will not only be honored as pillars; they will also be located "in the temple of my God." Here "temple" refers figuratively to the dwelling place or presence of God. All those who, like the believers in Philadelphia, persevere amid persecution are assured that they will have an honored place in the new heaven and new earth, where "God himself will be with them and be their God" (Rev. 21:3). Christ refers to his father as "my God" and does so strikingly no less than four times within this verse, stressing the close relationship he enjoys with God. This intimate connection in turn ensures Christ's ability to fulfill his promise to make the faithful Christian in Philadelphia a prestigious pillar in God's temple.

If the metaphor of a pillar conveys the *honored* aspect of the believer's place in the kingdom of God, the *guarantee* of that prestigious position is expressed in the additional clause: "and they will never again leave it." The clause as a whole is emphasized by an emphatic negation (BDF §365: the double negative *ou mē* with the aorist subjunctive)—the strongest form of negation in Greek: "they will *certainly/absolutely* not go out." Two adverbs reinforce this message. The one at the front of the clause (*exō*) emphasizes the idea of "going *out*," which is underscored by the related preposition in the compound verb *exelthē*. The adverb at the end of the clause (*eti*) should be translated after the two negatives as "never *again*" (BDAG 400.1.b; see also Heb. 8:12; 10:17; Rev. 18:21, 22, 23). This second adverb shows that the emphasized action of going out was, in fact, an actual occurrence in the past that would never be repeated.

Many commentators understand that past actual situation of "going out" to refer to a major earthquake that struck Philadelphia in AD 17 and forced its inhabitants to leave the city and live in the surrounding countryside. The ancient historian and geographer Strabo (63 BC–AD 23) refers to "the city of Philadelphia, full of earthquakes, for the walls never cease being cracked, and different parts of the city are constantly suffering damage. That is why the actual town has few inhabitants, but the majority live as farmers in the countryside" (*Geography* 13.4.10). Ramsay (1904: 306; 1994: 298) was apparently the first to connect this historical situation with Christ's promise in the Philadelphia sermon: "There is an obvious reference to this in a later sentence of the letter, where the promise is given to the faithful Philadelphians that they shall go out thence no more." Mounce (1977: 120–21) is typical of several scholars who have followed Ramsay's lead: "To a city that had experienced devastating earthquakes which caused people to flee into the countryside and establish temporary dwellings there, the promise of permanence within the New Jerusalem would have a special meaning" (so also, e.g., Caird 1966: 55; Hemer 1986: 156–57, 166, 175; Thomas 1992: 292n73; Kistemaker 2001: 164; Osborne 2002: 197; Wilson 2002: 275).

This proposed allusion in the clause "and they will never again leave it" to the dwelling of many citizens of Philadelphia outside the city walls due to the threat of earthquakes is attractive and in keeping with John's demonstrated practice of including local references in the sermons. Nevertheless, a few facts raise questions about the probability of this allusion. First, the AD 17 date of the earthquake is several decades earlier than the likely date of the book of Revelation and so raises the question of whether that past event was still a present reality for the recipients of the Philadelphia sermon. The counterargument is that this region lies on a major tectonic fault line, where earthquakes are an ongoing problem. The nearby city of Laodicea, for example, was severely damaged by an earthquake in AD 60, and this same natural disaster may have also done harm to Philadelphia. Yet even this later date is still some three decades before the writing of the book of Revelation. Second, Philadelphia was only one among many cities in the region to experience disaster in the earthquake of AD 17. The ancient historian Tacitus refers to "twelve famous cities of Asia felled by an earthquake in the night" (*Annals* 2.47). A huge marble base for a statue of Tiberius found in Rome's port city of Puteoli contains a dedicatory inscription to the emperor from fourteen Asian cities who received substantial financial aid after several earthquakes that took place during AD 17–29 (*CIL* 10.1624). The question arises: Why, then, should Philadelphia be singled out among the seven churches with an allusion to this natural disaster? Third, Philadelphia was not even the city most negatively affected by the AD 17 earthquake. Tacitus informs us that "the calamity fell most fatally on the inhabitants of Sardis, and it attracted to them the largest share of sympathy" (*Annals* 2.47).

The sermon itself reveals that the biggest threat facing the Christians in Philadelphia was not ongoing earthquakes but the local Jewish community. More likely, Christ's promise that believers who will become prestigious pillars in God's temple "will never again leave it" alludes to the danger from "the synagogue of Satan." The local Jews rejected the gentile Christians' claim to being members of God's covenant people and of his kingdom and the object of his divine love, and the local Jews had recently expelled Jewish Christians from the synagogue. To such Christ followers, whether gentile or Jewish, it would be deeply comforting to hear Christ promise them not only an *honored* place but also a *guaranteed* position within the kingdom of God. Christ had opened a door for them to be full members of God's covenant people, and no one, not even the local Jewish community, would be able to close that door and keep them out.

The second, symbolic act that Christ will do also guarantees the persecuted believers' membership in the kingdom of God: he will write on them three names. It is, of course, most fitting that those in Philadelphia who have been commended by Christ because they have not denied his name (3:8) will be rewarded by Christ's writing three names on them. The Greek text is ambiguous about whether these three names will be written on the victorious believer ("on the person") or on the pillar ("on it"); since it has just been stated that the believer will become a pillar, the latter option is more likely. Furthermore, it was a common practice in the ancient world to inscribe an honorific text or name on a pillar. Several different backgrounds have been proposed for the resulting image of a pillar on which are written three names.

1. Solomon had the names "Jakin" (probably meaning "he establishes") and "Boaz" (likely meaning "in him is strength") written on two key pillars in the portico of his temple (1 Kings 7:21; 2 Chron. 3:15, 17), leading some scholars to claim that the two promises here in the Philadelphia sermon "are drawn together by the recollection that the twin pillars in Solomon's temple had 'personal' names" (Farrer 1964: 81; see also Swete 1911: 57).

2. Another explanation is that the image of an inscribed pillar originates from the so-called king's pillar in the temple of Solomon (Wilkinson 1988). The king's pillar—possibly one of the "Jakin" and "Boaz" pair—was a special place reserved for Israel's ruler, where the monarch stood during temple ceremonies, including coronations (2 Kings 11:14; 23:3; 2 Chron. 34:31). The pillar promised in the Philadelphia sermon thus has kingship and coronation allusions that identify the victorious believer as royalty.

3. Some have claimed an allusion to a local custom of the imperial cult in which the priest, at the end of his year of service, would set up in the temple

a statue of himself and inscribe on it his name, the name of his father, his place of birth, and his year of service (so Moffatt 1910: 369; Charles 1920: 91–92; Kiddle 1940: 53–54). Against this proposal, however, are the facts that the parallel is not exact (it involves a statue instead of a pillar), the imperial cult was not set up in Philadelphia until more than a century later (AD 213), and the historical evidence for this practice is questionable (Hemer 1986: 166).

4. Some understand here a possible allusion to the gold plate inscribed with the phrase "Holy to the Lord," fastened on Aaron's priestly headdress and worn on his forehead (Exod. 28:36–38; so, e.g., Aune 1997: 242; Hemer 1986: 166; Osborne 2002: 197). This proposal finds some support in other texts in the book of Revelation where a seal or God's name is placed on the foreheads of saints (7:3; 14:1; 22:4; contrast 17:5), but it does not account for the metaphor of the pillar in God's temple.

5. Another claimed parallel involves a lengthy recording of the military exploits of Simon Maccabaeus and his brothers, which grateful Jews had inscribed "on bronze tablets and put it on pillars" in the Jerusalem temple (1 Macc. 14:26–48; so Beasley-Murray 1978: 102n3). Once again, however, the parallel with the Philadelphia sermon is not exact: there the inscription is on the pillar itself rather than on bronze tablets, and it consists not of the believer's accomplishments nor even of his name but rather that of God, of the new Jerusalem, and of Christ's new name.

6. The metaphor of the victorious believer as an inscribed pillar may continue the allusion in the third Christ title to Isa. 22:15–25, which tells how Shebna will be replaced by Eliakim as the master of the household of King Hezekiah and be given a powerful symbol of his newfound authority, "the key to the house of David; what he opens no one can shut, and what he shuts no one can open" (Isa. 22:22). The immediately following verses state that God will "drive him like a *peg* into a firm place" (22:23), thereby bringing honor to his offspring, but that after a while "the *peg* driven into the firm place will give way" (22:25), meaning that he, along with his family members, will lose this position of honor. A few Greek translations of these Isaiah verses (Vaticanus, Origen, Q) have the word "pillar" instead of "peg," which leads Beale (1999: 295) to explain the metaphor of the inscribed pillar in the Philadelphia sermon as follows: "In contrast to Eliakim's dependents, who eventually lost their glory and position in the palace when he was finally removed (cf. Isa. 22:23–25), the followers of Jesus will never be removed from their position in the temple/palace because Jesus, the 'true' Messiah, will never lose his regal position in the presence of his Father ('pillar' is metaphorical of permanence)" (see also Mounce 1977: 121; Michaels 1997: 85–86). Although this proposal is supported by the earlier allusion to Isa. 22:22, it rests on

the dubious assumption that John knew and was influenced by an alternative, minority reading of the Septuagint. The proposed OT background also does not explain the writing of names on the pillar.

7. It may well be that the image of a pillar on which names are inscribed does not allude to anything specific but simply reflects a widespread practice in the ancient world by which important individuals were remembered and honored. Many inscriptions on pillars were intended as reminders of significant events connected with the construction of the building where the column was located or the history of the local city. There is the example of the so-called Talking Pillar from the temple of Artemis in Sardis.

Figure 6.3. Two Doric pillars, part of the Prytaneum (city council building) in Ephesus, inscribed with names of the priests of Artemis.

This massive Ionic column contains an inscription given in the first-person voice: "My torus [foot] and my foundation block are carved from a single block of stone. Of all the pillars I am the first to rise." In the Asia Minor city of Euromos, located about twenty-five miles inland and southeast of the port of Miletus, a pillar in the agora (marketplace) contains a lengthy inscription about the financial aid given to the city by Callisthenes, an important figure who accompanied Alexander the Great during his Asian expedition.

Another type of inscription commonly found on pillars consisted of the names of those who paid for the erection of the column. Herodotus (*Histories* 1.92) claimed that Croesus, king of Sardis, dedicated many pillars in the building of the first temple of Artemis in Ephesus (550–520 BC)—a claim that was proved true in 1872, when a piece of one of its original marble columns was discovered with the inscription "King Croesus dedicated [this]." Two pillars from the Temple of Artemis in Sardis contain the name of the individual who donated them to the sanctuary. In the city of Euromos are the remains of one of the best-preserved Corinthian temples in Asia Minor, which was dedicated to Zeus. Sixteen of its impressive pillars still stand, and inscriptions on twelve of them record the names of its leading citizens who commissioned their construction.

The type of pillar inscription that most closely parallels the reward promised to the victorious believers in Philadelphia involves the names of individuals worthy of special honor carved into a column located in an important building within the city. One of the prominent pillars from the temple to Apollo at Claros, a key religious site in Asia Minor, includes an honorary inscription dedicated to Sextus Appuleius, a relative of Augustus who served as proconsul of Asia (23–22 BC). In the entrance hall of the Prytaneum (the city council building) in Ephesus, two very tall Doric pillars contain long lists of the names of *kourētes*, priests connected with the world-famous temple of Artemis. These priests performed both religious and civic duties, and their important service was recognized and honored by having their names inscribed on these pillars (see fig. 6.3). Even these few examples cited above justify the claim of Wilson (2002: 276): "So the imagery of pillars inscribed with names was familiar to the Asian believers." The honorific aspect of this metaphor also needs to be fully recognized. Christ's promise that victorious believers will be an inscribed pillar in God's temple would further reassure these oppressed church members in Philadelphia that they not only belong to God's people but even have a privileged place in the kingdom of God.

On the victorious members of the Philadelphian church, Christ will write not one but three names, none of which includes that of the individual believer. This threefold inscription is not redundant but emphatic. Since having the name of some person or thing involves belonging to that person or thing, the writing of three names stresses that those who persevere in the face of persecution belong to God ("the name of my God"), belong to the heavenly city or kingdom of God ("the name of the city of my God, the new Jerusalem, which is coming down out of heaven from my God"), and belong to Christ ("my new name"). As Hendriksen (1940: 75) puts it: "In other words, to the conqueror will be given the assurance that he belongs to God and to the New Jerusalem and to Christ, and that he will everlastingly share in all the blessings and privileges of all three."

The first name given is "the name of my God." This agrees with other texts in the book of Revelation where believers have the name of the Lamb and the name of his Father (14:1) written on their foreheads in contrast to the followers of the beast, who bear the beast's name (13:17; 14:11). It echoes generally the OT idea that God places his name on every Israelite and that his covenant people bear his name (Num. 6:27; Deut. 28:10; Isa. 43:7; Dan. 9:19; cf. James 2:7). Judging by the many citations and allusions to Isaiah earlier in this Philadelphia sermon, there may be a more specific echo of

Isa. 62:2, where God promises to give his people a "new name" (which could be, as asserted here in Revelation, the name of God himself) as part of their end-time vindication.

The second name given is "the name of the city of my God, the new Jerusalem." The fuller meaning and significance of having the name and thus also citizenship in "the new Jerusalem" is spelled out later in the book of Revelation, in the vision of chapters 21–22. There the brief and cryptic phrase "the new Jerusalem" is again mentioned (21:2) along with the additional description of this city as "coming down out of heaven from my God," which is repeated virtually word-for-word both in the introduction of this vision (21:2) and again later in its contents (21:10). This later vision about "the new Jerusalem" highlights the many blessings enjoyed by those living in the holy city, the preeminent benefit being the constant and unmediated presence of God with his people. The notion of a new, or heavenly, Jerusalem originates from Ezekiel's vision of an eschatological temple in Ezek. 40–48, especially its final and climactic verse that "the name of the city [i.e., the new Jerusalem] from that time on will be THE LORD IS THERE" (Ezek. 48:35). The expectation that followers of Christ would have membership in the new or heavenly Jerusalem and enjoy the blessings that come from life in that holy city is one that John shares with other NT writers (Gal. 4:26; Heb. 12:22; cf. Phil. 3:20).

The third name given to victorious believers is "my new name," that is, the new name of Christ. It is not stated here or elsewhere in the book of Revelation what this new name of Christ is. The description of his coming on a white horse to defeat the beast states that "he has a name written on him that no one knows but he himself" (19:12). The identity of this name seemingly will remain hidden until it is revealed at his glorious return. The key point here is not the identity of Christ's new name but the reassuring promise that victorious believers will be given that new name, confirming that they belong to Christ.

Many commentators follow Ramsay's suggestion (1904: 397–98, 409–12) that the promise of being given three new names would have special meaning for the Christ followers in Philadelphia since their city had been renamed twice: the first time it was given the new name "Neocaesarea" (new Caesar), to honor Tiberius for his generous financial aid following the devastating earthquake of AD 17; the city was rechristened a second time with the name "Flavia," in honor of the family name of Vespasian during his reign of AD 69–79 (so, e.g., Aune 1977: 244; Hemer 1986: 157–58, 176; Keener 2000: 152; Kistemaker 2001: 164; Osborne 2002: 198). Mounce (1977: 121) counters that this historical fact may be interesting but "adds little to our understanding of the verse." Although the significance of the city's double name change for the interpretation of 3:12c should not be overstated, it nevertheless does show that the act of renaming—whether a city or an individual—was recognized in that day as important. Hence the three new names that Christ promises to inscribe on those who persevere in the face of persecution would have been viewed by their recipients as no mere token gift but a momentous blessing.

The Contemporary Significance

Introduction

Many American cities have a nickname. New York is well-known as "the Big Apple," Chicago is "the Windy City," Las Vegas is "Sin City," Detroit is "the Motor City," and Philadelphia is widely known as "the City of Brotherly Love." Actually, that is not the nickname of Philadelphia but the literal meaning of its name: "Philadelphia" is the Greek word for "brotherly love."

Why give this name to a city? Why call a city "Philadelphia," that is, "brotherly love"? The answer is because the founders of this city wanted it to be a place where people love each other, a place where people act in a loving way like family, as brothers are supposed to act toward each other but often fail to do. It is a sobering truth that, ever since the time of Cain and Abel, brothers have been fighting each other more often than loving each other.

That is why the ancient world commemorated and celebrated the loving relationship that existed between two brothers who were sons of a king. The names of these two brothers were Eumenes II and Attalus II, and their family ruled over the city kingdom of Pergamum. Pergamum, of course, is the place to which the third sermon of Jesus was directed. Eumenes was the older brother, and so he logically became king instead of Attalus. Two events happened during the older brother's reign that resulted in the younger brother demonstrating "philadelphia," brotherly love. The first event involved a distant battle from which it was reported that Eumenes had been killed while fighting, and so Attalus was declared king in his dead brother's place. The report, however, turned out to be false, and Eumenes returned from the battle still very much alive. Although it was tempting for Attalus to fight against his older brother and selfishly hang on to power, he willingly handed the rule back to him as the rightful king. The second event occurred when the Romans secretly contacted Attalus and promised to help him overthrow his brother so that he could assume power, but Attalus refused Rome's offer and again demonstrated "philadelphia," brotherly love. Eumenes was so thankful for the loving actions of his younger brother that he took one of the cities in their kingdom and changed its name to "Philadelphia," to honor forever the love that his brother demonstrated.

Yet in the ancient city of Philadelphia, the city of brotherly love, there was no love for the followers of Jesus. The church of Philadelphia was being persecuted not only by the local Roman authorities but even more aggressively by the local Jewish community. The Christians in Philadelphia were being strongly persecuted for their faith, but they persevered. They were not like most of the other churches in Asia Minor who compromised their faith to avoid suffering at the hands of their pagan and Jewish neighbors. And so, in our message for today, I introduce you to the church of Philadelphia, or, as it can be justly called, "the church of the persevering persecuted."

The Christ Title (3:7b)

All seven sermons begin with the Christ title. Before Jesus says anything to the church of Philadelphia, he introduces himself using three titles. All of them come from the OT and so are especially effective as a polemic against the local Jewish community, which was particularly aggressive in persecuting the Philadelphian church.

Jesus introduces himself in the first Christ title as "the Holy One" (3:7b). This title appears often in the OT—including some twenty-five times in Isaiah—as a key title for God. Jesus's use of this divine title to describe himself is a not very subtle way of saying something important about who he is, that he is God. Before you too quickly dismiss this truth as something you already know and believe, remember what the Christians in Philadelphia were facing: strong opposition from the local Jewish community, who were vehemently denying the claim that Jesus is God. It would be especially comforting for the persecuted Christians in Philadelphia to hear, at the very beginning of this sermon, that the Jesus for whom they are suffering is "the Holy One," that is, God.

In the second Christ title, Jesus introduces himself as "the True One" (3:7b). This too involves a polemical argument against the local Jewish community, whom Jesus later in this sermon calls liars (3:9a), who vehemently deny that Jesus is the true Messiah. These Jews view Jesus as merely a pretend messiah, a fake messiah, a messianic wannabe. Once again, it would be especially comforting for the persecuted Christians in Philadelphia to hear at the very beginning of this sermon that the Jesus for whom they are suffering is "the True One," who is indeed the Messiah.

In the third Christ title, which is significantly longer, Jesus introduces himself as "the one who has the key of David; what he opens no one can shut and what he shuts no one can open" (3:7b). This Christ title closely echoes the words of Isa. 22:22. The backstory of this not-so-well-known passage from Isaiah goes like this:

In ancient Israel, no one could have direct and immediate access to the palace and the king; people instead had to go through the MOP, the Master of the Palace. He had the key, which meant total control over who could enter the palace and meet with the king. In the days of good King Hezekiah, the person who held the powerful position of MOP was a man named Shebna. Shebna revealed his vanity and selfish ambition by having a grave made for himself, cut out of solid rock, in a place where only the kings had graves. God was so displeased with Shebna's arrogant action that he promised to give the powerful position of MOP to someone else. This new person was promised "the key of David," a powerful symbol of his authority as MOP. In fact, this person would have such total control over who had access to the palace and the king that "what he opens no one can shut, and what he shuts no one can open."

This backstory explains the meaning of the third Christ title: Jesus is now the MOP, the Master of the Palace, the one with total control over who has access to "the city of my God, the new Jerusalem," as it is called later in the sermon (3:12). Jesus is the one with absolute authority over who can enter the kingdom of God.

This third Christ title also involves an important polemic against the Jewish community in Philadelphia. Judaism was officially recognized as a protected religion by the Roman state. Special arrangements with the Roman authorities allowed the Jews to meet in their synagogue buildings and be exempt from participating in pagan sacrifices, which were a big part of everyday civic life and were the way citizens publicly demonstrated their loyalty to Rome. Christianity, however, was not an officially recognized religion, and so when the Jesus followers similarly refused to participate in pagan sacrifices, they were persecuted. To avoid this persecution, many Jewish Christians continued as members of the local synagogue, taking advantage of the fact that most people could not distinguish Christianity from Judaism. Over time, however, the Jewish leaders realized that the Christians in their synagogues were taking advantage of the protection that Judaism afforded, and so they took steps "to close the door" on these Jesus followers, to excommunicate them from synagogue membership.

In the third Christ title, Jesus is telling the Christians in Philadelphia: "You may have been kicked out of the synagogue, but you have not been kicked out of the kingdom of God. Remember that I have the key of David. Remember that I am the MOP, the Master of the Palace. I have opened the door for you to approach God fully and freely and to enter God's kingdom, and what I open, no one can shut—neither the Roman authorities nor the leaders of the local Jewish synagogue."

The Commendation (3:8–11a)

After the Christ title, the second item typically found in each of the seven sermons is the commendation. Here Jesus praises the church of Philadelphia for what they are doing right. That this commendation is three and a half verses long (3:8–11a)—longer than any other commendation in the seven sermons—shows how pleased Jesus is with this congregation. Jesus gives them a double thumbs-up sign as he says, "Great job, church of Philadelphia! You have persevered in your faith even in the face of severe persecution!"

In fact, Jesus is so pleased with the church of Philadelphia that he keeps interrupting his commendation of what *they* are doing right in order to tell them what *he* in turn has done or will do for them. Three times Jesus switches from pointing toward them and commending them for their good works (using the second-person pronoun "you") to pointing toward himself and telling them what he has done or will do in response (using the first-person pronoun "I").

So what does Jesus commend the Philadelphians for doing right? Jesus says: "I know your works. . . . You have little power, yet you have kept my word and have not denied my name. . . . You kept my word to endure patiently." The church of Philadelphia has little power; that is, it is small in number and lacks political clout and influence in their community. The church of Philadelphia has also not denied Christ's name, which suggests that pressure was put on them in a public setting to renounce their faith in Christ. In the next verse, the reference to the "synagogue of Satan" and "those who call themselves Jews" strongly suggests that the local Jewish community made an official charge against Christians before the city council, accusing them of practicing an unapproved religion and engaging in treasonous activity. Yet despite such attacks, the church of Philadelphia refused to deny the name of Christ, and so Jesus says: "Great job, church of Philadelphia! Way to go, Church of the Persevering Persecuted!"

Jesus not only commends them but even interrupts his commendation three times to tell them what he has done or will do for them. The first interruption goes like this: "See, I have set before you an open door, which no one is able to shut" (3:8a). If we were looking at a letter of Paul, the "open door" metaphor would refer to evangelism—the opportunity to share the gospel. But we are not looking at a letter of Paul; we are hearing a sermon of Christ to the church of Philadelphia, and in the book of Revelation the "open door" metaphor refers to entrance into heaven (4:1), or what is referred to later in this sermon as "the city of my God, the new Jerusalem" (3:12)—images for the kingdom of God.

Don't miss the fact that Jesus sets before the church of Philadelphia not only a door that is open but also a door "which no one is able to shut." Here again is an allusion to Isa. 22:22 and how Christ is the MOP, the Master of the Palace, the one who controls access to the palace and the king. Here again is a local reference to the excommunication of Jewish Christians from the synagogue in Philadelphia. Christ's first interruption, therefore, would have been most comforting to the persecuted church of Philadelphia. They may have been kicked out of the synagogue, but Christ has the "key of David," which guarantees them full and free access to God and entrance into his kingdom, and what Christ opens, no one, not even the "synagogue of Satan," can shut.

Christ's second interruption of his commendation goes like this: "See, I will make those of the synagogue of Satan, the ones who call themselves Jews though they are not but are false—see, I will make them come and fall down at your feet and acknowledge that I love you" (3:9). On the basis of many OT texts, there existed a widespread expectation that the gentiles, who in this present age persecuted the Jews, would in the coming age fall down in humiliation and submission before God's people. Christ's second interruption comforts the persecuted church of Philadelphia by flipping this widespread expectation on its head: it is now the local Jewish persecutors who will be forced to fall down in humiliation and submission before the Jesus followers in Philadelphia, thereby vindicating their faith in Christ.

For yet a third time Christ interrupts his commendation of the church of Philadelphia: "I will also keep you from the hour of trial that is going to come on the whole world to test the inhabitants of the earth" (3:10b). The persecution that the Jesus followers in Philadelphia are enduring now is just a small and local foretaste of a larger and global type of persecution yet to come. There is "the hour of trial" that all Christians will face before the return of Jesus and the restoration of God's kingdom here on earth. Here we see the lie of the "health and wealth gospel"—the false claim that, if you believe in Jesus, all your troubles will go away: you'll never be sick, you'll never be poor, and you'll never face any trials. The Christians in Philadelphia knew from painful, firsthand experience that this is simply not true; those who proclaim the name of Jesus should expect to be persecuted. But amid these troubles, there is the comforting promise that Jesus will "keep you from the hour of trial"—not that Jesus will "remove us from" the hour of trial but that Jesus will "protect us in" the hour of trial. He will give each of us what we need to persevere in our faith.

The Complaint—None!

The third item that typically appears in the outline of each sermon is the complaint. After commending a church for what it is doing right, Jesus normally spells out what they are doing wrong. That's why what comes next in the sermon to Philadelphia—or more precisely, what *does not* come next—is so significant: the complaint is missing! Jesus utters no criticism at all about the church of Philadelphia. Normally, the Bible is significant for what it says; here is a rare instance when the Bible is significant for what it *does not* say. Only two of the seven churches are spiritually healthy; the majority are spiritually sick with significant problems. The missing complaint shows that the church of Philadelphia belongs to the select group of healthy churches (the only other member in this group is the church of Smyrna), which we should try to emulate. We also are called to persevere through whatever persecution may come our way and live such faithful lives that Christ would have no complaint at all to bring against us!

The Correction (3:11b)

It is not surprising that the lack of a complaint in this sermon also alters the fourth thing that is typically found in each message: the correction. If the church of Philadelphia is not doing anything wrong, then Jesus has no need to command them to repent, as he demands of the unhealthy churches. Instead, Jesus commands these believers to continue their commendatory conduct by persevering in their faith: "Hold fast to what you have" (3:11b).

What does the church of Philadelphia have, to which they must hold fast? They have the three wonderful gifts Christ has just named in his three interruptions. First, they have an "open door"; that is, they have full and free access to God through Jesus, the MOP, and membership in his kingdom, and when Jesus opens this door, no one— neither Roman rulers nor Jewish persecutors—can close it. Second, they have Christ's promise of vindication: their Jewish opponents, whose evil acts against the local Jesus followers reveal their true identity as the "synagogue of Satan," will be forced to recognize the church of Philadelphia as the object of Christ's love. Third, they have Christ's promise of protection in the worldwide persecution of the church. These are the three wonderful blessings that the church of Philadelphia must tenaciously cling to as they continue to face strong pushback from their pagan and Jewish neighbors.

The Consequence (3:11c–12)

The fifth and final item in the outline for all seven sermons is the double consequence: first, a negative consequence, describing the punishment that the church faces if it fails to follow Christ's correction; second, a positive consequence, describing the reward the church will receive if it responds to Christ's correction.

Negative Consequence (3:11c)

The church of Philadelphia is a healthy congregation, with whom Jesus has no complaint, and so the negative consequence is not nearly as strongly worded as it is in most other sermons: "in order that no one may take your crown" (3:11c). This crown is not a royal tiara with all kinds of precious jewels worn by kings and queens;

rather, it is the wreath made up of palm branches worn by victorious athletes and generals. The ancient world was as obsessed with sports as we are today, and the city of Philadelphia had a stadium where athletic contests were regularly held, so the image of a crown—or more accurately, a victory wreath—would have been familiar to anyone in the first century. The Christians in Philadelphia would interpret the reference to a victory wreath as a metaphor for the spiritual blessings they had received and a reminder of their need to "hold on to what you have" despite persecution, lest this victory wreath and the blessings it represents be taken away.

Positive Consequence (3:12)

The sermon to Philadelphia ends in the same way all the sermons have ended thus far: with the victory formula. Since this is now the sixth time that we have heard Jesus refer to "the one who is victorious," we remember that the Greek word used here is also the name of a popular sporting goods company, Nike. The company chose the name to connect the use of their sports equipment and apparel with winning.

The important question that our text raises is this: Are you a Nike Christian, that is, a victorious Christian? Are you able to persevere through whatever persecutions come your way? The good news of the gospel is that the answer to this question can be a resounding "Yes!" You and I can be Nike Christians and win the victory—not because we are so talented or hard working, but because Christ has already won the victory, and we who belong to Christ have his Spirit living in us. This divine Holy Spirit gives us the power not to be intimidated or afraid to live out our faith, no matter what kind of pushback comes our way.

What is the reward of the Nike Christian? Jesus says, "As for the one who is victorious, I will make that person a pillar in the temple of my God, and they will never again leave it" (3:12a). The Nike Christian who perseveres in faith despite persecution will be turned into a pillar. This may not initially sound like much of a reward, but Christ is promising us an *honored* and *guaranteed* place in the kingdom of God.

The idea of honor is conveyed by the pillar image because pillars were impressive pieces of architecture in the ancient world. They were typically made of marble or other expensive material and served the crucial purpose of holding up a building. The pillar as an image of honor is still found today: someone who is highly respected may be called a "pillar of the community." The location of the pillar also stresses the idea of honor. If the three most important things in real estate are "location, location, location," then the Nike Christian is going to be a pillar in the most honored location anywhere, in the temple of God. In other words, those who persevere in faith will enjoy an honored place in the presence of God and in his temple, that is, in his kingdom.

Christ promises not only an honored place in God's kingdom but also a guaranteed place. The guarantee is expressed in the emphatic phrase "and they will never again leave it." Here we have yet another allusion to the local situation of the church of Philadelphia and the excommunicating of Jewish Christians from the synagogue. It would be deeply comforting for these rejected and persecuted believers to hear Christ promise them not only an honored position in the kingdom of God but one that is also guaranteed. Christ is the MOP, the Master of the Palace, who opens the door for them to have full and free access to God and to his kingdom, and no one, not even the local Jewish community, can close that door and force them to leave.

Christ further comforts the Nike Christians in Philadelphia by promising to carve three names on their pillar: "And I will write on them the name of my God, and the name of the city of my God—the new Jerusalem, which is coming down out of heaven from my God—and my new name" (3:12b). To have the name of some person means that you belong to that person, and so the persecuted believers in Philadelphia have a further guarantee of their privileged position: they belong to God, they belong to the heavenly city or kingdom of God, and they belong to Christ, and these blessings belong to them.

Conclusion

What about the church in the twenty-first century? What word more accurately describes Jesus followers today: "persecuted" or "privileged"?

The word that accurately describes the global church is "persecuted." Because the Western press rarely reports on the oppression of Christians around the world, most of us are unaware of the suffering that so many of our spiritual brothers and sisters endure every day. The Pew Research Center has recently reported that in 128 countries—about 65 percent of all countries in the world—Christians face some form of persecution and that Christians are targeted for negative treatment more than any other religious group. This persecution may not always involve death and martyrdom, but it can still be painful and hard to endure. The phone calls and emails of Christians are often monitored by local government officials. Paid informants infiltrate churches, report on Christian worship services, and keep track of what pastors are saying to their congregation. Christians are ostracized by family members and prevented from having any contact with beloved relatives. Christians may not be hired for a job simply because of their faith, or their business may be shunned by the larger non-Christian community and suffer financially. Church buildings are burned or bombed, sometimes with Christians still inside. Many governments in predominantly Muslim countries use anti-apostasy or anti-blasphemy laws to arrest Christians and suppress the Christian faith.

Persecution is a painful reality for many fellow Christians around the world, making the sermon to Philadelphia especially relevant for our spiritual brothers and sisters in the global church who are suffering for their faith. They need to hear the gospel message that they can be Nike Christians, persevering in the face of persecution and having Christ's Spirit living in them to give them power not to be intimidated or afraid to live out their faith, no matter what kind of pushback comes their way. These realities should also motivate us to act on behalf of our persecuted brothers and sisters. The writer of Hebrews gives this clear command: "Continue to remember . . . those who are persecuted as if you yourselves were being persecuted" (Heb. 13:3). We are called to remember, pray for, and support in whatever way we can our persecuted brothers and sisters in the global church.

The word that more accurately describes the Western church, however, is not "persecuted" but "privileged." Far from suffering for our faith, most of us have benefited from our faith. We live in a country that historically has identified itself as a Christian nation and where the dominant religion by far is Christianity. This means that for a long time the Western church has been in a privileged position: the unique beliefs and distinctive ethics that we as Jesus followers profess have been supported by the broader culture in which we live.

But this privileged position is quickly changing. As our culture becomes increasingly secular, it is also becoming more hostile to the Christian faith. Christians are portrayed in television and film in an unflattering way as self-righteous, bigoted, and hypocritical. The sobering reality is that we live in a society rapidly becoming not just less Christian, but even anti-Christian. It may be only a matter of time before the word "persecuted" accurately describes not just the global church but the Western church as well.

When our faith is tested and persecution comes our way, how are we going to respond? Let us be like the church of Philadelphia, "the church of the persevering persecuted." Let us recommit ourselves to Jesus Christ, the Master of the Palace, who sets before us an open door by which we have full and free access to God and his kingdom. Let us by the power of Christ and his Spirit hold on tenaciously to the rich spiritual blessings that we have so that no one will take our crown, our wreath of victory.

"Whoever has ears to hear, let them hear what the Spirit is saying to the churches!"—not only the ancient church of Philadelphia but also the church of Jesus Christ today.

7

Laodicea

The Church of Vomit and Vanity

The Christ Title (3:14b)

The sermon to Laodicea begins in the same way that all the preceding six messages do, with a title that Christ gives to himself and that in some way anticipates the message he is about to give. Here, the title provides a threefold description: "These are the words of the Amen, the faithful and true witness, the ruler of God's creation" (3:14b). This is the only Christ title that does not stem from the opening vision in 1:9–20, but there are potential links with earlier verses in chapter 1 where Christ is described as "*the faithful witness*" and "the *ruler* of the kings of earth" (1:5) and the twofold affirmation "*Amen*" appears (1:6, 7).

All three descriptions of Christ likely echo Isa. 65:16–17. This passage twice describes God as "the God of Amen," and both times the Greek Septuagint translates the Hebrew "Amen" as "true." Furthermore, this text refers to the theme of new creation. Most commentators therefore see this OT reference as the background of the Christ title in Rev. 3:14b (see esp. Beale 1999: 298–300). That the Christ titles in four other sermons are also drawn from Isaiah makes the allusion here to Isa. 65:16–17 more probable (see Smyrna: "the First and the Last" [Isa. 41:4; 44:6; 48:12]; Pergamum: "the sharp, double-edged sword"

231

[Isa. 11:4; 49:2]; Sardis: "seven spirits" [Isa. 11:2–3]; Philadelphia: "the Holy One" [25× in Isaiah]). The likelihood that Isa. 65:16–17 is the background behind the Christ title in the Laodicean sermon gains further strength from the fact that John alludes to this Isaiah passage earlier in his book (Rev. 2:17; 3:12) in reference to receiving a new name (see Isa. 65:15, "to his servant he will give another name") and later (Rev. 21:1) in reference to the new heaven and earth (see Isa. 65:17, "See, I will create a new heaven and a new earth"). So John is clearly familiar with this chapter from Isaiah.

The first Christ title involves a very common Hebrew word used here in a rare way. The Hebrew word "Amen," literally meaning "true," occurs about 130 times in the NT. The vast majority of these occurrences involve a strong affirmation of what has just been stated ("That's true! Let it be so!"). John uses the word as a response at the end of a doxology (Rev. 1:6) or when affirming the truth of what has just been professed or heard (1:7; 5:14). Jesus sometimes prefaced his statements with either a single (Matthew, Mark, Luke) or double (John) "Amen" to signal the importance of the truth he was about to convey. Out of all the occurrences of this word in the NT, however, there is only one instance where it functions as a name: here in the Christ title in the sermon to Laodicea. The fact that Isa. 65:16 is the only place in the whole OT where the word "Amen" functions similarly as a name provides the strongest evidence that the first Christ title echoes this Isaiah passage.

Since Isa. 65:16 refers to God as "the God of Amen," John's use of this word to refer to Christ clearly asserts his *divinity*: Christ is God. As Aune (1997: 255) observes: "Christologically this title is significant since it attributes to Christ a title associated only with God." But this title does not just assert Christ's divine status; it also conveys something about his *character* as "the Amen"—namely, that he is the true and faithful one. This additional significance to the title "the Amen" is suggested by the context of Isa. 65:16: God's people can confidently either invoke a blessing in his name as "the God of Amen" or take an oath in his name as "the God of Amen" because he not only knows the truth in these matters but will also faithfully act according to that truth. Similarly, the Laodicean church ought to take seriously that Christ is not only speaking the truth to them in the words of judgment and grace that follow but will also faithfully carry out his threats of judgment and promises of grace. Beasley-Murray (1978: 104) recognizes this meaning of the first Christ title: "As surely as God's own character stands behind his word, so Jesus is the guarantee of the truth of his message."

The second Christ title confirms and reinforces this emphasis on Christ's divinity and character. The phrase "the faithful and true witness" is not introduced with the conjunction "and" but is instead placed in apposition to the first Christ title, indicating that it is intended to explain the preceding name, "the Amen." This conclusion is further supported by the fact that the Greek Septuagint translates the Hebrew "amen" with two adjectives: "faithful" (*pistos*) and "true" (*alēthinos*). The reference to "the faithful witness" in this second Christ title echoes the opening of the book of Revelation (1:5), where this same expression appears. In both instances "the faithful witness" refers not to the verbal testimony that Christ gave during his earthly ministry but to his words in the revelation transmitted through John in this book, both generally (1:5) and specifically in the sermon to Laodicea (3:14). Since the adjective *pistos* in Revelation always means "faithful, trustworthy" (1:5; 2:10, 13; 3:14; 17:14; 19:11; 21:5; 22:6) and the adjective *alēthinos* describes what is "true," it is the reliability and truth of Christ's forthcoming words that are being emphasized in the second Christ title. Jesus is about to speak as "the faithful and true witness," and so his message to the Laodiceans—no matter how stinging its complaint or how surprising its grace-filled consequences— should not be rejected or doubted but instead received as reliable and accurate.

The third Christ title has been variously interpreted. Is Christ "the *beginning* of God's creation" (KJV, ASV, NASB, NLT, ESV), "the *origin/originator* of God's creation" (GNT, NRSV, NET, LEB), or "the *ruler* of God's creation" (NIV, NCV, CEB)? All three meanings are possible because the Greek noun *archē* is used elsewhere with each of these senses (BDAG 137–38). Most commentators interpret the noun in this passage in connection with Paul's statements in Col. 1:15 and 1:18, which describe Jesus Christ as the "firstborn" (*prōtotokos*) and "beginning" (*archē*) of all creation. In support of this interpretation, it is noted that the cities of Laodicea and Colossae were close geographically (only about ten miles apart in the Lycus Valley) and that the churches in each city exchanged letters (Col. 4:16), with the result that the Laodicean Christians would be familiar with Paul's assertion about Christ in his Colossian letter (so, e.g., Charles 1920: 94–95; Mounce 1977: 124; Beasley-Murray 1978: 104; Hemer 1986: 185; Thomas 1992: 302; Kistemaker 2001: 169; Osborne 2002: 204). The meaning of *archē* here in 3:14 is then interpreted as emphasizing either Christ's temporal priority to all creation ("beginning") or Christ as the source or cause of all creation ("origin/originator"). A few commentators (Ladd 1972: 65; Aune 1997: 256; NET Bible footnote) choose the latter of these two possibilities on the grounds that this verse is connected not to Paul's word about Christ in the Colossian letter, but to the prologue of the Gospel of John, which claims that the Word was "with God in the beginning [*archē*]" and that "all things were made *through* him" (John 1:1–3).

Rather than interpret the third Christ title in light of distant connections to another author (Paul) or another document (Colossians or the Gospel of

John), it is better to view it in light of its closer link within the opening of the book of Revelation. We have already noted connections between the first two Christ titles (3:14) and this opening section (the twofold occurrence of "Amen" in 1:6–7 and the reference to "Christ, the *faithful witness*" in 1:5), which strengthens the likelihood that the third Christ title similarly looks back to the description of Christ in 1:5 as "the *ruler* of the kings of earth" (*archōn* shares the same root as *archē*). This in turn suggests that the third Christ title highlights neither Christ's temporal priority ("beginning") nor his role as the source of creation ("origin") but instead declares his authority or rule over creation. Hence this title is best rendered as "the ruler of God's creation." This interpretation is strengthened by the potential link with the positive consequence at the end of the sermon: victorious Christ followers "will be given the right to sit with me *on my throne*" (3:21). Since only kings and sovereigns sit on a throne, this closing reward presupposes that Christ is "the ruler of God's creation" and adds the promise that victorious believers will share in Christ's authority and rule over creation.

The Commendation—None!

In the previous six sermons, the transition from the opening Christ title to the next unit is signaled by the simple formula "I know." This second formal unit of the sermon typically contains the commendation, where Christ praises the church for what it is doing well. Consequently, when the believers in Laodicea hear Christ say "I know your works," they naturally would expect him to extol their good deeds and praiseworthy spiritual condition. The unanticipated deviation from this pattern in the sermon to Sardis should have caused some in Laodicea to wonder whether Christ would praise them or do what he did earlier and launch immediately into the complaint. The words of 3:17a ("You say, 'I am rich and have become wealthy and I do not need anything'"), however, make clear that the church in Laodicea was vain, overly confident of their superiority to other churches and of their self-sufficiency. Sadly, they were blind to their true spiritual condition (3:17b).

This is why what comes next would have been so surprising and shocking to them. What follows are not the expected words of commendation but the unanticipated words of complaint: "I know your works, namely, that you are neither cold nor hot. I wish you were cold or hot. So, because you are lukewarm and are neither cold nor hot, I am about to vomit you out of my mouth" (3:15–16). The situation at Laodicea is so serious that Christ is not able to say anything commendatory about them. It is not merely that Christ skips opening pleasantries and "gets straight to the point" (Thomas 1992: 304). Rather, the situation is much more serious: this deliberate omission involves an obviously negative judgment and strong rebuke. Here again we see that there are times when what the Bible does *not* say is as important as what it does say. Just as the omission of the complaint section in the sermons to Smyrna and Philadelphia reveals how *positively* Christ evaluates those two congregations, so the omission of the commendation section in the sermons to Sardis and Laodicea highlights how *negatively* Christ evaluates these two congregations. A literary parallel to this situation occurs in Paul's Letter to the Galatians, where the apostle is so concerned about their accepting a false gospel that he feels compelled to replace the typical thanksgiving section with a rebuke section (Gal. 1:6–10).

Yet the parallel between the Sardis and Laodicea sermons is not exact. Although the commendation section is omitted from both messages, the Sardis sermon contains an important concession that not everyone in the congregation is included in Christ's complaint (3:4a, "But you have a few names in Sardis who have not soiled their clothes"). Laodicea, by contrast, contains no such concession; Christ's complaint is directed toward the whole church. Furthermore, the complaint against Laodicea (3:15–17) is longer than that found in any of the other sermons (2:4, Ephesus; 2:14–15, Pergamum; 2:20, Thyatira; 3:1–2b, Sardis; Smyrna and Philadelphia have no complaint). Though it is hard to imagine hearing something worse than Christ's complaint that the Sardis church—or more precisely, the majority of that congregation—was spiritually dead (3:1), Christ's judgment against the entire Laodicean church seems just as bad: they make him want to vomit (3:16). As Charles (1920: 96) observed a century ago, "The Laodiceans are not only denounced, but denounced with the utmost abhorrence. Such a denunciation is without parallel in the other Epistles" (so also other commentators, e.g., Hemer 1986: 191: "No other church was condemned in terms so strong"; Thomas 1992: 304: "a rebuke that is the most scathing of any of the seven"). All these factors lead to the conclusion that the Laodicean congregation was the worst of the seven churches, which almost certainly explains why it stands last among the seven sermons. The order of these sermons does not stem primarily from the natural travel routes of that day, as is commonly asserted, because once the letter carrier left the island of Patmos and arrived in the port city of Ephesus, the order could easily have been reversed or changed. Rather, the order is intended to portray the poor condition of the Christian church in Asia Minor, with the two healthy congregations as exceptions hidden among the majority of unhealthy churches, and the worst church, Laodicea, standing in the climactic final position.

The Complaint (3:15–17)

Since the usual second unit, the commendation, is strikingly absent, the complaint comes immediately after the opening Christ title (3:15–17) and, as already noted, is the longest and harshest of the seven sermons. This complaint consists of two main parts, together validating our proposed title for this sermon: "Laodicea: The Church of Vomit and Vanity."

First Complaint: The Church's Vomit-Inducing Works (3:15–16)

The first complaint brought against the Laodicean church uses the striking metaphor of lukewarm water inducing a violently negative reaction from Christ: "I know your works, namely, you are neither cold nor hot. I wish you were cold or hot. So, because you are lukewarm and are neither cold nor hot, I am about to vomit you out of my mouth" (3:15–16).

There are two main interpretations of the meaning of this lukewarm metaphor. The older, traditional view is that the three temperatures of cold, hot, and lukewarm refer to different levels of spiritual fervor and commitment to Christ and the gospel: the Laodicean church is accused of having a lukewarm spirituality—a middle-of-the-road, indecisive faith that was neither bad ("cold") nor good ("hot"). Ladd (1972: 65), for example, states: "They [the Laodiceans] were not characterized by the coldness of hostility to the gospel or rejection of the faith; but neither were they characterized by a warm zeal and fervor. They were simply indifferent, nominal, complacent." Beasley-Murray (1978: 104–5) similarly asserts: "The Laodiceans do not reject the gospel of Christ, nor do they affirm it with joy. They maintain it without conviction, without enthusiasm, without reflection on its implications for life" (see also, e.g., Charles 1920: 95–96; Caird 1966: 56–57; Krodel 1989: 142; Thomas 1992: 304–7).

This interpretation, however, suffers from a couple of problems. First, the use of the adjectives "cold," "hot," and "lukewarm" to describe a person's spiritual fervor is virtually unparalleled. There are no other biblical examples of the adjectives "cold" and "lukewarm" being used in this way, and the same is true for the adjective "hot," although the participle of a related verb for "enthusiastic/excited" is used to describe Apollos (Acts 18:25) and the Christians in Rome (Rom. 12:11; see Rudwick and Green 1957–58; Hemer 1986: 187, 276n39). The second and greater problem is that "cold" along with "hot" are *both* presented as positive alternatives to the negative category of "lukewarm." According to the old or traditional view, this means that Christ would rather have the Laodicean church outright reject the gospel (be "cold") rather than be indifferent to it (be "lukewarm"). A few commentators boldly accept this interpretation without hesitation, despite its problematic implications. Krodel (1989: 142), for example, states: "Here Jesus is saying something that no preacher would dare to say if the Lord had not spoken it first; namely, that ice-cold atheists are preferable to him than lukewarm Christians." Most commentators from the traditional camp, however, recognize the weakness of their interpretation and so devote much effort to explaining how being "cold" could be preferable to being "lukewarm." Thomas (1992: 306) typifies this approach:

> How then is the objection that Christ would not want a church to be cold to be answered? The best suggestion is that spiritual coldness, even to the point of open hostility, is preferable to lukewarmness and repulsive indifference because it at least suggests that religion is something to be in earnest about. From an ethical standpoint, a frank repudiation is at least more promising than a half-and-half attachment. To prefer outright rejection over a half-way response is startling, to say the least, but to profess Christianity while remaining untouched by its fire is a disaster. There is more hope for the openly antagonistic than for the coolly indifferent. The state of coldness is more conducive to a person's coming to Christ than the state of lukewarmness, as illustrated in the conversion of Saul of Tarsus.

The majority of Revelation commentators, however, have not found such explanations convincing and are instead drawn to a different interpretation. It was first tentatively proposed by Rudwick and Green (1957–58) some sixty years ago, then further developed by Hemer (1986: 187–91) and Porter (1987), and is now adopted by most contemporary interpreters (so, e.g., Mounce 1977: 125–26; Aune 1997: 258, 263; Michaels 1997: 88; Beale 1999: 303; Keener 2000: 159; Osborne 2002: 205–6; Wilson 2002: 276; Beale and Campbell 2015: 91). This alternative interpretation connects the meaning of "lukewarm" to the water supply of Laodicea, which stood in contrast to that of the neighboring cities of Hierapolis and Colossae. Although the text of the sermon makes no explicit mention of water, such a reference is strongly implied by three things: (1) "vomit you out of my mouth" suggests that something disagreeable has either been eaten or, as the following two points suggest, drunk; (2) the adjectives "hot" and "lukewarm" are usually applied to liquids, especially water (Hemer 1986: 276); and (3) the mention of "hot" in the geographical setting of Laodicea would naturally suggest the renowned hot springs of nearby Hierapolis, located a mere six miles across the Lycus Valley, directly opposite and easily visible from Laodicea.

Although Laodicea enjoyed a favorable location at an important junction of roads (see esp. Ramsay 1994: 303–5), there was no spring nearby, and the two

Figure 7.1. Aqueduct at Laodicea. A double pipeline of stone blocks brought water into the city.

small rivers (the Asopus and the Caprus) that surrounded the city on either side and emptied into the Lycus Valley were insufficient to meet the water demands of the city's growing population (note the observation of Strabo, *Geography* 12.8.16: "Though formerly small, it [Laodicea] grew large in our time and in that of our fathers"). Vast amounts of water were needed not just for the daily consumption of its citizens but also for the multiple public baths and ornamental fountains in the city. Consequently, water was brought into Laodicea by aqueduct from a source south of the city, likely from a hot mineral spring some five miles away, near the modern city of Denizli. This aqueduct was a double-pipeline of stone blocks (see fig. 7.1) using the inverted siphon system, by which water was brought to nearby water towers and distributed throughout the city. There were at least two twenty-three-foot water towers—a smaller one located near the stadium and bath/gymnasium on the south side of the city, and a larger and more complex one located near the city center. A marble inscription dating to AD 114 has recently been discovered in Laodicea with laws about the use of water in the city and listing heavy penalties for those who damage the aqueduct or its sealed water pipes. That these laws were inscribed in marble, presented for approval to the proconsul in Ephesus, and accompanied by severe penalties for breaking them (fines of 5,000–12,500 denarii) reveals how crucial water was to the well-being of this city.

Since one of Laodicea's main water supplies was a hot mineral spring some five miles away, the water would cool as it traveled along the aqueduct and would arrive in the city no longer hot but lukewarm. There was a high amount of mineral content in this water (calcium carbonate), as evidenced by the heavy calcification of the pipes in the aqueduct and the city's water towers, but it was still drinkable. Strabo, the ancient geographer, affirms these two qualities about the water in Laodicea, stating that it was very hard ("the water turns to stone") but "potable" (*Geography* 13.4.14). The problem Christ identifies, however, was not the water's mineral content (as is frequently claimed by commentators) but its temperature—it was lukewarm.

The meaning of this metaphor is made more difficult to discern by the fact that the adjective "lukewarm" (*chliaros*) occurs only here in the entire Bible and is extremely rare in all time periods of ancient Greek literature. Yet there is suggestive evidence that lukewarm water was viewed in the ancient world as less desirable than cold or hot water. Herodotus (*Histories* 4.181.3–4) tells us that the temperature of the Ammonians' hot spring in North Africa changed drastically throughout the day and that the local citizens used the water when it was either cold or hot but not when it was lukewarm. Xenophon (*Memorabilia* 3.13.3) indicates that cold water is useful for drinking and hot water for washing, but lukewarm water is good only to give to the household slaves. Seneca (*On Anger* 2.25.1) claims that it is pointless to get angry when a slave is too slow in doing something, or when one finds the couch messy, or when the water one is about to drink is lukewarm. The key idea of the metaphor, then, is that just as lukewarm water is useless—in contrast to cold and hot water, which both have beneficial applications—so also the works of the Laodiceans are useless.

Both ancient and modern commentators have adopted this understanding of the text. In his commentary on the book of Revelation, Tyconius (AD 370–390), a church father from Carthage, asserts that the phrase "neither cold nor hot" means "it is useless" (Gumerlock 2017). In more recent times Ramsey Michaels (1997: 88) has offered the following explanation: "Either cold or hot water is good for something, but lukewarm water is not. The point of the rebuke is not lack of zeal or enthusiasm. If it were, 'lukewarm' would at least have been better than 'cold'! The point is rather the utter worthlessness of what the congregation has done and is doing." Keener (2000: 159) similarly states, "The point of lukewarm water is simply that it is disgusting, in contrast to the more directly useful 'hot' and 'cold' water; all the churches would plainly understand this warning."

The metaphor becomes more pointed when it is understood in its geographical context. Most commentators see intended contrasts between the

lukewarm water of Laodicea, the hot
water of Hierapolis, and the cold water
of Colossae. The churches in these tri-
cities of the Lycus Valley were closely
connected not only because of their
proximity to one another (Laodicea
was six miles from Hierapolis and ten
miles from Colossae) but also because of their joint ministry. All three
churches were likely established and

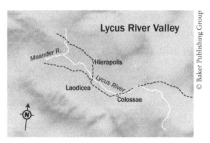

Figure 7.2. The tri-cities of the Lycus River
valley: Laodicea, Hierapolis, and Colossae.

overseen by the same person (Epaphras: Col. 1:7; 4:12–13). Their close relationship is further suggested by the fact that the churches of Laodicea and
Colossae were instructed to exchange the letters Paul had sent to each (Col.
4:16). In his complaint that Laodicea was lukewarm, Christ is deliberately
alluding to the contrasting hot waters of Hierapolis; this member of the
tri-cities was renowned in the ancient world for the healing effects of its hot
springs. Hemer (1986: 188) notes that Hierapolis's "prosperity as a health
centre and its obtrusive proximity to Laodicea corroborate this application."
Even today the bright white escarpment of Hierapolis, the result of calcium-
rich water cascading down into the Lycus Valley, is impossible to miss when
standing on the opposite side of the valley in Laodicea. The city's modern
Turkish name, Pamukkale ("Cotton Castle") alludes to these brilliant white
terraces.

In contrast to Hieropolis's famed hot springs are those of Colossae, the
other member of the tri-cities, located directly below Mount Cadmus (8,000
feet high). Throughout the year this city enjoyed an abundant supply of cold,
fresh water, devoid of heavy mineral content and immediately useful for drinking. Given the intended contrast between the hot water of Hierapolis and
the cold water of Colossae, the meaning of the lukewarm metaphor for the
Laodicea congregation becomes clear: "The church should not have matched
its water supply. The Laodiceans should have been known for their spiritual
healing (like Hierapolis) or their refreshing, life-giving ministry (like Colossae). Instead, as Jesus's next statement reads, they were 'lukewarm.' They
were devoid of works and useless to the Lord" (Osborne 2002: 206).

What were these works of the Laodicean church that Christ knows ("I know
your works") and judges to be lukewarm and useless? The complaint section
of other sermons typically identifies a specific problem or problems. To the
church in Ephesus Christ says, "You have abandoned the love you had at first."
Members of the Pergamum and Thyatiran churches were eating food sacrificed to idols (= idolatry) and committing sexual immorality. The problem

at Sardis is a bit vague—"You have a reputation of being alive, but you are dead"—but for the Laodicean church, no particular sinful act is mentioned in this lengthy complaint unit (3:15–17), nor can it be confidently inferred from the correction unit that follows (3:18). Any assertion about the nature of the problem in the Laodicean church, therefore, is just an educated guess (e.g., Beale 1999: 302, "The problem with the Laodicea Christians probably arose from willingness to identify in some way with the trade guilds and their patron deities"). The problem at Laodicea may well be similar to what was occurring in other churches in Asia Minor, but we cannot be certain.

What is beyond doubt, however, is the seriousness of the situation. This is clear from Christ's violently negative reaction to the Laodicean church's conduct: "I am about to vomit you out of my mouth." Virtually all the leading English translations soften this shocking image by rendering Christ's response merely as "I am about to *spit* you out of my mouth" (NKJV, CSB, LEB, and The Message have "vomit"; KJV and ASV have "spew"). The Greek, however, is unambiguous: the verb used here is not the softer *ptyō* ("to spit, spit out," BDAG 895) but the much more vivid *emeō* ("vomit, throw up," BDAG 322). Christ's complaint against the Laodicean church is severe, and despite modern sensitivities, only vivid verbs like "vomit" or "throw up" will alert the contemporary audience to the gravity of the situation.

A story from Aesop's Fables similarly links lukewarm water with vomiting. The collection of stories attributed to Aesop, a slave living in ancient Greece in 620–564 BC, was originally handed down orally until the stories were eventually transcribed and collected some three centuries after Aesop's death. One of these fables (*Life of Aesop* 2–3) recounts how two of Aesop's fellow slaves stole and ate two of their master's delicious figs and then tried to hide their guilt by accusing Aesop of the crime. To prove his innocence, Aesop drinks lukewarm water, puts his fingers down his throat to induce vomiting, and throws up only water. His two fellow slaves are then also forced to drink lukewarm water and to vomit, and their guilt is revealed when they throw up the just-eaten figs.

Second Complaint: The Church's Vain Attitude (3:17)

The causal *hoti* that opens verse 17 shows how the second complaint relates to the first: the lukewarm or useless works of the Laodicean church stem from the congregation's attitude of smug self-sufficiency: "For you say, 'I am rich and have become wealthy and do not need a thing'" (3:17a). How people act is intimately connected with how they think; thus Christ identifies the root cause of the problem in the Laodicean church. These believers will never be able to replace their useless, vomit-inducing works with truly praiseworthy ones unless they first change their misguided and sinful mentality.

The arrogance or vanity of the Laodicean church stemming from their wealth is emphasized in this second complaint in several ways. First, it is stressed rhetorically by stating essentially the same claim three times: "I am rich and have become wealthy and do not need a thing." Second, emphasis is shown grammatically in Greek by placing the adjective "rich" before the verb in the first clause (lit., "Rich I am"), by using the rarer and weightier perfect tense in the second clause ("I have become wealthy"), and by altering the word order in the third clause (lit., "not a need I have"). Third, the sequencing of the three claims may reflect the literary device *hysteron-proteron* (latter-former), which reverses the logical order to stress a point. Here the second clause ("I have become wealthy") should logically come before the first clause ("I am rich"; so Swete 1911: 61; Thomas 1992: 311; Aune 1997: 258–59; Osborne 2002: 207n11; this figure of speech also occurs in Rev. 3:3, 19; 5:5; 6:4; 10:4, 9; 20:4–5, 12–13; 22:14). Fourth, emphasis is also achieved by the intentional contrast with the poverty of the Smyrna church. The threefold reference to the wealth of the Laodicean church would immediately cause hearers to recall Christ's earlier commendation of the Smyrna church, whose members are economically poor but spiritually rich (2:9, "I know your poverty—yet you are rich").

Several commentators hear an echo of Hosea 12:8, where Ephraim, another name for Israel's Northern Kingdom, expresses a similar attitude of foolish confidence in wealth: "Ephraim has said, 'Surely, I have become rich; I have gained wealth for myself; in all of my gain no offense has been found in me that would be sin.'" Beale (1991: 304), for example, states, "The unique wording and thought in common between these texts suggest that it is more than a mere coincidental parallel, as many think, and that John has intentionally alluded to Hosea" (so also, e.g., Charles 1920: 96; Beasley-Murray 1978: 105; Hemer 1986: 191; Kistemaker 2001: 170; Beale and Campbell 2015: 92). However, this parallel is close only in the Hebrew Masoretic Text of Hosea 12:8; the connection in wording with the Greek Septuagint translation is not nearly as strong. Additionally, statements similar to the mentality reflected in the words of the Laodicean church can be found in other writings from the ancient world. Epictetus records the words of an imperial bailiff, which provides an even closer parallel to the words of the Laodicean church: "But I am rich and I need nothing" (*Diatribes* 3.7.29). Another parallel is found in 1 Enoch (97.8–9a): "Woe to you who gain silver and gold by unjust means; you will then say, 'We have grown rich and accumulated goods, we have acquired everything that we have desired. So now let us do whatever we like.'" It may well be that the arrogant self-assessment of the Laodicean church does not allude to Hosea 12:8 but rather echoes a conventional or proverbial saying of the rich whose hubris or vanity is rooted in their wealth (Aune 1997: 258).

The statement "I am rich and have become wealthy and do not need a thing" also reflects the local historical setting. About Rev. 3:17a, Charles (1920: 96) notes, "The allusion to the material conditions of the city cannot be ignored." Hemer (1986: 191–95) similarly observes that the complaint of verse 17, along with the correction of verse 18, is "rich in local allusion" and proceeds to catalog, in compelling detail, the wealth and self-sufficiency of Laodicea. At the end of the first century BC and the beginning of the first century AD, Laodicea had several citizens who were extremely wealthy, the "Bill Gates" of the Lycus Valley. Strabo (*Geography* 12.8.16) states, "The fertility of the country, *and the prosperity of some of its citizens*, made it [Laodicea] great." Strabo refers to a Laodicean local named Heiron, who supported many public building projects during his lifetime and upon his death left the city 2,000 talents (millions of dollars in today's currency). Another remarkably rich resident was Nicostratus, who was wealthy enough to finance the magnificent 900-foot-long stadium located in the south part of the city. There may well be a proud tone in the inscription (*CIG* 3935) recording this act, which says that he did so "out of his own resources." Yet another rich native of Laodicea was Flaccus, who generously heated the covered walks and provided piped oil at the baths. The inscription (*IGRR* 4.860) recording these acts has a similarly proud tone: the expression "by himself" occurs no less than four times in one sentence. Laodicea was also the hometown of the Zenoid family, which was among the greatest families in all Asia Minor (Ramsay 1895: 42–45; Hemer 1986: 192). The patriarch Zenon was a political orator in Laodicea, and later generations of his descendants served as vassal kings of different regions in Asia Minor under Roman control at the same time that many extended family members of this powerful and wealthy dynasty continued to reside in Laodicea.

Figure 7.3. Marble base (AD 30) for a statue of Tiberius found at Puteoli, port city of Rome. It displays a dedicatory inscription to Tiberius from fourteen cites of Asia Minor for his giving financial aid after several earthquakes that took place from AD 17 to 29 (National Archaeological Museum of Naples).

Sailko, CC BY-SA / Wikimedia Commons

Laodicea's wealth and its attitude of smug self-sufficiency stemming from that wealth are perhaps most evident in its action after a particularly devastating earthquake in AD 60, which destroyed many cities in the region. Laodicea is located on a major fault line and, along with all the nearby cities situated along this north-south fault line, was constantly vulnerable to earthquake activity. When they occurred, it was common for Rome to provide financial help to affected cities so that they could rebuild and recover from the damage. This is what happened in AD 17, when Laodicea and eleven other cities in Asia Minor were given earthquake relief funds from the emperor Tiberius (Strabo, *Geography* 12.8.18; 13.4.8; Suetonius, *Tiberius* 8; Tacitus, *Annals* 2.47; Dio Cassius, *Roman History* 57.17.8). After a major earthquake in AD 60, however, Laodicea apparently refused to accept any relief funds from Rome. Tacitus (*Annals* 14.27.1) reports: "Laodicea arose from the ruins by the strength of its own resources, and with no help from us." Tacitus's comment suggests that this was highly unusual and noteworthy. Laodicea's rebuilding itself without Rome's financial help became so well-known in Asia and areas beyond that it is likely alluded to in the Sibylline Oracles (ca. AD 80): "Wretched Laodicea, at some time an earthquake will throw you headlong and spread you flat, but you will be founded again as a city, and stand" (4.137–39). This text does not explicitly mention the rebuilding of Laodicea without Roman assistance, but the writer chooses to mention the reconstruction of Laodicea rather than that of any of the other important cities of the region that similarly had to rebuild after earthquake damage, suggesting that there was something special and noteworthy about it.

The statement of Tacitus proves that Laodicea was wealthy enough to rebuild itself without help from Rome, but this rejection of Roman assistance may also be evidence of Laodicea's pride and attitude of smug self-sufficiency. If so, this correlates closely with the inappropriate attitude of the Laodicean church that Christ complains about (thus many commentators). As Wilson (2002: 276) notes: "The Laodiceans prided themselves on their self-accomplishments and financial independence. This attitude seems to be reflected in the church." Hemer (1986: 195) ends his careful review of the ancient historical evidence as follows:

> I conclude that there is good reason for seeing Rev. 3:17 against the background of the boasted affluence of Laodicea, notoriously exemplified in her refusal of Roman aid and her carrying through a great programme of reconstruction in a spirit of proud independence and ostentatious individual benefaction. The flourishing church was exposed as partaking of the standards of the society in which it lived. It was spiritually self-sufficient and saw no need of Christ's aid.

The vanity of the Laodicean church and its deluded sense of independence is abruptly exposed by Christ, who describes their real situation and status: "But you do not know that you are wretched and pitiful and poor and blind and naked" (3:17b). This statement creates a sharp and shameful contrast between Christ's knowledge and the church's ignorance: Christ as "the Amen" and "true witness" (3:14) knows the real value of their deeds (3:15, "I know [*oida*] your works . . ."), while the Laodicean believers remain oblivious to their true spiritual condition ("but you do not know [*oidas*] that . . . ," 3:17). Christ uses five adjectives to convey the devastating truth of how serious the situation is. In Greek the five adjectives are closely connected to each other by a single article that introduces them all, thus powerfully presenting these five descriptors as a collective whole. But the first two adjectives ("wretched and pitiful") are distinguished from the remaining three ("poor and blind and naked") in a couple of ways: (1) the first two have a literal meaning, while the final three are used metaphorically; (2) the final three adjectives reappear in the correction unit that follows (3:18–19) and thus are emphasized.

Complaint Unit	Correction Unit: "I counsel you to buy from me . . ."
"poor"	"gold refined in the fire so that you can become rich"
"blind"	"salve to put on your eyes so that you can see"
"naked"	"white clothes to wear so that you can cover your shameful nakedness"

The first adjective (*talaipōros*) expresses the strongly negative state of being "*miserable, wretched, distressed*" (BDAG 988). It occurs elsewhere in the NT only in Rom. 7:24, where Paul's lengthy discussion about the power of sin that prevents one from obeying God's law leads to the desperate exclamation, "What a *wretched* person I am!" The noun form of this same adjective occurs twice: in Rom. 3:16 it is paired with the noun "ruin" in an OT quotation ("ruin and *misery* mark their path"), and in James 5:1 it describes the future miseries of the rich. The verb form of this adjective occurs only one time in the NT, in James 4:9, where it is paired with the verbs "to mourn" and "to weep" ("*Feel miserable* [i.e., lament] and mourn and weep!"). The second adjective (*eleeinos*) means "deserving of sympathy for one's pathetic condition, *miserable, pitiable*" (BDAG 315) and is based on an important verb that appears frequently in the NT and means "to have compassion/mercy/pity on." Its only other occurrence in the NT is in Paul's frank concession in 1 Cor. 15:19: if Christ has not been raised from the dead, then "we are most *pitiful* of all people." These first two adjectives are likely intended to be synonymous and help to intensify the contrast between the Laodicean church's misguided attitude of vanity and smug self-sufficiency based on their wealth

(3:17a) and the harsh reality of Christ's assessment that they are actually "wretched and pitiful" (3:17b).

The last three adjectives ("poor and blind and naked") also describe the real condition of the Laodicean church, but as already noted, they are picked up in the correction that follows and so are discussed in the next section.

The Correction (3:18–19)

As offensive as the vomit-inducing works of the Laodicean church and its attitude of vanity are to Christ, he has not given up on these believers. The fact that there even is a correction unit should be seen as evidence of the grace of Christ for the worst of the seven churches. There is still an opportunity for the believers in Laodicea to repent and respond appropriately to their spiritual poverty, blindness, and nakedness by following Christ's corrective commands.

There are three significant things about the seemingly innocuous phrase "I advise you to buy from me," which introduces the correction. The first is the understated tone of this exhortation (Osborne 2002: 208). The verb *symbouleuō* means "advise someone (to do) something" (BDAG 957.1) and occurs only once elsewhere in the NT with this meaning, to describe how the high priest Caiaphas "advised" the Jews at Jesus's trial, saying that it was better to have just one person die for the people (John 18:14). Christ's understated exhortation is surprising not only because the seriousness of the situation would naturally require a blunt command rather than diplomatic advice but also because the one speaking has already been identified as "the ruler of God's creation" and so has the power and authority to demand something from the Laodicean church.

The second significant thing about Christ's statement is the commercial connotation of the verb "to buy." Several commentators see a possible allusion here to the words of Isa. 55:1, which commands God's people in the messianic age to take advantage of his gracious provision and to "come, buy wine and milk without money and without cost" (so, e.g., Charles 1920: 97; Thomas 1992: 313; Aune 1997: 259; Kistemaker 2001: 172). Although this OT echo is possible, the verb "to buy" more likely was chosen because the Laodicean church already assesses itself in commercial terms ("I am rich and have become wealthy and do not need a thing"), and Christ's frank evaluation of their true condition ("poor") is similarly expressed. Christ's advice to this boastful church that sees itself as wealthy but is blind to its true poverty is ironic because they are commanded to purchase something they cannot actually afford.

The third significant thing about Christ's statement is the emphasis expressed by the prepositional phrase "from me." This emphasis is achieved through Greek word order (the prepositional phrase comes before the direct objects "gold," "white clothes," and "eye salve") and spelling (the emphatic form of the personal pronoun is used) and supports an important theological truth: despite their vanity and attitude of smug self-sufficiency, the Laodicean church is actually helpless and completely dependent on Christ and what he alone can give. Like the Laodicean believers before them, Christ followers today must eschew a "pull-yourselves-up-by-your-own-bootstraps" mentality that relies on natural ability and self-effort to overcome spiritual poverty. Recognizing their inability to solve the problem themselves, they must instead look to Christ, who alone can save them.

Most commentators find clear allusions to the local situation in the three adjectives ("poor and blind and naked") that describe the Laodicean church in the previous complaint (3:17b) and in the three corresponding antidotes here in the correction (3:18). Mounce (1977: 110–11), for example, states, "It is frequently noted that Laodicea prided itself on three things: financial wealth, an extensive textile industry, and a popular eye salve that was exported around the world. It is hard not to see here and in the following verse a direct allusion to Laodicea's banking establishments, medical school, and textile industry." Beale (1999: 306–7) similarly observes, "Some commentators rightly understand the accusation that they were 'poor, blind, and naked' and the threefold solution (v 18) against the background of (1) Laodicea's well-known banking institutions, (2) its medical school, known for ophthalmology, together with the region's well-known eye salve, and (3) the city's textile trade (Laodicea was famous far and wide for its woolen industry and tunics, which it exported)."

The many exegetes who believe that Christ's words are based on the local conditions of Laodicea base their conclusion primarily on the early observations of Ramsay (1904; 1994: 301–17) and especially the later analysis of Hemer (1986: 191–201). This conclusion, however, has been challenged by Koester (2003), who argues that the sermon to Laodicea makes use of common metaphors that are not specific to the local setting but would be readily understood in any community in the ancient world. This criticism by Koester is legitimate and should caution modern exegetes and preachers from overstating the local allusions in the metaphors of refined gold, white clothes, and eye salve. Nevertheless, some local connections justify seeing these vivid images as not just readily understandable by any of the communities in Asia Minor but as especially relevant to the local situation of Laodicea, making them particularly powerful word pictures for believers in that church.

The first of these three powerful word pictures involves "gold refined in the fire." Although there is little evidence for seeing exclusively a local allusion to Laodicea's financial institutions or to the city as a banking center, as is sometimes claimed (e.g., Charles 1920: 93; Mounce 1977: 111; Hemer 1986: 191, 196; Beale 1999: 307; Osborne 2002: 208–9; Beale and Campbell 2015: 92), the purpose clause that accompanies this metaphor ("in order that you may be rich") does clearly look back to the words of the church ("I am rich and have become wealthy and do not need a thing") and to Christ's assessment that they are in fact poor. In this way, the clause alludes, as do those earlier references, to the prosperity often associated with Laodicea. The evidence supporting both the city's wealth and its attitude of smug self-sufficiency stemming from its wealth has already been presented in our analysis of 3:17a and does not need to be repeated here.

The metaphor of refined gold refers to a process, well-known in the ancient world, by which this precious metal would be melted at extremely high heat so that any slag or impurities could be skimmed off the top and only pure gold would remain. References to "refined gold" or to this purification process thus became a common biblical metaphor for the cleansing of one's moral life by removing the impurities of sin (Ps. 66:10; Prov. 27:21; Isa. 1:25; Jer. 6:29; Ezek. 22:22; Zech. 13:9; Mal. 3:2–3; 1 Pet. 1:7; see also 2 Pet. 3:10, which is better understood as the world being purified by fire rather than being destroyed). The Christians in Laodicea can correct their spiritual poverty and become truly rich by removing all impure works from their current conduct, works that cause Jesus to vomit, leaving only obedient and holy deeds, which are more valuable than refined gold. Elsewhere in Scripture this metaphor sometimes refers to the purification process that takes place through trials or suffering (Zech. 13:9; 1 Pet. 1:7), so some commentators believe that the purification process of the Laodiceans will similarly involve persecution for their faith (Kistemaker 2001: 172, "These words hint at the fiery trial that the followers of Christ are to endure"; see also Thomas 1992: 313; Beale 1999: 305). Because the idea of Christian suffering is not found anywhere in this particular sermon, it is more likely that the metaphor of purified gold refers merely to the valuable character of the works that the believers in Laodicea are expected to produce.

The second of the three powerful pictures involves white clothes: "I counsel you to buy from me . . . white garments so that you might be clothed and the shame of your nakedness might not be seen" (3:18b). The Greco-Roman world did not at all connect shame with nakedness, and so the metaphor here is clearly drawing on an understanding stemming from the OT. The close link between shame and nakedness goes back all the way to Adam and Eve, who originally enjoyed a state of innocence in their physical relationship with each other (Gen. 2:25, "Adam and his wife were both naked, and they felt no shame"), but this innocence immediately turned to fear and shame after the fall (Gen. 3:7, 10, 11). In the OT, nakedness became a negative metaphor for sin and God's judgment on it (Deut. 28:48; Isa. 20:1–4; 47:3; Ezek. 16:36; 23:29; Nah. 3:5). Since a number of these OT texts involve the sin of idolatry, it is possible that this is the specific sin that is being addressed in Laodicea (Beale 1999: 306; Beale and Campbell 2015: 92). But although the complaint against the churches in Pergamum and Thyatira involves idolatry, and all seven churches surely faced this temptation, this sin is not specifically mentioned anywhere in the sermon to Laodicea. Hence it is better to view the negative metaphor of nakedness and shame as pertaining to any kind of behavior that Christ finds offensive and vomit-inducing.

The opposite of the shame that stems from being naked is the honor associated with receiving or wearing fine clothes, and this positive metaphor also stems from the OT. Joseph received a fancy coat from his father, signaling the boy's special status among his brothers (Gen. 37:3–4). Later in life, he also received robes of fine linen from a grateful Pharaoh for interpreting his dreams. Mordecai was honored by the Assyrian king, Ahasuerus, who gave him a royal robe to wear (Esther 6:7–11). The meaning of the second picture in the correction thus becomes clear: Christ views the church in Laodicea as being spiritually naked, that is, guilty of living a sinful life and in desperate need of clothing to hide their shameful conduct.

While any type of clothing would solve the problem of nakedness, Christ specifically exhorts the Laodicean believers to buy from him garments that are white. In the ancient world, soiled or dirty clothes have a negative connotation, often symbolizing immoral and irreligious conduct, while white or clean clothes signify ethical and religious purity. Several verses in the book of Revelation refer to white garments worn by the faithful followers of Christ: the few in Sardis who are not dying or dead but worthy (3:4–5); the twenty-four elders surrounding God, all seated on thrones (4:4); the martyrs under the altar (6:11); and the "great multitude that no one could count" who survive the great tribulation (7:9, 13, 14). The armies of heaven are not only riding on white horses but also wearing fine linen of white (19:14), clothing that is explicitly stated to be "the righteous acts of God's holy people" (19:8). The normal apparel in pagan cultic activity, not just for priests but for all participants, was white; worshipers did not dare come into the temple and the presence of their god wearing dirty clothes (so Keener 2000: 144n15, citing Josephus, *Jewish War* 2.1; Josephus, *Ant.* 11.327; Philo, *Contemplative Life* 66; Euripides, *Bacchanals* 112; Pausanius, *Description of Greece* 2.35.5;

6.20.3; Diogenes Laertius, *Lives* 8.1.33). Even Roman political candidates wore a *toga candida*, a "whitened toga" bleached dazzling white with chalk, to signify their virtue and honesty.

The metaphor of white garments may have been especially striking to believers in Laodicea, since their city was famous for its textile industry in general and for the softness and distinctive black color of its wool in particular (Trench 1867: 207; developed more fully by Ramsay 1904: 416–17, and in more recent times by Hemer 1986: 199–201). The ancient historian Strabo, who lived in Asia Minor in the early first century AD, wrote, "The country around Laodicea produces sheep remarkable not only for the softness of their wool, in which they surpass even that of Miletus, but also for its raven-black color. And they get a splendid revenue from it" (*Geography* 12.8.16). Vitruvius, the first-century BC engineer, describes breeding techniques that resulted in Laodicea producing lambs "as black as a raven" (*On Architecture* 8.3.14), further evidence that Laodicea was widely known for the unique color of its wool. Some have objected to the claim that a specific reference to Laodicea is intended here, arguing that "the figure of white garments as symbolic of righteousness is so widely used in Revelation that no local allusion is necessary" (Mounce 1977: 127) and that the production of wool and textiles was quite common to many of the cities of Asia Minor (Koester 2003: 420; Tonstad 2019: 95). Although the possible allusion to the local production of black wool should not be overstated, there is sufficient evidence that Laodicea was well-known for its unique production of raven-colored wool. So Christ's call to this specific church to buy white garments would be especially meaningful to those living in the city and to anyone familiar with the city's reputation for selling a unique textile product.

The third of the three powerful pictures in the correction involves eye salve: "I counsel you to buy from me . . . medication to put on your eyes so that you might see" (3:18c). Blindness is a common metaphor for ignorance and lack of discernment. It is not wealth itself that is the problem but the resulting attitude of vanity and smug self-sufficiency that has blinded the church in Laodicea to its true spiritual condition. Naively unaware of how serious their spiritual condition really is, they are "poor and blind and naked," but this need not be their permanent situation. Christ graciously offers a life-saving solution: believers in Laodicea can buy eye ointment from him, a spiritual salve that can cure their blindness and allow them to truly see. What Christ says here by way of a metaphor is similar to what he did and said during his earthly ministry through a miracle (John 9:1–41). Christ healed a man born blind, who then was able to see both literally and spiritually. The Pharisees believed themselves to have spiritual sight, but Christ exposed their spiritual blindness. Commenting on this miracle and how the religious leaders reacted to it, Jesus says, "For judgment I have come into the world, so that the blind will see and those who see will become blind" (John 9:39).

Like the two preceding images of purified gold and white garments, the image of eye ointment to heal blindness may have been an especially powerful metaphor for believers in Laodicea because of the city's famous medical school (Strabo, *Geography* 12.8.20), where a noted ophthalmologist practiced (so, e.g., Ladd 1972: 66; Mounce 1977: 127; Aune 1997: 259–60; Beale 1999: 306; Keener 2000: 160; Osborne 2002: 210; Wilson 2002: 278). Again some have objected to the claim of a local allusion by pointing out that several cities in Asia Minor had medical schools (Michaels 1997:89; Koester 2003: 417–18; Tonstad 2019: 96). It is true that the healing complex in Pergamum enjoyed a greater reputation, being the Mayo Clinic of the ancient world, but it is also true that Laodicea was especially recognized for its eye care (see esp. Hemer 1986: 196–99). The medical school of Laodicea followed the teaching of Herophilus of Chalcedon, a leading physician of the third century BC who is known to have written on ophthalmology. Galen, perhaps the most famous doctor of the ancient world, wrote, "And the eyes you will strengthen by using the dry powder made of Phrygian stone, applying the mixture to the eyelids without touching the membrane of the eye inside" (*Hygiene* 6.12). Although Galen refers to the province of Phrygia, he likely has in mind its leading city, Laodicea, and the famous medical school located there. The strongest evidence comes from another physician who studied at the Laodicea medical school, Demosthenes Philalethes, who was renowned as an ophthalmologist and wrote a standard work on eye care that was very influential in its day and still existed in translation in medieval times. Hemer (1986: 199) concludes his survey of the evidence by stating, "We thus find considerable circumstantial reason for connecting the 'eye salve' motif with Laodicea. The city probably marketed extensively and profitably an ointment developed locally from available materials, whose exact composition may have been kept secret from commercial rivals."

The correction continues with an unexpected statement: "Whomever I love, I rebuke and discipline" (3:19a). After the preceding harsh complaint of Jesus that he was about to vomit the Laodicean church out of his mouth, this shift to the language of love is sudden, surprising, and significant. The personal affection of Christ for this church, the worst of the seven, is stressed by the addition of a first-person personal pronoun, though already expressed by the verb, and its placement in the emphatic position at the head of the sentence. The deep emotion of Christ for the believers in Laodicea is further emphasized by the quantitative pronoun "as many as" or "whomever" (*hosous*), which is here combined with the generalizing particle *ean* to show that his love extends to each member of this church (*hosous* + *ean* makes "the expression more general *all those who, whoever*, lit. *as many as ever*," BDAG 729.2). In only one other sermon does Christ explicitly express his love for his readers (3:9, "they will know that I have loved you [the Philadelphian church]"), which means that his affection for the vomit-inducing and vain Laodiceans is as strong as his feelings for the persecuted and persevering Philadelphians. Some have claimed a distinction in meaning between Christ's use of the verb *agapaō* (3:9) with the Philadelphians and the verb *phileō* (3:19) with the Laodiceans, but these two verbs seem to be treated as synonyms in the Johannine writings (see, e.g., Hemer 1986: 281–82; Kistemaker 2001: 174; Osborne 2002: 210n22).

Christ's statement "alludes loosely" (Aune 1997: 260) to Prov. 3:12 LXX or is a "free rendering" (Thomas 1992: 317) of that passage: "For whom the Lord loves he disciplines; and he chastises every son whom he accepts." This OT text is cited word-for-word in three quite different writings (Philo, *Preliminary Studies* 177; Heb. 12:6; 1 Clement 56.4), which suggests that this verse was a well-known proverb among both Jews and Christians. The idea of "educative discipline" (F. Büchsel, *TDNT* 2:474), chastening someone out of love and for their ultimate good, is commonly used in the OT and Jewish literature to describe not only how parents should treat their children (Prov. 13:24; 23:13–14; 29:17; Philo, *The Worse Attacks the Better* 145) but also how God treats his people (Deut. 8:5; Job 5:17; Ps. 94:12–13; Prov. 3:11–12; Jer. 2:30; 5:3; Jdt. 8:27; Sir. 22:6; 30:1; Wis. Sol. 3:5; 12:22; 2 Macc. 6:12–16; 7:33; Pss. Sol. 3.4; 8.26; 10.1–3; 13.9–10; 14.1; see Aune 1997: 260; Keener 2000: 161n24). At first the church in Laodicea would have been hurt by hearing Christ's strong complaint against them, but now they can be comforted by realizing that his words about vomit and vanity, as shocking as they are, actually stem from his love for them. Christ's actions are like those of a caring parent, who disciplines a wayward child to lead them toward behavior that will ultimately result in their well-being.

The correction unit of 3:18–19 concludes with the kind of statement we have come to expect: "Therefore, be zealous and repent!" (3:19b). Every one of the five problematic or unhealthy churches is commanded to repent (Ephesus, 2:5 [2×]; Pergamum, 2:16; Thyatira, 2:21 [2×], 22; Sardis, 3:3; Laodicea, 3:19b), and so the presence here of the second command "Repent!" is hardly surprising. This compound Greek verb (*metanoeō*) literally means "to change one's mind." In colloquial terms, it involves engaging in a mental U-turn, recognizing the error of one's old way of thinking (and the actions stemming from it) and the need for a new and different perspective. In this context, repentance means that the Laodicean church must recognize the uselessness of their vomit-inducing deeds and the vanity of their attitude of smug self-sufficiency and immediately follow Christ's correction (the inferential particle "therefore" [*oun*] closely connects this command with the immediately preceding clause).

The first command to be zealous clarifies the second command to repent: this change of mind and obedience to Christ's correction must not be done reluctantly or half-heartedly but earnestly and fervently, as the seriousness of the situation requires. The word order of these two commands has perplexed some commentators; logically, repenting must precede adopting a zealous attitude and lifestyle. However, this may be another instance of the *hysteron-proteron* (latter-former) literary device, in which the logical order is reversed to stress a point. This device appears frequently in the book of Revelation (in addition to the comments above on 3:17a, see Rev. 3:3; 5:5; 6:4; 10:4, 9; 20:4–5, 12–13; 22:14; so Thomas 1992: 320).

Figure 7.4. *The Light of the World* (1853), by Hunter Holman. Keble College, Oxford. "Behold! I stand at the door and knock. If anyone hears my voice and opens the door, then I will come in and eat with that person and they with me" (Rev. 3:20). The door is overgrown with weeds, since it has not been opened in a long time. The door has no handle and can be opened only from the inside.

The Consequence (3:20–21)

Each of the previous six sermons has followed the same twofold pattern to bring the message to a close: first is a warning of the negative consequence if the church refuses to repent and heed Christ's correction; second is a promise of the positive consequence and reward if the church repents and with Christ's help conquers its particular sin(s). For one of the two healthy churches—Smyrna—the first negative consequence is replaced with a positive reward, but for the remaining five churches, the twofold pattern is consistently followed. This naturally leads us to expect the same pattern of warning and promise for Laodicea, the worst of the seven congregations.

First Positive Consequence (3:20)

The first four unhealthy churches faced a very serious negative consequence for their potential failure to repent and obey Christ's words of correction. Christ will remove the lampstand of the Ephesian church; that is, he will put the congregation out of existence (2:5b). He will come and fight against the Pergamum church with a sharp, double-edged sword protruding from his mouth (2:16b). Christ will throw Jezebel and her followers in the Thyatiran church into a sickbed, where they will suffer intensely, and he will kill her children (2:22–23). He will come not merely *to* but *against* the Sardis church like a thief (3:3b).

Given the severe threats that the other churches received from Christ, the Laodicean church must surely have been bracing for a strongly negative warning from Christ. After all, they were still coming to grips with the lack of any commendation and with Christ's stinging complaint about their vomit-inducing works and vain attitude. But the anticipated words of condemnation, though deserved, never come! Instead Christ speaks compassionate words of grace: "Behold! I stand at the door and knock. If anyone hears my voice and opens the door, then I will come in to that person, and I will eat with them and they with me" (3:20). The surprise of this grace-filled consequence is lessened a bit by the deep note of affection conveyed in Christ's preceding statement that "whomever I love, I rebuke and discipline" (3:19a). As stinging as Christ's complaint must have been, the believers should not interpret it as evidence of his rejection of them. On the contrary, Christ's sharp rebuke and discipline stem from his love for them, a love now expressed in the powerful metaphor of Christ standing and knocking at the door, seeking to reestablish not just fellowship with them but an intimacy characterized by the sharing of a meal.

The force of this metaphor is enhanced by a couple of grammatical features. First, Christ prefaces his statement with the interjection "Behold!" (*idou*: 26× in the book of Revelation, 6 of these in the seven sermons: 2:10, 22; 3:8, 9 [2×], 20), which not only sets apart this consequence section from the preceding correction but also draws attention to what he is about to say. Second, the opening verb "I stand" occurs in the less-used perfect tense, which "emphasizes the state of Christ standing, and functions to highlight Christ's climactic, present invitation to the readers as a powerful motivation to repent (v. 19)" (Mathewson 2016: 56).

There is disagreement about the source of the image of Christ standing and knocking at a door. Many assert that it stems from Song of Songs 5:2 LXX: "The voice is of my beloved. He is knocking on the door, 'Open to me, my darling'" (so, e.g., Charles 1920: 101; Thomas 1992: 321; Beale 1999:

308; Osborne 2002: 212; Beale and Campbell 2015: 93). In this view, Christ is presenting himself as a loving husband who stands at the door of his bride, the church of Laodicea. Others claim that this metaphor comes from the parable of the doorkeepers in Luke 12:35–36: "Be dressed, ready for service, and keep your lamps burning like servants waiting for their master to return from a wedding banquet, so that when he comes and knocks they can immediately open the door for him" (so J. Jeremias 1972: 55; Wilson 2002: 278; see also Aune 1997: 261; Beale 1999: 308; Keener 2000: 161n25). In this view, Christ appears as a powerful master knocking at the door of his own home and expecting his servants—the Laodicean believers—to open it immediately for him.

In both cases, the proposed source has only one element—knocking on a door—in common with Christ's words here in Revelation, an action that is not unique or distinctive. Furthermore, the context of the proposed sources differs from the Revelation passage. The text from Song of Songs conveys the perspective of the female inside the house, the male lover leaves before the woman can answer the door, and there is no mention of eating a meal together. In the parable of the doorkeepers, the master is coming home *after* a meal (a wedding banquet) and, acting as the host, will reward his alert doorkeepers by serving them a meal, whereas in Rev. 3:20 Jesus is seeking to share a meal as a guest of those inside (Wiarda 1995: 204–5).

Thus the image of Christ standing at a door and knocking probably does not stem from either the OT or a parable from the Gospels. Nevertheless, the meaning of the metaphor is easily understood and conveys Christ's deep affection for the Laodicean church. Despite their vomit-inducing works and vain attitude, Christ has not abandoned these believers but still loves them so much that he is willing to humble himself just to reestablish a relationship with them. After all, as the Christ title makes clear, he is "the ruler of God's creation" and thus has the divine power and authority simply to smash the door down and demand that the Laodicean church submit to him. Instead, Christ meekly stands at the door and politely knocks, requesting that they listen to him and let him in. As Mounce (1977: 129) observes, "In their blind self-sufficiency they had, as it were, excommunicated the risen Lord from their congregation. In an act of unbelievable condescension he requests permission to enter and reestablish fellowship."

Christ's deep affection for the Laodicean church is further evident from the fact that he is not satisfied with merely reestablishing his relationship with them; he desires an *intimate* relationship with them, expressed by the metaphor of a shared meal: "and I will eat with that person and they with me." Table fellowship in the ancient world had far more significance than it does in most places today. To eat and drink with another person was an act of acceptance and honor, a sign that intimate friendship existed between those dining together. As Tonstad (2019: 100) succinctly puts it: "'Eating' does double duty as a reference to eating and intimacy." The Jewish leaders complained that Jesus not only associated with tax collectors and sinners but also ate with them (Luke 15:2). The people in Jericho reacted very negatively when Jesus entered the house of Zacchaeus as a guest, which almost certainly meant sharing a meal with him (Luke 19:5–7). Jewish Christians in Jerusalem criticized Peter not because he preached the gospel to gentiles but because he entered gentile homes and ate with them (Acts 11:3). The negative consequence for the Laodicean church, therefore, is surprisingly positive: they have been given the gracious possibility of reestablishing a most intimate relationship with Christ.

In this promise of table fellowship, a few interpreters see an allusion to the Lord's Supper. Caird (1966: 58), for example, states: "The mention of a 'supper' with Christ could hardly fail to conjure up pictures of the last supper in the upper room and of subsequent occasions when that meal had been re-enacted as the symbol of Christ's continuing presence" (see also Mulholland 1990: 137; Beale 1999: 309). More find an allusion to the eschatological messianic banquet. Thomas (1992: 324) asserts: "Christ's present supping with believers is only a foretaste of the future. As part of the bride of Christ, believers will participate in the marriage supper of the Lamb (cf. Rev. 19:9) and in this manner celebrate in His future kingdom (cf. Luke 22:16, 29, 30). The language of this promise makes it impossible to rule out a primary reference to the future messianic kingdom" (so also, e.g., Beckwith 1919: 491; Osborne 2002: 213; for problems with this view, see Wiarda 1995: 204; Beale 1999: 308–9). In the context of the seven sermons as a whole, however, the reward of table fellowship with Christ is more likely a polemical contrast to the cultic meals that were a big part of the Greco-Roman religious world and were consequently a big temptation to John's readers (see esp. the complaint sections of the Pergamum and Thyatira sermons).

Second Positive Consequence (3:21)

The sermon to Laodicea comes to a close with the expected victory, or Nike, formula, which spells out the positive consequence if the church repents and overcomes its vomit-inducing works and vain attitude: "To the one who is victorious, I will give the right to sit with me on my throne, just as I was victorious and sat with my Father on his throne" (3:21). The distinctive feature and theological significance of this victory formula must not be missed.

Although each of the preceding six sermons similarly refers to "the one who is victorious," only here do we find the important addition "just as I was victorious." In other words, the believer's victory is ultimately due not to one's own talents or persistence but instead rests on Christ's previous victory. Only by virtue of their relationship with Christ and the empower-

Figure 7.5. A Roman coin (13 BC). *Left*: Bare head of Caesar Augustus. *Right*: Augustus and Marcus Agrippa, each wearing a toga, are seated side-by-side on a *bisellium*, or double throne.

ing presence of his Spirit can believers overcome their sin and be victorious. What is explicitly stated in a climatic manner as true for the seventh and worst church is also implicitly true for each of the preceding six churches. The positive consequence for each congregation should be viewed not as an earned reward but as an undeserved gift, a gift of grace given by Christ (note the words "I will give to him . . .").

The gracious gift that Christ will give to his victorious followers in Laodicea is "the right to sit with me on my throne." The image presented here is one where Christ followers sit not on their own thrones but beside Christ on his throne ("sit *with me* on *my* throne"). The *bisellium*, or "double-throne," was familiar in the Greco-Roman world. The coin in figure 7.5 depicts Caesar Augustus seated on a *bisellium* with his childhood friend and faithful general, Marcus Agrippa. This image was intended to show that the two men were sharing the rule of the Roman Empire and that Augustus had designated Agrippa as his successor. The Gemma Augustea (Gem of Augustus) is an onyx cameo famous for its detailed workmanship, which was produced in AD 10–20. The upper scene depicts the goddess Roma, a personification of the Roman state, seated alongside the emperor Augustus on a *bisellium*. Numerous Greco-Roman sources refer to two deities enthroned on a *bisellium* (see sources cited by Aune 1997: 262), and many ancient reliefs depict two gods seated together on a double throne, especially deities that are typically paired, such as Zeus and Hera, Demeter and Kore, and Hades and Persephone. An ornate *bisellium* made of bronze, with silver and copper inlays, was found in Pompeii in 1864 and is now in the Archaeological Museum of Naples (item 72992). The positive consequence promised to the Laodicean believers, therefore, is powerful: even members of the worst of the seven churches have the potential of sitting not merely on a throne but of sitting in an intimate and privileged position beside Jesus on his throne and sharing in his rule over God's creation.

The meaning and significance of this metaphor is better appreciated in light of several other biblical passages. Most relevant among these texts is the third of the Christ titles that open this sermon. The title "ruler of God's creation" not only authorizes the speaker but foreshadows the closing promise that believers will share in Christ's authority and rule over creation. Fanning (2020: 190) writes, "This promise that the overcomer will share Christ's authority returns to the theme of Christ's rule over all creation that the message started with (v. 14b)." The positive consequence offered the Laodicean church somewhat parallels the reward offered earlier to the Thyatiran church, though there the focus is less on Christ's kingly rule over the nations and more on the right to judge and destroy them: "He who is victorious and keeps my works until the end, I will give to him authority over the nations—and he will destroy them with an iron rod as ceramic pots are shattered" (2:26–27). The idea that Christ's faithful followers will share in his universal reign is expressed frequently in the book of Revelation (1:6; 2:26; 3:21; 5:10; 20:4, 6; 22:5). The apostle Paul encouraged persecuted believers with a trustworthy saying that also expresses this expectation of sharing in Christ's rule: "If we endure, we will also reign with him" (2 Tim. 2:12). Jesus promised his disciples: "Truly I tell you, at the renewal of all things, when the Son of Man sits on his glorious throne, you who have followed me will also sit on twelve thrones, judging the twelve tribes of Israel" (Matt. 19:28; cf. Luke 22:29–30). Several OT texts created the expectation that God's people would enjoy honored positions of power and judge their enemies in the coming kingdom (e.g., Ps. 149:4–9; Isa. 60:14; Dan. 7:14, 18, 27). But though the idea of believers enjoying a special status and role in the coming kingdom is expressed throughout Scripture, only here is it portrayed in such an intimate and privileged manner through the metaphor of sitting alongside Jesus on a *bisellium*, or double throne.

Hemer (1986: 205–6, 209) has proposed that the image of sharing a throne with Jesus has a special local connection, and a few other commentators have found this persuasive (so, e.g., Osborne 2002: 214; Wilson 2002: 278). The orator Zenon, briefly mentioned above in connection with Laodicea's great wealth (see on 3:17), played a key role, along with his son Polemos, in stopping a dangerous invader of Asia in 40 BC (Strabo, *Geography* 14.2.24). Rome gratefully rewarded Zenon by making him king of Cilicia and a few years later king of Pontus (Appian, *Civil Wars* 5.75; Dio Cassius, *Roman History* 49.25.4; Plutarch, *Antony* 38.3). Subsequent generations of this Zenoid family served as vassal kings of various regions of Asia Minor under Roman control, and many powerful and wealthy members of the extended family resided in Laodicea. This history, it is claimed, justifies identifying Laodicea as a "throne city" (Wilson 2002: 278) and suggests that Christ's promise that victorious members will sit with him on his throne alludes to the Zenoid family, who in a similar fashion received a throne as the prize of victory. Against the idea of seeing a local allusion in Christ's promise, however, is the fact that, as Hemer (1986: 205) himself concedes, very little is known about this dynasty beyond what is summarized above, and "nothing [is known] of their later relations with their city of origin." It is also questionable whether citizens of Laodicea in AD 95 would readily pick up such a veiled allusion to historical events that transpired many years before their own day. Additionally, the metaphor in 3:21 is not of a regular throne but the more specialized *bisellium*, which is not connected in any way with the history of the Zenoid family. Finally, a throne is a common metaphor for evoking a sense of power and privilege and would be readily understood by those in the ancient world, independent of any supposed allusion to Laodicea's local history.

The Contemporary Significance

Introduction

A sermon title should pique the interest of an audience, not offend them. Which of these two reactions do you have to today's sermon title: "Laodicea: The Church of Vomit and Vanity"? Some of you may well react negatively and object: "How can you use such vulgar language in a sermon title? The word 'vomit' has no business being used in a sermon or any part of a worship service!" But as offensive or shocking as that term may be, it is the word that Jesus himself uses to describe the church of Laodicea. They are a congregation whose actions and attitude are so upsetting to Christ that they make him want to throw up! This sermon constitutes a sobering warning not only to the church of Laodicea but also to believers today whose actions and attitudes fall similarly short of God's call to holy living.

Yet amid this language of vomit and vanity, dear friends, do not miss the good news of the gospel. In this sermon, Jesus speaks not only with stinging judgment but also with unexpected grace, expressing his love for you and his deep desire to enter into an intimate relationship with you. And so, in our message today, I introduce to you the church of Laodicea, or, as it can be justly called, "the church of vomit and vanity."

The Christ Title (3:14b)

The sermon to Laodicea begins in the same way as the preceding six messages, with a title that Christ gives to himself and that anticipates the message he is about to give. Before Jesus says anything to this congregation, he gives a threefold description of himself: "These are the words of the Amen, the faithful and true witness, the ruler of God's creation" (3:14b). All three titles have important implications for how the Laodicean church ought to respond to Christ's message, a message of both stinging judgment and unexpected grace.

The first Christ title identifies Jesus as "the Amen." In Isa. 65:16 the word "Amen" is used as a title for God, so when the word "Amen" is used here to refer to Jesus, it asserts his divinity: Jesus is God. The Hebrew word "amen" means "truth." When a congregation shouts "Amen!" to something the preacher says, they are really saying "That's the truth!" When Jesus says "I am the Amen," he is really saying "I am the truth. What I am about to say to you is the truth. No matter how stinging my words of judgment about you may be, don't reject them, because they are the truth. No matter how unexpected my words of grace about you may be, don't doubt them, because they also are the truth. I am the Amen! I am the truth!"

The second Christ title identifies Jesus as "the faithful and true witness." This second Christ title explains more fully the meaning of the Hebrew word "amen." When Jesus says to the church of Laodicea "I am the faithful and true witness," he is really declaring, "What I am about to say to you is faithful and true. No matter how stinging my words of judgment about you may be, don't reject them, because they are reliable and accurate. No matter how unexpected my words of grace about you may be, don't doubt them, because they also are reliable and accurate. I am the faithful and true witness!"

The third Christ title identifies Jesus as "the ruler of God's creation." This title highlights Christ's universal authority or absolute power, since he is the ruler not just of one nation or even of many nations but of all creation. Jesus was not exaggerating when he said before his ascension, "All authority on heaven and on earth has been given to me" (Matt. 28:18). When Jesus says to the church of Laodicea "I am the ruler of God's creation," he is really declaring, "I have authority over the whole of God's creation, including your church in Laodicea. That means that I have the authority to speak stinging words of judgment to you. That means that I also have the authority to speak unexpected words of grace to you. Don't reject or doubt what I am about to say to you in this sermon, since I am the ruler of God's creation!"

The Commendation—None!

At this point in the sermon, the Christians in Laodicea would be excited about what comes next. From the preceding six sermons they know that after the Christ title comes the commendation, when Jesus says something positive about what the church is doing well. They have already heard Jesus's commendation of the believers in Ephesus, Smyrna, Pergamum, Thyatira, Sardis (although it was a concession and not a commendation), and Philadelphia. What's more, the church of Laodicea was vain, overly confident of their superior status compared to other churches, and blind to their true spiritual condition (3:17b). All this would naturally lead them to expect glowing words of commendation from Jesus. But what actually comes next would surely have been surprising and disappointing to them. Instead of the expected words of commendation, they are given words of complaint: "I know your works, namely, that you are neither cold nor hot. I wish you were cold or hot. So, because you are lukewarm and are neither cold nor hot, I am about to vomit you out of my mouth" (3:15–16).

The commendation is missing in this sermon. The situation is so bad at Laodicea that Jesus cannot say anything positive about them, and unlike in the Sardis sermon, there is no concession that Jesus is pleased with at least some in the congregation. The Laodicean church is not the great and impressive congregation that they vainly thought they were; in fact, in Jesus's eyes, they are the worst of the seven churches.

The Complaint (3:15–17)

Since the expected commendation is disappointingly omitted, the sermon moves directly to the complaint, which is the longest and harshest of the seven sermons. The complaint has two main parts, each one justifying the title for this sermon to Laodicea as a church of "vomit and vanity."

The first complaint, found in 3:15–16, involves the church's vomit-inducing works. Christ accuses the Laodicean church of being neither cold nor hot but lukewarm. What does it mean to be a lukewarm church?

One common but unlikely answer is that a lukewarm church is a wishy-washy church with no passion or zeal for the Christian faith. A cold church is supposedly a congregation with no faith at all, which is obviously bad. A hot church is supposedly a congregation on fire for the Lord, which is good. But a lukewarm church, according to this line of thinking, is a congregation between these two extremes—a congregation that is indifferent, apathetic, and complacent. The problem with this interpretation is that Jesus seems to prefer a cold church to a lukewarm church. It is hard to believe that Jesus would rather have ice-cold atheists than lukewarm Christians.

A better explanation of what it means to be a lukewarm church links the various temperatures with degrees of usefulness. Evidence from the ancient world shows that both cold water and hot water were considered useful and thus preferable over lukewarm water, which was regarded as useless. For example, one ancient writer claims that cold water is useful for drinking and hot water is useful for washing, but lukewarm water is good only to give to the household slaves. Another ancient writer describes an unusual hot spring where the temperature changed drastically throughout the day; local citizens used this water when it was either cold or hot but not when it was lukewarm. The key idea of Jesus's first complaint, then, is that just as lukewarm water is useless compared with cold or hot water, so also the works of the Laodicean church are useless.

This understanding of the lukewarm metaphor seems also to be supported by the local geography. The city of Laodicea is located near two other cities along the Lycus River: Colossae and Hierapolis. These two cities, along with Laodicea, formed the tri-cities of the Lycus River valley. Colossae, ten miles south of Laodicea, enjoyed an abundant supply of cold water from the melting snows of a nearby 8,000-foot-high mountain. Hierapolis, six miles directly across the Lycus River valley from Laodicea, was famous for the healing effects of its hot springs. Laodicea's main water supply came from a hot spring five miles away; because the water cooled as it slowly traveled along the aqueduct, it was lukewarm by the time it arrived in the city. Given this geographical context, Jesus's metaphor of the three different temperatures would have been especially meaningful to the Laodicean believers. Jesus's first complaint is that, unlike the cold drinking water of nearby Colossae or the hot healing water of nearby Hierapolis, the Laodicean church's works were useless, like the lukewarm water that came into their city.

What works of the Laodicean church did Christ regard as lukewarm and useless? Although Christ's complaint here is longer and harsher than in any other sermon, no specific work is mentioned, so we simply don't know. We do know that the situation is clearly serious. This is signaled by Jesus's violently negative reaction to the works of the Laodicean church. He says, "I am about to vomit you out of my mouth" (3:16b). Most Bible translations soften the language here and say instead "I am about to *spit* you out of my mouth." But the original Greek text is crystal clear: Jesus will not merely spit them out of his mouth; he threatens to *vomit* them out of his mouth. Jesus is looking at the life and conduct of the Laodicean church, and their works are so offensive to him that he says, "Your congregation makes me want to throw up! Your works are so lukewarm and upsetting to me that they make me want to puke! You truly are a church of vomit!"

Jesus has a second complaint: they are not only a church of vomit but also a church of vanity. Their attitude of arrogance or smugness is revealed in the opening words of 3:17: "For you say, 'I am rich and have become wealthy and do not need a thing.'" Jesus knows that the way people act is intimately connected with how they think, and so he moves beyond his first complaint, dealing with the *actions* of the Laodicean church, to the second complaint, regarding the *thinking* of the Laodicean church. Jesus knows that they will never be able to replace their lukewarm, useless, vomit-inducing works with truly praiseworthy works unless they first change their vain attitude.

Their vanity stems from the mistaken belief that money is the answer to all their problems and the key to their happiness. They have an attitude of smug self-sufficiency, thinking that they don't need anything or anybody because of their financial wealth. The vain attitude of the Laodicean church may have been influenced by the vain attitude of the city of Laodicea. Several of the city's citizens were very rich; a few were multimillionaires—the Bill Gates of the Lycus River valley. What's more, on a few occasions the city and its rich citizens acted vainly because of their wealth. One notable incident involved a devastating earthquake that destroyed much of the city. Rome offered financial aid to Laodicea to help the city get back on its feet, but Laodicea smugly replied to Rome, "No thanks. We don't need your help. We can rebuild the city with our own money and resources."

The vanity of the church of Laodicea is exposed by Christ, the Amen, who is the truth and bluntly describes their true condition: "But you do not know that you are wretched and pitiful and poor and blind and naked" (3:17b). Of the five characteristics that Jesus lists in his second complaint, the last three are the most important. We know this because the last three descriptions in this complaint section, "poor and blind and naked," appear again in the correction section that follows. Let's move on, then, to the correction in order to see how not only the Laodicean church but also the church today can overcome its spiritual poverty, blindness, and nakedness.

The Correction (3:18–19)

Thus far Christ's sermon to Laodicea has consisted of stinging judgment on their vomit-inducing works and vain attitude, but Christ's strong judgment is now balanced by his unexpected grace. Even though they are the worst of the seven churches, Jesus has not given up on them but graciously provides a way to correct their spiritual poverty, blindness, and nakedness.

Their spiritual poverty can be corrected in this way: "I advise you to buy from me gold refined in the fire in order that you may become rich" (3:18a). This metaphor of refined gold refers to the process, well-known in the ancient world, of melting precious metal with extreme heat so that the slag or impurities can be skimmed off the top, leaving the purified element behind. "Refined gold" or the purification process itself became a common metaphor in the Bible for cleaning one's moral life by removing the impurities of sin. The church of Laodicea can correct their spiritual poverty and become truly rich by removing from their life all the lukewarm or useless works that are causing Jesus to throw up. The church must remove all of their vomit-inducing works until all that remains are the obedient, holy works that are more valuable than refined gold.

Their spiritual nakedness can be corrected in this way: "I advise you to buy from me . . . white garments so that you might be clothed and the shame of your nakedness might not be seen" (3:18b). Nakedness and white clothes are used throughout the Bible as metaphors for moral conduct. Nakedness is a negative metaphor for sinful actions; white clothes are a positive metaphor for obedient, holy actions. The useless, vomit-inducing, sinful actions of the Laodicean believers leave them spiritually naked. The church must repent of its sinful behavior and cover its shameful nakedness by putting on white clothes, by living lives characterized by obedience and holiness.

Their spiritual blindness can be corrected in this way: "I advise you to buy from me . . . medication to put on your eyes so that you might see" (3:18c). Blindness is used metaphorically in the Bible to describe ignorance and lack of discernment. The Christ followers in Laodicea are naively unaware of their true spiritual condition and that they justly deserve stinging words of judgment. Yet their dangerous spiritual condition need not become deadly, since Christ graciously offers them a life-saving solution: believers can buy eye ointment from Christ, salve that can cure their blindness and enable them to truly see.

As was true of the refined gold and the white garments, this eye-ointment is not widely available. In fact, these things can be bought from only one special person. As Christ stresses in this correction section: "I advise you to buy *from me*." The church of Laodicea may have lots of money, but all their wealth cannot buy them what they really need. Their vanity cannot hide the fact that they are actually helpless and completely dependent on Christ and on what only he can give them. There is no need for the Christians in Laodicea or for Christians today to have a self-sufficient, "pull-yourselves-up-by-your-own-bootstraps" attitude, relying on our own natural abilities or hard work to fix our spiritual poverty, nakedness, and blindness. We must instead fall on our knees and turn to Christ, who alone can save us.

Still more unexpected grace is found in the correction as Christ says, "Whomever I love, I rebuke and discipline" (3:19a). No doubt the church of Laodicea was at first hurt by Christ's stinging judgment about them in the complaint section. But now they are comforted by the realization that Christ's words about vomit and vanity, as painful as they are, flow from his love for them. Jesus is like a parent about to punish a child, who first says, "This is going to hurt me more than you." The wayward child facing punishment doesn't believe it, but that's exactly the way it is for dads and moms who love their children. They love their children too much to ignore their wrongdoing, but instead punish them out of the sincere hope that it will ultimately lead to their children's well-being and good. Jesus graciously reassures the vomit-inducing and vain church of Laodicea, the worst of the seven churches, by saying, "I love you."

The Consequence (3:20–21)

In all seven sermons, the fifth and final item in the outline is the double consequence: first, a negative consequence describing the punishment the church faces if it fails to heed Christ's correction; second, a positive consequence describing the reward if the church responds to Christ's correction.

First Positive Consequence (3:20)

The Laodicean believers must have been nervous about what Jesus was going to say next. After all, Jesus has already warned the four other unhealthy churches of the serious negative consequences they face. To the church of Ephesus, Jesus said "I will remove your lampstand" (2:5b)—that is, "I will put your congregation out of existence!" To the church of Pergamum, Jesus said, "I will fight against you with a sharp, double-edged sword coming out of my mouth!" (2:16b). To the church of Thyatira, Jesus said, "I will throw Jezebel and her followers into a sickbed, where they will suffer terribly, and I will kill all her children!" (2:22–23). To the church of Sardis, Jesus said, "I will not merely come *to* you but *against* you like a thief!" (3:3b). What will Jesus say to the church of Laodicea, the worst of the seven churches? They surely must have been bracing themselves for the very negative consequence that Jesus was about to pronounce against them.

But the anticipated words of condemnation never come; instead, Christ speaks more words of unexpected grace: "Behold! I stand at the door and knock. If anyone hears my voice and opens the door, then I will come in to that person, and I will eat with them and they with me" (3:20).

Dear friend: Don't miss the full force of Christ's grace and love expressed in this image! Don't forget the third Christ title, that Jesus is "the ruler of God's creation," who does not need to stand at the door and meekly knock. He has the divine power and authority simply to smash the door down and demand that the Laodicean church submit to him! But even though Christ has the power and authority to demand obedience, and even though the Laodicean church deserves to be treated that way, Christ comes instead with unexpected grace and love. He is like a sad-sack boyfriend who, despite being mistreated and cheated on by his girlfriend, nevertheless shows up at her door holding a bouquet of flowers in one hand and knocking on the door with the other, pleading, "Please let me in! I still love you!" It doesn't matter whether you're the worst church or the worst Christian. It doesn't matter what sinful things you've done. Jesus has unexpected grace for you and still loves you. He is standing outside your door and knocking because he wants to have a relationship with you!

More than this, Jesus wants an *intimate* relationship with you: he wants to share a meal with you. In the ancient world, and still today in many places around the globe, sharing a meal with someone meant enjoying close fellowship with that person. The Jewish leaders were upset with Jesus because he not only spent time with tax collectors and sinners but even ate with them (Luke 15:2). The Jewish Christians in Jerusalem were upset with the apostle Peter because he not only spent time with gentiles but even ate with them (Acts 11:3). The good news of the gospel is that it doesn't matter who you are or what you've done; Jesus has unexpected grace for you and still loves you. He is standing outside your door and knocking because he wants to have an intimate relationship with you!

Second Positive Consequence (3:21)

Christ's sermon to the church of Laodicea ends in the same way that all the sermons have ended, with the victory formula. This is now the seventh time that we have heard Jesus refer to "the one who is victorious," so we well remember that the Greek word used here is the name of a popular sporting goods company, Nike. The company chose its name because it wants us to associate their sports equipment and apparel with winning: if you use their products, you will be victorious, you will win!

The important question that our text raises is this: Are you a Nike Christian, a victorious Christian? Can you overcome the sin of being a lukewarm Christian, whose works are useless and so offensive to Christ that they make him want to vomit? Can you overcome the sin of vanity, smugly thinking that your wealth will take care of any problem that comes your way? The good news of the gospel is that the answer to these important questions can be a resounding "Yes!" You and I can be Nike Christians and win the victory, not because we are so talented or so hard working but because Christ has already won the victory, and we who belong to Christ have his Spirit living in us. This divine Holy Spirit gives us the power to repent of our sinful ways, commit or recommit ourselves exclusively to Christ, and live in ways that clearly show his grace working in us.

If you, then, are a Nike Christian, what is your reward? Christ answers with this promise: "To the one who is victorious, I will give the right to sit with me on my throne, just as I was victorious and sat with my Father on his throne" (3:21). The image here is of a double throne, a throne with two seats. Jesus sits on one seat, since, as the opening Christ title clearly asserts, he is "the ruler of God's creation." The other seat of this double throne is reserved for you. As a Nike Christian, you will sit beside Jesus on a double throne and share in his all-powerful rule over God's creation. Your status will be upgraded from being a vomit-inducing, vain sinner to being a coruler with Christ. What a positive consequence of unexpected grace!

Conclusion

The biggest danger facing the Western church today may be *physical wealth* that leads to *spiritual poverty*. Wealth itself is not bad. In fact, it is a huge blessing to be free from worry about our daily needs of food, shelter, health, and safety. Nevertheless, physical wealth all too often leads to spiritual poverty. A preoccupation with money and material possessions can easily cause us to become lukewarm Christians, so obsessed with our own financial success that we are useless in serving Christ and others. A preoccupation with wealth can easily cause us to become vain, persons who smugly think that we can handle the challenges of life ourselves without Christ's help. To all of us lukewarm and vain Christians, Christ the Amen speaks both a true word of stinging judgment, which would be dangerous to ignore, and a true word of unexpected grace, which would be foolish to doubt. Jesus loves you and is standing outside your door and knocking because he wants to have an intimate relationship with you. Will you open that door and with Christ's help become a Nike Christian?

"Whoever has ears to hear, let them hear what the Spirit is saying to the churches!"—not only to the ancient church of Laodicea but also to the church of Jesus Christ today.

Appendix

Grammatical Outlines

Grammatical Outline of Revelation 2:1–7 (Ephesus)

Main clause (command)	¹Τῷ ἀγγέλῳ τῆς ἐν Ἐφέσῳ ἐκκλησίας γράψον·
Main clause	Τάδε λέγει
Attributive participle	└ ὁ κρατῶν τοὺς ἑπτὰ ἀστέρας ἐν τῇ δεξιᾷ αὐτοῦ,
Attributive participle	└ ὁ περιπατῶν ἐν μέσῳ τῶν ἑπτὰ λυχνιῶν τῶν χρυσῶν
Main clause	²Οἶδα τὰ ἔργα σου,
Explanatory καί clause	└ καὶ τὸν κόπον καὶ τὴν ὑπομονήν σου,
Indirect discourse	καὶ ὅτι οὐ δύνῃ
Complementary infinitive	└ βαστάσαι κακούς,
Main clause	καὶ ἐπείρασας τοὺς λέγοντας ἑαυτοὺς ἀποστόλους,
Parenthesis	—καὶ οὐκ εἰσὶν—
Main clause	καὶ εὗρες αὐτοὺς ψευδεῖς·
Main clause	³καὶ ὑπομονὴν ἔχεις,
Main clause	καὶ ἐβάστασας διὰ τὸ ὄνομά μου,
Main clause	καὶ οὐ κεκοπίακες.
Main clause	⁴ἀλλ᾽ ἔχω κατὰ σοῦ
Indirect discourse	└ ὅτι τὴν ἀγάπην σου τὴν πρώτην ἀφῆκες.
Main clause (command)	⁵μνημόνευε οὖν
Interrogative clause	└ πόθεν πέπτωκας,
Main clause (command)	καὶ μετανόησον
Main clause (command)	καὶ τὰ πρῶτα ἔργα ποίησον·
Conditional clause (protasis)	εἰ δὲ μή,
Conditional clause (apodosis)	ἔρχομαί σοι,
Conditional clause (apodosis)	καὶ κινήσω τὴν λυχνίαν σου ἐκ τοῦ τόπου αὐτῆς,
Conditional clause (protasis)	ἐὰν μὴ μετανοήσῃς.
Main clause	⁶ἀλλὰ τοῦτο ἔχεις
Explanatory ὅτι clause	└ ὅτι μισεῖς τὰ ἔργα τῶν Νικολαϊτῶν,
Relative clause	└ ἃ κἀγὼ μισῶ.
Main clause (command)	⁷ὁ ἔχων οὖς ἀκουσάτω
Interrogative clause	└ τί τὸ πνεῦμα λέγει ταῖς ἐκκλησίαις.
Main clause	τῷ νικῶντι δώσω αὐτῷ
Complementary infinitive	└ φαγεῖν ἐκ τοῦ ξύλου τῆς ζωῆς,
Relative clause	└ ὅ ἐστιν ἐν τῷ παραδείσῳ τοῦ θεοῦ.

Grammatical Outline of Revelation 2:8–11 (Smyrna)

Main clause (command)	⁸Καὶ τῷ ἀγγέλῳ τῆς ἐν Σμύρνῃ ἐκκλησίας γράψον·
Main clause	Τάδε λέγει
Subject	└ ὁ πρῶτος καὶ ὁ ἔσχατος,
Relative clause	└ ὃς ἐγένετο νεκρὸς καὶ ἔζησεν·
Main clause	⁹Οἶδά σου τὴν θλῖψιν
Explanatory καί clause	├ καὶ τὴν πτωχείαν,
Parenthetical correction	├ —ἀλλὰ πλούσιος εἶ—
	└ καὶ τὴν βλασφημίαν
Prepositional phrase	ἐκ τῶν λεγόντων Ἰουδαίους
Indirect discourse infinitive	└ εἶναι ἑαυτούς,
Parenthetical correction	—καὶ οὐκ εἰσίν,
Parenthetical correction	ἀλλὰ συναγωγὴ τοῦ Σατανᾶ.
Main clause (prohibition)	¹⁰μηδὲν φοβοῦ
Relative clause	└ ἃ μέλλεις
Complementary infinitive	└ πάσχειν.
Main clause	ἰδοὺ μέλλει ὁ διάβολος
Complementary infinitive	└ βάλλειν ἐξ ὑμῶν εἰς φυλακὴν
Purpose ἵνα clause	└ ἵνα πειρασθῆτε,
Main clause	καὶ ἕξετε θλῖψιν ἡμερῶν δέκα.
Main clause (command)	γίνου πιστὸς ἄχρι θανάτου,
Main clause	καὶ δώσω σοι τὸν στέφανον τῆς ζωῆς.
Main clause (command)	¹¹ὁ ἔχων οὖς ἀκουσάτω
Interrogative clause	└ τί τὸ πνεῦμα λέγει ταῖς ἐκκλησίαις.
Main clause (emphatic negation)	ὁ νικῶν οὐ μὴ ἀδικηθῇ ἐκ τοῦ θανάτου τοῦ δευτέρου.

Grammatical Outline of Revelation 2:12–17 (Pergamum)

Main clause (command)	¹²Καὶ τῷ ἀγγέλῳ τῆς ἐν Περγάμῳ ἐκκλησίας γράψον·
Main clause	Τάδε λέγει
Subject	└ ὁ ἔχων τὴν ῥομφαίαν τὴν δίστομον τὴν ὀξεῖαν
Main clause	¹³Οἶδα
Locative clause	├ ποῦ κατοικεῖς,
Locative clause	├ ὅπου ὁ θρόνος τοῦ Σατανᾶ,
Main clause	├ καὶ κρατεῖς τὸ ὄνομά μου,
Main clause	├ καὶ οὐκ ἠρνήσω τὴν πίστιν μου
Adverbial phrase	καὶ ἐν ταῖς ἡμέραις Ἀντιπᾶς,
Apposition	├ ὁ μάρτυς μου,
Apposition	├ ὁ πιστός μου,
Relative clause	└ ὃς ἀπεκτάνθη παρ' ὑμῖν,
Locative clause	└ ὅπου ὁ Σατανᾶς κατοικεῖ.
Main clause	¹⁴ἀλλ' ἔχω κατὰ σοῦ ὀλίγα,
Explanatory ὅτι clause	└ ὅτι ἔχεις ἐκεῖ κρατοῦντας τὴν διδαχὴν Βαλαάμ,
Relative clause	ὃς ἐδίδασκεν τῷ Βαλὰκ
Complementary infinitive	└ βαλεῖν σκάνδαλον ἐνώπιον τῶν υἱῶν Ἰσραὴλ
Purpose/epexegetical infinitive	├ φαγεῖν εἰδωλόθυτα
Purpose/epexegetical infinitive	└ καὶ πορνεῦσαι·
Main clause	¹⁵οὕτως ἔχεις καὶ σὺ κρατοῦντας τὴν διδαχὴν Νικολαϊτῶν ὁμοίως.
Main clause (command)	¹⁶μετανόησον οὖν·
Conditional clause (protasis)	εἰ δὲ μή,
Conditional clause (apodosis)	ἔρχομαί σοι ταχὺ
Conditional clause (apodosis)	καὶ πολεμήσω μετ' αὐτῶν ἐν τῇ ῥομφαίᾳ τοῦ στόματός μου.
Main clause (command)	¹⁷ὁ ἔχων οὖς ἀκουσάτω
Interrogative clause	└ τί τὸ πνεῦμα λέγει ταῖς ἐκκλησίαις.
Main clause	τῷ νικῶντι δώσω αὐτῷ τοῦ μάννα τοῦ κεκρυμμένου,
Main clause	καὶ δώσω αὐτῷ ψῆφον λευκήν,
Main clause	καὶ ἐπὶ τὴν ψῆφον ὄνομα καινὸν γεγραμμένον
Relative clause	└ ὃ οὐδεὶς οἶδεν,
Exception clause	εἰ μὴ ὁ λαμβάνων.

Grammatical Outline of Revelation 2:18–29 (Thyatira)

Main clause (command)	¹⁸Καὶ τῷ ἀγγέλῳ τῆς ἐν Θυατείροις ἐκκλησίας γράψον·
Main clause	Τάδε λέγει
Subject	└ ὁ υἱὸς τοῦ θεοῦ,
Subject (attributive participle)	└ ὁ ἔχων τοὺς ὀφθαλμοὺς αὐτοῦ ὡς φλόγα πυρὸς
Verbless clause	└ καὶ οἱ πόδες αὐτοῦ ὅμοιοι χαλκολιβάνῳ·
Main clause	¹⁹Οἶδά σου τὰ ἔργα
Explanatory clause	└ καὶ τὴν ἀγάπην καὶ τὴν πίστιν
Explanatory clause	└ καὶ τὴν διακονίαν καὶ τὴν ὑπομονήν σου,
Verbless clause	καὶ τὰ ἔργα σου τὰ ἔσχατα πλείονα τῶν πρώτων.
Main clause	²⁰ἀλλ' ἔχω κατὰ σοῦ ὅτι ἀφεῖς τὴν γυναῖκα
Proper noun: apposition	└ Ἰεζάβελ,
Attributive participle: apposition	└ ἡ λέγουσα ἑαυτὴν προφῆτιν
Main clause	καὶ διδάσκει καὶ πλανᾷ τοὺς ἐμοὺς δούλους
Purpose/result infinitive	—πορνεῦσαι
Purpose/result infinitive	—καὶ φαγεῖν εἰδωλόθυτα.
Main clause	²¹καὶ ἔδωκα αὐτῇ χρόνον
Purpose ἵνα clause	└ ἵνα μετανοήσῃ,
Adversative clause	καὶ οὐ θέλει
Indirect volition infinitive	└ μετανοῆσαι ἐκ τῆς πορνείας αὐτῆς.
Conditional clause (apodosis)	²²ἰδοὺ βάλλω αὐτὴν εἰς κλίνην
	καὶ τοὺς μοιχεύοντας μετ' αὐτῆς εἰς θλῖψιν μεγάλην,
Conditional clause (protasis)	ἐὰν μὴ μετανοήσωσιν ἐκ τῶν ἔργων αὐτῆς.
Main clause	²³καὶ τὰ τέκνα αὐτῆς ἀποκτενῶ ἐν θανάτῳ.
Main clause	καὶ γνώσονται πᾶσαι αἱ ἐκκλησίαι
Indirect clause	└ ὅτι ἐγώ εἰμι ὁ ἐραυνῶν νεφροὺς καὶ καρδίας,
Main clause	καὶ δώσω ὑμῖν ἑκάστῳ κατὰ τὰ ἔργα ὑμῶν.
Main clause	²⁴ὑμῖν δὲ λέγω
Apposition	└ τοῖς λοιποῖς τοῖς ἐν Θυατείροις,
Correlative clause	└ ὅσοι οὐκ ἔχουσιν τὴν διδαχὴν ταύτην,
Relative clause	└ οἵτινες οὐκ ἔγνωσαν τὰ βαθέα τοῦ Σατανᾶ,
Parenthetical clause	—ὡς λέγουσιν—
Main clause	οὐ βάλλω ἐφ' ὑμᾶς ἄλλο βάρος,
Adversative clause	┌ ²⁵πλὴν ὃ ἔχετε
Main verb (command)	κρατήσατε
Temporal clause	└ ἄχρις οὗ ἂν ἥξω.
Hanging nominative	—²⁶καὶ ὁ νικῶν καὶ ὁ τηρῶν ἄχρι τέλους τὰ ἔργα μου—
Main clause	δώσω αὐτῷ ἐξουσίαν ἐπὶ τῶν ἐθνῶν,
Main clause	²⁷καὶ ποιμανεῖ αὐτοὺς ἐν ῥάβδῳ σιδηρᾷ
Comparative clause	ὡς τὰ σκεύη τὰ κεραμικὰ συντρίβεται,
Comparative clause	²⁸ὡς κἀγὼ εἴληφα παρὰ τοῦ πατρός μου,
Main clause	καὶ δώσω αὐτῷ τὸν ἀστέρα τὸν πρωϊνόν.
Main clause (command)	²⁹ὁ ἔχων οὖς ἀκουσάτω
Interrogative clause	└ τί τὸ πνεῦμα λέγει ταῖς ἐκκλησίαις.

Grammatical Outline of Revelation 3:1–6 (Sardis)

Main clause (command)	¹Καὶ τῷ ἀγγέλῳ τῆς ἐν Σάρδεσιν ἐκκλησίας γράψον·
Main clause	Τάδε λέγει
Subject	└ ὁ ἔχων τὰ ἑπτὰ πνεύματα τοῦ θεοῦ καὶ τοὺς ἑπτὰ ἀστέρας·
Main clause	Οἶδά σου τὰ ἔργα,
Explanatory ὅτι clause	└ ὅτι ὄνομα ἔχεις
Explanatory ὅτι clause	└ ὅτι ζῇς καὶ νεκρὸς εἶ.
Main clause (periphrastic participle)	²γίνου γρηγορῶν,
Main clause (command)	καὶ στήρισον τὰ λοιπὰ
Relative clause	└ ἃ ἔμελλον
Complementary infinitive	└ ἀποθανεῖν,
Main clause (explanatory)	οὐ γὰρ εὕρηκά
Supplementary participle/indirect statement	└ σου τὰ ἔργα πεπληρωμένα ἐνώπιον τοῦ θεοῦ μου.
Main clause (command)	³μνημόνευε οὖν
Interrogative clause	└ πῶς εἴληφας καὶ ἤκουσας
Main clause (command)	καὶ τήρει
Main clause (command)	καὶ μετανόησον.
Conditional clause (protasis)	ἐὰν οὖν μὴ γρηγορήσῃς,
Conditional clause (apodosis)	ἥξω ὡς κλέπτης,
Emphatic future negation	καὶ οὐ μὴ γνῷς
Indirect interrogative clause	└ ποίαν ὥραν ἥξω ἐπὶ σέ.
Main clause	⁴ἀλλ' ἔχεις ὀλίγα ὀνόματα ἐν Σάρδεσιν
Relative clause	└ ἃ οὐκ ἐμόλυναν τὰ ἱμάτια αὐτῶν,
Main clause	καὶ περιπατήσουσιν μετ' ἐμοῦ ἐν λευκοῖς,
Causal ὅτι clause	└ ὅτι ἄξιοί εἰσιν.
Main clause	⁵ὁ νικῶν οὕτως περιβαλεῖται ἐν ἱματίοις λευκοῖς,
Emphatic future negation	καὶ οὐ μὴ ἐξαλείψω τὸ ὄνομα αὐτοῦ ἐκ τῆς βίβλου τῆς ζωῆς,
Main clause	καὶ ὁμολογήσω τὸ ὄνομα αὐτοῦ ἐνώπιον τοῦ πατρός μου καὶ ἐνώπιον τῶν ἀγγέλων αὐτοῦ.
Main clause (command)	⁶ὁ ἔχων οὖς ἀκουσάτω
Interrogative clause	└ τί τὸ πνεῦμα λέγει ταῖς ἐκκλησίαις

Grammatical Outline of Revelation 3:7–13 (Philadelphia)

Main clause (command)	⁷Καὶ τῷ ἀγγέλῳ τῆς ἐν Φιλαδελφείᾳ ἐκκλησίας γράψον·
Main clause	Τάδε λέγει
Subject	└ ὁ ἅγιος,
Subject (apposition)	└ ὁ ἀληθινός,
Subject (apposition)	└ ὁ ἔχων τὴν κλεῖν Δαυίδ,
Subject (apposition)	└ ὁ ἀνοίγων καὶ οὐδεὶς κλείσει,
	καὶ κλείων καὶ οὐδεὶς ἀνοίγει·

Main clause	⁸Οἶδά σου τὰ ἔργα
Parenthetical clause	—ἰδοὺ δέδωκα ἐνώπιόν σου θύραν ἠνεῳγμένην,
Relative clause	└ ἣν οὐδεὶς δύναται
Complementary infinitive	└ κλεῖσαι αὐτήν—
Explanatory ὅτι clause	└ ὅτι μικρὰν ἔχεις δύναμιν
Explanatory ὅτι clause	καὶ ἐτήρησάς μου τὸν λόγον
Explanatory ὅτι clause	καὶ οὐκ ἠρνήσω τὸ ὄνομά μου.

Parenthetical clause	—⁹ἰδοὺ διδῶ ἐκ τῆς συναγωγῆς τοῦ Σατανᾶ
Attributive participle (apposition)	τῶν λεγόντων ἑαυτοὺς
Indirect discourse infinitive	└ Ἰουδαίους εἶναι,
Main clause	καὶ οὐκ εἰσὶν
Main clause (contrastive)	ἀλλὰ ψεύδονται
Resumptive clause	ἰδοὺ ποιήσω αὐτοὺς
Content ἵνα clause	└ ἵνα ἥξουσιν
Content ἵνα clause	καὶ προσκυνήσουσιν ἐνώπιον τῶν ποδῶν σου
Content ἵνα clause	καὶ γνῶσιν
Indirect statement	└ ὅτι ἐγὼ ἠγάπησά σε—

Causal ὅτι clause	¹⁰ὅτι ἐτήρησας τὸν λόγον τῆς ὑπομονῆς μου,
Main clause	κἀγώ σε τηρήσω ἐκ τῆς ὥρας τοῦ πειρασμοῦ
Attributive participle	τῆς μελλούσης
Complementary infinitive	└ ἔρχεσθαι ἐπὶ τῆς οἰκουμένης ὅλης
Purpose infinitive	└ πειράσαι τοὺς κατοικοῦντας ἐπὶ τῆς γῆς.

Main clause	¹¹ἔρχομαι ταχύ·

Main clause (command)	κράτει
Relative clause	└ ὃ ἔχεις,
Purpose ἵνα clause	└ ἵνα μηδεὶς λάβῃ τὸν στέφανόν σου.

Main clause	¹²ὁ νικῶν ποιήσω αὐτὸν στῦλον ἐν τῷ ναῷ τοῦ θεοῦ μου,
Main clause	καὶ ἔξω οὐ μὴ ἐξέλθῃ ἔτι,
Main clause	καὶ γράψω ἐπ᾽ αὐτὸν τὸ ὄνομα τοῦ θεοῦ μου
	καὶ τὸ ὄνομα τῆς πόλεως τοῦ θεοῦ μου,
Apposition	τῆς καινῆς Ἰερουσαλήμ,
Attributive participle	ἡ καταβαίνουσα ἐκ τοῦ οὐρανοῦ ἀπὸ τοῦ θεοῦ μου,
Direct object	καὶ τὸ ὄνομά μου τὸ καινόν.

Main clause (command)	¹³ὁ ἔχων οὖς ἀκουσάτω
Interrogative clause	└ τί τὸ πνεῦμα λέγει ταῖς ἐκκλησίαις.

Grammatical Outline of Revelation 3:14–22 (Laodicea)

Main clause (command)	¹⁴Καὶ τῷ ἀγγέλῳ τῆς ἐν Λαοδικείᾳ ἐκκλησίας γράψον·
Main clause	Τάδε λέγει
Subject	├─ ὁ Ἀμήν,
Subject	├─ ὁ μάρτυς ὁ πιστὸς καὶ ἀληθινός,
Subject	└─ ἡ ἀρχὴ τῆς κτίσεως τοῦ θεοῦ·
Main clause	¹⁵Οἶδά σου τὰ ἔργα,
Explanatory ὅτι clause	└─ ὅτι οὔτε ψυχρὸς εἶ οὔτε ζεστός.
Particle w/unattainable wish	ὄφελον ψυχρὸς ἦς ἢ ζεστός.
Particle w/causal ὅτι clause	¹⁶οὕτως ὅτι χλιαρὸς εἶ καὶ οὔτε ζεστὸς οὔτε ψυχρός,
Main clause	μέλλω
Complementary infinitive	└─ σε ἐμέσαι ἐκ τοῦ στόματός μου.
Causal ὅτι clause	¹⁷ὅτι λέγεις
Direct discourse	└─ ὅτι Πλούσιός εἰμι
	καὶ πεπλούτηκα
	καὶ οὐδὲν χρείαν ἔχω,
Main clause	καὶ οὐκ οἶδας
Indirect discourse	└─ ὅτι σὺ εἶ ὁ ταλαίπωρος καὶ ἐλεεινὸς καὶ πτωχὸς καὶ τυφλὸς καὶ γυμνός,
Main clause	¹⁸συμβουλεύω σοι
Indirect discourse infinitive	└─ ἀγοράσαι παρ' ἐμοῦ
Direct object	├─ χρυσίον πεπυρωμένον ἐκ πυρὸς
Purpose ἵνα clause	ἵνα πλουτήσῃς,
Direct object	├─ καὶ ἱμάτια λευκὰ
Purpose ἵνα clause	ἵνα περιβάλῃ καὶ μὴ φανερωθῇ ἡ αἰσχύνη τῆς γυμνότητός σου,
Direct object	└─ καὶ κολλούριον
Purpose infinitive	ἐγχρῖσαι τοὺς ὀφθαλμούς σου
Purpose ἵνα clause	└─ ἵνα βλέπῃς.
Conditional clause (protasis)	¹⁹ἐγὼ ὅσους ἐὰν φιλῶ
Conditional clause (apodosis)	ἐλέγχω καὶ παιδεύω·
Main clause (command)	ζήλευε οὖν καὶ μετανόησον.
Main clause	²⁰ἰδοὺ ἕστηκα ἐπὶ τὴν θύραν καὶ κρούω·
Conditional clause (protasis)	ἐάν τις ἀκούσῃ τῆς φωνῆς μου καὶ ἀνοίξῃ τὴν θύραν,
Conditional clause (apodosis)	καὶ εἰσελεύσομαι πρὸς αὐτὸν καὶ δειπνήσω μετ' αὐτοῦ καὶ αὐτὸς μετ' ἐμοῦ.
Main clause	²¹ὁ νικῶν δώσω αὐτῷ
Complementary infinitive	└─ καθίσαι μετ' ἐμοῦ ἐν τῷ θρόνῳ μου,
Comparative clause	ὡς κἀγὼ ἐνίκησα καὶ ἐκάθισα μετὰ τοῦ πατρός μου ἐν τῷ θρόνῳ αὐτοῦ.
Main clause (command)	²²ὁ ἔχων οὖς ἀκουσάτω
Interrogative clause	└─ τί τὸ πνεῦμα λέγει ταῖς ἐκκλησίαις.

Works Cited

Alford, H. 1976. *James–Revelation*. Vol. 4 of *The Greek New Testament*. Reprint, Grand Rapids: Guardian. Original ed., Cambridge: Deighton, 1866.

Allo, E. B. 1933. *L'Apocalypse due Saint Jean*. Paris: Gabalda.

Aune, D. E. 1997. *Revelation 1–5*. Word Biblical Commentary 52A. Dallas: Word Books.

Beale, G. K. 1984. *The Use of Daniel in Jewish Apocalyptic Literature and in the Revelation of St. John*. Lanham, MD: University Press of America.

———. 1999. *The Book of Revelation*. New International Greek Testament Commentary. Grand Rapids: Eerdmans.

Beale, G. K., with D. H. Campbell. 2015. *Revelation: A Shorter Commentary*. Grand Rapids: Eerdmans.

Beasley-Murray, G. R. 1978. *The Book of Revelation*. Rev. ed. Greenwood, SC: Attic.

Beckwith, I. T. 1919. *The Apocalypse of John*. New York: Macmillan.

Boxall, I. 2006. "Reading the Apocalypse on the Island of Patmos." *Scripture Bulletin* 40:22–33.

———. 2013. *Patmos in the Reception History of the Apocalypse*. Oxford: Oxford University Press.

Boyer, J. L. 1985. "Are the Seven Letters of Revelation 2–3 Prophetic?" *Grace Theological Journal* 6.2:267–73.

Brighton, L. A. 1999. *Revelation*. St. Louis: Concordia.

Caird, G. B. 1966. *The Revelation of St. John the Divine*. New York: Harper & Row.

Carson, D. A., and D. J. Moo. 2005. *An Introduction to the New Testament*. 2nd ed. Grand Rapids: Zondervan.

Charles, R. H. 1920. *A Critical and Exegetical Commentary on the Revelation of St. John*. 2 vols. Edinburgh: T&T Clark.

Chilton, D. 1987. *The Days of Vengeance: An Exposition of the Book of Revelation.* Fort Worth: Dominion.

Coles, R. A., et al., eds. 1970. *The Oxyrhynchus Papryi.* Vol. 36. London: Egypt Exploration Society.

Corsini, E. 1983. *The Apocalypse: The Perennial Revelation of Jesus Christ.* Wilmington, DE: Glazier.

Court, J. M. 1979. *Myth and History in the Book of Revelation.* Atlanta: John Knox.

Coutsoumpos, P. 1997. "The Social Implication of Idolatry in Revelation 2:14: Christ or Caesar?" *Biblical Theology Bulletin* 27:23–27.

Cowley, R. W. 1983. *The Traditional Interpretation of the Apocalypse of St. John in the Ethiopian Orthodox Church.* Cambridge: Cambridge University Press.

deSilva, D. A. 1992. "The Social Setting of the Revelation to John: Conflicts Within, Fears Without." *Westminster Theological Journal* 54:273–302.

Efird, J. M. 1989. *Revelation for Today.* Nashville: Abingdon.

Ehrman, Bart D., trans. 2003. *The Apostolic Fathers.* Vol. 1. Loeb Classical Library. Cambridge, MA: Harvard University Press.

Exler, F. X. 1923. *The Form of the Ancient Greek Letter.* Washington, DC: Catholic University of America Press.

Fanning, B. M., III. 1990. *Verbal Aspect in New Testament Greek.* Oxford: Clarendon.

———. 2020. *Revelation.* Grand Rapids: Zondervan Academic.

Farmer, R. L. 2005. *Revelation.* St. Louis: Chalice.

Farrer, A. M. 1964. *The Revelation of St. John the Divine.* Oxford: Oxford University Press.

Ford, J. M. 1975. *Revelation.* Anchor Bible 38. Garden City, NY: Doubleday.

Fotopoulos, J. 2003. *Food Offered to Idols in Roman Corinth.* Tübingen: Mohr Siebeck.

Friesen, S. J. 1995. "Revelation, Realia, and Religion: Archaeology in the Interpretation of the Apocalypse." *Harvard Theological Review* 88:291–314.

Garland, D. E. 2003. *1 Corinthians.* Baker Exegetical Commentary on the New Testament. Grand Rapids: Baker Academic.

Geil, W. E. 1896. *The Isle That Is Called Patmos.* Philadelphia: A. J. Rowland.

Gumerlock, F. X., trans. 2017. *Tyconius of Carthage: Exposition of the Apocalypse.* Fathers of the Church 134. Washington, DC: Catholic University of America Press.

Guthrie, D. 1990. *New Testament Introduction.* 4th ed. Downers Grove, IL: InterVarsity.

Hahn, F. 1971. "Die Sendschreiben der Johannesapokalypse: Ein Beitrag zur Bestimmung prophetischer Redeformen." In *Tradition und Glaube: Das frühe Christentum in seiner Umwelt; Festgabe für Karl Georg Kuhn zum 65. Geburtstag,* ed. G. Jeremias, H.-W. Kuhn, and H. Stegemann, 357–94. Göttingen: Vandenhoeck & Ruprecht.

Harnack, A. 1923. "The Sect of the Nicolaitans and Nicolaus, the Deacon in Jerusalem." *Journal of Religion* 3:413–22.

Harrington, W. J. 1993. *Revelation.* Sacra Pagina. Collegeville, MN: Liturgical Press.

Hemer, C. J. 1972–73. "The Sardis Letter and the Croesus Tradition." *New Testament Studies* 19:94–97.

———. 1986. *The Letters to the Seven Churches of Asia in Their Local Setting.* Sheffield: JSOT Press.

Hendriksen, W. 1940. *More Than Conquerors.* 2nd ed. Grand Rapids: Baker.

Hilgenfeld, A. 1963. *Die Ketzergeschichte des Urchristentums.* Hildesheim: Olms.

Horsley, G. H. R., ed. 1981. *A Review of the Greek Inscriptions and Papyri Published in 1976.* Vol. 1 of *New Documents Illustrating Early Christianity.* North Ryde, NSW: Ancient History Documentary Research Centre, Macquarie University.

———, ed. 1983. *A Review of the Greek Inscriptions and Papyri Published in 1978.* Vol. 3 of *New Documents Illustrating Early Christianity.* North Ryde, NSW: Ancient History Documentary Research Centre, Macquarie University.

Hort, F. J. A. 1908. *The Apocalypse of St John, I–III: The Greek Text.* London: MacMillan.

Jeremias, J. 1972. *The Parables of Jesus.* 2nd rev. ed. New York: Scribner's Sons.

Johnson, A. F. 1981. "Revelation." In vol. 12 of *The Expositor's Bible Commentary*, ed. F. E. Gaebelein, 397–603. Grand Rapids: Zondervan.

Johnson, D. W. 2004. *Discipleship on the Edge: An Expository Journey through the Book of Revelation.* Vancouver: Regent College Publishing.

Kane, J. P. 1975. "The Mithraic Cult Meal in Its Greek and Roman Environment." In *Mithraic Studies: Proceedings of the First International Congress of Mithraic Studies*, ed. J. R. Hinnells, 2:313–51. Manchester: Manchester University Press.

Keener, C. S. 2000. *Revelation.* NIV Application Commentary. Grand Rapids, Zondervan.

Keller, T. 2009. *Counterfeit Gods.* New York: Dutton.

Kiddle, M. 1940. *The Revelation of St. John.* Moffatt New Testament Commentaries. London: Harper & Brothers.

Kim, C.-H. 1975. "The Papyrus Invitation." *Journal of Biblical Literature* 94.3:391–402.

Kistemaker, S. J. 2001. *Exposition of the Book of Revelation.* Grand Rapids: Baker Academic.

Kloppenborg, J. S., and S. G. Wilson. 1996. *Voluntary Associations in the Greco-Roman World.* London: Routledge.

Knight, J. 1999. *Revelation.* Sheffield: Sheffield Academic.

Koester, C. R. 2003. "The Message to Laodicea and the Problem of Its Local Context: A Study of the Imagery in Rev. 3.14–22." *New Testament Studies* 49:407–24.

———. 2014. *Revelation: A New Translation with Introduction and Commentary.* Anchor Bible. New Haven: Yale University Press.

Krodel, G. A. 1989. *Revelation.* Augsburg Commentary on the New Testament. Minneapolis: Augsburg.

Ladd, G. E. 1972. *A Commentary on the Revelation of John.* Grand Rapids: Eerdmans.

Lenski, R. C. H. 1935. *The Interpretation of St. John's Revelation*. Columbus, OH: Lutheran Book Concern.

Lohmeyer, E. 1970. *Die Offenbarung des Johannes*. Handbuch zum Neuen Testament 16. Tübingen: Mohr.

Lohse, E. 1976. *Die Offenbarung des Johannes*. Das Neue Testament Deutsch. Göttingen: Vandenhoeck & Ruprecht.

MacKay, W. M. 1973. "Another Look at the Nicolaitans." *Evangelical Quarterly* 45:111–15.

Mathewson, D. L. 2016. *Revelation. A Handbook on the Greek Text*. Waco: Baylor University Press.

Metzger, B. M. 1994. *A Textual Commentary on the Greek New Testament*. 2nd ed. Stuttgart: Deutsche Bibelgesellschaft.

Michaels, J. R. 1997. *Revelation*. IVP New Testament Commentary Series. Downers Grove, IL: InterVarsity.

Moffatt, J. 1910. "The Revelation of St. John the Divine." In vol. 5 of *The Expositor's Greek Testament*, ed. W. R. Nicoll, 279–494. New York: George H. Doran.

Morris, L. 1969. *The Revelation of St. John*. Tyndale New Testament Commentaries. Grand Rapids: Eerdmans.

Mounce, R. H. 1977. *The Book of Revelation*. New International Commentary on the New Testament. Grand Rapids: Eerdmans. Rev. ed., 1998.

Moyise, S. 1995. *The Old Testament in the Book of Revelation*. Journal for the Study of the New Testament Supplement Series 115. Sheffield: Sheffield Academic.

Mulholland, M. R. 1990. *Revelation*. Grand Rapids: Zondervan.

Müller, U. B. 1975. *Prophetie und Predigt im Neuen Testament*. Gütersloh: Mohn.

Murphy-O'Connor, J. 1983. *St. Paul's Corinth: Texts and Archaeology*. Wilmington, DE: Glazier.

———. 2008. *St. Paul's Ephesus: Texts and Archaeology*. Collegeville, MN: Liturgical Press.

Newton, C. T. 1865. *Travels and Discoveries in the Levant*. London: Day & Son.

Osborne, G. R. 2002. *Revelation*. Baker Exegetical Commentary on the New Testament. Grand Rapids: Baker Academic.

Peake, A. S. 1919. *The Revelation of John*. London: Holborn.

Pliny the Younger. *See* Sherwin-White, A. N.

Porter, S. E. 1987. "Why the Laodiceans Received Lukewarm Water (Revelation 3:15–18)." *Tyndale Bulletin* 38:143–49.

———. 1992. *Idioms of the Greek New Testament*. Sheffield: JSOT Press.

Price, S. R. F. 1980. "Between Man and God: Sacrifice in the Roman Imperial Cult." *Journal of Roman Studies* 70:28–43.

Prigent, P. 1977. "L'Hérésie asiate et l'Église confessante de l'Apocalypse à Ignace." *Vigiliae christianae* 31:1–22.

———. 2001. *Commentary on the Apocalypse of St. John*. Tübingen: Mohr Siebeck.

Radt, W. 1988. *Pergamon: Geschichte und Bauten, Funde und Erforschung einer antiken Metropole.* Cologne: DuMont.

Ramsay, W. M. 1895. *St. Paul the Traveller and the Roman Citizen.* London: Hodder & Stoughton.

———. 1904. *The Letters to the Seven Churches of Asia and Their Place in the Plan of the Apocalypse.* London: Hodder & Stoughton. Reprint, Grand Rapids: Baker, 1985.

———. 1994. *The Letters to the Seven Churches.* Edited by M. W. Wilson. Updated ed. Peabody, MA: Hendrickson.

Robertson, A. T. 1933. *Word Pictures in the New Testament.* 6 vols. Nashville: Broadman.

Roloff, J. 1993. *Revelation.* Translated by J. E Alsup. Continental Commentary. Minneapolis: Fortress.

Rudwick, M. J. S., and E. M. B. Green. 1957–58. "The Laodicean Lukewarmness." *Expository Times* 69:176–78.

Saffrey, H. D. 1975. "Relire l'Apocalypse à Patmos." *Revue Biblique* 82:385–417.

Schürer, E. 1893. "Die Prophetin Isabel in Thyatira, Offenb. Joh. 2,20." *Theologische Literaturzeitung* 18:153–54.

Schüssler Fiorenza, E. 1973. "Apocalyptic and Gnosis in the Book of Revelation." *Journal of Biblical Literature* 92:565–81.

———. 1991. *Revelation: Vision of a Just World.* Proclamation Commentaries. Minneapolis: Fortress.

Scobie, C. H. H. 1993. "Local References in the Letters to the Seven Churches." *New Testament Studies* 39:606–24.

Scofield, C. I. 2003. *The Scofield Study Bible III: The King James Version.* New York: Oxford University Press. First published 1909.

Seiss, J. A. 1909. *The Apocalypse.* 3 vols. New York: Charles C. Cook.

Sherwin-White, A. N. 1985. *The Letters of Pliny. A Historical and Social Commentary.* Oxford: Oxford University Press.

Smalley, S. S. 2005. *The Revelation to John: A Commentary on the Greek Text of the Apocalypse.* Downers Grove, IL: InterVarsity.

Spitta, F. 1889. *Die Offenbarung des Johannes.* Halle: Buchhandlung des Waisenhauses.

Stuart, M. 1843. "The White Stone of the Apocalypse: Exegesis of Rev. ii.17." *Bibliotheca Sacra* 1:461–77.

Sweet, J. P. M. 1979. *Revelation.* Westminster Pelican Commentaries. Philadelphia: Westminster.

Swete, H. B. 1907. *The Apocalypse of St. John.* 2nd ed. London: Macmillan. 3rd ed., reprint, 1911.

Swindoll, C. R. 1986. *Letters to the Churches Then and Now.* Fullerton, CA: Insight for Living.

Tait, A. 1884. *The Messages to the Seven Churches of Asia Minor.* London: Hodder & Stoughton.

Thomas, R. L. 1992. *Revelation 1–7*. Wycliffe Exegetical Commentary. Chicago: Moody.

Thompson, L. L. 1990. *The Book of Revelation: Apocalypse and Empire*. New York: Oxford University Press.

Tonstad, S. K. 2019. *Revelation*. Paideia Commentaries on the New Testament. Grand Rapids: Baker Academic.

Trebilco, P. R. 2004. *The Early Christians in Ephesus from Paul to Ignatius*. Tübingen: Mohr Siebeck. Paperback ed. Grand Rapids: Eerdmans, 2007.

Trench, R. C. 1867. *Commentary on the Epistles to the Seven Churches in Asia: Revelation II. III.* 3rd ed., rev. London: Macmillan.

———. 1880. *Synonyms of the New Testament*. 9th ed. London: Macmillan.

Tyconius of Carthage. *See* Gumerlock, F. X.

Vincent, M. R. 1924. *Word Studies in the New Testament*. 2nd ed. New York: Scribner.

Wall, R. W. 1991. *Revelation*. Understanding the Bible Commentary Series. Grand Rapids: Baker.

Wallace, D. B. 1996. *Greek Grammar beyond the Basics: An Exegetical Syntax of the New Testament*. Grand Rapids: Zondervan.

Walvoord, John F. 1966. *The Revelation of Jesus Christ*. Chicago: Moody.

Weima, Jeffrey A. D. 2016. *Paul the Ancient Letter Writer: An Introduction to Epistolary Analysis*. Grand Rapids: Baker Academic.

Wiarda, T. 1995. "Revelation 3:20: Imagery and Literary Context." *Journal of the Evangelical Theological Society* 38:203–12.

Wilkinson, R. H. 1988. "The Στῦλος of Revelation 3:12 and Ancient Coronation Rites." *Journal of Biblical Literature* 107:498–501.

Willis, W. L. 1985. *Idol Meat in Corinth: The Pauline Argument in 1 Corinthians 8 and 10*. Chico, CA: Scholars Press.

Wilson, M. W. 2002. *Revelation*. Grand Rapids: Zondervan.

Witherington, B., III. 2003. *Commentary on Revelation*. New Cambridge Bible Commentary. Cambridge: Cambridge University Press.

Wong, D. K. K. 1998. "The Hidden Manna and the White Stone in Revelation 2:17." *Bibliotheca Sacra* 155:346–54.

Wood, P. 1961–62. "Local Knowledge in the Letters of the Apocalypse." *Expository Times* 73:263–64.

Worth, R. H. 1999. *The Seven Cities of the Apocalypse and Greco-Asian Culture*. Mahwah, NJ: Paulist Press.

Yamauchi, E. M. 1980. *The Archaeology of New Testament Cities in Western Asia Minor*. Baker Studies in Biblical Archaeology. Grand Rapids: Baker.

Zahn, T. 1924. *Die Offenbarung des Johannes*, vol. 1. Kommentar zum Neuen Testament 18. Leipzig: Deichert.

Subject Index

acropolis, 24, 95, 104, 178–79
Adam and Eve, 49, 50, 58, 164, 248–49
adultery, 139, 144, 147
Aesop's Fables, 241
affliction, 64–66, 74–75, 84, 144
altar, 96–97
ancestor worship, 125–26
angel (*angelos*), 28, 168, 170–71
Antiochus III, 178
Antipas, 100–101, 120
Apollo (Tyrimnos), 130–31, 219
Apollonius, 80
apostle, 32–33
Apostolic Decree, 106, 149, 163
ark of the covenant, 114, 124
Artemis, 14, 49–50, 58, 218
Asclepius, 96–98, 99
athletics, 47, 79, 213, 227

Baal, 135, 138, 157, 160
Balaam, 94, 101–2, 108, 122, 155–56
banking, 247
Bar Kokhba, 156
Barnabas, 33, 68
bisellium. See double throne
blasphēmeō, 68–69
blindness, 246, 250–51, 264
book of life, 185–86, 193–94

Caesar Augustus, 98, 130, 257
chalkolibanos, 132
child/children of Jezebel, 144–45

Christ
affections of, 251–52, 255, 257
authority of, 61–62, 93, 153–55, 189, 198,
    223, 234, 260
coming of, 111, 183, 192, 209–10
discipline of, 252, 264
divinity of, 62, 126, 146, 196, 232, 260
grace of, 257, 263, 264, 265
as judge, 92, 111, 120, 130, 158–59, 161
messianic rule of, 156, 198
name of, 115, 219, 220
power of, 29, 52, 63, 265
preexistence of, 233
presence of, 30, 52–53
return of, 47, 192
sovereignty of, 61–62, 75, 86
standing at the door, 254–55, 265
as thief, 182–84
titles of
    Amen, 232, 245, 260, 263, 266
    eyes like a flame of fire, 131–32, 146, 158
    faithful and true witness, 232–33, 245, 260
    feet like burnished bronze, 132, 158
    first and the last, 61–62
    holding seven stars, 27–29, 52, 168, 170–71,
        189
    Holy One, 195–96, 222
    ruler of God's creation, 233–34, 260
    Son of God, 129–31, 158
    True/Trustworthy one, 196–97, 222
    walks amid the golden lampstands, 29–30,
        52–53